T0301444

LABORATORY OF SOCIALIST DEVELOPMENT

LABORATORY OF SOCIALIST DEVELOPMENT

Cold War Politics and Decolonization
in Soviet Tajikistan

Artemy M. Kalinovsky

CORNELL UNIVERSITY PRESS   ITHACA AND LONDON

Portions of the following articles are used in this text with permission.

"Not Some British Colony in Africa: The Politics of Decolonization and Modernization in Soviet Central Asia, 1955–1964." *Ab Imperio* 2013, no. 2 (2013): 191–222.

"Tractors, Power Lines, and the Welfare State: The Contradictions of Soviet Development in Post-World War II Tajikistan." *Asiatische Studien-Études Asiatiques* 69, no. 3 (2015): 563–592.

"Central Planning, Local Knowledge? Labor, Population, and the Tajik School of Economics." *Kritika: Explorations in Russian and Eurasian History* 17, no. 3 (2016): 585–620.

"A Most Beautiful City for the World's Tallest Dam: Internationalism, Social Welfare, and Urban Utopia in Nurek," *Cahiers du Monde russe* 57, no. 4, (2016): 819–846.

First published 2018 by Cornell University Press

Printed in the United States of America

Library of Congress Cataloging-in-Publication Data

Names: Kalinovsky, Artemy M., author.
Title: Laboratory of socialist development : Cold War politics and decolonization in Soviet Tajikistan / Artemy M. Kalinovsky.
Description: Ithaca : Cornell University Press, 2018. | Includes bibliographical references and index.
Identifiers: LCCN 2017056273 (print) | LCCN 2017057140 (ebook) | ISBN 9781501715570 (ret) | ISBN 9781501715587 (pdf) | ISBN 9781501715563 | ISBN 9781501715563 (cloth ; alk. paper)
Subjects: LCSH: Tajikistan—Politics and government—20th century. | Economic development—Tajikistan—History—20th century. | Communism and society—Tajikistan—History—20th century. | Elite (Social sciences)—Tajikistan—History—20th century. | Central-local government relations—Tajikistan—History—20th century. | Soviet Union—Politics and government—1953–1985.
Classification: LCC DK928.86 (ebook) | LCC DK928.86 K35 2018 (print) | DDC 958.608/5—dc23
LC record available at https://lccn.loc.gov/2017056273

For Jeske and Sophia Irina

KAZAKH SSR

UZBEK SSR

Leninobod Kanibadam

Shurab

KIRGHIZ SSR

Urateppe

Panjikent

CHINA

Gharm

Vakhsh

Dushanbe

Rogun

Tursunzade

Nurek

Nurek

Yavan

Kalininabad

Qurghonteppe

Khorog

Kulob

Shaartuz

Panj

Panj

AFGHANISTAN

PAKISTAN

Industries

Non-ferrous

Engineering and metalworking

Electrical engineering

Chemical

Mineral fertilizer

Building materials

Textile

Ginning

Cotton

Silk

Food

Hydropower stations

Hydropower plants

Agriculture

Cotton growing

Viticulture

Vegetable growing

Horticulture

Sheep breeding

N

| 0 | | 50 | | 100 mi |
| 0 | 50 | 100 | | 150 km |

Soviet Tajikistan: cities, major rivers, and industrial sites.

Contents

Acknowledgments

Any attempt to account for all of the debts accumulated in writing this book would quickly take a Borgesian turn, taking up many more pages than the work itself. Nevertheless, I am going to try.

My greatest debt is to the people who shared their time, experiences, and knowledge. I am particularly grateful to Azizjon Rahmonov, Munira Shahidi, Olle Andersen, Ravshan Abdullaev, and Hojamamat Umarov. Abudrashid Samadov shared his knowledge of Persian literature over the years and became an invaluable guide into the world of the Tajik-Soviet intelligentsia. In Nurek, Rustambek and Kurbon Ashurov were my initial guides. Ismoil Tolbakov, Zaragul Mirasanova, and the staff at the Institute of Party History in Dushanbe kindly provided access to the party archives. Tahmina and her staff at the Central State Archive of the Republic of Tajikistan provided invaluable assistance over the years. Many thanks also to the staff of the Indira Gandhi Library at the Academy of Sciences, who were unfailingly kind, welcoming, accommodating, and patient.

Since I started conducting research in Moscow in 2004 I have had the privilege of feeling at home in Russia, a feeling unavailable to many emigrants. This is largely because Evgeny Golynkin and Alla Shashkova have shared their home with me. I am also grateful to Mikhail Lipkin, Sergey Abashin, Natalia Kapitonova, Vladimir Shubin, Viacheslav Nekrasov, and other Moscow scholars who facilitated my research there and provided intellectual food for thought. Again, the staff at the various archives listed in the bibliography deserve special thanks.

Mentors new and old have helped me conceptualize this project and offered valuable criticism and advice. Odd Arne Westad has continued to provide encouragement, support, and feedback long after his formal responsibility to do so ended. David Priestland has also given invaluable advice and considered feedback on some chapters. Adeeb Khalid encouraged me to pursue this project and helped me sharpen my thinking in the early stages. Muriel Atkin has been one of my sharpest critics since I first sat in her Russian history course as a freshman and used her encyclopedic knowledge of Tajikistan to help me develop this project.

I have been shameless in asking friends and colleagues to read my work and offer feedback. Particular thanks to Flora Roberts, Patryk Reid, and Till Mostowlansky, who read earlier versions of this manuscript from beginning to end and offered helpful comments. Dina Fainberg read many of these chapters more than once; I cannot imagine finishing this project without her input. Same goes for

Vanni Pettina, who helped me see connections between what took place in Central Asia and the experience of development as far away as Latin America. David Engerman pushed me to sharpen my arguments at several points over the past few years and provided valuable feedback on the introduction. I feel a particular bond to the people I met "in the field." Talks with Masha Kirasirova, although infrequent because of geographical distance, provided food for thought and spiritual nourishment for many months. Particular thanks to Malika Bahovadinova and Isaac Scarborough, with whom I hope to collaborate for years to come. Conversations with Daniel Beben and James Pickett were always educational, and I am grateful to them for sharing their linguistic expertise over the years. Gabrielle van der Berg graciously responded to queries. Thanks to Christian Bleuer, a brilliant guide to Tajikistan's history, politics, and outdoors.

Academics are encouraged to go beyond their silos and engage other disciplines. Doing so involves finding experts willing to share their knowledge and offer a critical eye. This book would have been very different without the input of Julie McBrien and Yakov Feygin. I am also grateful to P. W. Zuidhof, Luiza Bialasiewicz, Sophie Roche, and Jeanne Feaux de la Croix. George Blaustein was my go-to source for all things American, whether he liked it or not. My thanks also to Shirin Akiner and Zayra Badillo y Castro for hosting me in London and engaging in very helpful discussions.

This project was first conceived when I was at the London School of Economics, but most of it was developed at the University of Amsterdam. My colleagues, and in particular Michael Kemper, have gone out of their way to be supportive and create a stimulating intellectual environment. I am forever grateful to Hanna Jansen, among the first to make me feel at home in Amsterdam. Many thanks also to Danis Garaev, Sara Crombach, Alfrid Bustanov, Erik van Ree, Ben de Jong, Marc Jansen, and Tatjana Das for their company and stimulating discussions over the years.

This research has received generous support from several institutions. An IREX grant allowed me to make my initial trip to Tajikistan in 2011, and the IREX office in Dushanbe continued to offer support in subsequent years. My thanks to Radik Naibullin and Ibrahim Rustamian. The bulk of this research was conducted with the support of a Veni grant from the Dutch Research Organization, NWO. The Dutch Royal Academy of Science provided support for a workshop on development in Central Asia held in 2015. The Amsterdam School of Regional, Transnational, and European Studies provided additional support as the project neared publication. My thanks to Christian Noack and Paul Koopman.

Ever since Roger Malcolm Haydon said "I hate book proposals" I knew this was an editor with whom I wanted to work. My thanks to him for taking a chance on the book and seeing the manuscript through. Many thanks also to production editor Sara Ferguson, Bill Nelson for the maps, Sandy Aitken for the index, and the two anonymous readers for their careful assessment and helpful comments. Brian Inman Becker continues to be a great friend and editor.

None of this would be possible (or worthwhile) without the support of friends and family. My grandmother, Irina Kronrod, and my father, Mikhail Kalinovsky, passed away before the book was completed. Whatever their feelings about the Soviet Union, they were Soviet people, shaped by that country's institutions and the particular kind of social mobility offered by those. Although they were from another "periphery" of that country, many of the questions I asked in my research inevitably reflected my contemplation of their life stories. Jeske Ruigrok did not bat an eye when I first asked her to come to Tajikistan and became as much an enthusiast for the country as I am. Indeed, her enthusiasm for this project sometimes seemed stronger than mine. Sophia Irina did nothing to speed the process along, but her appearance in our lives has made everything else better.

Transliteration

Tajik is a close relative of Persian and was written in Persian (Arabic) script until the 1920s. Orthographic reforms undertaken in the Soviet period led to the language being rendered in a modified Latin alphabet and then in a modified Cyrillic. (On the relationship between Tajik, Persian, and Dari, see James Pickett's "Categorically Misleading, Dialectically Misconceived: Language Textbooks and Pedagogic Participation in Central Asian Nation-Building Projects," [*Central Asian Survey* (2017): 1–20].) In transliterating Tajik words, I have generally used a simplified version of the Library of Congress (LOC) system, with Tajik ӣ rendered as ī, a soft x rendered as h but a harder one, х, rendered as kh. For Russian, I have also followed a simplified version of the LOC system, with ц as ts and и as i, with ий rendered as ii.

Tajik names pose a particular difficulty. During the Soviet period, most central Asians used Russianized patronymics and surnames. Since 1991, most individuals have retained surnames but have gradually dropped the use of patronymics. Some Tajiks have retained surnames but dropped the Russian ending (the current president, Emomali Rahmon, was known as Rahmonov until 2005) or added the Persian "zade" (born of) or the ending ī. Others have kept the name but changed the spelling. This means that some individuals published under one name during the Soviet period and under another after independence. I have generally stuck to the names used during the Soviet period but have provided both versions in some cases to avoid confusion.

LABORATORY OF SOCIALIST DEVELOPMENT

THE PROMISE OF DEVELOPMENT

This book deals with some of the central struggles of the late twentieth century. Could the benefits of industrial modernity become widely available? What political and economic system offered the best path? Was it possible to overcome the legacies of World War II and the Stalinist terror? How best to right the wrongs of European imperialism, including economic inequality and cultural domination? Could former colonies and former colonizers be allies in these struggles? On what terms? Could any of this be achieved without harming the earth's natural environment? Or would the path to prosperity for humans lead to the destruction of the planet?

Historians have grappled with these questions for some time. This book takes readers to a place that captures these modern political, economic, and environmental dramas: the Soviet Republic of Tajikistan. Although Tajikistan may seem like a remote part of the Soviet Union, its story illuminates the history of Soviet development as well as other twentieth-century efforts to transform economies and societies in the postcolonial world.

After World War II, leaders of newly independent states all over the world looked to radical economic development programs to transform their societies. Through a combination of land reform, agricultural modernization, and industrialization, leaders like Ghana's Kwame Nkrumah and India's Jawaharlal Nehru hoped to create modern nation states that would deliver prosperity to their citizens. Many Latin American governments pursued industrialization and an ambitious extension of the welfare state, challenging domestic elites and the region's economic relationship with the United States. The United States, the

1

Soviet Union, and, later, the People's Republic of China competed for allegiances in what became known as the "Third World," offering advice and resources to postcolonial leaders.

Between Joseph Stalin's death in 1953 and the collapse of the Soviet Union in 1991, Moscow embarked on a similar project of development in its own semi-colonial periphery—the republics of Central Asia. Although transforming "backward" areas of the former Russian Empire had been on Moscow's agenda from the time of the 1917 Revolution, this goal was pursued with renewed vigor after Stalin's death. The end of Stalin's terror changed both the politics and the local, lived experience of development. Local politicians took advantage of Moscow's growing interest in the Third World to argue for development in their own largely agricultural republics. Like leaders of postcolonial and developing countries, they hoped dam construction and irrigation schemes, industrialization, and education would radically transform their republics and make modern subjects out of their citizens. Moscow, in turn, presented Central Asia as a model of development for Third World countries to follow.

Ambitious politicians used the Soviet engagement with the Third World to articulate and lobby for new cultural and economic policies—and to advance their own careers. Tajikistani peasants, workers, scholars, and engineers negotiated Soviet economic and cultural development projects. But the environment itself is a protagonist in the pages that follow. Mountains, valleys, soil, and rivers were sometimes a resource and at other times a target of development schemes. Tractors, cotton harvesters, high voltage electricity lines, roofing materials, and schoolbooks were a part of this story too. These mundane items were not distinct from the lofty goals of development, but an essential component; we must keep them in view to appreciate the powerful hold that visions of socialist development had on the imagination of so many people, and the consequences of trying to realize those visions.

I came to this topic somewhat serendipitously. I first went to Tajikistan planning to study the role of the Tajik elite in Soviet politics. But conducting research in the archive of the Communist Party of Tajikistan was no simple matter. To put it plainly, no formal procedure existed for gaining access. During my first week in the country I had been advised to go directly to the party's headquarters and present my case, which I did. The party's offices occupy the second floor of what used to be the headquarters of the city party organization, back when republic-level party organizations were united under the Communist Party of the Soviet Union. Most of the floor is still under the nominal control of the party, but there is only one full-time employee, a former Komsomol activist named Zaragul who collects dues and oversees the organization of campaigns and congresses.

Although she was immediately sympathetic, it would still take me almost a month to get any access. I returned to the party offices every few days anyway; I had practically no contacts and no access anywhere else, and not much else to do. If nothing else, the cool hallways were a respite from the June heat.

It was frustrating to pass the time in the dark, dilapidated corridors and waiting rooms of the once powerful party's remaining offices, rather than looking through government documents in an archive, but there was an unexpected benefit. Activists from around the country came in to pay dues, pick up materials, or just catch up. One afternoon when I arrived to inquire as to the state of my request for access, Zaragul was talking to a white-haired man. She introduced him as one of the party's activists from Ayni (a mountainous district halfway between Dushanbe and the northern city of Khujand). His name was Nizomuddin. Perhaps eager to be rid of us both, Zaragul suggested I interview him. Nizomuddin was happy to tell his story, and we settled in the unoccupied office next door— I behind some apparatchik's old desk, he on the leather couch by the wall.

As it turned out, Nizomuddin was not, as I had first assumed, a long-time activist still clinging to the party. On the contrary, he had joined only after the collapse of the Soviet Union. But his family had a serious communist pedigree, of which he was very proud. Nizomuddin said that rather than flee to Afghanistan as some opponents of the Soviet regime had done in the 1920s, his grandfather gathered the peasants in the village and suggested voluntarily organizing a collective farm (kolkhoz). Nizomuddin's father had been a life-long party member. Nizomuddin himself had studied at university and found it difficult to join, because in the 1970s and 1980s the party wanted to fill its ranks with "workers" to avoid domination by white-collar professionals. I wondered what made him join the party when its heyday had long passed, and when membership was unlikely to provide any obvious material, political, or social rewards. His answer surprised me: "Today," he said, "our people go to America, and they say 'look, they have real communism there.' And I say 'yes, but at what cost?!'" At first, I could not understand what America had to do with communism. But as Nizomuddin explained, he was referring to the big buildings, the cars, the infrastructure—all those things that are associated with both Soviet and American visions of modernity. For Nizomuddin, the main problem seemed to be how to get there—without, presumably, the inequality and dislocation associated with capitalist progress.

The answer was illuminating. I had originally planned to write a straightforward political history of the Soviet provincial elite, but conversations like this one made me realize that visions of what we might call "development" or "modernity" are central to any story of the Soviet experience in the periphery. Visions of revolutionary transformation were central to the Soviet project from the very beginning, and they were an important justification for the regime's existence.

In the periphery, that is, in the former tsarist colonies, these visions offered the hope of entering industrial modernity free of imperialist domination. Nizomuddin's understanding of his and his family's place in that history, as well as his understanding of what communism was and should be, suggests that this vision was powerful. If we are to understand the local dynamics of the Soviet project, we need to start with stories like Nizomuddin's, however contradictory their reading of history might seem.

My research was inspired by several ongoing discussions about the Soviet Union, Central Asia, and the history of post-colonial and Cold War era development that rarely intersect.[1] Much of the early work on development and foreign aid during the Cold War focused on the history of US development efforts and modernization theory. These works showed how a mid-twentieth-century faith in US progress led scholars and policymakers to promote programs of social and economic transformation for postcolonial states. Since the mid-2000s, scholars have begun to write European and socialist bloc efforts into this history, which has in turn led to a new appreciation of the similarities and differences between (and within) First and Second World approaches to development.[2]

The idea that governments could use technology and social science to "improve the human condition" had its origins in the Enlightenment. In the twentieth century, European states tried to apply these insights domestically and in their colonies. In the post-war decades, development became the province of international organizations such as the World Bank, as well as foundations set up in an earlier period. Economic development was thought to require such varied infrastructure as roads, rails, and ports, as well as access to mineral resources, electric power, the rationalization of agriculture, and ultimately industrial production. Many theorists and practitioners also understood that for any of these development projects to succeed, there would have to be trained engineers, skilled workers, and administrators to see the projects through. Thus development also had to include education. In addition to their technical know-how, individuals would also need to learn the particular forms of optimism—faith in state institutions, discourses of self-improvement, and science and rational thought in lieu of traditions—often folded into the broader concept of modernization. The 1950s and 1960s were the heyday of development—not only did postcolonial elites find this range of programs possible and desirable, so too did a significant portion of the population whom the elite led, as well as the specialists and policymakers in international institutions, think tanks, universities, and decision-making bodies in the so-called First World. Social scientists spoke confidently about "traditional society" becoming "modern."[3]

By the late 1960s, this consensus about how to make the world a better place was coming apart. Billions of dollars seemed to bring few gains in either general economic output or standard of living. Some scholars began to question the premises of much development policy, arguing that the problem was not just a constitutional dissonance between developed and underdeveloped nations but the ongoing unequal terms of trade between them.[4] Others hypothesized that the optimistic visions of the 1950s and 1960s had underestimated the degree of social change required before a modern, industrialized economy could survive. In the next decade, organizations like the World Bank would shift their emphasis away from large-scale state-led development toward what they now called "basic needs."[5] Anthropologists and other social scientists began to question the premises of development thought. Eventually, some of them articulated a more fundamental critique of development endeavors, showing how such initiatives treated contemporary European modernity as the ideal end-state and tended to dismiss indigenous communities and destroy their livelihoods.[6] Development, by this logic, was imperialism by another name. Environmentalist critiques, particularly those directed against large-scale infrastructure projects like hydroelectric dams, further undermined the earlier consensus. Scholars argued that development acts to suppress political struggle by offering a kind of technocratic-universalist justification for the power of its practitioners.[7] These arguments overlap with critiques of the very idea of transforming society, most famously articulated by James Scott, as well as the ongoing debate on the very notion of "modernity."[8] As a rule, scholarship on twentieth-century US development aid has echoed these critiques, often taking an ironic or cynical tone.[9]

The story of Soviet development in Central Asia followed a similar arc. The Stalin era left the region a cotton producer with limited industrial production. In the 1950s, local and Moscow-based scholars and planners argued that the region was ripe for industrialization, pointing to the hydropower potential of its rivers and its abundance of labor resources. These projections were built on the idea that agricultural work would be mechanized and a stream of labor, male and female, would be available for new industries. Industrialization would facilitate the spread of the welfare state and education, lifting standards of living and making Central Asians proper Soviet citizens and socialist subjects. By the early 1970s, these assumptions were increasingly being questioned, both in Moscow and within the region. Central Asians seemed reluctant to join industries; cotton was still harvested using manual labor; and both the cotton economy and industrialization were destroying the environment. By the 1980s, some local critics were arguing that Soviet economic policy was meant to benefit only Moscow and was just another form of colonial exploitation.

Scholars who evaluated Soviet development in Central Asia from the vantage point of the late 1980s saw failure. The Soviet ethnographer Sergei Poliakov argued that the socialist way of life had barely penetrated the Tajik countryside, and that religious and family traditions continued to determine the choices of young people. Poliakov's views were a product of the late Soviet period, when many of the claims made by propaganda in previous decades were suddenly revealed to be false. If an earlier generation of ethnographers had been expected to show villages moving toward socialist modernity, Poliakov demonstrated the apparent failure of Soviet institutions to effect real social change in the countryside.[10] Some sociologists, meanwhile, noted that the Soviet Union had failed to create modern Central Asian subjects, who recognized their own individual importance and agency in political and economic life.[11] While some Soviet scholars lamented the lack of change, Western scholars emphasized the destructive nature of the Soviet experiment.[12] This crude dichotomy has thankfully disappeared from much of western historiography, although debates about the success or failure of the Soviet era continue to play an important role in politics within the independent Central Asian states and to inform those states' relationship to Russia.

Development, Modernization, Culture, Empire

Few concepts are as omnipresent and as problematic as modernity. The scholars who developed modernization theory in the mid-twentieth century could speak assertively with regard to economic life, political institutions, and religion's retreat from the public sphere as a set of characteristics that defined "modernity." Historians today do not have the luxury of such confidence. In the mid-twentieth century, "modernity" stood for European or Western accomplishments, and thus served to maintain a hierarchy first established by imperialism. Some scholars have identified multiple (e.g., Chinese, Islamic, Socialist) modernities, but as Frederick Cooper points out, "if any form of innovation produces modernity, then the term has little analytical purchase."[13] There is no equivalent in Russian or in Soviet discourse more generally, but the Soviet Union claimed to be building a new world substantially different from the one that came before, untethered to tradition and technologically advanced—in broad outlines, at least, a definition of modernity that was widely recognized for the bulk of the twentieth century.[14] Muslim thinkers, including Central Asian ones, had developed their own discourses on progress (*taraqiyyet* in Tajik) by the early twentieth century.[15]

Although discourses of progress were central to the Soviet project, Soviet officials did not generally talk about "development" or "modernization" as a concerted program aimed at moving society from one state to another. One could speak of "developing" a local industry, or "modernizing" an existing one, but not developing or modernizing society as a whole. Rather, the Soviet Union was building communism, which meant an industrialized society with high levels of social welfare and complete equality achieved by giving workers ownership of the means of production. Whether it was starting a university, building a factory, or expanding irrigation, the Union of Soviet Socialist Republics (USSR) was working toward that same goal. (Doing these things abroad was usually called "aid" or "cooperation"; and when one Soviet republic sent cadres or materials to another it was called "aid from a fraternal republic.") Nor did Soviet officials, party leaders, and scholars speak often of "modernity" as an aspiration. Once again, communism was the end goal. Nevertheless, what the Soviet Union did at home and abroad, the way it understood the societies it sought to transform, and the concept of an end goal often looked quite similar in practice. Throughout the book, therefore, I use the term "development" to refer to the initiatives under discussion, precisely to underline the similarity between what happened within the USSR and in those parts of the world that were subject to development interventions, whether socialist or capitalist. Even if Soviet officials defined their practices against their western competitors, they often had much in common. To put it another way, communism and its Soviet variant Marxism-Leninism were ideologies of development: history proceeded through stages, from feudalism to capitalism to socialism and finally to communism, and it was up to a vanguard to hurry it along to that final stage.

This ideology envisioned not mere economic change but a total transformation of social relations and the creation of a "new man." Soviet development, then, cannot be understood without reference to *kul'turnost'* (culturedness) in a way that overlapped with many elements of European modernity, or specifically notions of European middle-class modernity. The term had no precise definition. Rather, as Vadim Volkov argued, it reflected a "complex of practices aimed at transforming external and internal features of the individual which emerged following the urbanization of the late 1920s and 1930s."[16] In one sense, Soviet kul'turnost' was about turning peasants into good urban citizens.[17] It included modes of dress, behavior in public transportation, the use of free time (theaters and museums were cultured; drinking and brawling were not), and cleanliness in the home. Kul'turnost' referred to workplace behavior too, delineating the proper use of machinery and maintaining a clean workspace.

The concept of kul'turnost' was imprinted on most economic development plans discussed in the chapters that follow, including such projects as the creation of a new educated elite, urban planning and construction, and the attempt to mechanize agriculture. Yet like other Soviet notions, it was surprisingly mutable. Kul'turnost' emerged in the late nineteenth century among a Russian intellectual elite concerned about the country's cultural development relative to Western Europe and the education of the masses. Applying it to the Muslim periphery of the former tsarist empire created a different set of problems. The elitism of one group of Russians prescribing modes of behavior for another now took a colonial tone. Traditions and concepts of proper behavior were different, while a local intellectual elite had developed its own ideas about revolutionary social transformation by 1917. Sometimes, as we will see, local elites translated or adapted kul'turnost' in ways that accorded with their own goals; at other times, it was the different understanding of cultured behavior that seemed to bring the limits of the Soviet project into sharp relief.

One area where culture and economic development come together most clearly is in the construction of a welfare state. Welfare states commit to provide for the health and education of its citizens, and to save them from poverty by providing housing and other services. But the specific contours of each welfare state would develop through political struggles particular to that state's history and could vary even within states.[18] In belated bids for legitimacy, colonial powers sometimes tried to win over subject populations by offering welfare services. Anti-colonial movements and postcolonial states did the same.[19] In the Soviet Union, the welfare state was crucial for creating the new socialist subject—one who trusted in institutions and modern forms of knowledge, who was committed to self-improvement and Soviet conceptions of equality, and who was willing to sacrifice for the collective.[20] The Bolsheviks aspired to make the USSR a welfare state from the very beginning, but it was only in the post-Stalin era that the resources and organizational capacity to bring the country close to that goal became available. This is particularly true in the case of Central Asia, where it is only in the 1950s that we see the real spread of health clinics, schools, and other social services beyond the cities.

This book grapples with how universal ideas were negotiated locally and ultimately reshaped. It would be a mistake to assume that orders simply came from Moscow, leaving local politicians and residents the options of resisting or accommodating. As Nathan J. Citino argued with regard to US modernization efforts in the Middle East, "those strategies were made and remade at the point of contact."[21] The same holds true for the USSR. Whether out of intent or necessity, Soviet policy and ideology left plenty of room for maneuvering and improvisation. One thus has to look closely at the actors involved. Oppositions like "state" and "society" are misleading because they suggest one unitary actor confronting another. The state consisted of multiple agencies at various levels. At the level of republican and local administration, the state's offices were staffed by people from the communities they were meant to govern. All of this created ample room for negotiation and virtually guaranteed that big and small projects would change and be reshaped locally.[22]

This book also informs the debate around the nature of the Soviet Union's relationship to its own periphery, particularly its Muslim periphery. Most of what is today referred to as Central Asia (Kazakhstan, Kyrgyzstan, Tajikistan, Turkmenistan, and Uzbekistan) was conquered by the Russian Empire in the nineteenth century, with some parts annexed outright and some incorporated as nominally independent protectorates. The Russian Empire also established control over the Caucasus in a series of wars with the Ottoman Empire and Qajar Persia. These areas were reincorporated into the Soviet Union and divided into autonomous republics, whose names were supposed to reflect the majority ethnic group. The "titular nationalities" had priority access to education, culture, and administrative posts, in an arrangement Terry Martin famously called the "Affirmative-Action Empire."[23]

During the Cold War, scholars examining Soviet Central Asia debated whether the region could be understood as a colony dominated by Moscow or, as Soviet propaganda often claimed, a model for the Third World.[24] Those who supported the latter view, like Alec Nove and Donald Wilber, pointed to the USSR's success at developing the region and pointed out that figures for industrialization, education, and access to services compared favorably with indicators for countries like Pakistan, Afghanistan, and Iran.[25] As scholars like Gregory Massell noted, however, Soviet development practices and nationality policy in the periphery created their own contradictions, by promoting an elite that was encouraged to think of itself in "national" terms and that might ultimately challenge the legitimacy of a centrally controlled Soviet system.[26] Contemporary historians of Soviet Central Asia have returned to these questions, now armed with a richer theoretical apparatus informed by studies of postcolonialism, possibilities for comparison, access to archival records, and first person accounts unavailable to their Cold War era predecessors. But this broadening has not led to a consensus. Some scholars have argued that the Soviet Union was a colonial power, not only in the way it dominated the region politically but also in the hierarchical nature of relations between European Soviets and Central Asians.[27] These newer studies highlight the extent to which the Soviet era in Central Asia, at least in certain periods, was shaped by the pursuit of deliberately anti- or postcolonial policies, even as legacies of the colonial past proved difficult to overcome, and central control and the single-party system created their own quasi-colonial patterns. Other scholars have argued instead that the contours of Soviet modernization in Central Asia are best compared to those in other colonial development contexts, or to the experience of modernizing states like Kemalist Turkey.[28]

My approach is to incorporate this debate while posing a slightly different set of questions. It is clear that the Soviet Union retained many features of an empire.[29] The fact that it pursued economic or social transformation, that it built roads and schools, would hardly disqualify the USSR from that designation. The French and British empires did the same in Asia, Africa, and the Middle East in the twentieth century and used this commitment as a justification of their continued right to rule. Echoing more traditional colonial discourses of the "White Man's Burden," the Soviet promise to transform non-European peoples of the union is sometimes referred to as the "Red Man's Burden."[30] In his study on themes of exchange and captivity in Russia's relations with the Caucasus, the anthropologist Bruce Grant noted how central the notion of a "gift" and sacrifice by the imperial center to the newly conquered periphery was in various portrayals of the conquest and imperial rule; these themes carried over into the Soviet period, with revolution and economic development taking the place of earlier notions of "civilization."[31] As we will see, these "imperial" motifs abounded in Moscow's relationship with Central Asia as well, whether in discussions of how the Russian revolution brought electrification to the Central Asian countryside or how ethnic Russians endured personal hardship to help build roads, dams, and schools. Promoting kul'turnost' in the region implied a transfer of European modes of behavior and thought to supposedly uncultured subjects.

Yet the parallels should not be taken too far. Development in the case of European empires was arguably an afterthought, not central to their purpose and ideology the way it was for the USSR. And the Soviet Union claimed to be anti-imperialist. The attempt to fulfill decolonization within the early Soviet Union effectively came to an end by the early 1930s, with the elimination of indigenous intellectuals and communists, the Sovietization and expansion of the cotton economy, and the turn away from anti-colonial politics more generally. But it would be particularly important from the 1950s on, when the USSR began to engage in anti-colonial politics, ultimately entering a competition not just with Washington but also with communist China. The Cold War and decolonization intersected in often surprising ways.[32] The formal colonies of the Russian Empire were now on the front line of the Soviet Union's struggle for the Third World. What did this mean for Moscow's relation to the region? What did it mean for local political and intellectual elites who were mobilized to assist in this struggle? What did it mean for peasants and workers who were frequently reminded that they were at the forefront of a global struggle for equality, progress, and justice?

My goal in writing this book has been to situate the Soviet Union more firmly in histories of economic development and decolonization, while also showing how those histories help us make sense of Soviet history. Looking out from Tajikistan, we can gain a new appreciation for how the Soviet Union tried to balance its various domestic commitments, including promises of cultural autonomy and local development, with the goals of socialist unity and all-Union economic growth. We also see that the USSR's successes and failures, and the way experts of all kinds thought about them, were not unique, but had parallels all around the world. I discard rigid divisions between political, social, and cultural history in favor of an integrated approach that makes it possible to explore these crucial questions in all their complexity. Questions of culture concerned economists and planners, while poets and writers worried about questions of economic development.

This book analyzes these issues at three different levels. First, it looks at Soviet debates and struggles over development and economic relations at the level of all-Union and international politics. The experience of Soviet development at home has to be understood in the broader context of Cold War and postcolonial development schemes. Many of the goals Moscow had for the region were similar to those it and the United States pursued in the Third World. The debates about the relative importance of industrialization, urbanization, and demography that took place within the Soviet Union had their echoes in the West and the Third World. The chapters that follow draw comparisons and show how the Central Asian elite learned from and engaged with the debates on development and underdevelopment outside the USSR.

More broadly, the book emphasizes that the image of itself the USSR tried to show to the world (and to its own population) played an important role in actual developments. The promise of internationalism and social welfare was central to both the social contract that enabled Soviet rule in the periphery and how Soviet ideology was understood. As Michael David-Fox noted, ideology has too long been taken for granted in Soviet historiography, or understood simply as a "straitjacket" that limited how actors thought.[33] I treat Soviet ideology as dynamic: it shaped historical actors and was reshaped by them. Central Asian elites and ordinary citizens engaged with communist ideology in this period, transforming it in the process. The commitment to internationalism both drove and justified Moscow's foreign policy, from its many commitments of economic aid in the Third World to its military intervention in Afghanistan (1979–1989). The ideals of internationalism often were supposed to govern relations among the various ethnic groups within the Soviet Union. That ideology was particularly important for large development projects like the Nurek Dam, where labor and resources from across the USSR had to be mobilized for an initiative that was supposed to serve as a demonstration of Soviet ideals for domestic and foreign audiences. In both cases, the rhetoric of "internationalism" was addressed to two audiences: one domestic (the Soviet citizens sending their sons to fight in distant wars or going there themselves) and one foreign (on the receiving end of internationalist aid). Internationalism (sometimes celebrated under the slogan of "people's friendship") could be hierarchical—putting the Soviet Union above other socialist states or Russians above other Soviet nationalities—but it could also have a flattening effect, serving as a claim making device for those seeking to challenge existing hierarchies.[34]

Laboratory of Socialist Development examines the role of the "knowledge-producing" elite—especially social scientists, planners, architects, and engineers—in these struggles. The political space that opened after Stalin's death gave Central Asian elites the opportunity and the confidence to negotiate the contours of Soviet modernization, without rejecting its basic premises. Future scholars, engineers, and politicians were recruited from local populations and mobilized to advance the fight for socialist modernity at home and to demonstrate the Soviet commitment to anti-colonialism abroad. They thus took on the role of what Tanya Murray Li, in her study of development schemes in Indonesia, calls trustees, "a position defined by a claim to know how others should live, to know what is best for them, to know what they need."[35] As party leaders, economists, engineers, and architects, they saw themselves as a vanguard that could define the local variation of Soviet modernity and find the most effective way to implement their vision. By the 1980s, many of them had become disillusioned, believing that the Soviet Union had done too little to improve the region's economic conditions and preserve its cultural heritage. Their critique of the USSR during the late 1980s often drew on experiences of interacting with the postcolonial world. These individuals came to see their society as another colonized group, often borrowing the language of resistance Moscow had encouraged them to use against western colonial and neocolonial powers.

This book brings forth the everyday experiences of the people who were supposed to be the main beneficiaries of Soviet development in Central Asia. It complicates notions of resistance and accommodation that have been at the center of debates about Soviet history. Peasants, workers, and urban elites certainly resisted policies and initiatives. Resettled peasants sometimes abandoned their new collective farms and returned to the mountain villages, living largely outside the reach of the state. In other cases, they tried to limit the reach of the welfare state into their family lives. Urban elites challenged cultural policies that did not accord with their own understanding of national culture. Yet my research shows that marginalized individuals, including peasant women and young men from remote areas of the republic, often found the experience of joining large Soviet construction projects, such as the Nurek Dam, genuinely liberating and fulfilling. Many young men and women saw themselves as active subjects shaping their own and their republic's destinies. Sometimes this meant challenging their own family structures or breaking with their relatives. At the same time, these young men and women could use the social and political capital they had gained as a result of their participation in these projects to benefit their home villages and extended families. The relative ideological flexibility of the post-Stalin years made it possible to deemphasize some aspects of socialist ideology, such as atheism, in everyday life, and thus enabled individuals to straddle two worlds and even bring them closer together. But the contradictions inherent in the development project and Soviet economic management meant that some initiatives, particularly those targeting the rural peasantry, often reinforced inequalities and marginalization. Not everyone became "Soviet," and many people remained marginalized. Looking at those who were part of the system, however imperfectly they fit in, is fruitful precisely because it reveals not only what it took to become Soviet, but also how the system had to change to accommodate diversity.

Finally, looking at these three levels helps us appreciate how models of development and social welfare change over time. There is much discussion—both among scholars and in the popular press—about the abandonment of state-led development and the decline of the welfare state in Europe, North America, and parts of the global south, and the rise of new modes of economic governance privileging individual initiative, entrepreneurship, and financialization. These new form of economic governance are often referred to collectively as "neoliberalism." Although neoliberalism is often seen as a paradigm imposed by the United States and the international institutions it controls, a number of scholars have pointed to neoliberalism's origins in the socialist world and in the global south.[36] Johanna Bockman and Gil Eyal have drawn attention to the role of socialist economists and planners in turning to the market as they sought ways to make socialism work. Stephen Collier, meanwhile, argues that neoliberalism should be seen not as an attempt to destroy the welfare state, but rather to make it work more effectively through a better understanding of the needs and desires of the people it is supposed to help. Drawing on Michel Foucault's lectures on biopolitics—the way that the state manages the social, biological, and economic life of the population—Collier investigates how the critique of the social state developed. Whom did it benefit? How could policymakers know what a group, let alone a single individual, needed or wanted?[37]

Though I do not claim to have found a Central Asian origin for neoliberalism, the questions posed by these authors can help us understand what happened in the region as part of a broader transformation in development and welfare policies in the twentieth century. In this book I show how fundamental assumptions about the economy and social welfare changed over four decades as a result of an ongoing dialogue between central and local politicians and social scientists and their reflection on everyday experience. As already mentioned, planners and scholars who promoted industrialization in the 1950s thought that the Central Asian peasantry would flock to factory work and take advantage of educational opportunities to go into the professions. When the peasantry failed to do so, planners and scholars were forced to change their approach to studying the population, and ultimately to revisit some of their earlier assumptions. By the 1980s many Soviet social scientists had come to the conclusion that decades of education and industrialization policies had failed in both their economic and their social goals—billions in investment from the center had not produced viable industries, while the standard of living of the local population increased in absolute terms but fell ever further behind all-Union averages. In this context, a growing number of experts decided to champion individual or "cottage" labor as a path to economic empowerment and social mobility. This seemingly minor conceptual shift was actually part of a broader transformation in how the Soviet state thought about its population and what bound the people of the Soviet Union together. But the questions these planners and scholars asked echoed those asked by their counterparts in developing countries abroad, and some of the solutions they found corresponded to what we have come to call neoliberalism. By looking at development theory and practice over four decades, we can begin to write the history of Soviet efforts into the larger history of development and welfare in the second half of the twentieth century.

A Note on the Setting

This book is not a chronological history (although the sections do follow a rough chronology) nor is it a comprehensive history of Soviet Central Asia or even of Tajikistan. Most of the action takes place in the southwest corner of Tajikistan, roughly bounded to the north by the capital of the republic (Dushanbe, known as Stalinabad from 1929 until 1961), the border with Afghanistan to the south, the border with Uzbekistan to the West, and the foothills of the Pamir Mountains to the east.

The decades preceding Stalin's death in 1953 were as tumultuous in Central Asia as in the rest of the Soviet Union, and the events of the 1920s, 1930s, and 1940s are essential for understanding what came later. The national delimitation that created the five republics of Kazakhstan, Kyrgyzstan, Tajikistan, Turkmenistan, and Uzbekistan (and the struggle between developing national culture and Soviet culture) started in the 1920s and was completed in 1936. The geological surveys that analyzed the economic potential of this region took place in the late 1920s and 1930s, and some of these in turn built on knowledge acquired during the tsarist period. Most important, collectivization (1929–1933) and the terror (1936–1939) both left long-lasting marks, as they did elsewhere in the USSR. Again, these decades are crucial to a full understanding of the history of the Central Asian republics in the Soviet era, but I focus primarily on the era that followed Stalin's death—first, because of the importance of international politics discussed above, and second, because the capacity to make lasting changes in everyday lives without recourse to mass mobilization, mass incarceration, or terror was limited before the 1950s. Others have covered the earlier period much better than I could hope to do.[38]

Our contemporary understanding of Central Asia is largely the product of nineteenth-century imperial contests, popularly known as the "Great Game," involving Russian, British, Chinese, and European players. At the time, the region was controlled by several polities centered around oasis cities like Bukhara, Khiva, and Khokand. Russia's search for a "natural border" in the steppes south of Siberia, and its interactions with the semi-nomadic Turkic peoples in the area, ultimately led to the conquest of the region.[39] Some areas, such as Tashkent, were annexed outright; others, such as Bukhara, remained autonomous right up to the revolution. To the south of the Amu Darya River, the Afghan ruler had been forced to accept British control over his foreign affairs in the 1880s. Negotiations between Russia and Britain set the border of the region at the river, and in the East with the weakening Chinese Empire.

The revolutions of 1917 upended the arrangements that had kept the Russian Empire together. In Central Asia, this meant that local rulers who were still in place, like the emir of Bukhara, sought to assert their independence, while other political actors, including intellectuals who had been debating and pressing for social and educational reforms over several decades, hoped the fluidity of the moment would allow them to fulfill their goals. In areas with significant European settlement, like Tashkent, Russian workers took matters into their own hands, establishing soviets (councils) while continuing to disenfranchise much of the local population. The civil war that followed saw shifting alliances, but the ultimate result was that by 1924 the region had been integrated into the newly formed Soviet Union. Part of the reformist elite threw in their lot with the Bolsheviks, hoping to use the Soviet state to advance their own educational, cultural, and economic goals.

The Bolsheviks now had to reconcile their takeover of Russia's territorial empire with their avowed commitment to anti-imperialism. The solution was national delimitation—the creation of republics that reflected the majority ethnic groups within their borders. Although the Bolsheviks were against nationalism, they came to see the nation state as a necessary evil on the way to truly internationalist proletarian unity. In a process that involved Russian scholars, local elites, and party activists, new "republics" were formed throughout the former empire. As Adeeb Khalid argued, Uzbekistan's borders roughly reflected what reformers in the years prior to the revolution had wanted for the settled Turkic speakers around the oasis towns of Bukhara, Samarkand, and Tashkent.[40]

Tajikistan was initially envisioned as an autonomous republic within Uzbekistan; it encompassed mostly mountainous territory by speakers of a Persian dialect, as well as a significant portion of "Turkic" speakers in the valleys. Both groups were Sunni Muslims. The Pamir Mountains, in the republic's east, were (and are) inhabited by Ismailis who speak a group of Eastern Iranian languages that are not mutually intelligible with Tajik/Persian. The capital of the new re-public was a town called Dushanbe, named after the day of the week (Monday) when it hosted a market. In 1929, Tajikistan became a full-fledged Soviet Socialist Republic. Once established, the new republic acquired formal institutions of So-viet governance, as well as resources to develop a "progressive" national culture, including theater and opera. Over the following decades, the precise meaning of what constituted "Soviet Tajik culture" was hashed out among local elites, party officials, and European specialists who were supposed to help the Tajiks achieve cultural enlightenment. Soviet institutions provided venues for this struggle even as they ensured ultimate control from the center, Moscow. The institutions also served to cement a sense of Tajik identity and a sense of being part of a new elite among the local cadres.

Because much of this book is concerned with the consequences of Soviet efforts to transform society, it is useful to consider some basic characteristics. Some 80 percent of southern Tajikistan's population at the time of the national-territorial demarcation were mountain dwellers who tended livestock, which they moved to higher ground for grazing during the summer months. They also grew small amounts of cereals and fruits, to the extent allowed by the terrain. Some villages consisted effectively of one extended family, with power concen-trated in the hands of the most senior active male. Family life was organized around the household (*hovli*). A married son might eventually move out and build his own hovli, yet remain in the vicinity of his parents. The youngest son would remain with his parents, take care of them in their old age, and then inherit their property. In larger settlements, a cluster of such households is known as a *mahalla*—a kind of self-governing institution that can settle disputes, organize mutual aid, and enforce rules on its members. It has been argued that these in-stitutions essentially survived intact even after collectivization. The Soviet state acknowledged the mahalla, even going as far as to set up committees that were supposed to mediate between the state and the local mahalla. The mahalla might also maintain a mosque that doubled as a community center and as a club during the Soviet era.[41] In Soviet Uzbekistan mahalla councils were legally recognized and incorporated into local governance of the republic; in Tajikistan, although legislation provided for recognition of mahalla councils, they were not developed as intermediary institutions until late in the perestroika era. A village council (*kishlachnyi sovet*), which might cover a cluster of villages, served a similar func-tion, channeling citizens' demands toward party and state organizations and helping to mobilize residents for voluntary work.

Although elder males were the most respected figures in a given community, several sources of power existed. Wealth, for instance, guaranteed a position of influence. As in most Muslim societies, religious figures such as *imam*s would command some respect. Although they had to be accepted in the community and could be expelled, once they had become established, *imam*s were trusted to oversee the education of (usually) male children, at least in wealthier villages, and to mediate disputes. They were not the only religious authority, however. Many villages also had descendants of local saints, as well as families claiming descent from the Prophet Mohammed. Descendants of saints in particular were held in high esteem, as it was believed that they had inherited the spiritual powers of their forefathers. They maintained the burial sites (*mazar*) of their ancestors, which were the sites of pilgrimage for people in the surrounding area. At least among senior males, therefore, influence was somewhat fragmented.

These structures remained in place throughout the Soviet period but were significantly transformed. Collectivization and waves of persecution in the 1930s eliminated many of the Islamic scholars and *imam*s who provided spiritual leadership at the local level, as well as the wealthier landowners. Although some of the latter may have managed to survive and stay on in the collective farms as managers, it would be a mistake to assume that this was the rule rather than the exception. As for the Islamic scholars, starting in the 1950s, some of the survivors did begin to return and to reassert some influence. Yet they had to do so clandestinely, and even where they were accepted, they had to contend with the other figures of authority.[42]

In many cases, these Muslim dignitaries worked with the new Soviet authorities, sometimes enthusiastically. As Flora Roberts wrote in her dissertation on Islamic notables in the city of Khujand (Leninobod from 1936 until 1990), "The relationship between the old, pre-revolutionary elite and the Soviet regime was far more complex and productive than might be supposed."[43] Roberts found that the pre-revolutionary elite used their considerable social and cultural capital to enter Soviet educational and cultural institutions, professions such as medicine and academia, and sometimes the communist party itself. Although many fell victim to the purges, their children thrived in Soviet institutions after Stalin's death.

Resettlement, discussed in more detail in chapter 7, often reinforced the communal patterns outlined above. The expansion of cotton production, starting in the 1930s, brought with it a demand for labor that could be satisfied only by relocating the mountain dwellers into the newly irrigated valleys. Yet because it was entire households or even mahallas and villages that moved, traditional communal patterns quickly reestablished themselves. For those families who were not resettled, economic life sometimes changed remarkably little in the 1930s.[44]

And up until the 1950s, at least, the Soviet Union had few resources to penetrate these communities and effect any kind of "cultural revolution." While there were attempts to build schools and health clinics and to send teachers, doctors, nurses, and agronomists to the countryside, the means to carry out any meaningful social change were inadequate. It was only in the 1950s, where this book largely begins, that resources began to match these earlier ambitions.

This book is divided into three sections. The first three chapters are concerned with those people involved in articulating and debating visions of transformation, as well as the visions themselves. The next four chapters zoom in on the everyday experiences of Soviet development, the planning and construction of the Nurek Dam (chapter 4), the struggles over the Soviet welfare state and urbanization (chapter 5), the problem of labor and the subjectivity of local workers at the dam site (chapter 6), and the campaigns to mechanize agriculture, electrify the Tajik countryside, and deliver the benefits of the welfare state while developing the cotton economy (chapter 7). The last two chapters focus on the emerging challenges to the Soviet model of development in the 1970s and 1980s. Chapter 8 explores the circulation of ideas made possible by presenting Central Asia as a model to the developing world while the final chapter examines the environmental, cultural, and political critiques of Soviet development that became public during the perestroika.

1

DECOLONIZATION, DE-STALINIZATION, AND DEVELOPMENT

Over the course of the 1950s Central Asia became a frontline region in the ideological battle for the Third World. As Odd Arne Westad pointed out in his influential *Global Cold War*, the United States and the Soviet Union both had a major liability as they sought influence in the postcolonial world—they both had internal colonies.[1] For the United States, this internal colony was its disenfranchised black population. For the Soviet Union, this was the part of the country colonized by the Russian Empire. For the Soviet Union, though, these regions also provided an opportunity. As former colonial territories with cultural ties to South Asia and the Muslim world, the Central Asian republics could play a central role in the Soviets' contest with the United States, and later, China. Just as (some) US policymakers realized that they would need to support civil rights for African Americans if they hoped to gain allies in Africa, Soviet leaders grasped that overcoming colonial legacies in Central Asia and the Caucasus could help Moscow reach out to postcolonial states.[2]

The Soviet engagement with the Third World had important consequences for Central Asian politicians and the republics themselves. Three of Nikita Khrushchev's priorities in the 1950s and early 1960s—consolidation of power within the party, de-Stalinization, and engagement with the Third World—provided opportunities for Central Asian leaders to negotiate economic and cultural modernization in their republics. By becoming Khrushchev's allies in domestic power struggles and in Moscow's battle for the hearts and minds of the Third World, local politicians were able to negotiate the development of their republics away from agriculture (and especially cotton) toward industrialization and win support for greater cultural autonomy. The wave of decolonization occurring beyond the USSR's borders provided the impetus to complete the "decolonization" of the Central Asian republics within a Soviet framework.

The Political Legacies of Stalinism

In the wake of the Russian Revolution and Civil War, the Bolsheviks offered an alternative to anti-colonial politics to the peoples of the Russian Empire. Rather than seeking fully independent statehood, as the subjects of the former Austro-Hungarian and Ottoman Empires had done, the tsar's former subjects would get their own ethno-territorial units, led by representatives of their own nationality. The elimination of indigenous leaders (along with other old Bolsheviks) during the 1930s put an end to whatever claim the USSR could make to an alternative form of anti-colonialism. A major component of Nikita Khrushchev's attempts to overcome the Stalinist legacy in the 1950s was the promotion of a new group of indigenous leaders who could in turn help Moscow reach out to the post-colonial world.

Many of the Central Asians who sided with the Bolsheviks in the 1920s emerged from the milieu of reformers and intellectuals active in the late tsarist period.[3] Some of them were from among the jadids, people who had responded to Russian colonialism by advocating for reform, particularly of education, and opening up to models from India, the Ottoman Empire, and Europe to allow for as much cultural and technological borrowing as would be beneficial for their own societies.[4] Those who joined the Soviet regime did so because, in Adeeb Khalid's words, "They saw themselves creating a new civilization—modern, Soviet, Central Asian, Turkic, and Muslim all at once. They hoped to co-opt the state to the work of modernization that exhortations alone had not achieved in the prerevolutionary era."[5] Other indigenous communists, including the Tajik leader Shirinsho Shohtemur, had been educated in Russian native schools or had been radicalized laboring alongside Russian workers prior to the revolution. Both groups would perish in Stalin's purges of the Bolshevik elite 1930s.[6]

The elimination of the "old" communists made way for a younger generation raised primarily in Soviet institutions: educated in Soviet schools, trained in Soviet factories, or within the Red Army.[7] The careers of these individuals overlapped with those of local communists of the 1920s and 1930s, but whereas the latter were in positions of real power and responsibility, the former were cutting their teeth in the Komsomol, the youth wing of the Communist Party. The younger generation survived the purges and benefited from them, assuming senior positions in the republic while still in their early thirties or even late twenties.[8] At the same time, their ability to shape policy and negotiate for resources was limited. Kazakhstan, Kyrgyzstan, Tajikistan, and Turkmenistan were all led by Europeans, appointed by Moscow to execute the party line, for at least part of this period. No Central Asian was present in the senior decision-making body of the party (the Politburo, or presidium as it was known between 1952 and 1966) or had access to Stalin's inner circle.

As he consolidated control within the party leadership, Nikita Khrushchev sidelined many of the officials appointed under Stalin and replaced them with younger cadres. The motives for the changes varied. Some of the people removed during the 1953–1956 period were suspected of resisting de-Stalinization and other Khrushchev initiatives. Among the charges against the Uzbek first secretary Usman Yusupov, for example, was that he had continued to praise Stalin's lieutenant and secret police chief Lavrentiy Beria, whom Khrushchev had helped arrest, try, and execute in 1953.[9] Khrushchev's "secret speech," at the 20th congress of the Communist Party of the Soviet Union (CPSU), where he delivered a radical (if selective) criticism of Stalin's rule, and the campaign against the "cult of personality" that followed was not universally welcomed. By March–April of 1956, it was becoming clear that many rank-and-file party members were ambivalent about de-Stalinization, as were many segments of the Soviet population.[10] Khrushchev needed reliable people who would be able to mobilize support behind the broader de-Stalinization of Soviet society that he envisioned.

The individuals who climbed to the heights of republican leadership in the 1950s were people who had spent their entire adult lives within the Soviet system and were fully socialized within it. Speaking of this generation's intellectuals and writers, the literary historian Rasul Khodizoda wrote that their "service in the building and strengthening of the Soviet state, in the propaganda and agitation of communist thought and belief was sincere and self-sacrificing. To the end of their lives they were firmly grounded in this thought and spirit."[11] The same could be said of their counterparts in the political arena. At the same time, both the intellectuals and the politicians continued to champion their republic's cultural and economic interests (at least as they understood them) and could be dogged lobbyists for both.

At the time of the 20th Congress in February 1956, the Communist Party of Tajikistan was led by Bobojon Gafurov, a former journalist and party activist who had written on Tajik history.[12] Even during the Stalin era Gafurov had been a strong advocate for his republic's development, assembling cadres and pushing for resources to develop its cultural, intellectual, and economic potential. He had risen to the top post in the republic in 1946 and oversaw the formation of a Tajik Academy of Sciences and the Tajik State University.[13] In May 1956 he resigned from his position at the head of the Communist Party of Tajikistan and moved to Moscow, where he became the director of the Institute of Oriental Studies. Whether the move was a demotion followed by a soft landing or a kind of promotion which put Gafurov closer to the center of Moscow's new Third World policy is difficult to say. On the one hand, Gafurov was a product of the Stalin era. He praised Stalin as late as April 1955, calling him Lenin's "most loyal co-worker."[14] Khrushchev was wary of keeping Stalin loyalists at the helm of party organizations, at both regional and republic level. At the same time, there is evidence that Khrushchev and Gafurov actually had a favorable relationship in 1954 and 1955, with Khrushchev backing Gafurov in several disputes and praising him for agricultural experiments in the republic.[15] There is no record of Gafurov being criticized at the time of his resignation; on the contrary, E. I. Gromov, the party's Central Committee representative, explained that Gafurov was needed in Moscow to take charge of the Institute of Oriental Studies and develop academic expertise for Soviet foreign policy.[16] Even if it is true that Khrushchev did not want Gafurov in Stalinabad, he nevertheless promoted him to a position of some importance. Gafurov was a member of the CPSU Central Committee and he played an important role in developing Moscow's Third World policy.

Gafurov's replacement in Tajikistan, Tursun Uljaboev, had risen through the ranks of the Komsomol (which is also where he was working during World War II), and his party career had already taken off during Stalin's last years. At the time Khrushchev was consolidating his power, Uljaboev was rising through the ranks of Tajikistan's party organization. He earned praise for his management of the southern Kulob region, ran the Agitation and Propaganda sector in the Central Committee, led the economically productive Leninobod region in the north of Tajikistan, and became chairman of the Council of Ministers of the republic in 1955.[17]

It was the Uzbek politician Nuritdin Mukhitdinov whose star rose highest in this period. Mukhitdinov had served as an agitator during World War II and been wounded; after returning to Uzbekistan he embarked on a party career. In 1955, Khrushchev returned from his Asian tour via Tashkent, the capital of Uzbekistan, where he removed Amin Niyazov and promoted Mukhitdinov.[18] Mukhitdinov also came from the generation raised under Stalin's rule, and confesses in his memoirs to having been in awe of the leader, but growing disillusioned by 1953. Mukhitdinov became a candidate (nonvoting) member of the presidium in 1956 and a full member at the end of the following year, the first Central Asian to belong to the inner circle of party leadership.

As Khrushchev explained, Mukhitdinov was being promoted to help correct for Stalin's destruction of the Central Asian communists and his failure to include any of them in the Soviet leadership. Considering Moscow's new foreign policy ambitions, such a state of affairs was unacceptable: "In the center we don't have enough people from the East, or even enough people who know it. You are an Uzbek, an Asian, from a Muslim background, which means you understand these questions. Who else, if not you, should handle our Eastern policy?"[19]

Mukhitdinov's portfolio was not limited to foreign policy. Following the 20th party Congress, Mukhitdinov was assigned to help party ideologist Mikhail Suslov prepare a resolution "on overcoming the cult of personality and its consequences."[20] Mukhitdinov was encouraged by Khrushchev to think of himself not only as an Uzbek leader but an all-Soviet one, and to take active part in presidium discussions. Mukhitdinov, in turn, lobbied for the rehabilitation of the leaders shot in 1937–1938, and was able to announce progress on this front at the First Congress of the Uzbek Intelligentsia in October 1956. Uzbek communists Akmal Ikramov and Fayzullah Khojaev, who had been tried along with Stalin's adversary Nikolai Bukharin at a show trial in 1938, were rehabilitated thirty-two years before the rest of the codefendants.[21] Mukhitdinov also used his position to promote the study of national histories and Central Asia's role in the Soviet Union's battle for hearts and minds in the developing world.

As elsewhere in the Soviet Union, the loosening of cultural and political controls and the revelations in Khrushchev's speech at the 20th Party Congress led intellectuals and cultural figures to question certain aspects of the Soviet system that went beyond the criticism of the "cult of personality" and the excesses of Stalinism. Although Central Asians rarely attacked the system directly, they openly criticized aspects of cultural and intellectual life they most disliked. Composers and musicians challenged the superiority of European musical forms.[22] In Tajikistan's Union of Writers "jadidism" was discussed in a positive way for the first time since the 1930s.[23] At a congress of Tajik intellectuals in Dushanbe, the writer Jalol Ikromī delivered an impassioned speech about the lack of works in Tajik, and the poet Abdusalom Dehoti criticized the political leadership for having a poor command of literary Tajik. He even proposed having party leaders take a language exam—harking back to the more radical indigenization policies of the late 1920s, when officials were expected to learn and work in local languages within a year of their arrival.[24] Other intellectuals also began to talk openly about Central Asia's colonization during the tsarist era—an interpretation officially favored in the 1920s but then abandoned because it threatened to undermine the position of the party, which was, after all, dominated by Russians. As Mukhitdinov recalled: "Some [Uzbek intellectuals] called their region a colony, others talked about its seizure [zakhvat], a third group about its military conquest, a fourth about its accession [prisoedinenii], and a fourth about a voluntary union with Russia. Now it all came to the surface, and people started looking for the truth. They cited V. I. Lenin's statements on the Russian empire being the prison of nations, that the national politics of tsarism was the worst form of colonial oppression."[25]

These debates reflected a long-standing challenge for Soviet ideology: how to justify the incorporation of areas that had been conquered under the Russian empire. Although describing the Russian takeover of Central Asia in the nineteenth century as imperialist was tolerated and even promoted at certain points in the first decade of the USSR, this interpretation had been supplanted in the late 1930s by a narrative that emphasized the progressive nature of Russian conquest.[26] The relative freedom of the post-Stalin years forced officials across the country to confront conflicting interpretations of the imperial past and its meaning for the inter-ethnic relations in the USSR.[27]

Mukhitdinov and the other Central Asians promoted by Khrushchev were expected to oversee the process of de-Stalinization in their republic and manage the consequences. As part of his contribution to de-Stalinization in the republic, Mukhitdinov organized a congress of the Uzbek intelligentsia, where he and other speakers highlighted the achievements of the republic, criticized Stalin, and discussed the rehabilitation of communists who had perished in the purges. Although Mukhitdinov criticized British and American commentators who compared Uzbekistan to the "colonial states of Africa,"[28] in his memoir he admitted that among the delegates at the congress many people made the comparison as well.[29]

Anti-Colonial Politics Abroad and at Home

The shift of Cold War competition from Europe to Asia, Africa, the Middle East, and Latin America, made it imperative that the USSR to shed any appearance of colonialist behavior toward its republics. Stalin had largely avoided involving the USSR in anti-colonial struggles, but Khrushchev hoped to reclaim the leadership of socialist and anti-colonial revolution for Moscow. The freedom made possible by de-Stalinization and the centrality of anti-colonial rhetoric and policies in the 1950s threatened to highlight the Central Asian republics' own unequal status within the USSR.

There was much suspicion of both the United States and of the USSR in the postcolonial world, something that became apparent at the first Afro-Asian conference organized in Bandung in 1955. The attendees—representing twenty-nine countries and movements—were united in opposition to the East-West paradigm of the Cold War and in solidarity against all forms of colonialism. Being lumped together with the imperialist powers was frustrating to Soviet leaders.[30] The People's Republic of China, though, seemed to be finding a common language with countries gathered at Bandung. Like newly independent states that made up the core of the conference participants, China had suffered from European colonialism. The African American writer Richard Wright, who chronicled the congress, observed that "Russia had no defenders at Bandung."[31] But China's foreign minister Chou En Lai ably won over delegates, avoiding any discussion of Russia and instead focusing on a common history of oppression and the willingness to resist it. Wright noted that Chou En Lai made full use of the opportunity, and that the general feeling among the delegates was that the Chinese were the true anti-imperialists. "All he had said was that he and his fellow Chinese were suffering, were backward, were afraid of war. . . . No one could recall having heard a Russian Communist speak like that; no one could recall if the Russian Communists had ever accepted a programme drafted by others.'"[32]

Wright may have exaggerated the distance between Moscow and Beijing at the Bandung Conference. The USSR and China were still coordinating their policies at the time, and the PRC deferred to the Soviet Union on foreign policy questions through most of the 1950s.[33] Still, Wright was on point regarding Moscow's disadvantages in the fight for allies in the postcolonial word. Khrushchev, too, understood that the Soviet Union had to burnish its anti-colonial credentials. Outreach to countries like India could be much stronger if they came via Tashkent and Stalinabad rather than Moscow. In 1925, at the time of Central Asia's delimitation, Stalin had urged the Tajiks to draw on their history to help lead the liberation of the colonial world: "Show the whole East that it is you, vigorously holding in your hands the banners of liberation, who are the most worthy heirs of your ancestors."[34] Stalin had curtailed engagement with the East by the 1930s, and neither Uzbekistan nor Tajikistan became much of a model in the period.[35] But in the 1950s, this promise would begin to be (partially) fulfilled.[36]

For Khrushchev, whose understanding of non-Slavic cultures was hazy at best, it was not the specific shared cultural heritage of the Central Asian republics with decolonizing states that was important, but rather a shared history of oppression and underdevelopment, supposedly overcome within the USSR.[37] Central Asian politicians and intellectuals accompanied Khrushchev on his tour of Afghanistan, India, and Burma in 1955, allowing him to boast that "Our delegation includes . . . representatives of Uzbekistan and Tajikistan, whose peoples are of the Moslem creed. But in what way do Moslems differ from the other creeds in our country? In our country we have no such differences, because all peoples of our country are worthy members of the great Soviet Union and make a united family of the peoples of our country."[38]

Khrushchev's sojourns in Tashkent were high-profile affairs. On December 20, 1955, *Pravda,* the official publication of the communist party, reported thousands of people lining the streets to greet Khrushchev and Bulganin's motorcade when the two leaders arrived from Kabul. The Uzbek politician Rafiq Nishonov recalled Khrushchev stopping in Tashkent after a trip to Indonesia and delivering a rambling monologue against imperialism and colonialism to a crowd of 15,000 in the city center.[39] Uzbek and Tajik leaders would also use the language of national liberation to highlight the Soviet Union's positive contribution to the development of less developed nations and to mobilize their own people behind economic projects. Khrushchev frequently reminded Central Asian politicians that they had a particularly important role to play in Moscow's battle for the Third World. At a meeting in Uzbekistan in January 1957, for example, Khrushchev told party members "Your republic must play an important role in developing friendly relations of our government with the peoples of Asia, Africa, and Latin America liberating themselves from colonial oppression."[40]

Khrushchev's practice of traveling widely across the country—something Stalin had not done—raised the profile of republican leaders. His visits to the republics helped local leaders feel more connected and also gave them the opportunity to lobby him on individual projects.[41] Khrushchev elevated the prestige of the individuals he promoted and thus bound them closer to him.[42] In Central Asia and other former "colonial areas," decentralization helped demonstrate the political equality of these regions within the Soviet Union. This may have been a secondary consideration, but, in the context of the emerging battle for the post-colonial world, it was an important one.

Central Asian leaders used their new importance for Soviet foreign policy to renegotiate the place of their own republics and societies (and their own political careers) in the Soviet context. Such was the case with Sharof Rashidov, an Uzbek writer and party member whose rise in the 1950s tailed Mukhitdinov's, and who would eventually become one of the longest serving republic first secretaries in the USSR. Starting in 1955 Rashidov traveled to the Third World as part of various diplomatic missions that followed the Khrushchev-Bulganin tour. After one of these early trips to Pakistan, India, Afghanistan, and Burma, Rashidov drafted a memo outlining the problems the USSR faced in these countries. Rashidov felt the effect of Anglo-American propaganda everywhere his team went; people were under the impression that the USSR repressed religion, ignored national culture, and trampled on people's rights. One of the best ways to counter this would be to open Central Asia to people from these countries, to show them mosques, madrasas, and other religious institutions, and to revive publications about Soviet Muslims such as the outlet of the Spiritual Administration of Muslims of Kazakhstan and Central Asia (DUMSK), whose publication had been suspended in 1948.[43]

As Rashidov pointed out, making Soviet propaganda work would require changing the reality within the USSR. One of the ways to do this was to restore buildings that were part of Uzbekistan's cultural and religious heritage. "Many mosques, tombs, and religious monuments are in a state of neglect and are being used for purposes other than those they are intended for," he wrote.[44] As elsewhere in the USSR, religious buildings had been repurposed, sometimes for industry, schools, or storage. Rashidov insisted that these be turned over to the DUMSK, restored, and made ready to accept international visitors. He also proposed reopening a madrasa in Tashkent—not to increase the overall number of places for religious students, but rather at the expense of the Mir-i-Arab in Bukhara, the only official madrasa still active. The point was not simply to show that religious freedom survived in the Soviet context (something that could be more easily done using the existing infrastructure Bukhara) but rather that it thrived in Tashkent, as part of everything Soviet modernity had to offer.[45]

In the following years, the Soviet Union invested in central and republic-based academic institutions devoted to studying local cultures.[46] The state also became directly involved in the preservation and restoration of historical buildings, from the madrasas of Samarkand to older fortresses in the desert. Although plans for the restoration of some monuments had been made under Stalin, in the 1950s and 1960s such projects finally received sufficient investment for them to be carried out on much greater scale.[47] The importance of outreach to the Muslim world meant that religious institutions gained greater visibility even as Moscow began a renewed campaign against religion at home.[48]

Rashidov's involvement in anti-colonial politics catalyzed his career. Initially he had been promoted to chairman of the Supreme Soviet of the Uzbek SSR—a largely ceremonial post. When Sabir Kamalov—an old ally of Mukhitdinov's predecessor Yusupov—was removed in 1959, Rashidov was considered for the post of first secretary. At the party meeting where his candidacy was discussed, Rashidov pointed to his busy international schedule in the past year. He had attended the Afro-Asian People's Solidarity Conference in Cairo, accompanied the king of Nepal on a month-long tour, and helped host a conference of writers from Asia and Africa.[49]

The contest came down to Rashidov and Samarkand oblast's (region) first secretary Arif Alimov. Of the two, it was clearly Alimov who had the most experience managing cotton production, still the core of Uzbekistan's economy. In fact, Alimov had been assigned to Samarkand as a troubleshooter two years earlier, replacing a weak predecessor.[50] But it was Rashidov who had the larger national and even international profile. At a meeting of the Uzbek party buro (analogous to the all-Union Politburo at the republic level) several speakers pointed out that Rashidov "knew ideology." The outgoing Kamalov, by contrast, had to admit that he had spent too much time thinking about cotton and thus failed as first secretary. In summing up the debate, R. E. Melnikov, who had been chairing the discussion, pointed out that as competent as Alimov was, it was Rashidov who had the broader popularity in the republic.[51] No doubt that popularity stemmed in part from his work raising Uzbekistan's importance within the USSR and internationally, as well as what he had done to champion the "restoration" of Uzbek culture.

No one was better at this game than Bobojon Gafurov. Outside of Tajikistan Gafurov is best known for his publications on Tajik history and his work promoting Soviet Oriental studies, but he was in fact a career politician. His historical work, *The Tajiks*—first published in 1949 and expanded in subsequent editions—was one of many similar "national" histories written during the Soviet period, but was notable for connecting Tajikistan's history to broader Persian and South Asian culture.[52] In his scholarly publications and in his political work he sought to "recenter" Tajikistan, taking some glory from Tashkent and positioning Stalinabad/Dushanbe as the key Soviet capital for outreach to the Third World.

Gafurov fulfilled the hopes of the party leadership by becoming one of the most articulate intermediaries in Moscow's engagement with the Third World. Gafurov organized meetings to discuss the Bandung Conference and invited ambassadors from countries represented there; he even delivered the keynote speech on the conference's significance. These meetings, which had the support of the Ministry of Foreign Affairs and the international department of the CPSU Central Committee, became an annual affair.[53] In 1958 he drafted a Central Committee document that would serve as the basis for a comprehensive program of engagement with the developing world through scholarship, and in particular Orientalist scholarship. The changing world situation, Gafurov wrote, made the training of qualified Orientalists imperative. Soviet researchers needed to coordinate their work, engage with the international community of Oriental scholars, and participate in Soviet outreach efforts. He proposed measures including the creation of Oriental studies departments in the Tajik and Uzbek Academies of Science, the creation of a publishing house which could print works in Arabic, Hindi, and other "eastern" languages, and the development of expertise on Africa.[54] Elsewhere, Gafurov proposed ideas for engaging with India, Vietnam, and other countries. And he used his academic perch to point out the ways in which less-developed Soviet republics compared favorably with former colonies like India, both in terms of the development of national cultures and the growth of their economies, underlining in particular the transition from an agriculture and resource-based economy to industrial production.[55] Gafurov's imprint, in other words, could be found all over Soviet public diplomacy aimed at the postcolonial world. He remained a key figure in shaping Soviet policy toward the Third World until his death in 1977.

When it came to articulating the link between Soviet domestic development, its nationalities policy, and its engagement with the Third World, perhaps no one could match the eloquence of Tajik poet Mirzo Tursunzoda (1911–1977). A poet of some international renown, Tursunzoda played an important role in the formation of Soviet Tajik literature through his work in the Union of Writers, where he wrote about the anti-colonial struggle. Tursunzoda became the head of the Soviet Afro-Asian Solidarity Committee, established in 1956. He and Gafurov most likely had a hand in having the first international congress of the committee in 1961 hosted in Dushanbe.[56] Politicians and cultural figures like Tursunzoda and Gafurov became adept at making their republics central to Soviet foreign policy, and then using that centrality to advance their own vision for cultural and economic development.

Light unto the Nations

In January 1956 an Indian delegation came to Tajikistan. As part of its coverage of the visit, the party newspaper *Kommunist Tadzhikistana* featured an article by Tursunzoda. The Tajik poet waxed lyrical about the newfound freedom of Britain's former colony, the aid that the Soviet Union was providing, and the engagement of Soviet specialists in the construction of Indian dams. With the goals of the sixth five-year plan about to be announced at the party congress, the Soviet Union had the opportunity to surpass the "most advanced capitalist countries" in production, and thus serve as a model for countries like India. "The Tajik people (*narod*) are proud that they are one of the peoples of the Asian part of the great multi-national Soviet Union," Tursunzoda wrote. "Along with all the peoples of the Soviet Union, building socialism and moving now to the heights of communism, they understand their great responsibility—to be pioneers in relation to the peoples of the entire East, which is now waking from many centuries of confusion and rising toward freedom, to the battle for a happy life."[57]

Tursunzoda's article contained a contradiction. When he talked about the Tajiks' role in relation to the newly decolonizing states, he put the republic on the front lines; when he talked about Tajikistan's role in the Soviet economy, he was less ambitious. After discussing the great accomplishments that would take place under the sixth five-year plan, he went on to say that Tajikistan would also play its part, and the evidence of this was the success of the cotton workers in the previous five-year plan! "This confirms," he concluded "the enormous growth of our culture, national in form, socialist in content."[58] Yet producing agricultural products and exporting a commodity like cotton for processing outside the country was not the kind of achievement leaders of India, Pakistan, and other emerging nation wanted for themselves.

In the 1920s and early 1930s, Soviet leaders promised to raise the economic development of Central Asia to the level "of the most advanced districts of the Soviet Union." Central Asian leaders criticized economists who wanted to limit the region's industrialization, labeling calls to keep cotton mills within the RS-FSR, for example, "counterrevolutionary" and an example of Russian nationalism.[59] The political upheavals of the 1930s weakened the ability of local communists to define their republic's development. Fear of war in Europe pushed Stalin to launch a crash course of industrialization and subordinate everything to the goal of preparing the European part of the USSR for an eventual confrontation. The period saw some major infrastructure projects, like an automobile road to the Pamir Mountains (the "Pamir Highway") and irrigation works like Vakhshstroi and the Great Ferghana Canal.[60] But most of these were primarily geared to expanding cotton production and relied heavily on forced labor. By 1937, "elevating" the republic was considered treason: one of the accusations against Fayzulla Khodzhaev was that he tried to industrialize Uzbekistan, so that Uzbekistan would be "more economically independent than ever of the Soviet Union, at the end of the first Five Year Plan."[61]

The revival and acceleration of development projects within Central Asia could solve two dilemmas for Moscow. Rather than being perceived as a cotton colony and a backwater, Central Asia would serve as a demonstration to the USSR's own citizens that they were beneficiaries of and participants in the Soviet drive for material achievement and modernization. Moscow could show the world that whereas the "imperialist powers" offered only exploitation, the Soviet model offered development without domination and inequality. The benefits would be material as well as political: successful modernization projects would also demonstrate the superiority of the Soviet economic system and technological power over its American alternative.

Economic development emerged as a Cold War battleground because it overlapped with the goals of postcolonial leaders, who envisioned transforming their societies into strong nation-states with industrialized economies and highly productive agricultural sectors. The leaders of the National Liberation Front, leading the struggle against French rule in Algeria, also promised to "create a powerful industry, organise agriculture, engage in profitable economic exchanges abroad, [and] intelligently exploit our mineral riches. . . . Misery will be eradicated."[62] The United States and the Soviet Union jostled with one another to show that they could help the postcolonial states achieve those goals more efficiently and more equitably than the rival superpower. Nick Cullather argues that strategic considerations played a small role in US relations with India in the 1950s; by contrast, "By the beginning of the Kennedy administration the United States had staked its reputation as a nation builder on its ability to eradicate hunger in India."[63] In Afghanistan, both superpowers would commit to major dam-building, irrigation, and road projects.[64]

Dams played a particularly important role for postcolonial states: by redirecting the flow of mighty rivers they could expand agricultural production and make it more predictable. The hydroelectric power generated from these dams could help to forge new industries and bring electricity to citizens. Dams also had symbolic power: as grandiose projects that mobilized thousands of laborers to transform nature, they could serve as an ideal manifestation of a new state's power and legitimacy.[65] It is not surprising that some of the major postcolonial hydropower and irrigation projects were revivals or continuations of late imperial plans.[66] Large dams were among the most dramatic ways to demonstrate man's ability to dominate and transform nature, a significant consideration for postcolonial leaders who promoted dam projects and for Soviet leaders who were eager to demonstrate the superiority of socialism. In the 1950s, India was in the midst of constructing the Bhakra Dam that Nehru would eventually call "new temple of a resurgent India," Kwame Nkrumah was dreaming of Ghana's transformation with a dam on the Volta River to "jet-propel [Ghana] into modernity," and the United States was already helping Afghanistan construct a major hydroelectric and irrigation complex in the Helmand Valley. And Egypt, under Gamal Abdel Nasser, turned to the Soviet Union to complete the Aswan Dam.[67]

For their supporters in the Soviet Union, large dams had the attraction of providing a reliable source of energy without the hassle of finding and transporting fuel. Hydropower energy was considered cheap compared to other forms of electricity production. Dams were particularly attractive in Tajikistan, a mountainous republic with several large river systems but limited supplies of coal and other fossil fuels, especially in its southern regions.[68] Besides providing electricity, dams could also help divert water for agriculture, industry, and even residential use.[69]

Soviet geologists and economists had identified Tajikistan's immense potential for hydropower production back in the 1930s. Although Tajikistan had been allocated the role of cotton producer for the first five-year plan, the surveys carried out in those years confirmed vast deposits of metals and minerals which, combined with the hydropower potential of the Vakhsh River, made southern Tajikistan a good candidate for industrialization in the future.[70] With its headwaters in the Pamirs, the Vakhsh River flows through central Tajikistan until it meets the Panj River and forms the Amu Darya, the border between Afghanistan and the Russian Empire since the late 1880s. The Vakhsh was crucial to the agriculture of southern Tajikistan, where it brought silt and minerals along with water. At the same time, since the river was heavily dependent on melting snow and glaciers, its flow varied heavily throughout the year and limited the growing season. Soviet scientists seized on the idea of "regulating" the river's movement to make it more predictable and divert the water for irrigation.

Already in 1931, Soviet officials had launched a major irrigation project, Vakhshstroi, to divert the river and increase irrigable land in the Vakhsh Valley.[71] The goal was not the industrialization of Tajikistan but cotton independence for the USSR. A war scare in 1927 pushed Stalin to pursue industrialization and a rapid collectivization of agriculture, and the onset of the Great Depression encouraged him further toward economic autarky.[72] For the Central Asian republics, already important cotton producers during the imperial period, that meant diverting all available resources to cotton production. If the USSR was going to produce textiles without relying on world markets it needed its own supply of cotton, and it was up to the Central Asian republics to fulfill the union's needs.[73] The results of Vaskhstroi were catastrophic, but they set the stage for the transformation of southern Tajikistan from an area inhabited primarily by shepherds and agriculturists based in the mountains to cotton farmers living in the valleys.[74] The cotton push also created a situation where the Central Asian republics effectively became commodity producers for the Slavic republics. Ideas for hydropower- driven electrification and industrialization were postponed indefinitely.

The idea for a large hydropower dam on the Vakhsh River had been circulating for some time by Stalin's death in 1953. Two smaller dams were underway in the late 1950s: Perepadnia, with a capacity of 30 MW, began operation in 1958; Golovnaia, with a capacity of 240 MW, started producing electricity in 1962. But the real prize was a proposed 3,000 MW dam further upriver. For Tajikistan's leaders, a large dam on the Vakhsh promised to fulfill two goals: the massive expansion of irrigable land, and, through the cheap electricity provided by the dam, the republic's industrialization.[75] But the dam's significance reached beyond the republic itself—its electricity would feed into a planned grid that would cover the Central Asian republics and southern Kazakhstan. The mountainous republics, Kyrgyzstan and Tajikistan, would send electricity from their hydroelectric dams in the summer months, when water levels were high, while the downstream republics, Uzbekistan, Turkmenistan, and Kazakhstan, would provide electricity from their coal and gas fired plants.[76] The whole region would benefit from irrigation and have a reliable supply of electricity year-round.

Kyrgyzstani and Tajikistani leaders were not always so enthusiastic about dams. Gafurov, for example, had been skeptical about a dam at Kairakkum in the early 1950s, in part because it would have flooded lands in Tajikistan and irrigated lands in Uzbekistan.[77] Kyrgyzstan's party leadership enthusiastically supported the idea of a large dam at Naryn, but similarly wanted to avoid flooding its own lands to irrigate that of its neighbor. In subsequent years, Kyrgyzstani leaders also became more sympathetic to the plight of communities that had to be resettled to make room for dam reservoirs, and insisted that Moscow provide compensation.[78] The proposals for the Vakhsh River seem to have been more uniformly accepted by the Tajikistani elite, perhaps because the main benefits were expected to accrue to the republic itself.

Enthusiasm for large dams among planners in Moscow also fluctuated. Dams were attractive because the energy they produced was cheap—it did not require coal, gas, or any other inputs except for naturally flowing water. But by the 1950s it had become clear that the actual construction of large dams was so much more difficult than that of coal-fired plants as to put the actual savings into question.[79] Plans for a large dam in southern Tajikistan were thus repeatedly shelved. Tajikistan's party leadership had enthusiastically supported the idea but was constantly rebuffed: the dam was too expensive and too difficult, and in any case, what would an agricultural republic do with all that electricity?[80] In the 1950s, Tajikistani politicians would use anti-colonial arguments, with some success, in support of industrialization in their republic. The necessity of demonstrating development at home, dictated by the spread of the Cold War to the newly decolonizing world, gave them an opportunity to push projects that planners in Moscow had previously rejected.

At the same time, Moscow's demand for cotton was not going away. On the contrary, Khrushchev's commitment to raising standards of living and access to consumer goods, especially clothing, made the increase in cotton production ever more important. "People will be wearing short pants," Khrushchev supposedly said, "if we don't get cotton." In addition, cotton was exported to Moscow's East European allies and some of its Third World friends, such as India.[81] Most of the cotton was picked and dried in the Central Asian republics, but it then made its way for further processing to plants in the European USSR and eventually to textile mills.

The growing demand for cotton put increasing strain on Central Asian ecological and human resources. In order to get a higher yield, collective farms had to resort to use more and more fertilizer, abandon alternative crops, and expand land under irrigation. Cotton production was labor intensive, especially during the harvest. Soviet officials had begun setting the mechanization of cotton as a goal in the late 1940s, but key tools like cotton harvesters were not widely available and often broke down. Farm managers preferred to bring school-age students and even urban professionals for the harvest rather than risk dealing with the unreliable machines.

I explore the social dynamics of the cotton economy in more detail in chapter 7. For now, it is sufficient to point to the complicated political calculus cotton created for Central Asian leaders in the 1950s. On the one hand, they recognized that the cotton monoculture was damaging the soil, limiting social progress, and making the republics dependent on imports for food and nonfood items.[82] Cotton production was also of limited value to their budgets. When farms sold their crop to government agencies, Central Asian republics were allowed to keep 100 percent of turnover tax, which was based on the difference between cost of production and sale price. Since raw materials were excluded from the turnover tax in the USSR, the sale of raw cotton to enterprises in other republics contributed nothing to the republican budget. On the other hand, these politicians realized that their own political capital in Moscow was dependent on delivering ever higher cotton quotas, and that these achievements could be used to bargain for other kinds of investments. Other postcolonial leaders had made similar bargains. Kwameh Nkrumah, for example, hoped to fund Ghana's industrialization through the sale of the same commodity crop, cocoa, that Ghana had traded to British producers before independence.[83] In a sense, Central Asian leaders were pursuing a similar strategy, except that rather than relying on financial capital they were making a more explicitly political bargain.

Uljaboev, Tajikistan's first secretary from 1956, argued that the dam would become a catalyst for the industrialization of the republic, while also vastly expanding land that could be used for cotton. The dam would allow the irrigation of 80,000 hectares in the Dangara plain, to the southeast of the proposed dam site, by diverting water through an immense tunnel. One-quarter of this land would be suitable for the highly desired thin fiber cotton. It would regulate the flow of water to several canals, facilitate mechanical irrigation with the cheap electricity the dam would produce, minimize siltation, and eliminate flooding in the lower Vakhsh and Amu Darya.[84] Uljaboev lobbied leaders privately and in public appearances; in his speech at the 21st Party Congress in 1959, he emphasized that in a republic with little coal, such a powerful hydroelectric dam was the best hope for propelling industrialization. It would have the additional benefit of helping to irrigate virgin lands in Tajikistan, Turkmenistan, and Uzbekistan.[85]

But like Gafurov before him, Uljaboev had trouble getting the project through central planning organs. Khrushchev, too, was apparently skeptical at first. The dam could power industrial plants, but Tajikistan had little industry to speak of, and neither the resources for such a project nor, seemingly, the need. According to his colleagues, Uljaboev won Khrushchev's support for the dam by convincing the Soviet leader that the dam would make it possible to sell electricity to Kabul and serve as an example to the people of India and Afghanistan. "The East," he told Khrushchev, "needs such light."[86] It would take several more years of lobbying to win over the Council of Ministers and various agencies whose approval was needed before the project could get under way. Besides convincing skeptical officials in Moscow, Uljaboev and his colleagues had to overcome the opposition of other Central Asian leaders, who feared that investment in a large dam on the Vakhsh would deprive them of resources for their own major projects.[87] In 1960 workers finally began preparatory work at a site some seventy kilometers southeast of Tajikistan's capital. The dam would become known as Nurek, after the city that served as the headquarters for the dam builders.

Attracting investments from Moscow sometimes meant competing with other Central Asian republics. National delimitation had left Tajikistan with little productive land, virtually no major cities, and poor infrastructure.[88] Samarkand and Bukhara remained in Uzbekistan. Tashkent, a major city even before the Russian conquest, was the seat of the Central Asian Bureau in the 1920s and the most important city in Central Asia. The transfer of industrial plants during the war and the revival of construction in the 1950s put further distance between the two republics. In 1957 Khrushchev warned Mukhitdinov that other Central Asian politicians were becoming jealous because Tashkent and Uzbekistan had developed so much in the previous few years.[89]

Anti-colonial arguments could be invoked to improve Tajikistan's position vis-à-vis Uzbekistan, as Uljaboev did to secure the construction of a mining and processing plant within Tajikistan. Explorations for mercury had begun in the Leninobod region in the 1940s, and ore was already being excavated by the mid-1950s. When the question of developing a plant to process that ore came up, the Tajik leadership insisted it be located within Tajikistan, rather than near Samarkand. According to Nazarsho Dodkhudoev, who was the chairman of Tajikistan's Council of Ministers, Uljaboev told visiting Central Committee secretary Petr Rudakov that it was wrong to mine the ore in Tajikistan but send it out for processing to Uzbekistan. When Rudakov would not budge, Uljaboev chided, "This manner in which you conduct your relations is similar to the manner in which Great Britain conducts its relations with Africa."[90] Finally, the plant was built in Tajikistan.

Tajikistani party leaders envisioned dam construction as the catalyst for a broader transformation of the republic, and echoed anti-colonial arguments to justify their plans. Soon after his election as first secretary, Uljaboev, speaking to a group of Tajikistani intellectuals and professionals, exhorted them to do more to make Tajikistan self-sufficient in consumer products and in industry. Why were so many products being imported from other republics, he demanded—did Tajikistan not have the human resources to produce things domestically?[91] Uljaboev saw the republic's dependence for consumer goods as evidence of persistent *otstalost'* (backwardness). The dams, he argued, were the best way to accelerate the republic's development. Other Tajikistani politicians repeated these arguments. At a plenum in 1962, Jabbor Rasulov, who by then had replaced Uljaboev, also spoke about the changes dam building would bring, promising that the completion of the Nurek Dam would be followed by electronics factories, chemical plants, aluminum plants, and other enterprises. These in turn would provide opportunities to create more model cities and allow cities like Kulob and Kurgan-Tyube (later Qurghonteppa) to "grow beyond recognition."[92]

The construction of the Nurek Dam, its proponents hoped, could spur the republic's development, promote a vision of Soviet modernity to locals, and

FIGURE 1.1. Tursun Uljaboev, Nazarsho Dodhudoev, Mirzo Rahmatov, and the rest of Tajikistan's leadership receive the Order of Lenin on behalf of the republic from Nikolay Bulganin, the chairman of the USSR Council of Ministers. Stalinabad (Dushanbe), January 1957. Courtesy of the Russian State Archive of Photo and Video Documentation.

demonstrate Soviet achievements to the outside world. In 1961, Dushanbe hosted the conference of the Soviet Committee for Solidarity with Asia and Africa. Delegates traveled from Afghanistan, India, and other countries from Asia, Africa, Latin America, and the Middle East. Uljaboev, one of the keynote speakers, highlighted Tajikistan's industrialization and electrification, especially as compared to the limited industrialization of countries like Iran, Turkey, and Pakistan, and of course spoke about the promise of the Nurek Dam for Tajikistan's development.[93] Although workers had barely begun preparatory work, it was already being used for the USSR's public diplomacy.

Central Asian Politicians and Khrushchev's Power Struggles

By the late 1950s, Tajik and Uzbek politicians had achieved unprecedented levels of power, visibility, and influence for people from their region of the USSR.

During a conversation with New York governor Averell Harriman, then visiting the Soviet Union, Khrushchev listed Mukhitdinov as one of the younger communists who would play a leading role once he and Mikoyan, one of the last remaining leaders whose career stretched back to the immediate postrevolutionary years, passed from the scene.[94] But Uljaboev, too, was waiting in the wings, and apparently was being considered for the CPSU CC Presidium;[95] Gafurov and Tursunzoda were helping shape Moscow's Third World policy; and Jabbor Rasulov, who served as USSR deputy minister of agriculture from 1955 to 1958, was appointed ambassador to Togo in 1960. Khrushchev had promoted these people, listened to them, took them along on his international visits, and helped them get the resources they needed for projects like the Nurek Dam. They repaid him with support in his political battles, including his confrontation with three former allies in 1957.[96]

Khrushchev's leadership was challenged that June by Vyacheslav Molotov, Lazar Kaganovich, and Georgy Malenkov. These three men had helped Khrushchev get rid of Beria and had even supported his rise since 1953 but now felt he had amassed too much power. They first tried to remove Khrushchev in a session of the presidium, but he was able to outmaneuver them and take his case to a plenum of the Central Committee. Loyalists rushed to gather Central Committee members, many of whom were Khrushchev protégés, in Moscow. One aide compared it to a "crash campaign to bring in the harvest."[97] Mukhitdinov was inspecting sheep in the Ferghana Valley when he was called to Moscow, and other secretaries were similarly gathered up and brought to speak on Khrushchev's behalf. Eventually, Khrushchev was able to rally support and have the three conspirators labeled the "anti-party" group. All three were expelled from the leadership and party.

In his memoirs, Mukhitdinov claims a central role in forcing the discussion about Khrushchev out of the presidium to a plenum of the Central Committee, and turning the debate against the three conspirators and in favor of Khrushchev. Mukhitdinov almost certainly exaggerates: to the extent that any one individual was crucial in this turn of events it was Georgy Zhukov, a hero of the Great Patriotic War, who made it clear that the military did not support the actions of Molotov, Kaganovich, and Malenkov. Nevertheless, Mukhitdinov clearly did play a role, and it is interesting to look at what he, Gafurov, and Uljaboev said in support of Khrushchev.[98] At a presidium meeting, Mukhitdinov praised Khrushchev for his support of the republics' industrialization. At one point Mukhitdinov addressed Kaganovich: "You are accusing Nikita Sergeevich of giving away factories and enterprises to the republic, thus weakening the government. But we think of that as one of the great reforms which was immediately and with great satisfaction received by the republics. There are communists working there, and this elevated their role and responsibility for affairs. Is it not clear that the stronger the republics, the greater the Soviet government becomes as a whole? Instead of slowing down we should be speeding up this work, following it through."[99]

During the plenum, Mukhitdinov spoke up repeatedly against Molotov, Kaganovich, and Malenkov. Mukhitdinov criticized the conspirators for wanting to roll back Khrushchev's distribution of power to the republics. He praised Khrushchev for paying attention to the republics, for visiting Uzbekistan, meeting with party leaders and traveling to collective farms and enterprises, listening to suggestions, and providing resources to improve not just cotton, but meat and milk production as well.[100] Malenkov, Kaganovich, and Molotov were criticizing Khrushchev for spending too much time traveling to the republics, but Mukhitdinov claimed to speak on behalf of "the local workers" who "believed that one of the most valuable qualities of Nikita Sergeevich is that he is directly connected to the people."[101]

Uljaboev praised Khrushchev for helping elevate the standard of living in the republic. Unlike the conspirators, he went on, Khrushchev showed he genuinely cared about Tajikistan and was willing to listen to and learn from its own specialists. Molotov had never been to Tajikistan, but Khrushchev had already visited the republic twice since becoming first secretary. Malenkov, Uljaboev said, had ignored new methods developed on Tajik farms for the seeding of cotton, but Khrushchev came out to Stalinabad and insisted on seeing these experiments firsthand.[102] Khrushchev's opponents were criticizing him for paying too much attention to agriculture, but Uljaboev pointed out that Tajik industry had grown substantially since Khrushchev took over, and the standard of living was much higher than it had been in 1953.[103] Gafurov, too, threw his support behind Khrushchev, as did Kyrgyz party secretary Iskhak Razzakov.[104] With the exception of Razzakov, all these politicians had Khrushchev to thank for their rise, and had also found him receptive to their ideas and plans.

The alliance was not to last. In subsequent years Khrushchev's Central Asian allies would disappoint him, while his behavior alienated many of the people he had promoted. Khrushchev's drive to "catch up and overtake" the United States in agricultural production had perverse effects, such as the confiscation and slaughter of livestock by local authorities desperate to meet meat quotas. But it also led to downright fraud: kolkhoz managers embellished the volume of goods they were sending to the district, the district secretary padded the numbers a bit more, and so forth. The republic or region could then claim to have met or surpassed its target, and get more investments in return.[105] The discovery of this practice in Tajikistan led to a major shake-up in the republican party and may have contributed to the breakup of Khrushchev's Central Asian coalition.

The practice had begun soon after the 20th Party Congress, and increased year by year as benefits accrued seemingly without negative consequences. Everyone profited: the republic received a 10,000,000 ruble bonus in 1960 alone for surpassing its quota, the benefits of which trickled down in various ways to administrators and farm chairmen.[106] At the same time, livestock numbers were actually falling, and, as in Ryazan and elsewhere, much had been confiscated from farmers to meet quotas. The farmers often received no compensation, while the actual availability of meat and milk in the republic had dropped.[107] It seems that union authorities had become alerted to inconsistencies in Tajik figures sometime toward the end of 1960. Mukhitdinov was asked to troubleshoot, and at the end of January 1961 he went to Stalinabad to discuss Moscow's concerns and address party officials.[108]

Meanwhile, the investigations continued. On April 8, a delegation of top Tajikistani leaders was summoned to Moscow and confronted with the results of the investigation by inspectors of the CPSU's Central Asia section.[109] The next day, the Tajik Politburo met in the offices of second secretary Pëtr Obnosov to decide the fate of the party's leaders. Mirzo Rakhmatov, the chairman of the republic's soviet (parliament) spoke first in favor of removing Uljaboev, Obnosov, and other leaders from the party and handing their case over to the prosecutor's office. On April 12 Central Committee members gathered in an extraordinary plenum to air the results of the investigation and choose a new leadership in the presence of Khrushchev's protégé Frol Kozlov.[110]

There were plenty of mutual recriminations, but everyone blamed Uljaboev, insisting that he not only knew what was going on but in fact directed the process personally. Besides his awareness of and involvement in the scandal, Uljaboev faced the same accusations that Khrushchev himself would face three years later: that he had come to think of himself as too important, that he accepted no criticism, that he spent too much time traveling and delivering speeches.[111] Obnosov, a second secretary of the Central Committee, complained: "He [Uljaboev] stuck his nose absolutely everywhere, always flattering and trumpeting his connections; constantly he's talking to Moscow, one [official] is his friend, another is his brother. In other words, he gained an illusory, rotten authority and basically held everything with tight reins." But as Obnosov admitted, only a few months earlier everyone had nothing but admiration for Uljaboev: "With only a few exceptions, all the members of the buro fluttered: 'Tursun Uldzhabaevich, Tursun Uldzhabaevich, what a smart guy, what a great speech he made!' They carried Uljaboev on their arms."[112]

It is no surprise they did. Uljaboev had accomplished a great deal in his five years in office, at least in terms of getting Moscow to commit to Tajikistan's development. Even if this did not mean much to ordinary people in the republic, it certainly meant a great deal to other party members, who saw their leader's role, and by extension their own role, greatly elevated, and had real material accomplishments to point to. As for the corruption scandal, this may have been as much Khrushchev's fault as Uljaboev's. Khrushchev's pressure for results at all costs, even when advisers and economists warned him that the figures were completely unrealistic, encouraged falsification on the part of local leaders who did not want to disappoint their superiors.

Uljaboev maintained his innocence, admitting that he had been cheated by his subordinates. In his closing statement, he pleaded: "I ask again, believe me, that never in my heart or my soul was I against the party, I had no intentions, besides bringing good to our party and to my people. . . . Even [if I am forced out of the party] I will stay loyal to the party, send me to the most backward corner, so that I can correct the mistakes I allowed to happen as the first secretary of the Central Committee of the Communist Party of Tajikistan."[113] He would get his chance. Soon after his dismissal his family was moved out of their government apartment. Uljaboev spent several months unemployed before his successor, Jabbor Rasulov, finally assigned him to run a state farm.[114]

The investigation revealed how little had actually been done to change the lives of ordinary Tajiks along the lines envisioned by Khrushchev, Uljaboev, and others. The cotton industry was inefficient, even by Soviet standards, with the highest cost-per-ton of any of the cotton-producing republics. It had the lowest rate of mechanization, and still widely used schoolchildren (including those from primary grades) in the harvest, for periods as long as three and a half months.[115] Because the investigation involved an audit of the prosecutor's office, it also revealed that little was being done to address the treatment of women.[116] The promises of Soviet modernization, in other words, had thus far produced meager results.

The year of the Tajik scandal also saw Mukhitdinov lose his spot in the presidium. Sharof Rashidov became the sole Central Asian in that body, later to be joined by Kazakhstan's leader Dinmukhamed Kunayev. Gafurov lost his position on the Central Committee, but he remained director of the Institute of Oriental Studies and continued to play an influential role in Moscow's Third World policy through that institution and through the Society for Solidarity with Asian and African Countries. Of course, the Tajik party had the biggest shake-up; several hundred people ultimately lost their positions as a result of their ties, whether direct or indirect, to the scandal.

Khrushchev had encouraged leaders like Uljaboev to claim industrial and other development projects for their republics; they in turn used this opportunity to elevate their own status. Yet Soviet leaders worried that the economy could not operate on such narrow principles; specialization, they believed, was necessary if the socialist world would become as efficient as the capitalist world, a position that also informed their approach to East European allies (and caused significant friction). Uljaboev may have won the day by securing the construction of the ore-processing plant inside Tajikistan, but it probably would have made more sense to build it near Samarkand, as planners originally envisioned: the city was only a few hours away and had a larger existing industrial base and pool of workers.

Khrushchev was troubled by the uneven pace of development in the Central Asian republics, on the one hand, and by republican leaders' insistence that new enterprises be located within their own borders, on the other. The former was upsetting the political balance and complicating Khrushchev's political alliances, while the latter led to waste and corruption. In a lengthy memorandum prepared between two trips to the region in 1962, Khrushchev complained that the search for "independence" had gone too far: "in the industry of these republics there is a great deal of unnecessary parallelism. . . . Each one would rather do something poorly as long as they can do it themselves." Khrushchev proposed instead the creation of a single coordinating body for Kyrgyzstan, Tajikistan, Turkmenistan, and Uzbekistan.[117] This idea was taken up with the creation of a Central Asian party bureau, headquartered in Tashkent, at the end of 1962, and a Central Asian economic coordinating council (*sovnarkhoz*) the following year.[118] Similar structures were also created for the Caucasus.

Central Asian politicians resented Khrushchev's attempts to recentralize economic and political power in the region.[119] A Tajik economist later complained that the Central Asian sovnarkhoz had been "contradictory to the principles of Lenin's nationality policy," since it undermined local control.[120] Equally problematic was Khrushchev's zigzagging on questions of cultural autonomy, which paralleled his inconsistency on other questions of de-Stalinization and intellectual freedom. Khrushchev's fears about unleashing nationalism led him to propagate, at ideologist Mikhail Suslov's urging, a goal of *sliianie* (merging) of Soviet nationalities, and simultaneously emphasize the teaching of Russian language. The de-Stalinization program gave local intellectuals hope that they could articulate a cultural program with minimal interference from the center, but these initiatives seemed to portend the opposite.[121]

Khrushchev's erratic behavior, his imperiousness, and his unpredictability in both domestic and foreign policy alienated even some of his closest allies. By October 1964 a group led by Khrushchev's protégé Leonid Brezhnev was ready to remove the leader from power. Brezhnev and his allies were worried about their own fate under a leader who frequently became disappointed with underlings, ministers, and provincial leaders. They no longer had to fear the Gulag, but demotion or banishment to the political wilderness remained real possibilities.

When the conspirators finally moved against Khrushchev he seemed to have no supporters among the Central Asian leaders. There was little they could have done to save him, but by this point they seemed happy to be rid of him. Rashidov apparently flew to Moscow in October 1964 to attend a scheduled plenum of the CPSU with two versions of a speech—one with mild and the other with savage criticism of Khrushchev's initiatives.[122] At the presidium meeting on October 13, Rashidov was given the last word, and he tore into Khrushchev for undermining party authority with constant reorganizations.[123] The next day Khrushchev was formally removed at a plenum of the whole Central Committee. The Central Asian buro of the CPSU Central Committee and the Central Asian Economic Council (as well as analogous structures for the Caucasus) were abandoned within weeks. The decision to return to the pre-1962 status quo was presumably part of Brezhnev's alliance making and consolidation of power.

Neither Mukhitdinov, nor Uljaboev, nor any other republican leader thought in terms of "independence" in the sense contemporary anti-colonial activists and postcolonial leaders did. But they did think of themselves as champions of their republic's interest, and this in itself had interesting implications, both positive and negative. One was that they became lobbyists for projects that made little economic sense either from the point of view of their own republic's needs or the economic interests of the USSR as a whole. Another was that it led to inter-republic rivalry. These problems emerged as an unintended consequence of shifting Soviet approaches to managing the vast, complicated, multiethnic state.[124] More important, the politicians who rose to prominence in this period helped define their republics' economic development, their place in Soviet foreign policy, and the cultural policy that would be pursued more or less until the Soviet collapse.

Khrushchev was attacked not only for his personality and administrative reforms. His opponents also criticized him for wasting resources on the postcolonial world, whose leaders, "having eaten what we gave them, have turned away from us."[125] Yet in the next two decades the USSR would only deepen its commitment to the developing world. Similarly, the transformation of Moscow's relations with the Central Asian republics would not be undone. In many ways, some of the trends begun under Khrushchev—toward a greater emphasis on consumption, investment in the welfare state, and a commitment to industrialization, would only deepen in the following years. It is to the proliferating consequences of the changes brought in the dynamic 1950s that the book now turns.

AYNI'S CHILDREN, OR MAKING A TAJIK-SOVIET INTELLIGENTSIA

This chapter focuses on the people who negotiated and implemented ideas for social transformation in their republic—the technical and cultural elite. Two generations are of particular interest: the first includes those individuals born around the time of the revolution—contemporaries of the Russian group Vlad Zubok called "Zhivago's Children." Like their Russian counterparts, they too sought to connect a prerevolutionary cultural inheritance and idealistic sensibility to the realities of the Soviet system.[1] The second is the generation that followed, meaning those who entered university starting in the late 1950s, and whom Donald Raleigh has called the "Soviet Baby Boomers."[2] This generation, writes Raleigh, experienced "the rise of youth culture, the appeal of Western popular culture, more leisure time, a carefree attitude, economic growth, rising living standards and a consumerist culture, and the expansion of education." Like their American counterparts, the Soviet baby boomers "played a vital, even defining role, in transforming the climate of the contemporary world."[3]

Just as there are important differences between the American and Russian baby boomers—the much greater wartime losses in the USSR, postwar poverty versus American postwar prosperity, and the legacy of late Stalinism—any study of the postwar Central Asian professional elite needs to make sense of how being on the semi-colonial periphery of the USSR shaped the experiences and worldview of its members. As a group they share much in common with other postcolonial elites, including a sometimes ambivalent relationship toward the metropole and its standards of progress and culture and a sense of their own mission with regard to the broader society.[4] At the same time, this was a Soviet elite, and understanding this group requires looking at their experiences against the background of the Great Patriotic War, late Stalinism, the "thaw," and other milestones of Soviet history. We need to follow them outside the republic, around the USSR, and beyond. Many of these individuals were able to develop and take advantage of networks across all parts of the union. These networks helped them in their professional careers and affected how they saw the world and their place within it. Understanding the intelligentsia's experiences in the postwar decades will help us make sense of how they dealt with the dilemmas of modernization and "cultural construction" as they took on positions of responsibility in academia, publishing, and planning.

The sociologist Georgi Derluguian called the Soviet professional intelligentsia the "new proletarians" because they were brought from the peasantry into state industries and institutions. But he underlines that they were hardly the "hapless human material of Stalinist industrialization" or of postwar education and mobilization campaigns. Rather, Derluguian argues, the new proletarians took post-Stalinist Soviet ideology seriously, became socialized into urban Soviet life through education, and found ways to make claims on the state.[5] This conception of the "new proletariat" also holds for our case, although as we will see the boundary between the "proletarian intelligentsia" and the "bureaucracy" was porous.[6] The individuals that came of age in these decades ran the republic's newspapers, taught at its schools and universities, and debated and designed economic programs. Working in institutions like the State University, or the Council of Ministers of the Tajik SSR further encouraged them to think of "their" society as Tajik. In their progression through Soviet institutions and engagement with various forms of mobilization and cultural life, these individuals developed a sense of tangible responsibility for the future of their own society.

Making a National Intelligentsia under Stalin

The Bolsheviks had a complicated attitude towards the intelligentsia. Prior to the October revolution the term "intelligentsia" was used by the part of Russia's educated elite that saw itself as the conscience of the nation, defending the masses but not of them. The Bolsheviks needed the educated elite but reserved the role of leading the masses for themselves. As the historian Stuart Finkel points out, "The Soviet definition of intelligentsia was at once broader and more elemental [than the pre-revolutionary one] including all those who performed mental labor [*umstvennyi trud*] but rejecting the idea that the intelligentsia had any historic mission."[7] After the revolution the independent intelligentsia in Russia—the part of it that refused to side with the new regime—was largely eliminated, either through repression or forced exile.[8] To fill the gap, the regime sought to organize writers, artists, and other intellectuals within more tightly bounded ideological frames, while at the same time establishing control over the "technical intelligentsia"—engineers and other experts that were heavily represented among the bourgeoisie. In subsequent years, its dependence on people educated under tsarism declined. The consolidation of control over higher education helped ensure that a new generation of specialists would emerge and free the regime from its reliance on remnants of the old elite.

In Central Asia, part of the intellectual elite that had sought social reforms and revolutionary change prior to the revolution sided with the Bolsheviks and sought to promote these changes within the new Soviet context. As Adeeb Khalid shows in *Making Uzbekistan,* most of the pre-Soviet reformers were at best ambivalent about the Bolsheviks, and some were highly suspicious of the new regime. Many nevertheless chose to reconcile with the new regime because of the broader opportunities it provided for cultural and social development. Flora Roberts, in her study of the old elite of Khojent (Leninobod), showed how the older elite used their social and cultural capital to shape Soviet institutions of enlightenment.[9] At the same time, a new elite was being shaped by Soviet schools, the Komsomol, and other institutions. As in the rest of the Soviet Union, the older elite was targeted in two waves—first in the early 1930s, and then again during the great terror. The elimination of those individuals thus fractured an important link between Soviet Central Asia and its prerevolutionary reform path. Still, the legacy of those reformers lived on and continued to shape how Central Asians thought about their own societies and their role in them.

These links become clear when we consider the biographies of some of Tajikistan's elite families. For example, the engineer and Communist Party official Jura L.'s parents came from Bukhara, where his grandfather had been a poet and jadid sympathizer; one of his poems was even included in Sadriddin Ayni's famous anthology of Tajik poetry, *Namunai Adabioti Tojik* (1926). Jura L.'s father became a journalist, joining the newly founded *Pravda Bukhary.* After 1929, when Tajikistan became an independent republic, he moved to Stalinabad/Dushanbe. For the rest of his life he would work at the Lahuti theater while continuing to publish poetry in the new Tajik press and organizing drama circles for children at the local youth center, the House of Pioneers. Jura L. himself was born in Stalinabad just before World War II. He would grow up with the city, eventually attending the newly formed Polytechnic Institute when it opened in 1961. A construction engineer by training, he was recruited into party work, spending many years on various municipal committees.

The path from Bukhara to Stalinabad was not unusual. In fact, a large part of the "native" intelligentsia in Tajikistan through the 1950s were Persian speakers from Bukhara and Samarkand, two of the most important centers of learning in the region. They included pioneers of Tajik-Soviet culture, such as Sadriddin Ayni (1878–1954), who worked as educators and writers before the revolution, as well as younger intellectuals such as Ghani Abdullo and Jalol Ikromī, who made their careers after the Bolsheviks came to power.[10] People like Jura L.'s father came to develop theaters, teach in the schools, edit the republic's newspapers, and run its administration.

Some of those who came to Stalinabad from Bukhara or Samarkand in the 1930s, particularly in the wake of the 1936–1938 purges, found a shelter from the terror. For children of "enemies of the people," or for those who had fallen under suspicion but escaped imprisonment, Tajikistan offered the possibility of riding out the storm, and even being sheltered from prosecution by local officials desperate for qualified cadres. Yet living in Tajikistan did not shield one from the terror completely. The intelligentsia that had arrived since the late 1920s fell under suspicion and was persecuted by local authorities, just as their counterparts had been in Uzbekistan.[11] Those whose families had been ensnared by the terror elsewhere and came to Tajikistan for safety still carried the stigma of disgrace or being children of "enemies of the people." They lived on the margins and were often the last to receive housing or any other benefits the state could distribute. Thus the family of composer Ziaudullo Shahidi, whose father was labeled an "enemy of the people," lived in a one-room mudbrick house until 1943, when the Iranian-Tajik poet Abdulqasim Lahuti intervened with local authorities and helped the family get a larger apartment.[12] For others the label continued to cause problems well into the 1950s. The father of the literary historian Hursheda Otahonova, a communist, had been arrested in 1937. Although Otahonova's father was released during the war, he had not been reinstated in the party at the time of his death in 1952. Nevertheless, he remained a committed communist and sought repeatedly to have his expulsion from the party overturned. Otahonova sincerely believed in the party's mission as well, but her father's conviction precluded her entry into its ranks and may have also initially blocked her acceptance for graduate study, despite her being one of the top students in her class.[13]

Stalinism inspired fear and resistance but also fierce loyalty among some of the newer entrants into the party. The literary historian Hudoĭnazar Asozoda recalled that his father, a laborer who attended a Soviet school and became a village schoolteacher, "was a believer in Stalin. He really accepted the socialist order. He often reminded us that there had never been an order like this one in history."[14] When Stalin died in March 1953, the family was mourning an infant who had lived only eight days, yet Asozoda's father immediately began organizing a ceremony for the deceased Soviet leader at the local school.[15]

Although the region was far from the fighting, the Great Patriotic War played a crucial role in the formation of the Central Asian elite. As scholars have argued, the war was crucial for the legitimization of the Soviet system.[16] In this sense it may have played an even greater role in Central Asia, where the war effort, while imposing some additional hardships, also became a collective endeavor. The subsequent celebration of locals' role in the war cemented it in memory as a shared enterprise.[17] Marianne Kamp noted that soldiers came back from the war with a stronger sense of belonging in the USSR as well as greater openness regarding the role of women in the family and economic life.[18] The evacuation of people and industries brought specialists and cultural elites from Moscow and Leningrad to cities like Tashkent and Dushanbe. Although most would return to their places of origin, many would stay and work as engineers, teachers, and managers for decades after the war.[19]

The war was a fundamental experience for those who fought as well as for those who stayed behind. The future historian Aslamsho, who grew up in a village in the country's southeast, described the war as the most important influence of his life. "I was a seven- or eight-year-old boy working in the kolkhoz in place of those who went to the front. Not just me, others my age worked, too. What made us work so actively to help the front and restore the economy? Was it the party? No. The government? No. It was our highly elevated patriotic consciousness." Aslamsho was not just repeating slogans. His experience of the war was personal, as he explained, because his father was at the front and returned a decorated officer, and his two older brothers also were at the front: "They suffered at the front, they were wounded, and we here were hungry."[20] Memories of the war period, and persistent questions (why did this happen?), would lead him to study history in the 1950s.

It was not only party members in good standing who went off to fight. Over 260,000 young men from Tajikistan went to the front, at a time when the whole population of the republic was just under 1,500,000.[21] The future academic Mohammad Osimov (Osimī) had hoped to go to Leningrad for graduate work in physics, but instead found himself sent to command a battery defending the city.[22] While some may have volunteered out of a sense of patriotism, others hoped to erase the stigma of the terror. Ikromī recounts the stories of several intellectuals who volunteered for service because they had been accused of disloyalty and had been living under a cloud; they wanted to prove their loyalty to the party and rehabilitate themselves.[23]

The Soviet treatment of some veterans also underscored the cruelties of postwar Stalinism. Ashur Haydarov had studied drawing in his native Samarkand and was working as an artist in the Uzbek language newspaper *Lenin Yuli* when he heard the news that war had broken out between Germany and the USSR.

The next day he went to his editor, Sharof Rashidov (the future party boss of Uzbekistan), and told him, "Everything is boiling inside me, the whole day I'm thinking about one thing, I'm asking you to let me volunteer for the army." Two months later he made his way to training camp, along with Rashidov and another colleague. He was eventually sent to the front as a second lieutenant in the infantry.[24] In 1942, while fighting in Ukraine, Haydarov was taken prisoner and put in a POW camp. There he was compelled to join the anti-Soviet Turkestan Legion being formed with the help of some Central Asian émigrés. Haydarov claims he did so unwillingly, and escaped at the first opportunity. He joined partisans in Poland, finally spending the last months of the war fighting Ukrainian separatists with a detachment from the People's Commissariat of Internal Affairs (NKVD).

Demobilized at the end of June 1945, Haydarov made his way back to Samarkand. His father was still in Leningrad, one of his brothers was near Konigsberg, another had died near Stalingrad. Several days after his arrival, Haydarov was asked to come to the office of the local NKVD and questioned about his time as a POW. Although released, he was denied a passport and was told not to leave the city without permission. Nevertheless, despite the threat that seemed to be hanging over him and general postwar poverty, his return to civilian life went smoothly at first. In August 1945 he was invited to join the local Artists' Union, reuniting with some of his teachers and mentors from before the war.[25] Then, in 1949, he was suddenly arrested and sentenced to fifteen years for collaborating with the enemy—a not uncommon fate for those who had been prisoners of war and then escaped. Haydarov was relatively lucky—his drawings earned him some protection from the criminal leaders within the camp, while camp management put him in a brigade with artists. Still, he was shocked by the brutality, the forced labor, the depravity of some of the prisoners. He was finally released in 1955. Soon Haydarov returned to his work, and in 1957 was even taking part in the second Ten Day Festival of Tajik Culture in Moscow. He was able to rebuild his life in Stalinabad, eventually becoming one of the republic's most prominent visual artists. It was only during perestroika that he found out he had been completely rehabilitated in the 1950s.[26]

Haydarov's story illustrates some of the complexities of the war experience for Central Asian soldiers and civilians. Although Central Asia was far from the fighting, the war and postwar paranoia caused upheaval in people's lives. At the same time, there was a sense (actively promoted in postwar decades) that the whole region had taken part in a great battle against evil and helped the Soviet Union emerge victorious. Many of the returning veterans felt emboldened to play a more active part in shaping their republics in the subsequent decades. Scholars of the postwar Russian intelligentsia have noted that veterans of the Great Patriotic War played an important role in the reform communism of the post-Stalin years. They had seen European cities where the quality of life was much higher than what they knew at home, and their experience as veterans gave them the confidence (and political capital) to push for reform.[27] The same was true for some Central Asian veterans.

Haydarov himself remained proud of his military service and, until his death, stayed in close contact with some of his veteran friends from other parts of the union. Every interlocutor I spoke to who remembered the post-war period recalled a time of optimism. As Rasul Khodizoda noted, "After the war life was difficult, but we felt cultural, scholarly, and spiritual life in the political environment of the country growing, . . . The power of the Soviet government grew. . . . The influence of the government and communist party spread out over every part of the world."[28] Munira Shahidi explained that "the feeling of victory seemed to leave a mark on my whole generation. We felt that we were right. In any case, that was the ideology, that's what we were told (*chto nam vnushali*) and we believed it."[29]

Stalinabad was still a small city in the early 1950s, though increasingly cosmopolitan. It had once again become a refuge for some who were unwelcome elsewhere, including families of repressed old Bolsheviks and the prerevolutionary intelligentsia, Jewish professionals seeking shelter during the anti-cosmopolitan campaign, and Tajik-speaking elites from Samarkand and Bukhara. Finally, it became the home to Iranian leftists exiled after the shah's crackdown on the Tudeh Party in 1949 and again after the CIA-supported coup against Mohammed Mossadeq in 1953.[30] All of these people would play an important role in the city's postwar intellectual life.

Stalinabad's cultural and intellectual life in the postwar years took place almost entirely within a narrow band around the main street, Prospekt Lenina. Many of the families that represented the republic's cultural elite were housed in one of two nearby wooden apartment houses—one for writers and the other for musicians and theater directors. Munira Shahidi recalled that as a result her "childhood was happy—I lived surrounded by poets, writers, musicians, and artists."[31] Children imitated their parents, recreating their artistic world in the courtyard. Jura L. recalled: "All of the parents were actors and they would come home and say to each other, 'This evening will be a rehearsal of such a play or this evening such a performance will take place and so forth.' Well, we imitated them, we created a kind of *kruzhok* [reading circle] and tried to create a stage set and paint it."[32] By the 1950s, a new generation was growing up that could think of itself as native to the republic and model itself on the life being created by their parents.

At the same time, the growing cosmopolitanism of the city meant that the Tajik intelligentsia growing up in the postwar years had several points of reference for thinking about its role and mission. Those whose ancestors claimed status as Islamic notables drew on their own family histories, rearticulating a notion of "service to the people" for their work in Soviet academic institutions and in the professions.[33] Many intellectuals, especially those who came from Samarkand and Bukhara, looked to the jadids as modernizers who wanted to advance their culture. But since the late 1920s jadidism had become a byword for Pan-Turkism and any revival of it deemed anti-Soviet.[34] Mentioning the jadids became a taboo. The writer Sadriddin Ayni provided the ideal connection. While associated with the jadids in the pre-revolutionary period, he had managed to survive the political fluctuations of the 1930s and emerged as someone who connected this pre-Soviet past with the present of the new intelligentsia. Especially for those who had gone to university in the 1940s and 1950s, while Ayni was still alive, the writer and scholar served as a model and often as a mentor.[35]

The younger generation sometimes also looked to the Russian and Jewish intelligentsia that came to the republic in the 1930s and in the postwar period. These groups brought not just their professional expertise but a commitment to education, knowledge, art, and service. Many brought a personal or family history of repression that gave them a point of identification with some of the locals who had suffered in the 1930s. If there was optimism in these postwar years, it was tempered by poverty, the memory of the terror, and the paranoia of the late Stalin era. Shahidi remembered developing a great love for literature, "especially Russian literature," as a pupil in the 1950s, under the influence of teachers like Berta Gamarnik. "I was very lucky that I had a teacher who really loved her work," Shahidi explained. But she learned that they were also united by misfortune. According to Munira, Gamarnik was the daughter of a military commander who had been sentenced to a Gulag camp.[36] One day she asked Munira, "Did you know that your grandfather was sent to Siberia on the same day as my father?"[37] Such connections played a contradictory role—they encouraged identification, and even solidarity, with Russians, Jews, and other across the Soviet Union, binding people together, but it was a solidarity of suffering at the hands of an unjust regime.

One result of these interactions was that the emerging postwar educated elite acquired a sense of itself as a group that drew on diverse sources. There was the notion of service to the community (increasingly understood as the "nation") inherited from prerevolutionary elite who actively inculcated this notion to pupils in the new institutions of higher learning. But the passion for secular knowledge carried by newcomers to the republic also played a role. Finally, this emerging elite became increasingly transnational, in the sense that it traveled, studied, and established networks far beyond its own republic.[38]

Education and Social Mobility

In 1944, Rasul Khodizoda moved to Tashkent to start university. The timing proved fortuitous. Orientalists from Petersburg and Moscow had been evacuated to Tashkent during the war, and some of them were invited to lecture at the university. Khodizoda studied with luminaries such as Evgenii Eduardovich Bertels (1890–1957), Andrei Nikolaevich Kononov (1906–1986), and Mikhail Andreev (1873–1948). The latter seems to have played a particularly important role in Khodizoda's life. At Andreev's house Khodizoda saw a personal library the likes of which he had never seen before. Besides the vast collection of books, there were photo albums, including those documenting Andreev's travels in India. Andreev told Khodizoda about a kruzhok on oriental studies that he had organized in the 1920s, and, with Andreev's encouragement, Khodizoda revived the group.[39]

New institutions of higher education were created or expanded throughout the USSR in the postwar era. As Benjamin Tromly argued in his study of universities in Russia and Ukraine in this period, these institutions were "training grounds for the military-industrial complex, showcases of Soviet cultural and economic accomplishment, and, especially after Stalin's death, valued tools in Soviet cultural diplomacy."[40] The USSR was hardly alone in trying to use higher education to create a new elite; empires, anti-colonial movements, and post-colonial states all hoped to create technically competent individuals loyal to their particular projects.[41] The Soviet Union, the United States, and some European countries became involved in setting up universities in the developing world; their goal was not just to impart technical knowledge, but to create new kinds of subjects—thinking in terms of their nation rather than their home village or region, forward looking, and rational.[42] Within the Soviet Union, education was openly treated as an ideological activity meant to create technical skills, faith in the revolution, and loyalty to party and state. Yet the educational institutions set up by the Soviet state also allowed administrators, teachers, and even students significant room to define the specific content of courses and the overall experience of education. These institutions produced a national technocratic elite within a Soviet context.

Studying Tajik literature in Tashkent was a natural choice in 1944—even though that city was the capital of Uzbekistan. It was only in the postwar years, as higher education throughout the Soviet Union expanded, that Tajikistan got its own university (a medical school had been established in 1939). Gafurov, installed as first secretary after the war, seems to have played an active role in expanding higher education in the republic. In a note to Andrei Zhdanov in 1946

FIGURE 2.1.   Mohammad Osimov (Osimī) lecturing at the Polytechnic Institute in Stalinabad (Dushanbe), 1950s. Courtesy of the Russian State Archive of Photo and Video Documentation.

he emphasized that establishing a university in Stalinabad would help achieve Soviet foreign policy goals: "It is important to remember the geographical position of Tajikistan, that it is in the vicinity of Middle East Countries—Iran and Afghanistan—that have a population close to the Tajik in language and from an anthropological and ethnographic point of view. It makes sense to study the nature, economies, and populations of these neighbors not only from the center of the Union, but also from the Tajik SSR, where specialists from the local population make the best cadres for studying populations close in language."[43] Although it is unclear if Gafurov's appeal to Soviet foreign policy interests had any influence over officials in Moscow, the proposal was approved and the university established in 1948. The local branch of the Soviet Academy of Sciences became its own independent institution several years later, with Ayni installed as its first president. The 1950s saw the opening of a Polytechnic Institute and expansion of teacher's colleges and other schools.

For Gafurov, Ayni, and other Tajik intellectuals, expanding education fulfilled both economic and nation-building needs. As Ayni told Khodizoda, studying the history of Tajik literature meant "serving Tajik science and culture." "For that," Ayni said, "you need to be in the center of Tajik science and culture.... You have to go to Stalinabad ... where [Bobojon Gafurov] is making every effort to gather cadres for Tajik scholarship."[44] Similarly, Sulton Umarov, then the rector of Tashkent State University but later Ayni's successor as president of Tajikistan's Academy of Sciences, emphasized: "The road for all Tajiks now leads to Stalinabad. Bobojon Gafurov is following a wise policy of gathering all qualified cadres ... since the foundation of our university a number of people have been invited to Tajikistan or gone there on their own initiative. You are also a qualified Tajik cadre and your going there will be a benefit to Tajikistan and also to you."[45]

The new institutions broadened access to higher education. Children of the "old" elite continued to pursue university studies, but more and more students would come from poorer peasant families, even from the remote corners of the republic. Prior to 1948, an aspiring student's best chance at a higher education was to attend one of the teacher's colleges located around the republic; a few could then continue to a university education in Tashkent or one of the other Soviet cities. Graduate study always meant leaving the republic. The university and the academy of sciences, with its ability to supervise research and award *kandidat nauk* degrees, made it possible to pursue undergraduate and advanced study within the republic. These individuals quickly found work. The university's first class of philologists, for example, produced graduates who went on to key roles in publishing and academia within the republic in the postwar decades and into the independence period.[46]

For those without a family background in education—whether religious or secular—the university and technical schools presented a special attraction. Aslamsho, who came from a village in Darwaz in the foothills of the Pamir Mountains, contrasted life in the city with the poverty and closed-mindedness of his home village. In 1949, he recalled, after intensive agitation from party and Komsomol officials, two girls became the first to go to Dushanbe to study. As a result, their families were ostracized. "The old, feudal-patriarchal relations interfered and the clergy labeled them unbelievers (*kofir*) and forbade anyone to visit their parents," Aslamsho recalled. The girls studied at the pedagogical institute and returned to the village, presumably to assume teaching posts. "We looked at them lovingly and with jealousy, and the elders looked at them with hate. They returned as city people: their clothes, their hairstyle, their manner of speaking at such a high level, this striking beauty, all of this inspired in us the idea that it was also necessary ...

to go study, at any price."[47] In Stalinabad, Aslamsho explained, a young villager was exposed to things he or she had never seen before: "hot water, electricity, a dormitory, bedding that was changed every week, a cafeteria with food three times a day, and you could live there for free and they gave you a stipend on top of that." These conditions, in turn, further stimulated the desire to study.[48]

Aslamsho most likely exaggerated the conditions in the dormitories; it is clear that many of them still had trouble meeting these standards even in the 1970s, when resources were much greater than in the 1950s.[49] What is interesting is how important he believed the university experience to be in one's transformation from peasant to cultured urbanite. Certain kinds of dress, regularly changed clean bedding, and access to electricity were all accouterments of a "cultured" person and freed one to develop his or her intellectual potential.[50] The economist Rashid Rakhimov also recalled how much attention one of his Russian teachers paid to grooming. The teacher would periodically ask the boys to put their hands on the desk, then trim their fingernails or send them out to wash up. Although such behavior seems to carry colonial overtones, it was hardly different from what modernizing elites in other countries hoped to do through their educational institutions in this period. Emphasis on comportment and hygiene was not unusual for a school that was taking peasant boys and girls and preparing them to be white-collar professionals. Rakhimov viewed this attention to the length of his fingernails or the cleanliness of his hands as particularly important in helping restore normal civilian life after the war.[51] Shukur Sultonov, who taught at the university in Leninobod, similarly recalled that one of the university's strengths was that "teachers were interested in everything, from clothing and up to culture and worldview."[52]

Similar stories came from people with different backgrounds. Thus Manzar M., from Gharm, contrasted the closed-mindedness of his village, where, in his words, even wearing your hair slightly longer than normal could make you an outcast, with the broader horizons offered by study in the capital. By the time I interviewed him in 2012 and 2013 Manzar had grown increasingly critical of the Soviet Union, especially the enforced atheism and the corruption he says he observed from the late 1970s. Nevertheless, he spoke of studying in Dushanbe as a transformational experience. It was at the university that he met his wife, the daughter of a Tajik soldier who had been wounded at the front and the Ukrainian Catholic nurse who cared for him. Both Manzar and his wife became historians.[53] He taught at the university for many years, eventually going on to do graduate work at the Academy of Sciences. Inspired by the campaign for the industrialization of the republic, Manzar chose the history of the Southern Tajikistan Territorial Production Complex as his dissertation topic.

Whether entering the humanities and social sciences or more practical fields like engineering or architecture, many of the young men and women felt that education gave them a chance to be part of something bigger, to provide a larger service to their republic. It was a message actively instilled by their teachers. The point of literary research, Ayni explained to Khodizoda, was "to serve Tajik science and culture." In other words, it was a way to contribute to the articulation and dissemination of Tajik national identity and to link older Persianate traditions with the Soviet present. The notion of serving Tajikistan was not limited to those who went into the humanities. The students who chose technical subjects were attracted by taking part in another big project, namely the industrialization of the republic. For Jura L., studying in the construction faculty at the new Polytechnic Institute was exciting and "prestigious" because it was associated with the new, widely publicized projects that promised to transform the republic and lift standards of living.[54] Olimjon H., who had gone to school in Leninobod, decided to focus on industrial refrigeration. To him, studying this seemingly unglamorous topic pointed to the possibility of participating in the transformation of his city. "We had a canning factory, and the food industry was being developed, but there were no refrigerators, the big kind, and we wanted to be specialists in this sphere. . . . It was new."[55] Even seemingly mundane specializations enabled many students to take part in the most exciting projects of the day, whether the transformation of the republic through industrialization or the preservation and development of Tajik culture through research.

How successful were the universities in preparing the kind of technical, managerial, and cultural elite the republic required? In 1966, the republic was short some 32,000 specialists, meaning among other things that industrialization required importing people from other parts of the USSR or using underqualified cadres. The natural policy response was to try to expand the capacity of the institutes and access to education, but this was easier said than done.[56] By 1976, the republic's universities and institutes had 2,845 researchers and teachers, including 43 doctors of science and 783 with a candidate of sciences degree. Combined they enrolled a total of 40,867 students, of whom 24,091 were regular "day" students, 3,885 were taking night courses, and 12,891 were following "distance" courses.[57] But it was clear that the system could not keep up. Inspectors from Moscow complained that Tajikistan's universities and institutes "relied very heavily on recent graduates for teaching." Those sent to Moscow and Leningrad for graduate study—with the idea that they would return to Tajikistan and become lecturers—were poorly prepared compared to their Russian peers and needed a year of preparatory work to catch up. The problem was particularly acute in mathematics and the sciences.[58]

One issue was language. In theory, it was possible to study in Tajik or Russian, giving students who had attended Tajik schools, especially those from rural areas, a chance at a university education. But the quality of Tajik-language instruction was often poor, in part because there were few qualified instructors who could teach at a university level in the language and in part due to a lack of textbooks. One inspection from 1969 found that most courses taught in Tajik "are thoroughly lacking in the necessary literature, and an additional difficulty arises from the lack of Russian-Tajik dictionaries for specific terminology."[59] Although some work was being done to provide study materials in Tajik, another report six years later lamented that the "students of the preparatory division [of the Tajik Polytechnic Institute] are mostly supplied with high school textbooks and when it comes to math the Tajik-language groups have only half the textbooks and exercise books they need."[60] In addition, the republic had a perpetual shortage of qualified Russian teachers at the school level, and those who were available tended to stay in the larger cities.[61]

Preparatory courses were supposed to democratize access to the university-level education, giving students from weaker schools, or those who had entered the work force straight after school and now wanted to study, a chance to catch up. As the example of the textbooks shows they lacked the resources to overcome some of these inequalities. Between 1973 and 1978 almost one-third of students were unable to complete the preparatory studies at the Polytechnic (although the number was decreasing), and almost one-fourth of those who completed the courses dropped out of the institute, mostly as a result of poor academic performance.[62] The state university faced similar problems. Perhaps as a result, the number of applicants for the preparatory courses was decreasing, from a high of 711 applications per 275 seats in 1976 to 498 in 1977.[63]

Nor were these problems limited to the university-level institutions. The professional-technical colleges (*proffesional'no tekhnicheskoe uchilishche*), which were supposed to help draw rural youth into the skilled work force, also had trouble attracting students and, with those they did accept, producing graduates. As I show in the next chapter, the failure of these institutions became a growing concern for planners, economists, and sociologists in Central Asian republics and in Moscow, as it undermined their goals for social and economic transformation in the republic. The failures of these schools limited social mobility, and left the republic's nascent industry as well as its collective farms with a shortage of specialists. It also created yet another rift between those who were able to take advantage of the social mobility offered by the system and those who could not.

Beyond the Classroom

University life was not just about education and opportunity—it was a crucial step in socialization, especially for those students who did not come from elite families. Student groups within the universities and colleges and the growing range of arts and entertainment outside the institutions filled in the hours between classes and studying. Jura L., accepted into the first class of the newly formed Polytechnic Institute, recalled the influence of then rector Osimov (Osimī), the decorated war veteran who had studied physics in Tashkent and later earned a doctorate in philosophy.[64] According to Jura L., Osimī encouraged the institute to develop a lively cultural life, including amateur theater, sports, and literary events. Osimī also personally took groups of students to the theater.[65] Jura's contemporary Ibrohim, who studied journalism at the state university in the mid-to-late 1960s, also recalled the vibrant social life available to students in the city, including gatherings at dance floors. "Young people, at the end of the working day, whether students or not, would go to the dance floors to relax," Ibrohim said. Like Jura, he saw visits to the theater as particularly important: "people were taught to go to the theatre, watch a play, and then there would be discussions, including students. . . . I was also one of the active commentators, I took part in critiquing the actors, I couldn't do anything myself but I could critique others."[66] Later, when he himself became a teacher, Ibrohim also made a point of taking his students to the theater. Unlike Jura, Ibrohim did not come from an artistic or intellectual family—his father sold dried fruit at the bazaar and his elder brother was a miner. He emphasized the role teachers like Osimī and the city's cultural institutions played in his own transformation into a "cultured person."

Theater, film, and dance were not the only extracurricular activities available to students. Academic and semiacademic kruzhki were equally important. Such groups were supposed to be led by particularly eager students, with faculty mentors guiding their studies and work. Students in the natural sciences got a taste of doing advanced research work; those working in the humanities could participate in research on local history and culture. By the early 1970s there were 233 such groups in the republic, spread around its various institutes and two universities.[67] Students in archaeology kruzhki were particularly active as participants in expeditions, and were valued, no doubt, for the free labor they provided. Students in the natural sciences, too, were encouraged to present papers at annual faculty conferences.[68]

Literary evenings were a big part of social life both at the state university and especially at the Polytechnic. In 1964, a professor at the university opened a reading room, where he gathered books from around the world. One of his students recalled that "the atmosphere in the reading room was such that students would stay for hours."[69] According to Abdurashid Samadov, who studied literature at the university and was a student of Khodizoda, it was actually at the Polytechnic in the 1960s that one discovered the key Russian poets of the thaw, including

Yevgeny Yevtushenko and Andrei Voznesensky, as well as more controversial poets who were coming back into vogue like Marina Tsvetaeva and Sergey Yesenin.
At the same time, the thaw enabled the rendering of contemporary and classical
Persian poetry into the Tajik Cyrillic script, as well as its translation into Russian,
and also saw translations of works from Europe and the Americas, including
those by Walt Whitman and Pablo Neruda. All of these provided new inspiration
and points of reference to the young intelligentsia.[70] It was in these literary gatherings in the 1960s and early 1970s that some of the biggest names of postwar
Tajik literature also made their appearance—poets like Loiq Sherali, Bozor Sobir,
and Ubajd Rajab.[71] Such events helped socialize students into a certain kind of
intellectual life, and encouraged their self-identification as cultural leaders connected to other Soviet elites but with their own local mission. While inculcating a
Soviet notion of culturedness, which emphasized public engagement with literature and the arts, the content of these evenings often pushed the limits of Soviet
ideology, in ways that even people like Osimī probably could not have predicted.

Two other institutions played an important role for young specialists. Many
of the people I spoke with saw the Komsomol as an important stepping-stone in
their lives. For those who came from the remote parts of the republic, the Komsomol often played a crucial role in encouraging them to aim for an education,
even intervening with parents if necessary, and organizing their travel to the capital so that they could take entrance exams. Those who studied at the university
or one of the institutes in Dushanbe and Leninobod associated the Komsomol
with literary evenings, discussions with foreign socialist leaders, and excursions
throughout the republic and beyond. But many also praised the Komsomol for
helping to instill discipline, honesty, and initiative in its members, and saw it
playing an important role in their own formation. Working in the Komsomol
allowed one "to learn oneself."[72] For those who were truly active, the work provided valuable organizational experience, boosted confidence, and garnered attention from party leaders and managers. Along with the literary evenings and
theater outings, party and Komsomol meetings encouraged students and teachers to think of themselves as active agents not only in their own lives, but in the
ongoing transformations of their societies and the broader struggle for justice
in the world. Shukur Sultonov, a young teacher of history at the university at
Leninobod in the 1960s, recalled that "what was noteworthy [about the time]
was also the party and workplace meetings.... They were interesting and vividly
memorable. And even though in the political language of the day no one spoke
of 'pluralism,' 'democracy,' or 'glasnost,' people raised sharp, difficult questions."[73]

In the postwar years, service in the military became a regular rite of passage
for Central Asian males, as it did for all Soviet young men. Central Asians rarely
served in the elite forces, and many seemed to have been sent to construction

brigades.[74] Army service carried its own difficulties. For many it would be the first time in a primarily Russian-speaking milieu and could lead to cultural conflicts. Abuse in the Soviet military was rife, especially after the change from a three-year service to two gave rise to the phenomenon of *dedovshchina*, or hazing of more junior soldiers by the "grandfathers." Yet it also provided recruits with the opportunity to learn new skills, to improve their Russian, and to carry a certain pride at having completed the service. A good performance in the army could lead to a recommendation for party membership or further study.[75] According to some of my interlocutors, a man was considered proper marriage material only after he had served. Those who entered the military after the university did so as junior officers rather than enlisted men, something they were proud of. It was in the army that some got their start as managers within their chosen professions, whether as choral conductors, such as the future leader of the Ayni Opera and Ballet's choir, or engineers like Olimjon H.[76]

Decades later, my interviewees recalled that these institutions and extracurricular activities encouraged them to see culture and service as something that continued far beyond the university years. They would try to pass on these values as they in turn became teachers, administrators, and scholars. These shared experiences also gave them connections that proved useful throughout their careers.

To Moscow, Tashkent, or Stalinabad?

Ayni, Gafurov, and their successors hoped to make Stalinabad/Dushanbe a center of Tajik learning and culture. By the mid-1950s Stalinabad had a university, academy, museums, and cultural institutions, allowing it to claim status as a kind of modern successor to the ancient cities of Bukhara and Samarkand. At the same time, many young men and women now had the opportunity to study in other parts of the Soviet Union, including its most cosmopolitan cities, Moscow and Leningrad.

When Olimjon H. was choosing where to study, he desperately wanted to go to Leningrad Polytechnic. He explained that the idea had grabbed him when he was still in school and he wanted to go beyond his own city (Leninobod), and even Dushanbe or Tashkent: "I had never been to Moscow or Leningrad. But we had seen films, there were no televisions yet, we read about it in books, and we wanted to see it and live there for a while, to study in Leningrad."[77] Although he was not able to study at the Leningrad Polytechnic, he did manage to study in Moscow for several years.

Relatively few went to Leningrad or Moscow for their entire course of undergraduate study, although by 1966 there were over 500 Tajik students completing at least part of their degrees in Russia's major cities; out of those, over 400 did so in Moscow or Leningrad.[78] Many who had ambitions to do graduate work tried to go there. Studying in the Soviet "center" was prestigious and probably offered quicker career advancement then graduate work within the republic or even Tashkent. Cultural life in the Soviet capital was also attractive. Khodizoda recalled his excitement as he traveled to Moscow by train, interrogating his Russian fellow passengers about the city's theaters and museums.[79] Similarly, the future architect and city planner Naim Ëkubov recalled the five days of travel to Moscow as filled with "discussions of the future, the institutes where we would study, though we knew nothing about them . . . and finally [there was] Moscow, the city of my dreams, the city I had been thinking of all the previous days."[80] Qahhor Mahkamov, who would spend several decades at the helm of the republic's planning committee (Gosplan) and eventually became first secretary during perestroika, went to Leningrad with weak Russian—he had studied in a Tajik-language school—but recalled that while at the mining institute he and a friend "signed up for evening courses, where we studied literature and art. It was in Leningrad that I started to understand what opera, ballet, and art is."[81]

Many of the people I interviewed described the Soviet capital's cultural life as one of the most memorable aspects of their time there. As Mahkamov's reflection suggests, it was also part of the "working on the self" that young specialists were encouraged to undertake during their studies. But Khodizoda also pointed to something else he says he experienced for the first time in Moscow and Leningrad. Walking the streets of these cities, reading in the Lenin library, and visiting museums, he gained an appreciation for Russian history and resolved to continue studying his own: "The trip to Moscow and Leningrad brought me to another world and another atmosphere, which awakened in me the longing and desire to continue my scholarly work. I felt that this atmosphere of freedom for young people who are at the beginning of their life's path is very necessary. In a free atmosphere the road becomes clear, and obstacles to firm decisions are removed. In the new atmosphere of Leningrad my plans for future work gradually came into view and its approximate outlines gradually took shape in my thoughts."[82] This association of Leningrad with "freedom" may sound strange to a Western reader, especially considering that the author is talking about 1952—a period of heightened paranoia, suspicion, and the "Doctors' plot," in which Jewish physicians were accused of trying to poison party leaders. But what the city seemed to offer to Khodizoda were endless possibilities to study, to work, to improve himself, and to connect to a wider world, all while being of some use to his own society.

Studying in Moscow or other Russian cities was not without difficulty. First, families were often opposed to letting their sons, and especially daughters, study so far from home, something noted by sociologists and confirmed in my interviews.[83] There were several explanations for this—fear of delayed marriage, or worse, intermarriage with non-Tajiks, or that the son or daughter might stay away and thus deprive the family of needed labor. For those who did go, Moscow and Leningrad could be especially alienating, and there was usually no family support network to help in times of trouble, although older and more experienced students could be an important resource.[84] As Jeff Sahadeo has shown, migrants from Central Asia and the Caucasus could face discrimination and racial stereotyping. Poor knowledge of the Russian language might be a handicap in Dushanbe, but in Moscow it could turn one into a "nonperson," shunned by officials and ordinary citizens alike.[85] Clearly, many students from Tajikistan who managed to gain admission in Leningrad and Moscow, especially those who came to study technical subjects, found themselves unprepared. Returning home as a "failed" student was no doubt traumatic. Yet Sahadeo also found that on the whole these migrants were grateful for the social mobility that Moscow and Leningrad provided, and many also praised the liberating effects of being in these cosmopolitan cities. They were able to make these cities feel like home, in part by thinking of themselves as Soviet citizens who had more in common with the milieu they found there than with what they might find abroad.[86]

There was also the matter of being needed at home. Many of the university students and those who went to graduate study in Moscow or Leningrad were funded by scholarships from the Tajik republic. They were expected to return home as highly qualified specialists to build up educational institutions, conduct research, and manage the economy. After Khodizoda had completed his doctoral studies, he was invited to remain in Moscow and work in the Committee for People's Literature of the USSR Union of Writers. Ayni insisted that Khodizoda come back to Tajikistan. "You need to think of this not just in terms of what is beneficial for you, since you will advance more quickly in Moscow, and compared to Stalinabad life is easier there, but rather Tajikistan's need for people. . . . And after you have shown yourself well within Tajik society you can (after 3–4 years) go on to further doctoral studies."[87]

For those who studied in Moscow or Leningrad, the experience provided a lifelong network both intellectual and professional. These relationships were later developed through interactions in institutions like the writer's union, through professional seminars, and amid vacations in Soviet sanatoriums in places like Kislovodsk and Yalta. Khodizoda's time in Moscow helped him become a well-known figure in the USSR Union of Writers and a regular contributor to publications like *Druzhba Narodov*. As chapter 3 shows, economists and social scientists who spent time outside the republic later used the relationships established during their graduate studies to push their ideas in planning institutions. And in some cases, those contacts helped save intellectuals when they fell afoul of authorities in the republic. Thus, when the writer Juma Odinaev's novel satiriz-ing the party elite was pulled off the shelves on the day of publication in 1979, his main supporters were the Georgian singer-songwriter and novelist (and a fa-vorite of Russian intellectuals) Bulat Okudzhava, the (Russian) head of the USSR Union of Writers Georgi Markov, and the Orientalist scholar Iosif Braginskii.[88]

Beginning in the 1960s, other centers beyond Moscow and Leningrad increas-ingly beckoned for the postwar intelligentsia. Tajikistan, after all, had a special role to play in the fight against imperialism and the liberation of the (post)colo-nial world, and this was reflected in student life. The local branches of the Com-mittee for Solidarity with Countries of Asia and Africa, or the Committee on Women, mobilized university students for rallies, where the poet Mirzo Tursun-zoda was often a speaker. Writers, artists, and students signed messages declaring their solidarity with the peoples of Asia and Africa in their struggle for "complete liberation from imperialism."[89] Young men and women were encouraged to en-gage with the "awakening East," and this in turn lessened the hold of Moscow on their imaginations. Of course, "East" and "West" were not mutually exclusive. Munira Shahidi, for example, was working as a Komsomol translator, helping guide tourists around Tajikistan, when she was presented with the opportunity to travel to India as the translator for a delegation that included the India spe-cialist Yevgenii Chelyshev. The visit inspired her to devote her life to the study of the East. With Chelyshev's encouragement, she enrolled as a graduate student at the Institute of Oriental Studies in Moscow, although Gafurov persuaded her to focus on Tajik literature rather than Indian philology. For others, this "East," whether real or imaginary, became a repository of cultural values and traditions they worried were being lost in Tajikistan itself.

Divisions

In 1966, a letter arrived at Communist party headquarters in Moscow from eight Tajik communists complaining about "localism" in party work. Specifically, the petitioners insisted that party cadres from Samarkand and Bukhara were being pushed out and replaced by those from Leninobod: "In the collective organs of the republic, jobs are allocated according to a territorial principal, and as a reac-tion to this Leninobodi localism other localisms are forming, including Pamiri, Gharmi, and others." The issue was forwarded to the Tajikistani party organiza-tion, which took it up at a Politburo meeting in November. Jabbor Rasulov, the first secretary of Tajikistan's Communist Party, admitted that such a problem existed at the collective farm level and elsewhere in the republic, but insisted that the party was aware of the situation and was doing its best. This satisfied the inspectors in Moscow. At the dawn of the Brezhnev age, interference in local party affairs was kept to a minimum.[90]

The 1920s and 1930s had seen an influx of Bukharan and Samarkandi intellectuals who formed the intellectual and cultural elite of the Republic of Tajikistan. But the expansion of higher education decreased the reliance on these people as new, much larger, cohorts of cadres made their way through institutions of higher education and party organizations like the Komsomol. Since Leninobod was the most developed part of the republic it appears that it became, perhaps unintentionally, the source for personnel at the highest level and even for students.[91] In principle, the university and institutes were supposed to help erase such differences, promoting instead a more unified Tajik-Soviet identity. University officials tried to make sure that young people from one region did not share dorm rooms, but were rather forced to bunk with those from another part of the republic.[92] Yet both in university admissions and in management, the dominance of Leninobodis persisted, as did divisions among students, so that it was not unheard of to have "fights of a regional character between guys from one region and those of another."[93]

Already by the 1950s life in the larger cities of Central Asia—Stalinabad/Dushanbe, Leninobod, and Tashkent—was very different from that in the smaller provincial cities, let alone rural areas. The larger cities cultivated cosmopolitan atmospheres, bringing together not just people from around the republic and region but from the USSR as a whole. In the southern Tajikistani city of Kulob, by contrast, a future literary critic remembered only a handful of Russians, Ossetians, Tajik-speaking Jews from Samarkand and Bukhara, and Tatars. Almost everyone else was from the surrounding countryside. Improving his Russian was difficult, he recalled, because even the Russian children growing up in the city spoke Tajik.[94] Students from these smaller towns and villages arrived in Dushanbe already at some disadvantage. It is possible that the expansion of technical schools and teacher's colleges in smaller cities (Kulob, Kurgan-Tyube) and in the north further entrenched these regional divisions, encouraging aspiring students to stay closer to home.

As the letter above suggests, Bukharan and Samarkandi elites in Tajikistan often felt this division acutely. This was true also for their children. Certainly they were not completely disenfranchised, but they felt as if certain roads were now closed off to them. As Rashid Abdullo, the son of playwright Ghani Abdullo, recalled, his family became "like Jews," in the sense that they had to work twice as hard as others to get ahead and maintain a niche:

> I have a good biography, but my geography is bad. The first ones to really feel this were the Samarkandis, because they became unneeded,

and they had one path, like the Jews, to be specialists and a step ahead
of everyone, [because] only then will you be needed.... And in this way
they were, as they say, in demand and that's how it was for them with all
the local Tajiks. If he knows one language, you need to know two. If he
knows two, you have to know four ... and eventually if you cannot find
a place for yourself you go out into the bigger world.

If Bukharan and Samarkandi elites felt the loss of an earlier status, others, for example those from Gharm or Kulob, were frustrated by the lack of opportunity—
they found that senior positions in many institutions tended to favor Leninobodis. At the same time, while regionalism caused resentment, its importance
should not be overstated. As we will see, political elites from the north fought to
pour resources into developing the southern part of the republic, while economists hailing from the Pamirs or from Gharm thought about the prosperity of
their republic as a whole.

It was not only regional affiliations that divided the growing professional elite.
As elsewhere, Khrushchev's de-Stalinization campaign was not met with universal acceptance.[95] For those who had suffered under Stalin, or were children
of those who did, the changes were welcome, at least in so far as those changes
enabled people to return from camps or shed the burden of being children of
"enemies of the people." For others, who had made their careers under Stalin and
had actively contributed to the creation of cultural life in that period, the changes
were harder to swallow.

Arguably, these divisions overlapped with a generational change. Khodizoda
had noted that members of the preceding generation sincerely devoted themselves
to "service in the building and strengthening of the Soviet state [and] the propaganda and agitation of communist thought," whereas his own had largely grown
up in the system and believed in it. Many of the generation that followed—that is,
those who came of age during the thaw—would come to question the premises
on which people like Khodizoda had built their lives, namely that participating
in the Soviet project and developing one's own culture were not just compatible,
but necessarily tied together. As elsewhere in the Soviet Union, reckoning with
the Stalinist past also meant questioning what the Soviet experiment meant for
one's "national" culture and welfare—the ostensible goal to which these young
men and women were encouraged to devote themselves.[96]

We can see this generational split in the difference between the poet Mirzo
Tursunzoda and those of the thaw generation like Sherali, Sufieva, and Sobir.
Tursunzoda was most famous for his poems about India, and was known for
his anti-imperialist writings. A key figure in the USSR Union of Writers as well
as the Soviet Committee for Solidarity with Countries of Asia and Africa, he

epitomized the idea of Soviet Tajikness. The younger generation started their lives under the tutelage of people like Tursunzoda, and were sometimes known as "Komsomol poets" because of their progression through the institutions described above. They participated in the creation of a unified "Soviet" culture by translating their counterparts from Russia and other republics. Sherali, for example, was known for his translations of the Russian Poet Sergei Yesenin's work. They sometimes wrote on typical Soviet themes—Sherali penned a poem devoted to the Nurek Dam and Sufieva one to Rogun. Yet they also came to lament what they saw as the disappearance of Tajik as a language, the loss of connection to a broader Persian culture, and the dominance of Russian. These views would find particular resonance during the perestroika.

The notion of a generational split needs some qualification. Generational affiliation was not the only determinant of one's point of view, and at least in their early years, many younger writers were championed by their elders.[97] Even among the younger cohort of intellectuals there were differences in where their dissatisfaction with the Soviet system led them. For some, it was expressed in a Tajik nationalism defined first and foremost in anti-Uzbek terms. Others looked beyond Moscow or bypassed it for their own version of internationalism. For many it was expressed in subtler ways, such as the campaigns to bring "Tajik" traditions into public life. An example of this is the campaign to institute the Persian New Year, Nowruz, as a public holiday. In 1966 *Maorif va Madoniyat* (the local version of the educational weekly *Uchitel'skaia Gazeta*) became a focal point of the Nowruz campaign, which finally secured party approval in the early 1970s. From the 1960s, the newspaper gained a reputation for pushing ideological boundaries. The paper was led by Buriniso Berdieva, who took the reins in 1960 after graduating from the party's higher school in 1958. Throughout her tenure, *Maorif va Madoniyat* published writers and views that, while not completely beyond the pale, could not find platforms elsewhere.[98] Arguably the paper was analogous to the Russian "thick journals" that, from the late 1960s on, pushed the boundaries of discourse in more liberal and more nationalist directions.[99]

The generational rift went beyond the cultural sphere. By the 1970s and 1980s, the graduates of the 1950s increasingly took leading positions in the party, managed industry, staffed the research institutes and taught at the. To them, the Soviet Union often seemed a land of opportunity. They tended to assume that building schools and factories would be enough to attract people to the new way of life. They expressed frustration when this turned out not to be the case. Already in 1963 Rasulov complained about young people who were "whiners, complainers; young old men who are disappointed with everything, who are not impressed by anything. They are only interested in the consumerist side of life. They are not interested in what they themselves can do for society: they do not even want to think it. These people are used to thinking that all the good things in life which they use, which surround them—that's how it should be."[100] For Rasulov, who made his career during the difficult Stalin years, the new generation had it easy yet seemed to expect even more. As we saw earlier, the expansion of education created opportunities, but it also raised expectations while leaving many people behind.

The elite that emerged in the postwar decades fulfilled the general goals of Soviet education policies and the more specific ones of intellectual and political leaders like Ayni and Gafurov. Shaped by their experiences the new educated elite could devote itself to working for the economic and cultural life of their republic even as they sought to continue their own personal growth. They felt a connection to broader developments in the Soviet Union and even the world at large.

DEFINING DEVELOPMENT

Throughout the twentieth century, national governments turned to academically trained specialists for the theoretical and empirical knowledge to manage the different components of what increasingly became known as "the economy."[1] The expansion of the welfare state in the interwar period required experts to measure and predict developments in industry, commerce, agriculture, labor supply, and the health of the population and to offer policy interventions. Newly independent states looked to specialists to help them design policies and overcome the economic legacies of colonialism.[2] In the decades that followed, many of these experts joined the growing international bureaucracies of organizations like the World Bank and the United Nations, taking their expertise far from their homelands.[3]

The Soviet Union, too, relied on expert knowledge to manage its experiment in developing a socialist economy. But while Soviet economists like Wasily Leontieff made important contributions to international scholarship and the making of the early Soviet system, they were sidelined in the 1930s, along with other experts whose independence Stalin saw as a threat. It was only after Stalin's death that the field of economics recovered some of its independence and prestige. Simultaneously, it began expanding far beyond its original centers in Leningrad and Moscow. In the post-Stalin decades, Central Asian republics also required the expertise to create new industries, modernize agriculture, and study labor problems. From the late 1950s, Moscow invested in training economists and other social scientists. These specialists went to work in newly created or expanded research institutes and planning organizations, becoming an important voice in debates on all aspects of the economy in their own region and beyond.

Histories of Soviet economics, like those of economics more generally, tend to focus on outstanding individuals, whose name comes to stand for a whole school of thought. This approach obscures the larger networks of researchers and bureaucrats, working in relative obscurity, whose assessments and studies gradually dismantle one set of assumptions and lay the foundations for another. Some of the questions debated by Central Asian economists, such as reconciling the needs of the union economy with those of republics and regions, stood at the center of Soviet economic history for the USSR's entire existence.[4] Other problems took on particular importance in the Khrushchev and Brezhnev periods: reconciling the priorities of regional equality and all-Union growth, fulfilling the promises of Soviet nationality policy while pursuing all-Union interests, or raising living standards and expanding the military-industrial complex.[5] During these periods, economists' understanding of key ingredients like territory, population, society, and economy underwent subtle but important shifts. Throughout most of the 1960s, for example, Tajikistan's economists sought to show that the republic's rapid population growth made it an ideal target for industrial placement, despite its relatively remote location and other unfavorable factors. By the 1970s, the seeming failure of agricultural workers to switch to industry and of young people to take advantage of educational opportunities pushed social scientists in Moscow and Central Asia toward micro-level studies of social processes. Social scientists now had to grapple with factors like local traditions, culture, and values. Yet this focus on local particularism had a dangerous side—by the early 1980s some scholars and planners in Moscow began to use arguments about cultural difference to argue that industrial investment in republics like Tajikistan was pointless.

Following Central Asian scholars and planners will help us see what happened in the region as part of the broader story of development in the post-colonial world. Their engagement with problems of economic development, inequality, and poverty stemmed from personal experience. The peripheral position of these social scientists and the universal nature of the Soviet project—including Moscow's role as a development donor in the "foreign East"—made them local and global at the same time. The scholars in question were similar in their trajectories to colleagues from the Third World, and they sometimes actively engaged in debates about development and changed their views based on what they heard from colleagues in developing countries such as India. Their evolving conception of the economy demonstrates, in microcosm, the fate of the larger Soviet project in the periphery and its significance to the global history of development.

Generations of Tajik Economists

The economics profession got a boost during the 20st Party Congress in 1956 and at the 21st Party Congress in 1959. Party leaders called on economists to improve their efforts and integrate their views into planning. Economists in Moscow used this call to expand old institutes and create new ones, a process that was then repeated in the republics.[6] Economic "sectors" within the republican academies were transformed to full-fledged institutes.

The growth of economics as a profession within Tajikistan began in the late 1940s and early 1950s with the creation of the Tajik State University and the local branch of the Soviet Academy of Sciences becoming its own, semi-independent institution. The profession's major surge took place in the early 1960s when political changes and plans for industrialization created the demand for more competent cadres to take part in planning at all levels. In other words, the development of a "national" economy produced the need for specialists to oversee it, and these specialists would then use their positions to articulate new visions for that economy. Tajikistan's Institute of Economics was set up in 1963, and its main tasks were research on the placement of productive forces within Central Asia, the rational use of labor, and patterns of economic development in a communist society.[7]

Understanding the commitment of these scholars to industrialization and development is impossible without reflecting back on their biographies. Some of the foundational figures of Western development economics, many of whom had fled Nazi Germany, were motivated by their émigré condition to tackle the causes of poverty and inequality.[8] Arthur Lewis and Raul Prebisch drew on experiences and observations from their youth and early careers. Central Asian economists and social scientists also drew on their own mix of experiences. For some, the childhood experience of rural poverty influenced their approach to economic questions. Typically for the intelligentsia discussed in the previous chapter, most also subscribed to an optimistic view of Soviet development and an understanding of their role in making it possible.

As of the late 1950s, young Tajikistani economists who wanted to do graduate work had to go to Leningrad, Moscow, or Tashkent. Among these scholars was Ibadullo Kasimovich Narzikulov. Born in Samarkand in 1909, Narzikulov lost his father, a craftsman, when the latter was forty-four, and the future economist entered the workforce at age thirteen. He joined the Komsomol in 1925 and the Communist Party in 1929. After completing an engineering degree at Leningrad's M. I. Kalinin Industrial Institute in 1935, he worked in Tajikistan's state planning committee (Gosplan), ultimately becoming its chairman. In 1946 he left Gosplan to pursue a research career, completing his dissertation, "The Development of

Socialist Industry in Tajikistan," at the Institute of Economics at the Academy of Sciences. In 1954 Narzikulov became the rector of Tajik State University and, simultaneously, the first chairman of the Department of Industrial Economy. In subsequent years he would play a leading role in the development of Tajikistan's Academy of Sciences and the Council for the Study of Productive Forces (SOPS) within it. He also returned to working in Gosplan, combining his research and practical interests.[9] By 1963 academics in Moscow saw Narzikulov as "one of the most qualified" economists in Tajikistan, and recommended him for further graduate work (*doktorantura*). The advanced research degree would allow him to supervise graduate students and thus develop his own "school" within the republic.[10]

Central Asian economics, and the idea of placing industry in Central Asia, got a big boost from the economic geographer Nikolai Nikolaevich Nekrasov (1906–1984), a senior figure in the all-Union SOPS.[11] Nekrasov was a tireless proponent of spatial approaches to economic planning, and of the development of economic geography as a discipline with a greater voice in planning. For Nekrasov, economic geography was a way to make planning holistic—taking account of resources, human capacities, demographic patterns, and even the need to protect environmental resources. Nekrasov was an early champion of investment in Central Asia, which he considered to be an economic region with unique potential in terms of natural and human resources.[12] Nekrasov and Narzikulov appear to have had a close relationship. Nekrasov wrote warm introductions both for a posthumous book about Narzikulov and for Narzikulov's collected works.[13] Nekrasov's works on planning were enthusiastically reviewed by Tajikistani economists and often cited. The research of Narzikulov and his Central Asian colleagues extended the analysis of Moscow-based planners like Nekrasov, providing additional empirical information as well as pushing the center toward new approaches to understanding of space, labor, population, and equality. Narzikulov also worked with Nekrasov in Moscow, chairing the Central Asia commission of the USSR Academy of Sciences Research Council on the Placement of Productive Forces, formed in 1963.[14]

Between the late 1950s and his death in 1973, Narzikulov pursued work on three fronts: developing the field of economics within Tajikistan, mobilizing economists to improve planning within the republic, and boosting the republic's voice within central planning organs. In the early 1960s he helped create a working group to develop proposals for the eighth five-year plan (1966–1970),[15] and organized studies on the economic possibilities opened up by the construction of the Nurek Dam.[16] These issues continued to be the focus of Narzikulov's work in the last decade of his life. In this period he also turned increasingly to the problem of labor and its relation to the issue of territorial planning.[17]

Narzikulov's mission was to convince Soviet planners that Tajikistan could and should be transformed into an industrial republic. Opponents of industrialization would argue that the republic's poor transport links and lack of pre-existing infrastructure made it a poor candidate for investment. Having worked in the planning organizations himself, Narzikulov understood the importance of countering such perceptions when it came to lobbying for resources and investment. One of Narzikulov's projects was a 200-page Atlas of the Tajik SSR, which appeared in 1968 and contained maps and detailed information regarding the natural resources of the republic.[18] By all accounts, the atlas was one of Narzikulov's main priorities in this period, and he clearly meant to popularize the idea of a Tajikistan as a land wealthy in resources and ripe for investment. Narzikulov also published a work called *Lenin and the Development of Productive Forces of the USSR*, where he used the Bolshevik leaders' statements on the placement of industry to underline the necessity of developing industry in Tajikistan.[19] Like the atlas, the book was intended to reach beyond professional economists to party members, planners, and even the general public from Tajikistan to the broader USSR.

Narzikulov helped mentor a new generation of economists who would continue his work. Rashid Rakhimov, who had grown up in the north of the republic, studied at the Plekhanov Institute for the National Economy in Moscow in the 1950s, worked briefly at the closed "nuclear city" of Chkalovsk (Buston), where uranium was mined and processed. He then began graduate work at the Academy of Sciences in Tajikistan. Although Narzikulov, whose main institutional base at the time was the university, was unable to supervise his thesis, Rakhimov credited Narzikulov with helping him find a topic and mentoring him. Rakhimov defended his dissertation in 1958, and in 1963 he became the director of the newly founded Institute of Economics, remaining at the post until 1993.[20] Another Narzikulov student, Nazarali Khonaliev, continued his mentor's inquiries into labor and planning and argued that industrial territorial planning should better reflect the distribution of population within the republic. Born in the Shugnan district of Badakshan in 1940, Khonaliev graduated from Tajik State University's Economics Faculty in 1965, worked for several years in the human resource department of Shirin, a candy factory in Dushanbe, and then went to work for SOPS, simultaneously pursuing graduate work under Narzikulov. After Narzikulov's sudden death in 1973, there was no one left to supervise his topic, and Khonaliev had to defend his dissertation in Kazakhstan, a reflection of how much Narzikulov still dominated the study of economics in Tajikistan and the subfields relating to labor, population, and planning in particular.[21] Other young economists continued their graduate work in Moscow, at the Institute of Economics of the Soviet Academy of Sciences.

Labor, Industry, and Population

By the late 1960s, Central Asian economists had already become established as a professional group with a recognized academic status and a strong voice in policy debates.[22] Their ideas made their way into policy documents, and their findings were cited in correspondence with central planning institutions.[23]

For Central Asian economists, as for many of their counterparts in republican capitals across the USSR, the main unit of development was their own republic. Like their fellow intellectuals in other fields, they took seriously the idea that they were working for the benefit of their society and that they should do this through Soviet institutions. They did not seem to be affected by the regional divisions discussed in the previous chapters. In their research and recommendations, scholars from various regions, as well as those who came from outside the republic, tended to think of Tajikistan as a whole.[24] They also focused their efforts on those parts of the republic considered most "underdeveloped." But thinking of development in territorial terms often meant treating the natural environment and human population as resources. Over time, economists would change their approach, putting more emphasis on groups and individuals as both subjects and objects of development, and the need to make sure that the benefits of development reached all Tajikistanis.

One set of questions that occupied Central Asian economists in this period was how to make the best use of the region's booming population. During the 1920s, Soviet economics had identified "disguised unemployment" in the countryside—some peasants simply did not produce as much as others, and lived off the surplus of those who did. One way to rapidly industrialize the USSR was to draw this "surplus" labor into the industrial workforce, while squeezing the profits of the rest of the peasantry for investment. Stalin's collectivization and industrialization program was essentially an extreme version of this proposal, and it brought famously disastrous results. The notion of "disguised unemployment" or "surplus population" continued to play a central role in debates about development economics after World War II.[25]

For developing countries and development specialists, large populations could be seen as either a blessing or a curse. In the neo-Malthusian view, a large and rapidly growing population made raising standards of living all but impossible—a conclusion that would lead some countries to promote family planning and even forced sterilization.[26] For some economists, including Paul Rosenstein-Rodan and Lewis, a large agricultural population provided ideal conditions for industrialization, as capitalists could take advantage of low labor costs.[27] Marxists believed that the industrial labor force would ultimately lead a revolution and take control of industries. Economists like Lewis, Rosenstein-Rodan, and

Prebisch did not see the need for a complete takeover of power. Nevertheless, they hoped that the industrial labor force would eventually earn higher wages, become more politically active, acquire skills, and force the creation of a more just and equal society.[28]

Within the USSR the population debate became increasingly important in the postwar period. Even as population growth slowed or fell to negative levels in the Baltic republics and the RSFSR; it was booming in Central Asia and parts of the Caucasus. What was the proper policy prescription? According to some demographers based in Moscow, a unified policy for the entire USSR made little sense, since it would encourage population growth in regions with an "excess" supply of labor and discourage it in regions where the birthrate was falling. A differentiated policy, by contrast, was politically difficult, and generally opposed by Central Asian scholars and politicians, since they saw the subsidies provided to large families as an important tool for raising living standards.[29]

From Moscow, the population problem looked different from the way it looked from Dushanbe or Tashkent. Moscow-based demographers often divided the Soviet Union into three zones: a western zone, where industry was located but the labor force was shrinking; an eastern zone—Siberia, which contained great mineral and hydrocarbon wealth and seemed to represent the greatest opportunity for future development; and a southern zone—Central Asia and parts of the Caucasus, which were relatively underdeveloped but had booming populations.[30] Ideally, people would move from the southern zone to the eastern zone, where they were most needed.

For Central Asian economists the question was not so much how to move the population to the European regions of the USSR or to Siberia but rather how to engage them in productive industry within the republic itself. Like their counterparts in other Central Asian republics, Tajikistani economists were concerned with how to ensure a rising standard of living for a rapidly growing population while drawing that population into the industrial workforce. They saw some benefits in migration, and their plans presumed that young Tajiks would go to work in enterprises across the USSR, eventually bringing their skills back to their home republic. Tajikistani economists did not see migration as solving the broader problem of living standards in the republic, and they believed that Tajikistan possessed sufficient natural resources to justify using the labor force closer to home.

These issues were at the heart of Narzikulov's research and that of his students. Narzikulov argued that Tajikistan and Central Asia were ideal locations for industrial development precisely because of their rapidly growing population and labor force. At a time when the Soviet Union was facing an increasing imbalance in its labor supplies, Narzikulov offered a seemingly easy solution: "In the future, the labor resources of Tajikistan and all of Central Asia will greatly increase thanks to the rapid natural growth of the population, and the introduction ... particularly into agriculture, of complex mechanization, automatization, and the decrease in the share of the population not engaged in material production. This means that even the rapid growth of the economy is not going to lead to problems in satisfying the demand for labor resources."[31] In other words, Tajikistan and Central Asia had ample labor, which the more developed regions lacked; this in turn justified industrialization. Narzikulov would return to these themes repeatedly in the following decade, as would his students.

The views of these economists, and the regional political leaders who generally supported them, were similar to those of the colonial and postcolonial elite in places like India, Ghana, Mexico, and many others.[32] Industrialization was not just an end in itself, but a path to raising standards of living for the population, and even toward transforming consciousness. The socialist state was an instrument for the pursuit of development. While the state may have been an instrument of development, development was clearly one of the things that legitimized communist rule, especially in the periphery. Once the consensus on development began to come apart in the 1980s, it put the very legitimacy of Soviet rule in question.

Equality and Industrialization

Economists, planners, and party leaders who argued for the industrialization of Central Asia assumed that industrialization would lead to higher standards of living as peasants left the relatively low paying work in collective farms for the more advanced world of the factory. By the late 1960s, as the Central Asian republics—and Tajikistan in particular—seemed to be falling behind the rest of the union, economists began to question this premise. How were equality and standards of living to be understood? Was progress simply a matter of increasing electricity production or industrial output per unit of population? Such questions—and the shortcomings of the Lewis model of development—had already led western experts and even the World Bank under president Robert McNamara to change their understanding of what was meant by "development," moving beyond indicators like GDP growth to focus on questions of poverty, inequality, and eventually "basic needs."[33] Critics argued that broad generalizations and indicators such as GDP per capita were insufficient to address the wide variety of problems experienced by developing countries, and specialists began to pay more attention to factors such as "nutrition, public health, education, and housing."[34] A similar paradigm shift happened in the Soviet Union, as the assumptions of the

1950s no longer seemed adequate. In other words, just as disappointment with the 1960s "development decade" led to a paradigm shift in international development thought, so too did disappointment with the "industrialization decade" in the USSR lead scholars and planners to rethink their earlier assumptions and to look for new tools to understand the causes behind the lack of change.

Industrialization had spurred the development of economics within the Central Asian republics in the 1950s and 1960s, and economists in the republics became active proponents of industrialization. They argued that industrialization was crucial to achieving equality across the Soviet Union, bringing the level of development in relatively backwards regions up to those of the most developed parts of the country.[35] To do so, proponents of industrialization had to overcome calls from some central planners for greater specialization among the republics and against inefficient "parallelism" in the placement of industry. While celebrating the gains Tajikistan had made since the October Revolution, proponents of industrialization also highlighted ways in which the republic remained behind the rest of the union, a backwardness that would be eradicated by rejecting narrow specialization and instead developing all sectors possible given a region's resources.[36] Such works underlined the fact that the Soviet Union's claim to being truly anti-colonial was not to be taken for granted; rather, it was the task of the union to overcome inherited inequalities.

The debate on specialization also got at the heart of what socialism, and economic development, was supposed to be about. In their insistence on developing industry within the republic and going beyond "narrow specialization," Tajikistani economists echoed the views of contemporaries, who were making similar arguments about countries participating in the world economy: namely, that specialization benefited advanced economies much more than peripheral commodity-producing ones. The debate about specialization was not limited to the Third World; it was a contested issue within the Council for Mutual Economic Assistance. Soviet planners encouraged their allies to specialize and trade with each other for products they did not produce themselves, but national planners feared that overspecialization would undermine their broader development goals and thus resisted Soviet plans.[37]

In 1957, Khrushchev had promised Soviet citizens that their standard of living would catch up with and overtake that of the United States. Although the USSR never came close, in the following two decades standards of living—as measured by access to housing, consumer goods, and food—did rise substantially. But the benefits were not spread evenly. If anything, rising standards of living in the European USSR, and particularly major cities like Moscow and Leningrad, only accentuated the gap between those parts of the USSR and the Central Asian republics. For planners this posed a conundrum—they had assumed that industrialization would drive an improvement in the standard of living of both the rural and urban populations, setting off a virtuous cycle of development. Were Central Asians to wait until this finally happened, or could standards of living be raised before the republics were industrialized, thereby encouraging even rural residents to become better Soviet citizens?

In the early 1970s, Tajikistani economists entered the debate by arguing for greater attention to consumption as an indicator of the USSR's success (or lack thereof) in achieving the kind of broad-based equality the system promised. In a wide-ranging article that appeared in 1970 in the *Bulletin of the Academy of Sciences of the Tajik SSR*—the flagship journal for social science research in the republic—Rakhimov and his one-time student, who had trained in Leningrad and then in Dushanbe, Ia. T. Bronshtein, addressed questions that related to the further development of Tajikistan.[38] Among other things, they insisted that planners should pay attention to not just how much each republic was producing but also how each republic's citizens were living: "The essence and goal of evening out the economic development of regions is not in 'equal' levels of production, but in equal possibilities for consumption and equal levels of welfare. And from this point of view, only once we have provided for the population of Tajikistan in the same measure as the populations of other regions and the country as a whole, do we have the right to speak about reaching an equal level of development."[39] This was a significant shift even from Narzikulov's earlier conceptions that saw production and standard of living as rising together and took it for granted that industrialization would raise living standards. Rakhimov and Bronshtein were careful to point out that theirs was not a call to shift investment priorities—quite the opposite.[40] In the past, Tajikistan lagged in its development because it had been passed over in the rush to industrialize other regions. Now, they argued, it was time to shift attention back to the republic. Raising living standards did not mean dependency; rather, living standards could rise even as the republic's contribution to the broader Soviet economy grew: "Sometimes there is disagreement with this position, [with some] pointing to the fact that a lower national income means a smaller contribution into the common effort (*obshchee delo*) and, therefore, a certain 'dependency' of a less economically developed region. This, in our view, is a disputable question. . . . In particular, some of the backwardness in the production of national income by Tajikistan is connected to a significant degree with the fact that we have not developed our natural resources."[41] The authors argued that regardless of Tajikistan's overall contribution to the Soviet economy, the center had a responsibility to ensure the welfare of Tajikistani citizens on a par with those of other republics, especially because, as they suggested, it was the center's earlier unwillingness to invest in industrialization that had left Tajikistan behind. Once again, the Soviet Union was being called on to fulfill its promise as a developmental, postcolonial state.

"You Cannot Study These Things from Moscow . . ."

The model used by proponents of industrialization presumed that people would leave relatively low-paid agricultural labor to work in factories. This assumption required some historical amnesia. Peasants in England—the first industrial power—did not seek work in industry voluntarily, but were pushed from the land by the enclosure movement of the eighteenth century. Industrialization and urbanization in the Soviet era were driven by a more extreme attack on the peasantry, namely Stalinist collectivization. Although some level of compulsion was certainly used in resettling peasants, the kind of coercion employed in the 1930s was no longer an option after Stalin, and the plans of the 1950s and 1960s assumed peasants would shift to industrial labor because it offered attractive wages and other conditions (for more on this, see chapter 7). By the early 1970s, it was becoming clear that Central Asian peasants showed little interest in industrial labor, forcing scholars and planners to revisit their earlier assumptions and develop new methodological tools to understand the population.

The debate on labor within Central Asia began to change. Now it was no longer just a question of creating industry for the republic, but of understanding why locals were not joining the workforce.[42] As late as 1970, party and state officials in Tajikistan regarded the problem as one of inadequate information, and they directed agencies to organize meetings and advertising campaigns calling on youth from the countryside to join the workforce in either the smaller cities or the more developed industrial centers of Dushanbe and Leninobod.[43] In the following years, by contrast, attention turned to diagnosing why such measures tended to magnify the problem rather than solve it.

Prominent specialists in Moscow were crucial in highlighting the needs for more "local" studies across different disciplines, not just economics. For example, Boris Urlanis, a leading Soviet demographer who frequently alerted officials and the public to the population problems in the European parts of the USSR, also became a vocal critic of how his colleagues studied these questions. At a meeting of the Academy of Sciences social science section in 1968, Urlanis complained about the limits of his discipline and the academy's failure to invest in studying local demographic change. "Ethnography is also an important science, and ethnographers also send tens, hundreds of expeditions to study the ways of life and morals of people who live in prehistoric times. But when the question is about how people are living now, how to deal with the acute demographic situation, how to study the problem with the modern population, no money is provided for this and the Academy is completely indifferent."[44] Despite his apparent confusion about what ethnographers actually did, Urlanis was making an important point about the shortcomings of demographic knowledge as gleaned from aggregate statistics.

Nekrasov echoed Urlanis's comments. Highlighting the diversity of conditions even within individual Central Asian republics, Nekrasov argued: "You understand that one cannot study these questions from Moscow. You have to study this question more holistically and in a wider form together with sociological investigations. We have to engage the scholars who are studying these questions in the union republics."[45] Nekrasov and Urlanis thus offered two correctives to the way that Soviet social scientists and planners looked at demographic questions. First, they recognized that the way things looked from Moscow was not how they might look from Dushanbe or Tashkent. Second, they criticized a certain kind of quantitative empiricism that was predominant in social science and called for more qualitative study of social relations.

Such arguments empowered scholars in the republics and also contributed to a shift in how questions of labor, population, and planning were studied. To improve their understanding of local conditions, Central Asian economists and planners had to turn to sociology, a social science just beginning to resurface in the Soviet Union. After suppression under Stalin, the discipline of sociology saw a revival during the thaw. Nevertheless, according to one of its practitioners, in the 1970s the discipline was under constant pressure from party officials who were frightened by the consequences of what such research might uncover. The results of studies could be suppressed not just from the public but even part of the leadership. In the meantime, the party tried to appropriate the discipline by conducting its own surveys and publishing them in the field's main journal, *Sotsiologicheskie Issledovaniia.*[46] In Kyrgyzstan, a sociological laboratory was organized in the mid-1960s and by the 1970s began playing an important role in studying industrial as well as ethnic relations.[47] In Tajikistan, the Academy of Sciences opened a sector for sociological research, but the republic initially had no trained sociologists. Thus, "sociological" surveys were carried out primarily by labor economists and researchers based in the philosophy department of the Academy of Sciences. Recognizing the importance of sociology for "economic and cultural construction," the Central Committee of Tajikistan's Communist Party called for the professionalization of the discipline within the academy and within state organs.[48]

With support from figures like Urlanis and Nekrasov, Moscow-based specialists and local scholars carried out major expeditions in 1968, 1970, and 1972 to collect demographic information and assess attitudes to family size throughout rural and urban Central Asia.[49] In subsequent years, local scholars continued these inquiries, asking questions about attitudes toward education, labor, migration, and gender norms. The terms of the debate on labor thus began to shift—it was no longer a question simply of developing industry but figuring out how to attract young people to participate in it. Although only a handful of specialists worked on this issue, in the 1970s for the first time we see the appearance of studies that try to understand attitudes of youth in the Tajik countryside and their reluctance to move to the cities.[50] In a study completed in 1974, Sh. Shoismatullaev, a young sociologist who had trained in Dushanbe and Moscow, researched the attitudes of school graduates in rural Tajikistan and found that few of them expressed any interest in technical education. Shoismatullaev also looked into the reasons that these young men and women preferred to stay in the countryside, and found that while socioeconomic factors were important, the hold of traditional values likely played an even greater role.[51] Ideological control notwithstanding, such studies could undermine the consensus among Central Asian planners, suggesting that the reasons that Tajiks were not entering the industrial workforce or moving to cities might be more fundamental than simply access to education or the placement industry.

The Family, Cottage Labor, and Economic Development

The work of Shoismatullaev and his counterparts in other republics inaugurated a whole series of studies that introduced new questions and new vocabulary into the understanding of labor problems, including the role of "values" and the family in determining life choices.[52] Inevitably this new research program led to questions about how much rural society had to change to adapt to new circumstances and how much state policy would have to adjust to accommodate itself to reality. If, as some studies showed, rural youth in Central Asia were often deficient in Russian, should professional-technical schools (PTUs) do more teaching in local languages? Would studying in Tajik or Uzbek leave graduates unprepared to work in national industries, where the main language of interaction was Russian?[53] The new sociological studies convinced scholars there was much more to be learned about how people lived before planning could effectively take cultural factors into account. As one economist complained at a conference in 1974, "We do not know our population well enough. We study and know the economy better than we know the main productive force [i.e., the working age population]. We have only started studying the influence of national traditions and psychology on the mode of reproduction of the population and the use of labor resources."[54]

Western development specialists, too, were concerned with how family ties affected developmental outcomes. Like their Soviet counterparts, they believed that the entry of women into the workforce was a crucial step in the developmental process. Thus Lewis, in his famous 1954 essay on "Economic Development with Unlimited Supplies of Labor," noted: "The transfer of women's work from the household to commercial employment is one of the most notable features of economic development."[55] Lewis's reasoning was that most of the work done by women in the home could be more effectively organized outside the house, thus contributing to overall wealth. Some modernization theorists went further, arguing that extended families slowed development because they bound people within a set of mutual obligations that discouraged individuals from pursuing their own interest. A 1960 book noted that the extended family "is, more often than not, unfavorable to economic growth . . . family loyalty and obligations take precedence over other loyalties and obligations . . . the extended family tends to dilute individual incentives to work, save, and invest."[56] In other words, family connections were a source of strength and resilience, but they also kept individuals from developing themselves, thus keeping their societies form entering the developmental path.

The Bolsheviks had radical ideas about transforming family life, rejecting both traditional patriarchal models as well as the bourgeois nuclear family. Writing in the 1970s, social scientists in the Soviet Union no longer felt the need to talk about a "break" with older forms of family life, and instead focused on ways that the family could be influenced and integrated into the socialist state. One conclusion that Tajik economists drew, for example, was that if the population in their republic did not want to move, perhaps it was better to bring development to the population. From the 1930s, agricultural development in the mountainous republic had been based on the principle of moving mountain dwellers to the valleys. This required massive displacement of peasants in the short term and in the long term often led to conflicts among settlers. From the 1960s, Narzikulov and others began to question the wisdom of this policy. Narzikulov organized a research program within SOPS to study the potential for developing mountain regions. In 1972, he and a colleague presented their first results, pointing out that the favoring of valleys made sense in an earlier period, but now the valleys were overcrowded whereas the mountain areas had enormous potential for agriculture and tourism and were in any case more pleasant to live in. They advocated a program of research and investment to prepare some of these districts for modernized agricultural production and even light industry.[57] Other economists further developed this line of thinking, also arguing that industry needed to be located where people were already concentrated.[58] Although their prescriptions did not always become policy, chapters 5 and 6 show how activists and party leaders at the Nurek Dam drew similar conclusions about the need to understand local conditions and family structures, and act on that knowledge to find a bridge between their goals and those of local communities.

Scholars also began to articulate a more fundamental critique of the industrialization program. Once again what happened in the USSR tracked developments elsewhere. In 1970, the Danish economist Ester Boserup published *Women's Role in Economic Development,* an overview of the effect of imperial and post-imperial development schemes on women. Boserup, who had worked at the United Nations in the postwar period and then as a consultant on numerous development projects, drew on her own research and findings from across the social sciences. She underlined that blindness to the role of women in economic production had repeatedly led scholars and policymaker to devise programs that weakened women's positions and sometimes hindered development more broadly.[59]

Boserup's book sparked further research into gender and labor and forced planners to rethink their approach to development. Her work also complicated the assumptions behind terms like "surplus labor" and "disguised unemployment." Among Boserup's many findings was that in many conditions women avoided the factory and preferred cottage labor, which gave them more control over how they used their time and allowed them to combine household duties while earning an income.[60] Although anthropologists had been aware of this, economists relegated such activity to the inefficient "traditional" sector. Influenced in part by Boserup's book, the United Nations declared 1975–1985 the Decade for Women and set aside resources to help women produce and market handicrafts.[61]

In the USSR, too, some scholars were reaching similar conclusions. The Uzbek economist Rano Ubaidullaeva defended her dissertation on the role of women in the collective farm in 1966.[62] It seems that she had set out expecting to find that women were taking on management roles and jobs that required technical training. Frustrated at the lack of adequate statistics on gender and labor in Tashkent, she took her research to the field, studying several collective farms near the city. What she found contradicted her initial hypothesis—women were largely engaged in manual labor, and the skills of women who had studied for more technical jobs often went unutilized, as men took those jobs for themselves. Ubaidullaeva, one of the few female economists in Central Asia, continued her research on gender and labor in subsequent years, working at the intersection of economic, sociology, and demography.

By the early 1980s, Ubaidullaeva had grown critical of the assumptions made by some of her colleagues. She argued that while more could be done to draw young men into the industrial workforce, in reality limitations existed to how much of the rural population could or should be recruited. At a meeting of

Central Asian economists and their counterparts from Moscow in 1981, she criticized her colleagues for inflating the level of "disguised unemployment" in the countryside by including women with multiple children. There was good reason, she pointed out, they preferred to engage in cottage labor—with large families, entering the industrial labor force and being away from home for long periods of the day was simply impractical. The state should instead encourage cottage labor, both to help rural women earn a living and fill gaps in production. No doubt, the ability to collect taxes from these producers was an additional benefit from the point of view of government officials, although not the main consideration.

Many peasant communities—not just in Central Asia—supplement their income from farming or animal husbandry with household production. In the early 1920s Soviet officials had tried to integrate these laborers into the socialist economy by organizing cooperatives called *artels* to market their handicrafts. Artels continued to function in the decades that followed, with laborers sharing a workshop and sometimes working from home. Many more did not participate in any formal artels but produced for the "grey economy."[63] Some rural families used this labor to supplement their earnings in the collective farms, for others, particularly those who moved to towns and cities, it may have even been a crucial source of income.[64]

Cottage labor provided a crucial supplement to family income, but it also helped plug gaps in the consumer economy. Family laborers produced clothing, household items like blankets, and other products that were notoriously difficult to get in state shops. If state factories and workshops mostly produced "European" clothing, it was cottage labor that filled the need for "national" clothing favored by rural residents. Malik Abdurazzakov, a senior Uzbek party official complained at a plenum in 1959: "In our cities and especially in the rural areas many people wear robes. Keeping in mind the local climate and work conditions, they wear *tubiteyki* boots, and women wear national dresses and *kamzula,* in the villages over 90 percent wear [this form of dress]. Where do they get this clothing, if state enterprises and artels of industrial cooperation do not make it? This clothing is sewn and sold for insane (*beshennye*) sums by privateers, who are mostly not registered either by the Ministry of Finance or the prosecutor's office."[65] In other words, not only was the practice widespread, but the state exercised no control over it and collected no taxes from the sale of these goods. Abdurazzakov could have also pointed out that this "private sector" production required inputs, including cotton, destined for other uses by the state sector.

Abdurazzakov was not suggesting that people should not have these items, but rather chiding state producers for not providing them and finance officials for losing track of the gray market. Khrushchev had made a bold promise to raise standards of living, and to "take and overtake America in twenty years," but he did not envision doing this through any kind of mixed economy. On the contrary, he wanted to prove that the state sector was better placed at fulfilling the demands of consumers than the market economy. Despite periodic crackdowns, the practice continued in subsequent years. As with other elements of "grey economy" in the Soviet Union, officials occasionally railed against the practice but recognized that eliminating it was in no one's interest.

By the late 1970s, a number of Russian economists had already proposed de-emphasizing factory labor for women and offered work at home as an alternative. Some argued that the necessity to provide employment for citizens, enshrined in Soviet law, forced planners to create economically unviable enterprises and also increased the burden on social welfare services such as day care. Others hoped that having fewer women in factories might lead to higher birth rates. They apparently envisioned women working from home but as part of the formal economy, fulfilling orders from local factories. These ideas were accepted by policymakers by the mid-1970s, although the practical consequences appear to have been limited. [66]

In Central Asia the path to a cottage labor policy was somewhat different. As we saw earlier, economists there in the 1950s and 1960s thought primarily in terms of drawing women into factories and the service sector. It was only when economists and sociologists like Ubaidullaeva turned to investigating why the rural population failed to join the industrial labor force, going beyond the figures collected in central offices and out to the villages where people lived, that they started to pay more attention to cottage labor. Like Boserup, Ubaidullaeva was not suggesting that women should not enter other sectors, or that cottage labor was the only form of work they should pursue. She too remained committed to the idea that women should be able to enter other professions. But she saw cottage labor as a step that would allow some women to raise their family income.

Not everyone agreed that promoting cottage labor was a wise policy. The Tajikistani academic Rashid Rakhimov delivered an impassioned speech against the proposals being put forth by Ubaidullaeva and others. "I will explain my reasoning to you," he told his colleagues. "Home labor in the conditions of Central Asia is economically effective only on the surface. There is a major social cost here. In the conditions of Central Asia, in small and medium sized cities child labor is [already] being used. This has to be kept in mind. It means being taken away from school, from gaining relevant knowledge, and so on."[67] Although he did not say so to his colleagues, Rakhimov spoke from experience—as a child in the 1940s, he and his siblings had been pulled in to help their mother with production of blankets that she then sold.[68] It was hard work that made keeping up with school assignments difficult. As an economist, Rakhimov had envisioned a future where such labor would no longer be necessary. He and many of his colleagues believed that industrialization would transform the economic and social lives of the peasantry, stimulating changes in educational attainment, gender equality, and raising the standard of living. Rakhimov did not reject a cottage labor policy outright, but warned that it had to be approached carefully "so that in the race for a superficial economic effect a future generation is not pulled away and distracted from schooling."[69] Child labor was a bad enough problem in Central Asia, and poorly reflected in official statistics. Rakhimov was concerned that promoting cottage labor would make things worse.

The split revealed a growing divergence of views not just on the economic rationality of industrialization, but on the social goals of economic policy. Boserup had largely assumed that the biggest issue for women in development remained access and opportunity; later feminist critics would point out that the modern economy subjugated women.[70] Ubaidullaeva also focused on access to jobs in her early research; by the 1980s, she was more concerned with the exploitation of women within the socialist economy. For Rakhimov and like-minded scholars, economic policy was inseparable from the broader goals of social transformation and emancipation. Not only would industrialization ultimately lead to abundance, it challenged a patriarchal order. The proponents of a cottage labor policy did not reject these goals, but believed that the experience of the last twenty years showed that a new approach was necessary. Cottage labor might not be a path to radical social transformation, but it allowed families to earn additional income; and by encouraging the practice among women, it could actually to serve the goal of female empowerment.

Debating and Planning

Starting in the 1960s, Tajik economists created a body of research that informed debates within the republic and gave the republic's leaders material they could use in negotiations and debates with Moscow. Personal connections, such as the friendship between Narzikulov, Rakhimov, and the influential Nekrasov, ensured that local voices got heard. There were also strong institutional links that provided for regular exchanges of information and ideas. Every year a delegation from the republic's Gosplan would come to Moscow and present their projects for the coming year. Republic-level Gosplan officials sought out their friends from university and graduate school working in the central apparat.[71] SOPS within Tajikistan maintained close relations with the republic's Gosplan and with the same institution in Moscow. Tajikistani economists and planners could also push their ideas during discussions on five-year plans and fifteen-year development schemes, through budget committees within the Supreme Soviet, and by appealing to party organs. A review of correspondence on planning from Gosplan and the USSR Council of Ministers shows that the economists' recommendations informed what politicians and planners from Tajikistan said to Moscow, and that their ideas often received a sympathetic hearing. But their claims on resources had to contend with all-Union priorities, as well as more politically powerful neighbors like Uzbekistan.[72]

The biggest problem was the "path dependency" that followed from the construction of the Nurek Dam and the subsequent decision to use its electricity to power several industrial giants, including an aluminum factory and a chemical plant. These capital-intensive plants required a relatively small but skilled workforce. To meet production targets, managers tried to attract experienced workers from across the Soviet Union, and proved reluctant, at least in the beginning, to hire locals, especially those from outside the immediate area. Although the ideas of Tajik planners—that industrial placement should be more dispersed to draw in the local population—found support among senior Soviet officials, the decision to build the plants could not be undone, and the general preference of Soviet planners for large industrial plants, on the basis that they made for a better investment, often contradicted the goals of drawing the rural population into factory work.

Khrushchev's call for better coordination, discussed in chapter 1, served as a stimulus for Tajik planners to put together a coordinated long-term program for development. Drawing on the various studies conducted since the 1930s and ideas developed by Nekrasov, Narzikulov, and others, they responded to Khrushchev's call by offering a long-term program of industrialization and presenting the many advantages Tajikistan possessed across numerous sectors: soil rich in precious metals, and possibly oil and gas; a large working-age population, and, most important, the availability of cheap electricity from the Vakhsh Cascade, including Nurek, Rogun, and a series of smaller dams.[73] The document paid lip service to inter-republic coordination, promising irrigation and electricity for Tajikistan's neighbors.[74] With an appendix that included proposals for dozens of factories, mines, and transport projects, it responded to Khrushchev's call for better coordination between republics by arguing that Southern Tajikistan could be treated as a coherent whole.[75]

This seems to have worked, as Tajikistan succeeded in having Moscow recognize the creation of a "Southern Tajikistan Territorial-Production Complex."[76] In Soviet planning, such complexes were organized around a particularly rich source of energy—such as the Vakhsh River, in the Tajik case—to take advantage of a particular region's natural and human resources.[77] The idea of complex development was similar to Rosenstein-Rodan's theory of the "Big Push"—a factory without a road would never be able to market its production; a road built for one factory made little economic sense, but a road (or an electric grid, or any other mix of necessary infrastructure) that could serve many factories simultaneously was much more efficient. The specific contours of the Southern Tajikistan Territorial Production Complex remained undefined and would be subject to ongoing negotiation over subsequent decades. At the heart of the debate were different understandings of the ultimate purpose of such a complex, and of industrialization in general. Was the primary purpose to fulfill needs in the all-Soviet industrial supply chain? To produce for local needs? To raise the standard of living in the republic?

Party leaders and central planners had been won over to the Nurek project in part because it provided the cheap electricity needed for major aluminum and chemical plants, then considered crucial to the region but also Soviet industry as a whole. At least some Tajikistani leaders preferred a more diversified development program that would employ the rapidly growing working-age population. There are two different stories regarding the reasons that the aluminum and chemical plants ended up dominating the early years of the complex's development, one that comes from archival sources and one that comes from memoirs. Tajikistani leaders, following the advice of their leading economists at the time, tried to lobby Moscow for a reorientation toward light industry and "machine building" which could be more broadly placed around Southern Tajikistan. The response from Gosplan reads almost like a caricature of Soviet planning: "To use the electricity that would be freed up in case the aluminum factory was not built, it would be necessary to construct over ten large machine building plants. However, the necessary prerequisites for such construction—raw materials, a qualified work force, and consumers—are currently lacking in Central Asia."[78] In other words, the aluminum factory would have to be built because nothing else was going to use up all the cheap electricity. Yet it was precisely to create a qualified work force and stimulate other industry (i.e., create consumers) that Tajikistani planners and economists like Narzikulov, Rakhimov, and Khonaliev asked for more diverse investment.

In another version of this story, it was Tajikistani planners themselves who demanded the aluminum factory. According to Qahhor Mahkamov—the chairman of the republic's Gosplan in this period who served as first secretary of the Communist Party of Tajikistan in the Gorbachev era—Abdullahad Kakhorov, the chair of the Council of Ministers, came to Moscow to lobby for the aluminum factory to be built in Tajikistan rather than Uzbekistan. After winning over Gosplan chairman Nikolai Baibakov, who agreed that the cheap electricity provided by Nurek made the placement of the aluminum factory in Tajikistan sensible, the two went to see Alexei Kosygin, the chairman of the USSR Council of Ministers. Kosygin asked Kakhorov whether Tajikistan really needed such a large factory.

"It's most necessary, dear Alexei Nikolaevich," Kakhorov replied. "How are we going to use up the 2.7 billion kilowatts and 12 billion kilowatt hours that we will produce every year? Of course, to use this energy we need an energy intensive factory. We will produce so much electricity, that we will turn the wheels of the factories, and the welfare of the fatherland will become inevitable. The aluminum factory will become like Nurek, something invaluable, a source of friendship and the brotherhood of the peoples."[79] Kosygin then called Leonid Brezhnev, the general secretary, and told him the factory should be built in Tajikistan rather than Uzbekistan.

The two versions of this story may not be mutually exclusive.[80] It is possible that while some Tajik economists and planners preferred a more diversified industrialization from the beginning, they also saw the value of a giant like the aluminum plant, which would demonstrate Tajikistan's status as an industrialized republic.[81] If the aluminum plant had gone to Uzbekistan, the dam would have been using Tajikistan's natural resources to power industry in another republic. And the Gosplan document, after all, did not reject the construction of other plants outright—it simply pushed them into the distant future. Tajikistani planners may have well chosen to secure the aluminum plant now and leave the fight for a broader industrialization for another day.

Yet the consequences of this decision would be felt soon. By the mid-1960s, the construction of Nurek Dam was well under way and work on the aluminum plant was gaining momentum. Both of these required a massive influx of workers from European parts of the USSR, while hiring locals proved to be a challenge. A 1966 report by Gosplan concluded that the migration of workers from the RSFSR to the Central Asian republics was actually depressing levels of employment among the local population. The more qualified European workers were an important factor in "creating a situation where there is a much higher proportion of the [local] population not engaged in the social economy or in education." Despite rapid population growth, even in cities that had trouble filling vacancies, "it was difficult to employ young people of the indigenous nationality."[82] As the report suggests, the problem was not simply one of Central Asians being unwilling to enter the industrial workforce, but also of managers preferring to hire workers they knew had the right skills and would require less training. The internationalist prerogatives of training an indigenous proletariat had to contend with the need to fulfill quotas and plans.

In September 1974, Rahmon Nabiyev, the chairman of the Council of Ministers of the Tajik SSR, wrote to Kosygin about the tenth five-year plan (1976–1980). His requests reflected what Tajikistani economists had been saying. He expressed "deep concern" regarding the republic's relative poverty compared to the rest of the Soviet Union, whether measured by per capita income, industrial production per inhabitant (which had declined from 49.7% in 1963 to 37.4% in 1973 relative to the union average), the percentage of people employed in industry (4.4%), urban living space, or the number of people not involved in "social" production—all this with the highest population growth in the whole USSR at 3.2 percent per year, with the working age population expected to grow by 64 percent by 1990. Expanding cotton production further was not an option, Nabiyev argued, because there was little land that could be used that was not being used already. Expanding light industry and food industry was also not an option, since raw materials for these industries were not going to expand any further. Nabiyev asked Kosygin to speed up the construction of the aluminum and chemical plants. Most important, he asked Kosygin to include a range of factories located near small and medium-size cities, where most of the indigenous working population lived.[83] Kosygin instructed Baibakov to consider Nabiyev's requests in the preparations for the tenth five-year plan, but it appears that few of them were implemented. Once again we see that the ideas of the economists were picked by the senior politicians in their own republics and even got consideration from officials like Kosygin.

At the same time, Tajikistani economists grew frustrated that Moscow's "bird's-eye view" kept obscuring local patterns. They saw that the failure of locals to enter industry was part of a complex set of problems that included questions of language, housing, and family—not a simple willingness or unwillingness to work in industry. And they felt that experience had shown that industrial location made a huge difference. Ironically, the aluminum and chemical plants proved their point. Both were located in smaller towns some distance away from Dushanbe and were forced to rely on the local population for labor. By 1979, 82.6 percent of the aluminum plant's employees were Tajiks or Uzbeks.[84] And at the chemical plant in Ëvon, on the job training programs were moving ethnic Tajik and Uzbeks from unskilled positions to those requiring more advanced skills.[85] But the total number of employees these plants hired was small—the aluminum plant had a total of 3,815 workers. Whatever their successes, these capital-intensive plants made a small dent in the overall labor problem.

Tajikistani and other Central Asian economists continued to have supporters in Moscow, and by the 1980s they would get many of their earlier demands included in investment plans. In the meantime, many officials in Moscow were growing increasingly skeptical that industrialization would make economic sense or could help solve the local or national labor problem, an issue I return to in chapter 9.

The story of Central Asian social scientists and their role in economic debates tells us something important about the nature of planning itself. Although the

idea of a planned economy presumed extensive technocratic knowledge concentrated in a central decision-making body, the acquisition of that knowledge
required a dispersal of resources to acquire the necessary information. Inevitably,
planning became a field of political struggle as much as a technocratic process,
allowing different groups to make arguments for or against investments, targets,
and so forth. Starting in the 1960s, Central Asian economists initiated or engaged in many of the key debates surrounding their region's development. They
were able to do this in part because Soviet institutions (like Gosplan, SOPS, and
the Institute of Economics) were replicated in each republic, providing a venue
for discussion to take place. At the same time, the focus and character of these
institutions was determined not just by Moscow but the initiative of people like
Narzikulov and his students. Their insistence on studying local conditions and
adjusting development plans to their findings often challenged the bird's eye perspective of planners in Moscow. The post-Stalin USSR, with all of its sometimes
contradictory priorities and commitments, also created the institutions to challenge and redefine priorities emerging from the center.

Central Asian economists were of course limited by their training and socialization as Soviet economists, by the language of the field they worked in, and
by institutions that were modeled on similar structures in Moscow. Yet the very
existence of these institutions provided them with an opportunity to engage in
debates and question decisions emanating from Moscow. The multidisciplinary
nature of economics as practiced within the Soviet Union also pushed them to
view development in a more holistic way.

By turning to demography, geography, and sociology, Central Asian economists helped shift the debate on the meaning of development. If development
from the 1930s to the 1950s largely meant the agricultural development of the
territory, in the 1960s it became the industrialization of the republic. By the
early 1970s this picture became more nuanced, as economists began to rethink
how territory, industry, and agriculture had to interact if they were going to develop not just Tajikistan but Tajiks. Though they succeeded to a considerable
degree in getting support for their views, the Soviet planning system ultimately
proved too inflexible to respond and balance the social and economic goals of
its constituencies.

The shift to studying "local factors," meant to facilitate industrialization and
development ultimately proved dangerous. By the 1970s, social scientists in the
periphery and the center were both producing research that showed that culture
and values helped explain the failure of locals to join the industrial workforce.
Yet the conclusions they drew from these findings were very different. A growing
number of scholars and planners in the center came to see these "cultural" factors
as fixed and largely unchangeable, meaning that continued industrial investment

would be throwing good money after bad. For most of the Central Asian social scientists discussed here, these were factors that needed to be understood and acted on. In their view, low mobility meant that industry had to be located where people preferred to live, while investment in the welfare of rural residents would help transform their "cultural" level and make them better prepared for industrial labor and increasingly mobile. Although questions of cultural specificity affected debates about domestic equality and social welfare in the United States and European countries, the implications for the USSR were much more serious. The notion that all people could develop along similar lines was central to the Soviet idea. Abandoning this notion put the whole Soviet social contract in jeopardy. In the late 1980s, claims about cultural particularism would be used by activists in the periphery to claim autonomy, but also by nationalists in Russia and the wealthier republics to argue against investments in the Soviet south.

PLANS, GIFTS, AND OBLIGATIONS

The city of Nurek lies some seventy kilometers southeast of Dushanbe, on the right bank of the Vakhsh River at an elevation of 860 meters. To get there from the capital, one goes east toward Ordzhonikedzeabad (known today as Vahdat) and then south through the city and over the Zardolu Pass at 1,600 meters, after which the road rapidly descends before leveling out as it enters the vicinity of the Vakhsh. Then the road forks: one can go right and on to the cotton plains of Dangara, or left, toward Nurek. From there, a straight path takes one past the remnants of the Nurek Sovkhoz (State Farm), set up in the 1960s to provide food for dam builders; soon after, on the outskirts of the city itself, is the bustling market. In the distance are the mountains of Sanduq and Nor. Here the road becomes Lenin Street, the town's main thoroughfare, which runs roughly parallel to the river. On the right is a stadium, a park, and a playground. A few hundred meters further one encounters the main square of the city, which includes administrative buildings, a hotel, and, most impressively of all, a giant statue of Lenin. His arms are at his sides, but as is usually the case with monuments to the great leader, he appears to be mid-stride, or mid-speech. It is surprising, though, that he is not looking at the dam, which is further up the road, but rather back, toward Dushanbe. Perhaps Lenin is meant to be greeting arriving visitors, but it is almost as if, having seen the dam, he is eager to return back to the capital, where the real action is.

As late as the 1950s Nurek was a sleepy town with mudbrick homes, two stores, one high school, and a few administrative buildings.[1] Other villages spread out on both sides of the Vakhsh and smaller ones, some of only ten or fifteen households, in the higher altitudes far above the river, reachable only by winding and

FIGURE 4.1. Mountain climbers building dam. Courtesy of the Tajikistan State Archive of Photo and Video Documentation.

often treacherous paths. The population was mixed between local Uzbeks (Laqai) and Tajiks, some of whom had been resettled there during the 1930s.[2] Nurek (Norak) can mean "white light" in Uzbek, which is most likely the reason that the name of the town also became the name of the dam.[3] Some local residents who lived closer to the river grew tobacco or tended sheep and cattle, while others had been resettled there in the 1930s to mine gold. Further upstream the rock face on both sides curved toward the opposite shore; a wooden bridge connected the two banks of the river at that point. The place was known as "pul-i-sangin," or "Stone Bridge." As the river was narrower at that point, it was also a natural place to erect a dam, and this is where the first engineers and builders began arriving in 1960 to start work on a project that was supposed to transform southern Tajikistan and help bring light to all of Central Asia.

The nation-building discourses that surround the dam effectively serve to depoliticize the questions of its construction. Large dams are the epitome of what James Scott called "high modernism," expert led attempts to improve nature and society while shutting people out of decision making. Dams were meant to demonstrate the power and prestige of a foreign colonial power or a national postcolonial one.[4] And histories of dams tend to emphasize the environmental and social costs involved in their construction and continued operation. Dams block the nutrients carried by rivers, leading downstream lands dependent on chemical fertilizer; they disrupt fish migration patterns; they flood irrigable land and destroy the habitats of land animals. Their construction often involves the resettlement of thousands of people, usually ones whose livelihoods were dependent on the river being transformed.

In May 2013, having spent many months over the previous two years working in party and state archives in Dushanbe and in Moscow, I began traveling to Nurek to collect oral histories from the residents of the city and the surrounding villages—anyone who had worked on the dam or been affected by it and who would be willing to talk. (On many of the trips I was accompanied by Malika Bohavodinova, an anthropologist interested in labor migration in the Soviet period and the present day). I had expected to find evidence of opposition to the dam, or at least to the local resettlement that it caused. After all, people depended on the river, and the village of Tutkaul, which was to be submerged with its cemetery, had been occupied for many generations. In Iusuf Akobirov's novel *Nurek,* a local resident explains that while scientists and engineers called the Vakhsh "wild" and promised to tame it, to locals the river was "holy," even though its ebbs and flows sometimes brought catastrophe.[5] Nonfiction accounts, such as journalist Lydia Korobova's *Proshchai Tutkaul,* also acknowledged the pain of leaving Tutkaul.[6] Despite reviewing the records of the local party organization from the decade before construction up until the Soviet collapse, I found no evidence of open resistance—no reports of confrontations with party workers or instructions on how to deal with recalcitrant peasants. Absence of evidence is not evidence of absence, and it is possible relevant records could have been lost or destroyed. Yet one would expect to see at least some echoes in the party records, which are extensive. Some remembered their families reluctant to be resettled; yet no one seemed to remember any incidents of outright resistance. With time, it seemed, the pain of abandoning the ancestral village had receded.

How to explain the fact that trepidation about the dam did not translate into outright resistance? Memories of the Stalin era and its violence—still fresh in the late 1950s and early 1960s—probably precluded any attempt or even discussion of outright resistance. But this is not the end of the story. When people spoke about the dam, they sometimes reproduced the official line about the dam's economic importance for Tajikistan and Central Asia as a whole, but they also cited elements that were only tangentially related to the dam itself. They pointed to the wide availability of construction materials for their homes, or the arrival of running water and electricity, the opportunity to earn high salaries, or the new schools and medical clinics that appeared. Although they did not try to resist the social and environmental changes in any organized way, an examination of their stories and the archival record shows a whole range of strategies and responses to the evolving situation.

"The gift of empire," writes anthropologist Bruce Grant, "builds on a logic that to better the lives of others is a godly practice; it encompasses those to whom gifts are intended; and it can ratify many forms of sovereign rule."[7] Soviet propaganda often spoke about what Soviet rule had given to the peoples of the former Russian empire, underlining the loyalty those people owed to Moscow. But Soviet ideology, and in particular the oft trumpeted values of internationalism, also emphasized mutual obligations in a way that complicates familiar understandings of gift giving as a practice of power. In getting central authorities to approve the dam (and other investments) republic-level leaders did not shy away from reminding Moscow what it owed to the Central Asians in return for their loyalty and role in the Cold War struggle. In similar ways, people made claims on the state in their daily interactions with its representatives and institutions.

In order to examine more closely what these obligations meant in terms of everyday life, I look at the way that changing realities of planning in the post-Stalin era, the commitment to the welfare state, and internationalism conditioned the strategies of all actors involved. Placing Nurek in the context of two similar projects—the Tennessee Valley Authority (TVA) and the Helmand and Arghandab Valley Authority (HAVA) in Afghanistan—will highlight ways in which Soviet efforts resembled and differed those undertaken with and by the United States. Like all big dams, Nurek caused displacement and dislocation for the area's residents, but it also brought major investment in roads, schools, electrification, and health clinics to the worker's settlement and city of Nurek and (eventually) to the surrounding villages. At the same time, the particular inefficiencies and waste endemic to such a large construction site (and Soviet processes of procurement and delivery) actually provided opportunities for local farmers who now had captive consumers in the local market, residents who wanted materials to improve their houses, and local leaders who could use these conditions to fulfill their ambitions. If we are to understand the way the dam impacted local communities, we first need to understand the day-to-day reality of construction, and its challenges and impact from the point of view of managers, workers, and local residents.

The Hiding Hand

It is useful to go back to an insight offered by the economist Albert Hirschman about how development actually happens. Hirschman had spent many years as an adviser in Colombia, Nigeria, and other countries before settling down to an academic career in Princeton, and had plenty of firsthand experience dealing with fashionable trends in American development thought of the postwar decades, as well as the problems of development encountered by planners and practitioners in practice. In the mid-1960s Hirschman was hired by the World

Bank to help improve its evaluation of projects. Hirschman found that while development schemes rarely followed the course set by planners, the creativity of individuals in solving unforeseen obstacles often led to novel solutions. Although the result was not what was originally envisioned, it did not mean that the initiative was a failure. On the contrary, the intermediate steps could provide their own lasting rewards. In a 1967 article, Hirschman called this principle the "Hiding Hand": "since we necessarily underestimate our creativity it is desirable that we underestimate to a roughly similar extent the difficulties of the tasks we face, so as to be tricked by these two offsetting underestimates into undertaking tasks which we can, but otherwise would not dare, tackle. The principle is important enough to deserve a name: since we are apparently on the trail here of some sort of Invisible or Hidden Hand that beneficially hides difficulties from us, I propose 'The Hiding Hand.'"[8]

If all costs were calculated beforehand, Hirschman argued, people would avoid undertaking tasks that seemed too difficult or expensive. The key, then, was to commit to a project, and in this sense underestimating difficulties and costs was actually crucial for development. In his work for the World Bank, Hirschman also argued that one benefit of large infrastructure projects was that they would create conflicts which would alter the initial plans and force a more inclusive approach. Irrigation works, for example, raised questions of land use and tenure, and engaged farmers, administrators, engineers, and other experts, creating space for bargaining and negotiation.[9]

Hirschman's principle does not predict the kind of solutions that people in a given system or society might reach for. Creativity may be a universal human trait, but it is expressed differently in different contexts. The broader social and political consequences of development interventions always depend on the political and social context in which they are made. One only needs to consider the Nurek Dam's predecessors and contemporaries to see technology could just as easily reify inequalities and social divisions as overcome them. In the interwar period, it was the United States that was the world leader in building large dams. During the Great Depression, the federal government provided resources to build dams for electricity and irrigation in different parts of the country. The Grand Coulee Dam in Washington state, built between 1933 and 1942, became the tallest, at 168 meters. In the southern states, the government secured support for a development scheme in the Tennessee Valley—one of the most economically depressed areas in the country. The Tennessee Valley Authority oversaw irrigation, road building, health services, and the construction of fertilizer plants to help poor farmers.

But the TVA was more than economic program—its chairman called it "laboratory for the nation," while the *Washington Post* described it as the "greatest experiment in social reform."[10] The dams themselves were crucial—not just as engines of economic growth, but as lodestars guiding people toward modernity. In the context of the Great Depression they were to help Americans overcome "fear itself," identified by President Roosevelt as the greatest impediment to the nation's recovery. David Lilienthal, a TVA administrator who would go on to lead development projects in the Third World, believed that "If a great dam or new system or roads inspires people in a country with a feeling that this is theirs, and that it provides an opportunity, a leverage by which they and their young people can look to the future with hopefulness in specific ways, then that great dam as an inspiration will produce more than electricity and irrigation, the road network more than transport. It will produce a change in spirit, a release of energies and self-confidence which are the indispensable factors in the future of that country."[11] The dam was not just a tool in economic development, but a way to mold modern subjects and accelerate social change. But setting up the TVA involved assembling a political coalition that included some of the most hardened supporters of Jim Crow racism. It is not surprising then that the TVA's benefits accrued predominantly to white farmers. African Americans were largely cut out of vocational training and higher skilled jobs. The planned communities set up by the authority were either segregated or excluded African Americans altogether.[12]

Stalin also pursued dams and large irrigation works in this period. If such programs reified racial divisions in the United States rather than overcoming them, Soviet initiatives reflected the chaos and terror of Stalin's reign. The Belomor (White Sea) Canal, designed to connect the White Sea and the Baltic, was hailed as a project that would demonstrate Soviet achievements in technology and organization and create new people. In practice it mostly involved manual labor by prisoners, thousands of whom perished from disease and accidents. In the end the canal was too shallow for most heavy shipping. Similar problems plagued dams on the Volga River and irrigation in Central Asia. In the Vakhsh Valley, Soviet engineers tried to create a major irrigation network, relying on forced resettlement and labor. Starvation and disease were common, and many of the resettled families fled. When construction was almost finished floodwaters washed away most of the work. Hundreds of officials and engineers were arrested. "After seven years of costly construction work and difficult attempts at colonization," notes Christian Teichmann, "the Vakhsh project had transformed the river valley into a wasteland of salty marshes and swamps."[13]

In the postwar era, both the United States and the Soviet Union would take their development practices abroad, and the USSR would return to its underdeveloped periphery with plans that were far more ambitious than Vakhshtroi. The TVA, for all of its problems, became a powerful myth about the power of grassroots development both within the United States and in its engagements abroad.

It inspired many imitations around the world. The myth of the egalitarian and efficient TVA, like all myths, could inspire as well as obscure.[14]

About an hour's flight south from the Afghanistan-Tajikistan border, one passes over the province of Helmand. Here, starting in 1946, American engineers and development specialists tried to help the ruling dynasty achieve its goals for modernization by building large dams on the Helmand and Arghandab Rivers, which would irrigate thousands of acres of farmland throughout southern Afghanistan. Seminomadic tribesmen could be settled, their children sent to state-sponsored schools, and taught to think of themselves as "Afghans." Living in the shadow of the dam, exposed to the ways of American engineers, and feeding themselves from land irrigated with their help, these Afghans would start changing their views about the state, education, and their own possibilities in life.

The Helmand project was run by Morrison-Knudsen (MK), the US engineering firm that had built the Hoover Dam, with financial and diplomatic support from the US government. The company had successfully gathered some of the most experienced engineers and agronomists it could find, in some cases recruiting individuals who had worked on the fabled TVA. These individuals were reminded that they were "pioneers, like in our own early west," by the president of MK. Their ability to transform the landscape was a social responsibility and foreign policy priority, they were told: "We can do much to help these backward people. Just remember you are from the United States. To these Afghans you represent America."[15] The project soon ran into trouble as the water table rose and patches of salt appeared on the soil. And yet rather than tearing the dam down and starting over, the project was folded into the emerging American development apparatus.[16]

The Helmand Valley scheme was no less ideological than Nurek. The US government's decision to help fund the venture after 1949 was a direct result of its Cold War politics and its postwar optimism about development interventions, inscribed in President Harry Truman's Point IV program. As the dam ran into difficulties, US officials encouraged further financial commitment, pointing out that "Abandoned MK camps will stand as monuments of American inefficiency. Arghandab and Kajkai dams would be monuments [to] American ability. Only loan making possible continued MK employment and completion Helmand project can avoid reduced US prestige and cooling of present cordial Afghan-US relations."[17]

At one level, then, the projects in Helmand and in Nurek were similar. In both cases, the transformation of nature was supposed to be the first step of a larger transformation of society. US officials talked of the Helmand Valley Authority as "a major social engineering project," responsible for river development but also for education, housing, health care, roads, communications, agricultural

research and extension, and industrial development in the valley."[18] Both fulfilled
only part of their intended purpose. The Helmand and Arghanab River dams
did help irrigate thousands of acres of farmland in southern Afghanistan and
increase food production, but this land could not always be used, and when it
was, the facilities for transporting the produce were often unavailable. An MK engineer complained in 1954 that the dam "had a great deal more water than could
be effectively used, it irrigates more land than can be cultivated, and there were
no roads by which the produce of the irrigated lands could be got out. It looked
as though, after all this work had been done, there was very little actual use of
it."[19] Although some of these problems would be dealt with through yet more
loans and investments, the project never lived up to the dreams of its visionaries.

Nor did the HAVA create the kind of "modern subjects" that prophets of modernization had envisioned. Throughout the 1950s and 1960s, the social goals of
American development planners and the monarchy were at odds. While the
former had envisioned community development, the building of schools and
4-H clubs for young farmers, and engaging with the local clergy, Afghanistan's
leadership sought primarily to bring in settlers who would be a bulwark against
uncontrollable semi-nomadic tribes. Although Western-educated members of
the ruling elite viewed their people as backward and envisioned a mental transformation, they were more concerned with establishing and maintaining control.[20] The HAVA did very little to change the balance between landowners and
tenants, or between rich and poor—something characteristic of other initiatives
to transform agricultural production that western aid organizations pursued in
this period.[21]

The Afghan case shows the downsides of Hirschman's model. By refusing to
abandon their dam, American engineers and aid workers and the monarchy only
deepened the social and environmental problems the project caused. The United
States was able to export its technical expertise, but, as happened back home, the
actual benefits of the endeavor accrued to one group more than others. If the
story of Nurek was different, it was because, in one way or another, party officials,
engineers, and managers were not trying to repeat the experience of the 1930s,
but rather to start anew and redeem the Soviet Union.

To Build or Not to Build?

Nikolay Savchenkov had nearly a decade of experience as an engineer by the time
he came to work in Nurek. A graduate of the Moscow Institute for Irrigation
Engineers, he worked for Semen Kalizhniuk laying irrigation in Turkmenistan
in the 1950s.[22] When Kalizhniuk became the first director of the Nurek Dam,

Savchenkov followed him to Tajikistan. The difficulty of the task presented a particular attraction to a young engineer. The project was so complex that it was far from clear whether it would ever be completed. A debate on the economic efficiency of dams had raged in the late 1950s, and although Khrushchev had ultimately backed plans for Nurek and other large dams around the USSR, opponents continued to claim that they were far too expensive and difficult, while final costs were inevitably much greater than initial calculations and much harder to predict compared with fossil fuel plants. Nurek, which was to be the highest dam in the world in a seismically active area in a remote part of the USSR's poorest republic, was bound to embody all these problems. A young engineer who chose to go to such a site thus risked spending several years of his life on a mission that would never be completed. But Savchenkov's boss believed that he could avoid this fate. According to Savchenkov, Kalizhniuk's aim was to get the construction underway as quickly as possible, so that the USSR's leadership would effectively have little choice but to see it through. A friend in the Central Committee had apparently encouraged Kalizhniuk to keep cost estimates down to get the plan approved, and then revise the plans after Moscow had firmly committed to the project.[23]

Kalizhniuk was an experienced engineer who had spent the better part of his career in Central Asia. Born in 1900, he had worked on Vakhstroi in the 1930s and like many of the other professionals involved in that disaster he was arrested and spent twenty-six months in jail. After he was released he tried to avoid working as an engineer. He later recalled that he found a job as a librarian because at least that way, he though, he could live without the fear of arrest.[24] Eventually he worked on irrigation in Kattakurgan (Uzbekistan) and later in Turkmenistan. Kalizhniuk had already retired by the time Nurek got underway, but came out of retirement to oversee the dam's construction. As the playwright Sotym Ulugzade remarked on meeting the engineer, Nurek would be Kalizhniuk's crowning achievement.[25]

Even as Kalizhniuk and his assistants began preparatory work and the first laborers arrived in 1960, the dam's future remained unresolved. Over the next eight years the project would be reassessed three times—in 1960, 1964, and again in 1967. In each case, the issues were similar. First, it was clear that costs had been underestimated, and they rose with each reassessment. Second, there was continued disagreement about what materials to use for the dam itself. One group of engineers favored a cement construction, while another preferred using primarily local materials. As late as 1967, this question remained unresolved, with some engineers making a passionate plea to use the more "modern" materials—cement and reinforced concrete.[26] Even the supporters of using local materials had to admit that the initial quarries they had located near the construction site provided rock of poor quality, forcing the builders to go further afield and construct yet more roads to get the rock to its ultimate destination.[27]

In these early years, rumors swirled around the construction site that the whole plan would be abandoned. It seems that after construction got under way the enthusiasm of officials in Moscow for the project cooled considerably. Yet there was also a coalition whose commitment to the dam never wavered, which included Tajikistan's politicians, economists, builders like Kalizhniuk, and officials, such as the chairman of the Soviet State Committee for Power and Electricity, Petr Neporozhniy. For these individuals and the institutions they represented, the benefits of the dam far outweighed the costs. Together they managed to get Moscow to maintain its commitment to the dam and to accept cost estimates as they were being revised upward. The cost had already more than doubled, from a projected 273 million rubles in 1960 to 595 million rubles according to 1967 estimates.[28]

By 1964, the chances that the dam would be abandoned had shrunk considerably, since construction of the aluminum plant in southwestern Tajikistan and a chemical plant in Ëvon were getting underway. These two capital-intensive plants were both designed to take advantage of Nurek's supposedly cheap energy, and could not be conceived independent of the dam. With the 1967 review completed and approved, the builders got a new boost. The following year Premier Alexei Kosygin, the most important economic decision maker in the Soviet Union, made an official and highly publicized visit to the construction site, touring the dam and the worker's town, meeting with republic and local officials, and encouraging them to be more ambitious not just in their approach to the dam but to the surrounding town and welfare facilities for workers and local peasants in the surrounding villages. Kosygin's visit served as an important signal—not only was Moscow fully behind the dam, it would commit even more resources than it had already.[29] Kalizhniuk's gamble had paid off. Although the dam was already behind schedule—according to earlier plans, it should have already been completed in 1968—and cost far more than initially promised, it was too late to scuttle the project.

In the meantime, Kalizhniuk had fought to concentrate more control over the dam's design and construction, and his struggles help illuminate the actual functioning of the Soviet economy. It is no secret that the "planned economy" in the Soviet Union was at best an aspiration, and at worst an illusion. Five-year plans were less the outcome of technocratic calculation than the result of central organs reconciling the demands of interest groups from around the country. Officials from the level of the village all the way to republic planning organs and sectoral industries lobbied those above them to secure funding and materials for irrigation, clubhouses, schools, roads, factories, and so on—it was a constant game of "making it into the plan" (*popast' v plan*).[30] In this context, officials and

managers tried to carve out the maximum amount of autonomy possible without losing the crucial support of the center.

Theoretically, Nurek was to be built according to plans reviewed and approved
in the center, with the details worked out by the Central Asian branch of the
Gidroproekt, the planning, surveying and research institute based in Moscow.
Saogidroproekt, as the Tashkent branch was known, sent its plans and instructions on to the management in Nurek, which was supposed to oversee their ex-
ecution. From the beginning, a conflict developed between Kalizhniuk and the
institute in Tashkent. Kalizhniuk insisted that his colleagues in Uzbekistan's capital were poorly placed to draw up plans for Nurek, as they were always working
from a distance and stubbornly held to textbook assumptions whereas Kalizhniuk's team was gaining new insights on a daily basis. Kalizhniuk complained
about the quality of plans produced in Tashkent and insisted that an independent
team be set up right in Nurek to take up planning work. Although Kalizhniuk's
requests were originally rejected, he successfully demonstrated that his own team
was best placed to not just execute construction but also oversee its planning.[31]
Kalizhniuk was not just fighting bureaucratic turf wars. His claim that the Nurek
team should be more involved in planning, because it had the best knowledge of
the local landscape and the evolving construction process, allowed him to claim
more autonomy, which in turn made it possible to have more influence with
central ministries and planning organs.

Kalizhniuk's authority was restricted not just by Tashkent and Moscow, but
also by the local party organization. In the early Soviet period, the party was supposed to oversee the work of "experts," many of them holdovers from the tsarist
government and suspicious of the Bolsheviks, making sure that they conformed
to the revolution's goals. By the 1950s the USSR had educated its own specialists in all fields, and many of them were party members. Still, a certain division
between party work—focused on various forms of mobilization and ideological
policing, and technical work persisted. This was certainly true at Nurek, where
the importance of the local party organization, overseen from 1963 by a young
party worker named Pavel Gorbachev, grew with the project. The party became
involved in questions of labor recruitment, management, housing, urban planning, and life in the surrounding villages. Although the head of the party was
Russian, most of the active members were Tajiks—some sent from other parts of
the republic and others who joined locally. A few dedicated themselves to party
work full-time; the rest were involved in politics alongside their day jobs as teachers, engineers, or construction workers.

The locally recruited cadres often acted as spokesmen for their communities.
Locals may have been powerless to stop the building of the dam, even if they had
tried, but that does not mean that they had no say in how it was built, by whom,

or how construction would affect them. Party gatherings, meetings of the village council (*kishlachnyi sovet*), and informal lobbying all served to channel resources and, sometimes, to resist the reach of the state.

The Frustrations and Benefits of Inefficiency

The Vakhshtroi experience was the opposite of everything Soviet modernity promised. Instead of anti-colonialism there was forced resettlement and forced labor; instead of technological prowess there was chaos. Mastery of nature was just a distant dream. The post-Stalin era was different, and not just because the terror was over. The endless reevaluations of the plan, the attempts to negotiate with local authorities, the willingness to assert expert primacy were a far cry from Stalin-era shock construction. Certainly the engineers were better prepared; not only did they have the experience of Vakhshstroi as a cautionary tale, they now had decades of measurements to work from. There was still enormous inefficiency and learning on the spot. This time, at least, the effects of this inefficiency were not uniformly negative.

In Hirschman's conception of the "Hiding Hand," the solutions that managers found to their initial problems begat their own problems, and called for yet more creativity. In the case of the paper mill, the plant first tried importing pulp, which was expensive, then set up an organization to collect bamboo in villages throughout the country, and, most important, "started a research program to identify other fast growing species which might to some extent replace the unreliable bamboo as the principal raw material base for the mill."[32] In other words, faced with the failure of their original raw material supply, plant management found creative solutions by broadening their linkages with potential suppliers, and stimulated technological innovation to find a more reliable source of bamboo. Similar processes were at work in Nurek, and they were shaped by the twin (evolving) commitments to the welfare state and internationalism. At the same time, local officials could often display a remarkable ideological flexibility without losing sight of their broader modernization goals.

Soviet managers may have dreamed of a "rhythmic" process that allowed construction to proceed at a constant pace, but this was rarely if ever achieved. Instead, construction moved in fits and starts. The work was hazardous. Mountain climbers had to rappel down the rockface to drill holes which could then be blasted with dynamite; other teams then turned these initial openings into tunnels. Danger was everywhere, and periodically a climber fell or a worker was buried under rock. The biggest obstacle to rhythmic work was securing construction materials. The initial quarries that were supposed to help fill the dam proved to

FIGURE 4.2. Dump trucks unloading dirt to fill in the dam, 1966. Courtesy of the Tajikistan State Archive of Photo and Video Documentation.

have the wrong kind of rock, and new quarries further afield had to be found and mined. Existing factories, like the cement plant in Dushanbe, had to be expanded, and new ones, like the plant for residential construction (*domostroitel'nyi kombinat*) in Ordzhonikidzeabad, built.

Supplies coming from further afield were an even bigger problem. Nurek had to compete with hundreds of other large construction projects which often required the same kind of materials or tools. Not surprisingly, lack of materials could slow construction for days or weeks at a time. It also encouraged managers to request much more than what they actually needed.[33] Like other Soviet managers, the engineers trying to build the Nurek Dam knew that cost overruns would be ultimately covered, and so it made perfect sense to put in orders for materials that might not be used. In doing so, they were not acting as profligate managers, but rather trying their best to overcome the inefficiencies of the supply chain to complete the job.

These problems provided an unintended benefit to local residents. Starting in the late 1960s, the Soviet Union began investing heavily to support rural construction, including residential construction. Records from Tajikistan show that the agencies tasked with helping peasants build new homes lacked the capacity to fulfill all the demands for materials and work they received.[34] Villagers from around Nurek found that they could get building materials such as wood or siding from the dam site itself. Managers often had plenty of such stuff available when it was used at intermediate stages of the construction process, or simply because they consistently ordered too much of it.[35]

A related issue was transport. Constructing a reliable road and rail network in the mountainous republic had been a challenge for all economic development schemes going back to the 1920s.[36] By the 1960s, the republic was connected by rail only in the relatively flat north (today's Sughd Region) and in the southwest, through Dushanbe, meaning that traveling by rail from the capital to the north meant traveling through Uzbekistan. The automobile routes went over mountain passes and were often closed in winter. The roads that had been built in earlier decades had not been designed for heavy trucks carrying industrial machinery. Within Nurek, a fleet of high capacity dump trucks was required to move dirt and bring in the rock that would fill in the dam and carry away dirt. At the peak of construction in the late 1960s and well into the 1970s this fleet worked on a continuous loop, putting enormous stress on the machinery, the mechanics who had to keep it operative, and the drivers who had to navigate the enormous trucks on treacherous paths that ran above the river. Fatal accidents took place several times a year. Machinery broke down and sat idle while mechanics waited for spare parts.[37] A new road had to be constructed from Ordzhonikidzeabad, near

Dushanbe, up to Nurek, which cut travel time from four hours to under two and also improved the link between the capital and southern districts.

Finally, the arrival of thousands of workers reoriented the local agricultural economy. A new state farm, the Nurek Sovkhoz, was organized to provide food for the workers, but its production was never sufficient. Workers complained constantly about the poor quality and selection of food in cafeterias, as did managers. Food had to be brought in from as far away as Kurgan-Tyube (know today as Qurghonteppa). Eventually, Nurek would get the status of "Moscow provisioning," meaning its stores got priority on products from across the USSR.[38] Meanwhile, the arrival of workers proved a boon to those farmers and traders able to sell their produce on the market. A 1967 report complained that on the kolkhoz market in Nurek, "prices for vegetables, potatoes, and fruits are 1.5–2 times as high as in Dushanbe, Kurgan-Tyube, and other cities in the republic. . . . No measures are taken by the police (*militsia*) to stop this speculation."[39] The most likely reason that measures were not taken, of course, is that without this trade feeding the workers would have been even more difficult. While the state farm struggled, peasants had an opportunity to market food grown on their personal plots.

For Hirschman, such unintended consequences were a feature of development, not a bug. Soviet officials, bound to the notion that planning was superior to the market, could never openly admit such a thing; the notion was anathema to them no less than to the World Bank officials who rejected Hirschman's findings. Trying to understand why inefficiencies weren't rectified or wasteful managers punished, to search for the intent behind such an action or the lack of action, would be to miss the point, which is that this was part of how things were done. However imperfectly, the system worked, not just to build the dam, but to make it palatable to the population most immediately affected by it. A functioning dam was still a distant dream in the 1960s. It was precisely these unplanned effects of planning that brought tangible improvements to people's lives—in the form of better roads, building materials, and new markets for farmers. These effects were maximized in the Soviet case, where the rigidity of planning and distribution led to inefficient allocation. Such by-products of dam construction were the "gifts" that drew the web of relations binding local residents with the party, state, and construction organizations.

Internationalism, Labor, and Mutual Obligation

Whether or not their provision was intentional or planned, building materials, new roads, even new factories, were gifts from Moscow to locals. Such things arrived from somewhere else, or were built by experts from other republics. But the very notion of a "gift"—a selfless provision of goods or knowledge with an implied but unstated return obligation—was undercut by the notion of internationalism, which also played a power role on the construction site. If Moscow's gifts could be used to remind locals what they owed to the Soviet Union, internationalism reminded Moscow and local officials what they owed to the people they claimed to liberate.

Once again, the problems of planning and ideological frameworks interacted in productive ways. At first, when planners were promising to get the dam finished quickly, they had envisioned recruiting a temporary workforce from across the USSR. Although Tajikistani workers, especially ones from the area, were employed from the very beginning of the project, the desire to complete the dam quickly led to an emphasis on recruiting specialists and workers from across the Soviet Union. Between primitive living conditions (most workers had to live in tent cities in the first few years), the difficult work encountered at the site, and rumors that construction would be abandoned, turnover rates were high—officials complained constantly that they were losing as many workers as they were recruiting.[40] These problems led to several decisions: first to build a real, planned city that would be attractive to the workers coming from elsewhere, second, to recruit more heavily among the local population, and third, to provide training opportunities so that both Central Asian and European workers already at the site so they could be promoted, making management less reliant on recruitment from outside the republic.

By the late 1960s, as the problem of drawing locals into the labor force was becoming an increasingly controversial issue in debates about investment and placement of industry, the recruitment and advancement of local workers in Nurek took on ever-greater importance. Nurek was supposed to be the centerpiece of the republic's industrialization, and its successes and failures could be generalized. Hundreds of young men, and very few women, did join construction crews from the very beginning. In the mid-1960s officials boasted that "The Tajik people (*narod*) is sending 2,500 of its best sons to the energy giant on the Vakhsh." They emphasized also the transformative nature of work on the dam: "Yesterday's farmer and shepherd is becoming a highly skilled specialist, getting behind the controls of a bulldozer, excavator, becoming a director and organizer of production. For their growth and training there is every opportunity and big opportunities."[41] The reality was that few of these laborers acquired skilled professions, and even fewer took on leading roles as managers or party activists. Pavel Gorbachev complained at a 1966 plenum: "Tajikistan is now preparing specialists of a wide range of construction-related professions, including hydrotechnicians (*gydrotekhnikov*). But we can count the graduates of Tajik institutes, especially those of the local nationality, on our fingers. Let's look—who from this group is working in a managerial position in the different divisions of NurekGesStroy—3, 4 people. We need to sound an alarm through the Central Committee of the Communist Party of Tajikistan and use the most energetic measures to overcome this deficiency."[42] In fact, this would be an ongoing refrain. At a 1969 plenum, V. Davidov pointed out that the Tajik and Uzbek share of the workforce had grown from 10 percent in 1961 to 29 percent by 1969. Yet still this was not enough, Davidov pointed out—why were specialists being recruited from cities all over the USSR when there was so much potential so close to home?[43]

The growth of the party organization in Nurek and the ideological importance of the entire project ensured that the issue would get increasing attention as time went on. As Gorbachev explained, this was not just about getting the dam built: "We need to understand that the political importance of this question is no less than the construction of the dam itself, and it is the task of the city committee of the party, the primary party organizations, and each communist to see the preparation and growth of dam builders from the local nationality from the state's point of view (s gosudarstvennoi tochki zreniia), decisively suppressing any deviation from the party line."[44] As Gorbachev's words suggested, this meant not only enticing Tajiks into the workforce, but also making sure managers accepted them and helped them grow. (For more on the subject of "shaping" workers, see chapter 6.)

From at least 1961 managers petitioned Moscow for resources to pay workers a premium for working in a place where the summer temperature could reach 42 degrees Celsius in the shade.[45] In these petitions, managers cited the suffering of (European) cadres, noting that since there were few "qualified workers" they would have to be recruited from the "central districts" of the USSR.[46] Yet when this premium was approved, it was granted not just to the European workers but also to all locals who came to work on the dam site, and eventually it would be provided to everyone who worked in Nurek, including schoolteachers and retail personnel.[47] Managers could also reward workers by being liberal with bonuses, as well as taking a lax attitude toward absenteeism.[48] The practice was hardly unique to Nurek—salaries within the USSR were highly equalized, and managers used "soft budget constraints" to help retain labor and reward favored workers. Yet we should not underestimate the impact that this had on people. For locals, especially, the opportunity for a family member to supplement their relatively low farm income with a relatively high salary could mean a serious improvement in the standard of living.

The turn toward local labor also led managers to rethink their approach to finding skilled workers. If in the early years of construction they had preferred

FIGURE 4.3. Leonid Brezhnev, accompanied by Yuri Sevenard and Jabbor Rasulov (pointing), tours the Nurek Dam, 1972. Rahmon Nabiyev is to Brezhnev's right. Courtesy of the Tajikistan State Archive of Photo and Video Documentation.

to find workers who had already trained elsewhere in the USSR, by the mid-1960s they had come to prefer recruiting workers they already had and locals for further training. One way to improve workers' skills was to increase the number of on-the-job training programs. But creating managers and engineers required more formalized training, and in 1967 a technical college was organized right in Nurek. Its record was decidedly mixed—by 1980 it had prepared 710 specialists, of whom only 65 were "of local nationality."[49] Its recruitment in local schools proved problematic, in part because instruction at the technical college was in Russian.[50] Even with a year of preparatory courses the students struggled and many ultimately dropped out. Some transferred to more prestigious institutions of higher education, such as the Polytechnic Institute in Dushanbe. These difficulties also had an effect on local managers and party leaders, who began to take a more active interest in local education starting in the early 1970s, and diverted manpower and material to help build new schools.[51]

The labor question was increasingly discussed in terms of internationalism, which was a form of discipline that bound the actions of both employees and managers, including party officials. Thus, workers were enjoined to think about "internationalism" in the work place, which primarily meant identifying with workers of different nationalities on the basis of class and membership in the Soviet family. "International" brigades were particularly celebrated. By the early 1970s, officials claimed that out of 220 brigades, almost each one had representatives of at least five nationalities. A brigade led by Muhabbat Sharipov was among those most often lauded in the local press for being "truly international" because it included "Tajiks, Russians, Tatars, and Ukrainians."[52] Working side by side in the international brigades, workers were expected to learn about each other, form bonds, and grow as individuals.[53]

Managers too had to prove their internationalism by hiring and promoting workers from the local population, setting up international brigades, generally making sure that everyone benefited equally from the dam. Those who failed to do so were chided for "failing to understand the political significance" of their actions.[54] They could also come under attack from subordinates or residents for favoring "Russians" in employment or in choosing which schools, roads, and settlements would receive investments. The local party organization served as disciplining agent, reminding managers to look beyond their purely technical goals and remember the broader social goals they were supposed to serve. Sometimes managers resented the norms of internationalism, especially if they felt like these norms interfered with their professional qualifications and authority.[55] But others seem to have internalized the ideals of internationalism and came to see it as an important part of their job.[56]

Internationalism was also used to mobilize resources beyond labor. The dam required sourcing materials and parts from across the Soviet Union. From the start of construction, Nurek's managers had to deal with the usual shortages endemic in the Soviet economy and to compete for specialized equipment with some of the other large dams under construction at the same time. By underlining "internationalist cooperation" and "socialist competition" officials politicized the economic relationship to mobilize workers across a range of industries. Internationalism was celebrated and promoted through meetings and exchanges. As one official noted in 1972, "A great deal of attention at the construction site is dedicated to internationalist cooperation in work with supplying factories. In this half year delegations from factories in Kharkov, Sverdlovsk, and Zaporozhye came to discuss results of our competition. These meetings give good results, facilitate the fulfillment of obligations, and strengthen friendship and brotherhood."[57]

Internationalism had its limits and peculiarities. On the one hand, it applied to both "Europeans" and "locals." The former were encouraged to engage with local workers, to think of them as belonging to one family, to exchange skills and participate in a shared social life. On the other hand, the road to internationalist community was easier for the "Europeans" than for the locals. The most obvious example of this concerns language—to take part in economic and social life, locals were expected to learn Russian, but newcomers were not expected to learn Tajik. This changed in the perestroika era, when Tajik language courses were organized for Europeans.[58]

Nor did the stated goals of internationalism preclude racism and discrimination at the work-site.[59] When I conducted interviews in Nurek, my subjects—both local and Europeans—insisted that ethnic tensions simply did not exist, at least until the 1980s. Similarly, the extensive party records I consulted have only vague references to the need for better "internationalist education" and occasionally to hooliganism. Yet several of my interlocutors did admit that fights regularly broke out between Europeans and locals at the Friday night dances organized by the local Komsomol. One Russian woman admitted being horrified by the "sea of black faces" she found when she first arrived to join her husband in Nurek, although she insisted that she quickly overcame her prejudice.[60] More subtle forms of discrimination were present as well—for example, in terms of European managers being reluctant to hire Tajik workers. However, such reluctance was treated as a violation of norms, of a refusal to live up to the European manager's side of the obligation to locals.

A Bottomless Gift of Nature?

So far we have discussed the gift and the plan in the context of human relations at the dam. Yet this leaves out a crucial player in the story—the natural environment. If the inefficiency of planning had some happy consequences for the people affected, the same could not be said for the rivers and soil transformed by Soviet development. This was not because engineers or others failed to recognize an obligation to act as stewards of the environment. Rather, the illusion of planning led officials to ignore how water would actually be used.

Hirschman's "Hiding Hand" model failed to account for the environmental damage that might be caused by the persistence and creativity of planners and engineers, and the reality of dam construction in the USSR illustrates all too well how the impact and ecological footprint of large construction projects tends to be much larger than calculated in initial plans. To understand the broader consequences of irrigation and dam building, we need to look beyond the dam itself. Of course, Nurek caused many of the same problems associated with large dams everywhere—the storage basin actually raised temperatures, the minerals that had been carried by the Vakhsh and fertilized surrounding fields instead built up as silt behind the dam wall, and the construction process itself caused harmful chemicals to be released into the water.[61] And the human cost was significant as well. Thousands of people would have to be resettled to make room for the new city and the reservoir. Taming the Vakhsh and bringing in industrial production meant profoundly changing the way people interacted with the river.[62]

As the Soviet irrigation system developed, engineers and managers believed that they could make efficient use of water by using mapping and monitoring techniques that would make clear when, where, and how water was being used. Water conservation had already become a major concern of scientists and officials in the Khrushchev era. A conference of specialists in 1961 urged Khrushchev and other Soviet leaders to remember that "the Soviet Union is not so rich in water resources that they can be viewed as some bottomless gift of nature"—an important intervention, since this was precisely how many proponents of dam building and large scale irrigation spoke of water.[63] The scientists' proposal envisioned ambitious technical solutions, such as redirecting rivers. Most important, they argued for centralized control and more extensive knowledge of natural and manmade waterways within the Soviet Union.[64] The logic of these and other such schemes was that knowledge and technical skill would make it possible to continue making use of the union's water resources in novel ways while preventing pollution and waste.[65]

By the 1970s, three major problems had developed. The first had to do with the overuse and misuse of water. Officials complained that while the republic had made great strides in making water available, the use of water at the kolkhoz level was "uncultured" and in on some state and collective farms was "the same as in the prewar years."[66] In fact, there seemed to be a kind of water-hoarding taking place, as "many districts took 1.5–2 times the allowed volume of water, but used only 50–70%." At the same time, farm managers failed to maintain the pumps, filters, and drainage system as a whole. The result was that these mechanisms became clogged and sometimes failed, contributing to water pollution and soil erosion. In some cases, the high demand for water led to the breaking (*proryv*) of canals, accidents, and the breakdown of the drainage system.[67] Investigations also faulted brigade leaders for taking the diversion and release of water into their own hands.[68]

How had this situation come about? Republic-level officials identified several tendencies that seemed to predominate at the farm level. One was the primitive state of communications systems, which made coordination between brigade leaders, mechanics, and others responsible for water use difficult. Another problem was the absence of qualified personnel to oversee the water use. Was it not paradoxical, one official wondered, that while the farms had veterinarians, mechanics, and economists, they lacked water engineers and technicians, let alone brigadiers and irrigators who had a "bare minimum of theoretical knowledge and practical experience in irrigation and melioration"?[69] Of 765 workers and specialists employed to manage the distribution of water, only 8.8 percent had higher technical qualifications, while almost one-half (347) employed as "engineers" did not even have basic specialized training.[70] Salaries for such specialists were raised in 1971, but officials recognized that it would be years before they could fill all of the positions with qualified personnel, especially as the irrigation system within the republic continued to grow.[71]

Ultimately, the problem lay with the farm managers themselves. Until 1956, farm managers had to account for all the water they used, but in that year, as part of a series of measures meant to give them more responsibility and control, such reporting requirements were lifted. Officials in the Ministry of Melioration insisted on introducing penalties for the misuse of water, but the problem was so widespread such measures would have been of dubious effect. (A law on water gave republic-level planning organs the right to determine water fees and penalties).[72] From the farm managers' point of view, the specialists, monitoring equipment, and other measures meant to decrease water use were another cost that made little sense as long as water continued to flow. And there seemed to be no question of turning off the water, since that would mean putting the farms, and therefore district and republic targets at risk.[73]

Even as some farms were becoming more efficient in their use of water, the drive to expand cotton production created new possibilities for waste. Some farms, on their own initiative or under pressure from local party secretaries, began to plant cotton on slopes. Such experiments began already in the 1960s and increased in the 1970s. The slopes were intended for grapes and other horticulture, but farms were using them instead for cotton. Yet the method for irrigation was the same as for flatland, despite the fact that gravity changed the speed and absorption of water. Brigades compensated by drawing on more and more water to irrigate these fields, letting polluted water run into the drainage system and on into the rivers, leading in the meantime to the erosion of furrows and other water channels.[74]

Water was not just being wasted, it was becoming increasingly polluted. The cement plant in Dushanbe, so crucial to housing and industrial construction in the republic, was one of the early culprits. The plant's location was unfortunate. From 1962 to 1965, a series of filters to keep the waste products from being dumped into the Varzob River was implemented in the plant, as well as a system to recycle water being used in the production process and limit intake of fresh water to a minimum. Both of these had collapsed by the 1970s. The cement plant was hardly the only polluter. Oil refineries, meat processors, canning plants, and tanneries were all dumping waste into rivers, taxing and occasionally overburdening the water filtration systems. All of them were found to have filtration systems that had long stopped working and not been repaired. Ministry of Irrigation officials complained that plant managers repeatedly ignored warnings to repair their filtration systems, even when faced with fines. Meanwhile, several water hungry enterprises were coming on-line, including the aluminum smelter and chemical plant that were the centerpieces of southern Tajikistan's industrialization. Although these had been designed to minimize wastage through recycling and pollution through filtration systems, we saw already how these mechanisms quickly failed in other plants. The chemical plant and the aluminum plant would become among the worst polluters. Meanwhile, the demand on Tajikistan's water resources nearly doubled over sixteen years from 8 km^3 in 1960 to 10 km^3 in 1970 and 14.2 km^3 in 1976—and officials expected it to rise to 20 or 25 km^3 shortly thereafter.[75] But farms were themselves major polluters of water. To keep up with the ever increasing cotton targets, farms used more and more pesticides and chemical fertilizers, which then entered streams, rivers, and ultimately drinking water. As a result, drinking water was also becoming polluted.[76] Still, officials seemed quicker to recognize the dangers of industrial pollution: in 1975, the Council of Ministers approved a 44,000,000-ruble plan to build various filtration and purification systems for the republic's growing industry but did not include collective farms.[77]

Planners and engineers had created a system that farms were ill equipped to use properly. Even the ministry officials themselves lost track of water channels. Older canals, some of them predating the Soviet period, were supplemented by newer ones, and both were sometimes repaired and modified without the changes being registered. "As a result," inspectors found, "the collective farms and state farms that are using their internal [irrigation] networks are left without design and executive documentation. . . . In many farms there are no water technicians and plans of water use are not compiled."[78] A system that required up to date plans and records and specialists that could read plans and make them a reality failed because both were lacking. Officials in Dushanbe were powerless to do anything because the neat plans they had assembled had little to do with a reality that was always shifting as farm workers and brigade leaders made many minor adjustments to the network and used the water as they saw fit. As a result, farm workers were left to deal with the situation as best they could. A brigade leader remembered that in the 1980s, shortages of water had become endemic, leading her brigade to improvise measures to keep the crop from failing: "It even got to the point that during the hot season the canal ran dry. Much of the harvest was lost on account of the fact that the crops were left for hours without water in the heat of the day. We were forced day and night to take turns at the head of the canal to make sure our water did not go elsewhere."[79]

It is not surprising that water became one of the central concerns for environmentalists in the Tajik SSR and beyond. Some of the economists and geographers working in the state planning system and research institutes had already begun questioning the wisdom of constructing large dams in the republic and ever expanding irrigation of the lowlands for cotton. Even Nikolai Nekrasov, usually sympathetic to placing industry in Central Asia, worried that chemical plants in particular would "ruin Central Asia" and lead to a situation where the factories would have to be decommissioned and the water supply system rebuilt.[80] In the 1960s, and especially in the 1970s, the protection of water resources became a part of state discourse and policy.[81] It forced economists and other specialists to rethink questions of pricing and resource allocation. As elsewhere in the Soviet Union, problems caused by the effects of these technologies created a new environmental consciousness. These issues would become heavily politicized during perestroika, but already in the 1960s we see a kind of alliance between ministry

FIGURE 4.4.   The Nurek Dam, 1974. Courtesy of the Tajikistan State Archive of Photo and Video Documentation.

officials and semi-independent environmentalist groups. Yet these individuals were powerless as long as they failed to win over the farm managers and those responsible for using water locally.

Viewing the case of the Nurek Dam alongside its contemporaries such as the HAVA points to the possibilities for comparison between socialist "internal" development and "international development" as practiced by the United States, European countries, and even the Soviet Union itself. Such a comparison highlights the similarities of Soviet and US views on development in this period, both in terms of the emphasis on transforming nature and in the expectation that large development schemes would transform people as well as economies. Yet the Nurek case also demonstrates the limits of this comparison. The practices of construction and the experience of people caught up in it were tied to the possibilities offered by ideological flexibility, commitment to social welfare, and internationalism reinvigorated by Cold-War competition that was characteristic of the 1960s and 1970s.

The post-Stalin era saw a new social contract between the government and the people, and culminated under Brezhnev in what Sovietologist James Millar famously called the "Little Deal." In exchange for loyalty, the regime found ways to satisfy the needs the material needs of the population. Millar's conception, though, presumes a depoliticized population and an elite that deemphasized ideology (beyond sloganeering) in favor of technocratic management. Yet the Nurek case shows something more complicated. Material goods and mutual obligations were in fact highly politicized, because the question of their provision was at the very heart of Soviet claims to equality and modernity, and the fairness of mutual obligations between the state and the local population at the dam.

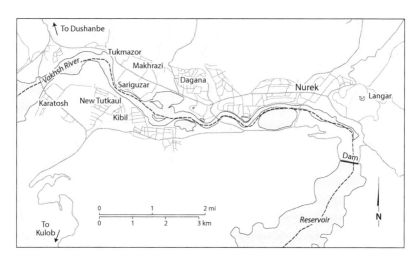

Nurek and its satellite villages after the damming of the Vakhsh River.

NUREK, "A CITY YOU CAN WRITE ABOUT"

In March 1961, the engineer Semen Kalizhniuk met with the leading writers of Soviet Tajikistan, including the bard of Soviet anti-colonialism Mirzo Tursunzoda, to tell them about the construction of the Nurek Dam. It was not just a dam that was being built, Kalizhniuk promised: "We are planning a city that will be the prototype for future cities. The city will meet the requirements of the future of our communist society. Everything must be taken into account: height, capacity, the thickness of the walls, the circulation of air, temperature and so forth. It will be the kind of city, I think, that you can write about."[1]

Why would Kalizhniuk feel the need to promise a group of Tajik writers that, besides building the tallest dam in the world, he would also build a beautiful city? Planners and visionaries around the world had wrestled with how to organize urban space so that the achievements of modernity were available to workers and not just capitalists. For Soviet architects and urban planners, the city was also crucial for shaping modern men and women. City planning under Khrushchev was intimately tied to the other promises of the era: raising standards of living, overcoming regional inequality, and making the Soviet Union a model for the postcolonial world.

Nurek was one of dozens of new cities built in the 1960s to house workers for shock construction campaigns. Their construction was part of the Khrushchev-era drive to develop new territories and industries through mass mobilization rather than terror. With their modern infrastructure, comfortable housing, and urban amenities, these cities were supposed to attract and keep specialists and

FIGURE 5.1.   The poet Mirzo Tursunzoda and other Tajik writers meeting with a delegation of builders working on the Nurek Dam, 1972. Courtesy of the Tajikistan State Archive of Photo and Video Documentation.

workers. As a number of scholars have argued, those amenities often came late, long after enthusiasm had turned to disappointment and cynicism. Paul Josephson notes that Soviet urbanization "was plagued by irrational planning and shortages, and everywhere its supposed benefits—museums, public transport, access to good medical care inexpensive housing—reached the residents least and last."[2] Although Nurek would eventually become a showpiece city, getting to the vision outlined by Kalizhniuk was not a straightforward process. Kalizhniuk himself often resisted investing in urban construction, preferring instead to direct all resources to the dam.

The most interesting thing for us, though, is the struggle that took place around those utopian ideals, and what it reveals about how the post-Stalin USSR tried to reconcile its promises of social welfare, internationalism, and equality, with economic goals.[3] As the city grew, it exposed inequalities between newcomers and locals, and led local activists to press for more investment in the surrounding villages. The city and the surrounding villages were shaped and reshaped by hundreds of compromises and negotiations between planners, builders, party officials, workers, and local residents as officials tried to attract and keep labor, meet production targets, and live up to the ideals of Soviet labor culture and internationalism. A widely accepted set of ideas about "cultured" urban life determined what the city would become. Nurek was shaped by the way party activists,

construction officials, workers, and local leaders responded to problems of disorder, disease, social welfare, and coexistence by falling back on these ideas; the
solutions they found emerged from within the logic of postwar Soviet modernity
and welfare state, but that welfare state in its localized form was itself shaped by
these struggles. Even in the absence of a single utopian plan for the city or its satellites, large and small solutions that were part of a larger utopian project shaped
the urban and rural space.

Urban Utopias and Social Welfare

Urban utopias had played an important role since the revolution—how people
lived was at the center of the Bolshevik's goals of industrialization and social
transformation. The right kind of urban planning could help avoid the pitfalls
of industrialization in the capitalist world, including overcrowding and urban
inequality. In the 1920s, some of the more radical thinkers of the "dis-urbanist"
movement hoped to close the gap between the cultured but overpopulated and
unhealthy town and country by eliminating the former and spreading industry
and labor throughout the countryside. Their opponents, the "urbanists," dreamt
of the elimination of the family unit, which would be replaced with communal
living in large blocks of residences with daycare, schools, and kindergartens.[4]
Both of these schools were sidelined in the 1930s as Stalin favored a more conservative, monumental vision for cities inspired by the "City Beautiful" movement,
which had its roots in the United States.[5] These utopian ideas were nevertheless
absorbed in later Soviet city planning, giving rise to, among other things, the
ubiquitous but varied Soviet *mikroraion,* itself a variant of the "Garden City"
envisioned by British and American planners at the turn of the century.[6] Utopian
visions also influenced the planning of industrial cities, like Magnitogorsk, during the 1930s.[7]

   The original model for Soviet company towns was Nikolay Miliutin's "linear
city," which he outlined in his 1930 book *Sotsgorod.* Miliutin's plans drew on
Fordist and Taylorist ideas about industrial production, but also sought to in-
sulate residents from industrial pollution, provide all necessary social services,
and extend these to the surrounding countryside.[8] Such cities were built not just
to accommodate workers, but also to make them class-conscious, enlightened
(*kul'turnyi*) and politically conscious citizens.

   The Khrushchev era saw several population trends that had important implications for city planning and housing. First, the opening of the Gulags and
the easing of restrictions on former prisoners meant that many of those who
had been resettled in the country's resource- rich but inhospitable areas were

leaving.[9] At the same time, as peasants left the countryside for the cities, planners and demographers worried that too many people and too many factories were being concentrated in the largest cities of the country, a trend that would become even more accentuated in the 1970s. The Soviet regime thus tried to promote the settlement and exploitation of distant areas by promising housing and amenities that were in short supply in the more overcrowded cities of the European USSR.

The 1950s also marked a transformation in the regime's relationship with workers. A mass housing program, discussed under Stalin but implemented only under Khrushchev, gave millions of families their first opportunity at an individual urban apartment. As Mark B. Smith points out, while "the dogma of paradise- using housing to create a way of life appropriate to communist ideals" existed in various forms from 1917 through the Stalin era, it was under Khrushchev that "housing was a mechanism for pushing society from socialism to communism. While paradise was always the ultimate goal, it was an explicit and immediate target only in the third stage of this scheme."[10] At a conference on city planning in 1961, architects and officials discussed ideas from the 1920s, as well as British "new towns"—themselves descended from the "Garden City" concept)—at length.[11] Following the conference, a joint resolution of the Central Committee of the Communist Party of the Soviet Union and Council of Ministers called for "complex planned construction with capital investments . . . for housing, communal, cultural, and health services" on construction sites of particular importance located far from existing cities.[12] The resolution left plenty of room for officials to decide just how planned and "complex" a city had to be.

The 1950s and 1960s were the heyday of Soviet "company towns." Some of these were labor camps that became cities with relatively high standards of living, such as Vorkuta or Ozersk, a center of Soviet plutonium production.[13] Others were "new towns" such as Togliatti or Naberezhnye Chelny, created to house the workers for a given industry.[14] In many of these smaller Soviet towns, the local industry also provided many social-welfare services, either directly or indirectly.[15] Urban construction also became part of the Cold War competition. The construction of "socialist cities" was encouraged in the new "people's democracies" such as Poland, where the settlement of Nova Huta grew up around a new steel plant outside of Krakow.[16] Large-scale development projects such as dams or industrial towns brought new cities in their wake. Like the dams themselves, these new towns were supposed to demonstrate the best features of the donor country. In Afghanistan, the development of the Helmand Valley Authority was accompanied by the construction of an "American Town" with evenly spaced private houses that seemed to come straight from Phoenix, Arizona, while the Soviets built a district in Kabul still known today as Mikroraion, which was a replica of contemporaneous Soviet urban mass housing. Both American Town and the

Mikroraion were originally intended for the foreign staff coming to deliver aid, but eventually came to house local elites.[17] If such towns were supposed to show the best of the superpowers features, they could also show the worst, as Robert Vitalis shows in his masterful study of segregation in the towns built for US oil workers in Saudi Arabia.[18]

In the 1960s and 1970s, Soviet and other Eastern bloc architects fanned out across the postcolonial world to help build cities that would in turn shape citizens of these new states.[19] One reason they were in demand was their expertise in combining nationalist culture with socialist content—a priority for postcolonial leaders who sought unifying symbols that could be imprinted on everything from currency to forms of dress. At the same time, socialist architects supposedly knew how to build for the masses. The right kind of housing and urban planning could help eliminate the inequalities and indignities of industrial modernity and ensure a just distribution of its benefits (whether achieved through socialism or capitalism). Yet it was not just cities built abroad that served to showcase these different modernities—city building within the Eastern and Western blocs also served to demonstrate the benefits of one or the other system.

In Central Asia, the situation with housing and city planning was slightly different from the European or Siberian parts of the USSR. Local politicians and planners saw the growth of cities as crucial to raising the standard of living in the republics. Like western modernization theorists and many postcolonial elites, they believed in drawing people out of what they saw as an overcrowded countryside into industry. The local elites were often the most enthusiastic proponents of expanding and modernizing existing cities like Tashkent.[20]

But there were several problems that plagued city building in the region. First, there was very little of the migration from the countryside to the cities seen in the European USSR. The large cities, like Dushanbe and Tashkent, were still settled primarily by migrants from outside the region. Since plans for industrialization had assumed a large local workforce, the failure of Central Asians to urbanize and enter the industrial workforce became an argument against further investment in industry among skeptics in Gosplan and other central Soviet bodies during the 1970s. Many officials in Moscow were wary of sending labor to the region when it was increasingly seen as scarce in the European parts of the USSR and especially in Siberia. Finally, there was a perception among locals that the cities were being developed primarily for Russian speakers. Housing was limited, and what was built went to the specialists and workers who were brought to the republic from outside. Tajiks and other Central Asians tended to stay away from the cities, and were often disadvantaged in the distribution for apartments when they did move there.

It is worth considering the history of Tajikistan's capital in more detail. At the time of the revolution it had been the site of a fort and a village with some 10,000 residents, and it was chosen as a capital for the new republic primarily for its central location. The Soviet city's original layout in the 1930s actually owed something to Miliutin's *Socialist City,* with the main thoroughfare (Prospekt Lenina, naturally) part of the emerging highway connecting the north and south of the republic and running parallel to the Varzob River. The main administrative and cultural buildings were all designed by architects from Moscow and Leningrad, and followed what might be called the "Oriental Stalinism" pattern—neoclassical buildings with archways and windows evoking the styles found in Bukhara and

FIGURE 5.2.   The Rohat Teahouse, with its hand carved wooden ceilings executed by local craftsmen, was celebrated for its fusion of modern and traditional architectural styles. Courtesy of the Russian State Archive of Photo and Video Documentation.

Samarkand. The opera theater (1940), the central committee of the communist party (1957), and the original home of the university (1948) were all stretched out along the main road.

Beyond these main administrative buildings, Stalinabad was hardly fit to be the capital of a republic. It remained, in the 1930s, a collection of mud-brick buildings. In the following years the city grew. A cement plant completed in 1956 made construction easier. Investment in industry and education brought thousands of workers and professionals to the city. A population of 92,000 in 1940 had exploded to 330,000 by 1966, and was growing at between 4.5 percent and 5 percent per year. Between 1959 and 1965 alone thirty-five new schools and forty preschools were erected. Land on the right bank of the Varzob River had been reclaimed for new residential neighborhoods.[21] Although the city had lost the look of Miliutin's "linear city," the 1966 plan, which envisioned the city growing to 460,000 residents, nevertheless maintained the division of industrial, residential, and rest and recreation zones.[22] The city was becoming a pleasant provincial capital whose streets were lined with sycamores, maples, and poplars; these trees provided shade even in the intense summer heat, when temperatures often reach forty degrees centigrade.[23] It was a city that could and did serve as a destination for tourists on their Central Asian tours and as site for international conferences, although it was dwarfed in that role by Tashkent. At the same time the new industrial zones undermined one of the key goals of the linear city—to keep pollution away from the residential and rest areas. The cement plant was situated at the north end of the city, where the main road began its long climb through the Varzob Valley. Winds coming from the north regularly carried the plant's emissions over the rest of the city.[24]

Yet though the city was the capital of Tajikistan, it was not very Tajik. As was already discussed, the industries being developed in the republic did a relatively poor job recruiting Tajik workers. This was equally true of the industries that had been set up in Stalinabad/Dushanbe, including a cable plant, a factory that made tractor parts, a factory that made "Pamir" refrigerators, and several others. Since housing was often allocated on the basis of one's place of employment, the Europeans who worked in these factories also ended up occupying much of the new housing that was being built. As elsewhere in the USSR, residence in a city required a registration (*propiska*), which was provided by one's employer or educational institution. And without adequate housing, Tajiks were reluctant to move to the city and look for a job. Those apartments that were available were rarely large enough for families with more than two or three children, meaning that for larger Tajik families staying in the city sometimes became untenable.

Besides, the layout of apartments was based on ideals of European urban life and intended for nuclear families. Houses throughout most of Uzbekistan and

FIGURE 5.3.   Prospekt Lenina, main thoroughfare view from Ayni Square, Dushanbe, 1960s. Courtesy of the Russian State Archive of Photo and Video Documentation.

Tajikistan consist of rooms built around and inner and an outer courtyard—an architecture that helps maintain notions of propriety and gender segregation. Most family life goes on in the inner courtyard; a guest room (*mehmonhona*), which does not provide access to the rest of the compound, opens into the outer yard. In most Soviet apartments, doors opened to a common hallway or were connected to each other; the windows opened onto the street or a common courtyard. Of course, families found creative ways to approximate their notion of proper layout; for example, by segregating part or all of the common room (*gostinnaia*) so that guests could visit without seeing the rest of the house. Nevertheless, the fact remained that feeling at home in such an apartment took a major adjustment.

In a sense, the Soviet Union solved one problem of industrial urbanity—there were virtually no slums—but created another, that of urban exclusivity, that took on a colonial shade in republics when the *propiska* (urban registration) seemed more easily available to Russians than locals. At the same time, the "Russianness" of the city should not be exaggerated. Tajiks who entered the expanding higher educational institutions, or those who worked for one of the city's cultural or administrative institutions, made a home in the city, and the latter often found housing in specially designated buildings. (Until the late 1950s, when the city could build little housing of its own, important artists and intellectuals were rewarded with plots of land where they could build cottages, which were often roomier than the standard apartments in the housing units. This meant that by the 1960s a significant portion of the cultural and intellectual elite clustered on neighboring streets to the north of the administrative center and east of the main road, Prospekt Lenina.) By the 1980s the advantage of Russian speakers in securing apartments or other goods was diminished, because the bureaucracy was increasingly staffed by Central Asians. The sociologists Victoria Koroteyeva and Ekaterina Makarova, in their studies of Uzbek cities, found that Central Asians, who were more likely to be able to call on family connections, had to spend half as much on bribes as Russian residents.[25]

Still, many Tajiks I spoke with noted how foreign Dushanbe seemed to them, at least when they first came into contact with it. The language spoken on the streets was usually Russian, the buildings were unfamiliar, and finding housing meant dealing with an often indifferent and hostile bureaucracy. Similar patterns held up in other republic capitals, like Tashkent and Frunze (Bishkek), the capital of Kyrgyzstan. City officials were aware of this problem, but what was the solution? Tajikistani party officials promoted the celebration of literary heroes with statues and monuments as one way to anchor the city in the republic's history, but this was not going to be enough.[26] By the 1970s, Central Asian architects were becoming more vocal in calling for more innovative solutions. Tajikistan's senior architect, Vsevolod Veselovsky, a Russian who had worked in Tajikistan since 1937, published an article in January 1979 where he called on his colleagues to look for new national forms without sacrificing modern construction methods, blindly copying classical forms, or imitating what was already being done elsewhere.[27] Many responses followed, from younger architects working in the republic. Among the most vocal was Rustam Mukimov, who called on planners to work together with sociologists, artists, and architectural historians and study the historical experience of traditional Tajik residential construction as well as the needs of people.[28] The debate over how to move forward and what was holding back new residential construction continued over the following years.[29]

In fact, the debate was ongoing not just in Tajikistan but also in other republics. Tashkent, as usual, was far ahead of other major cities in the region. Architects there had been trying to find new forms not just for administrative and cultural buildings, but to integrate traditional Uzbek living patterns into the modern apartment block. The 1966 earthquake cleared entire neighborhoods but also drew resources and attention, making the city a fertile ground for these experiments. Among the most audacious was a building with a "vertical mahalla," where apartments that could accommodate larger families were situated around an inner courtyard.[30] Tajikistani architects came up with interesting ideas of their own. Mukimov, for example, urged his colleagues to think about ways that the Tajik tradition of building on hillsides could be used to develop the hills around Dushanbe—and many such apartment buildings were planned.[31]

The problem with these proposals was that they actually did little to address the immediate problem, which was how to build as much housing as quickly as possible. Construction in Dushanbe was already more expensive and time-consuming than in other Soviet cities, due in part to seismic vulnerability—buildings had to be built to withstand earthquakes of up to the ninth intensity degree on the Medvedev—Sponheuer—Karnik scale, a requirement that became even more important after the 1966 catastrophic earthquake in Tashkent, which registered at 8–9. The quickest way to erect new buildings was to modify the existing models that could be easily put together with steel beams, window panes, pipes, and other part already produced in factories throughout the USSR.[32] Mukimov's ideas may have helped the city look more Tajik, but they would make the solution of the housing problem all the more difficult. Engineers and planners sometimes grew frustrated with their more creative colleagues.[33]

Going into the 1980s, the problem in Dushanbe appeared intractable. Though it housed Tajik cultural and administrative elite, it still felt like a colonial city to some residents, and the housing shortage perpetuated the problems of labor recruitment and industrialization that was irritating central planners as well as locals. This was why the development of smaller industrial cities was particularly important. As was discussed in chapter 3, Tajik economists were pressing their own republican leaders and planners in Moscow to shift investments from "established" cities like Dushanbe to smaller towns in the republic since at least the early 1970s. They believed that situating industry closer to the rural areas would make it easier to draw local workers into the industrial workforce and raise the standard of living in the countryside. Cities like Nurek promised industrial employment for a population that remained in villages but could commute easily to work, while bringing the benefits of Soviet modernity to where these workers lived.[34]

Construction Site to City

When construction began, Nurek was a small town on the right bank of the Vakhsh River with a tobacco field and cemetery on its northern outskirts. The area designated for the new city contained several surrounding villages: Dissabur, Langar, and Sary-bolo. All of these would eventually have to make way for the new Nurek, with the residents resettled in one of the surrounding villages or the city itself. Tutkaul, one of the larger villages in the area, would ultimately be submerged by the dam's reservoir, and its residents were resettled onto the left bank into a village called New Tutkaul.

Constructing a model "city of the future" was neither an obvious nor an un-contested choice. A broader debate went on among Soviet city planners regarding priorities in industrial and urban development. One school argued for laying the groundwork of the city first, to attract and keep good workers; another preferred to focus resources on developing industry, even if quality of life had to suffer.[35] This divide was also visible in Nurek: despite Kalizhniuk's promise to Tajik writers to create a "city of the future," it appears that not all managers and leaders actually agreed on the extent to which resources should be devoted to urban construction. According to Marat Khakel, an engineer who worked on Nurek in the 1960s, there was an ongoing debate between the directors of construction on the one hand and local party and executive authorities on the other regarding the priorities of city building. "The [dam] builders, including head of construction S.K. Kalizhniuk, were in favor of quick (skorospeloe) housing. . . . Local administrative and party organs were interested in building a real [capital] city with modern brick and panel housing and cultural-communal facilities. The building of houses was slow, there was a catastrophic shortage of housing, and people were settled in tents, yurts, and wagons."[36]

Utopian visions for Nurek—as a city that met workers' needs while helping raise them to a new cultural level—were in consideration from the earliest days of construction. In practice, construction of housing, parks, and other facilities had to compete for resources and labor with the construction of the dam itself, as well as with housing construction elsewhere in the republic. In addition, there were rumors that the project would be abandoned—it was far behind schedule, and many officials in Moscow were skeptical about the value of large dams in general and Nurek in particular.[37] Pavel Gorbachev, the first secretary of the local party organization, recalled that many officials doubted whether building a city was even necessary.[38] Kalizhniuk made it clear that the first priority was getting workers out of the elements—city building would have to wait.[39] Early plans therefore focused on building temporary housing as a stopgap measure—primarily yurts of the kind produced by a factory in Charjou and wooden eight-apartment houses that had housed dam builders on the Volga.[40] At the same time, local construction organizations and officials in Moscow agreed that Nurek would one day have to include schools, daycare centers, movie theaters, libraries, and so on.[41]

Workers usually came by train to Dushanbe and then from there traveled to Nurek, often by hitchhiking. They gathered by a teahouse (chaykhana) nicknamed "Kazanskii Vokzal," after the train station that served as the departure point for Central Asia–bound travelers from Moscow. Many had been recruited directly out of the army and sent to their destinations in entire brigades, arriving in their uniforms.[42] Khakel saw a scene of chaos during his first trip to Nurek; the workers looked more like refugees with no clear sense of the future awaiting them than enthusiastic builders doing their internationalist duty: "At the entrance to Nurek we saw an unhappy picture. Under the Chinar trees by the chaykhana and nearby, wherever there was even a little bit of shade, on suitcases and bags (*na uzlakh*) sat workers who had come from all over the Soviet Union. Many had families and children. And there was not yet enough work for everyone."[43]

The village of Tutkaul became the home for many of those who decided to stay. Some rented from local residents, but not all were so lucky. According to Khakel, "A significant part of our workers settled in this village. For this the space of a former animal farm was rebuilt and converted to temporary housing. Some of the [arriving] families were lodged with local families. In the center of the *kish-lak* (village), near the road, was a *stolovaia* (cafeteria) and a summer [outdoor] movie theater, surrounded by a clay *duval* (fence). This is where our workers from gidrospetsstroi [the organization building the dam] went with their stools to watch films." Another young, recently married engineer recalled that when he arrived in March 1962 he found that "there was no city and it would have to be built. In the place of the city were just a few dusty kishlaks, there was nowhere to live, no potable water and [in general] practically nothing."[44]

There was little differentiation between how workers and management lived in these early days. While some specialists and directors whose daily presence was not required could commute from Dushanbe, others settled in the same space as the workers.[45] Yuri Sevenard, then a young engineer and one of the first on the site, found some laborers to build a room for him in the ruins of an old school in Nurek. The room, 2.5 by 1.5 square meters, served as Sevenard's office and bedroom for his first two months in Nurek.[46]

Ultimately it was difficult to manage a construction site where workers found living conditions unacceptable. Relatively high salaries meant little when one could not get shelter or decent food, let alone entertainment or consumer goods. Many workers left within weeks or months of arrival. There were very few apartments as late as 1964, and even getting a spot in a dormitory could be difficult, meaning that some workers spent months or years in tents.[47] Those lucky enough to get a spot in one of the dormitories found conditions barely acceptable. An inspection found that "in the larger dormitories the basic conditions are still not being met—there is no boiled or warm water, no closets for work clothes and clean clothes, no storage space and frequent delays and irregularities with changes of bedclothes, even though just this year the ZhKK [the housing and services offices] received more than 4,000 sheets and other bedding."[48] A Komsomol inspection similarly found that dormitories lacked "chairs, hangers, closets, dressers; the sinks do not work, and two weeks or more pass before bedding is changed."[49] Another report noted that in the men's dormitories, "dirt and unculturedness rule."[50] Workers were apparently stealing wood from the construction site so that they could burn it and keep warm in the winter months.[51]

As with many construction sites where thousands of young workers gathered, drinking and hooliganism were a big part of daily life in Nurek in the early 1960s. A Komsomol report noted that "The lack of basic cultural facilities is leading people to drunkenness and crime. The amount of alcohol per person consumed in Nurek has doubled between 1962 and 1963, and is twice the volume consumed in Dushanbe."[52] Over 1,000 people, roughly every one-fifth resident of Nurek, were arrested over the course of the year for "disturbing the public order." Drunkenness and hooliganism made it difficult to maintain an orderly construction site and contributed to absenteeism. Although officials rarely stated this in their reports, such behavior caused strains between the newly arrived workers and the local residents, thus undermining the "internationalism" of the whole project. The republic newspaper, *Kommunist Tadzhikistana,* chided local officials for failing to provide decent living conditions and especially opportunities for "cultured relaxation."[53]

Officials understood the problem to be lack of cultural activities and facilities where workers could spend their free time. The solution, party and Komsomol officials believed, was to find a way to divert the energy of young people to more "cultured" activities, like movie screenings, dances, concerts, and organized sports. They pressed for the construction of dance floors, libraries and a stadium.[54] Officials were seeking solutions to practical problems, but evoking utopian reasoning to find them. Like the prefabricated panels used to assemble new housing, these were ready-made elements of cultured urban life that officials reached for almost instinctively.

Poor living conditions, disease, and boredom, all led to a high circulation of cadres, and party activists criticized managers for failing to pay attention to residential construction. "Hundreds of experienced specialists are leaving the construction site," a communist named Gamianova complained at a party meeting in August 1962, addressing Kaliuzhniuk, "They are leaving because they are not given the minimal conditions for work."[55] As late as 1967 officials were complaining about severe labor shortages, and especially the turnover of qualified labor.[56] That year, out of a total workforce of 9,514 people engaged in various enterprises related to Nurek, 4,387 had quit or been fired and 4,526 were newly hired.[57] Nurek was neither a closed city nor a Stalinist work camp, and workers were free to come and go. Party activists like Gamianova connected labor turnover with problems of housing, provisions, and quality of life. Enthusiasm and the promise of high wages were enough to attract workers, but not to keep them.

The City of the Future

Gradually, construction officials like Kalizhniuk and his successors, who had the most say in the distribution of funds and materials between urban construction and the main dam site, came around to the point of view of party activists who believed the city and the dam had to be built together. They too began to push for constructing something like the "city of the future" envisioned earlier, even if it meant taking resources away from the main construction site. Whether or not they bought in to the broader ideological goals behind the idea of creating a model city, these officials saw the need to provide a city with enough amenities, shelter, and entertainment to keep workers for the duration of construction. By 1964, construction engineers were begging Moscow and Dushanbe to invest millions more in housing, schools, and medical facilities.[58] A *Pravda* report mocked those who had favored temporary housing: "There was an idea to build the Nurek GES quickly. And if so, then what's the point of building housing? The builders can live in yurts. Well, life has laughed at those who supported this strange idea." But the article also mocked those who wanted to go in the opposite direction. Referring to Manilov, a character from Nikolai Gogol's *Dead Souls* who thought up projects that could never be fulfilled, the paper wrote: "The planners hit the other extreme. They showed incredible *manilovschinu*, drawing a picture of Nurek, the 'city of the future' on their drafting paper."[59]

Even when managers committed to building housing or other facilities, shortages of labor, materials, and problems with transport made it hard to bring plans to fruition.[60] The republic's construction industry could barely keep up with the regular demands of an expanding urban population, let alone the construction of a new city. A new factory to produce housing materials was being built in Ordzhonikdzeabad, but it would be a while before it could operate at capacity. The rush to build housing led to shoddy construction throughout the city, necessitating fundamental repairs.[61]

Construction officials had come to think of the workers as an urban population, and of the workers' health, comfort, and family life as falling within their sphere of responsibility. They petitioned republic and Soviet authorities to allocate additional funds for residential construction, medical and service facilities, and entertainment venues.[62] Gradually, conditions began to improve. The tent cities gave way to dormitories, and then the first apartment blocks. Khakel recalled that "imperceptibly, Nurek started to acquire traits appropriate for a city. On the main street (as always, named after Lenin), multi-story buildings arose, on one of which a color mosaic panel was raised, showing a worker walking with the dam in the background and the words of the poet Vladimir Mayakovsky "I know there will be a city!" Nurek also started getting the cultural and

educational facilities, including a new ten-year school and a summer movie theater. "[Although] in many places people were walking ankle deep in dust, the
kishlak was slowly disappearing."[63] E. K. Sedykh, Nurek's representative in the
Tajik SSR Supreme Soviet, boasted in a 1967 *Pravda* article titled "The Diamond
of the Vakhsh": "Nurek already exists. In the place of the mudbrick kishlak a
modern city with a population of almost 20,000 people has arisen."[64]

Ironically, the failure to get the dam built quickly made the construction
of a planned permanent city possible, even necessary. Gorbachev, who seems
to have been one of the early proponents of building a permanent city, wrote:
"No doubt, if construction lasts only three to five years, and the district has no
chance of further economic development, one can and should focus on temporary housing." But if the project lasts longer, for ten to fifteen years, then one
has to think not just about the construction site but about urban formations.
People may arrive as single demobilized soldiers or recent graduates of technical
institutes, but if they stay long enough they will form families. In an apparent
rebuke to those who had argued for holding off on urban construction, Gorbachev asked: "Can you deny builders basic conveniences? Can you deny the
children of builders their swing-sets, slides, and swimming pools? In place of
the 'theory of the temporary' there comes a sober and serious calculation: labor
turnover is more expensive then swing sets, a fountain, and even a modern
House of Culture!"[65]

By 1967, the situation had changed in a number of ways. First, though labor turnover was still a problem, more workers were staying. In fact, they were
forming families. A city of 11,967 had 4,356 children—more than one-third of
the population. Earlier delays in construction meant that the city had not even
reached its peak population. To get the first turbine functioning by 1970, as called
for at the 18th Party Congress, would require a doubling of the workforce. By
1967 the debate over what kind of city to build had been settled. The new workers would not have to live in tents; instead, officials would do what they could to
have dormitories and apartments ready for them.[66]

Finally, the place of Nurek in the development of southern Tajikistan had
changed over the course of the 1960s. Although the energy from the Nurek dam
had always been intended for several industrial giants to be built in southwestern
Tajikistan, it was only gradually that the idea of a "Southern Tajikistan Territorial
Industrial Complex" took hold among local planners and won approval from
Moscow. Early discussions about Nurek presumed that it would be either a settlement for construction workers or at most a "maintenance town" for the staff who
would stay behind to operate the dam after construction. Although the precise
details of the complex were to be debated and contested until the collapse of
the USSR in 1991, there seems to have been agreement that Nurek should itself

become a minor industrial city within a broader network of small cities built around industries.

The Model City

Tajikistani proponents of Nurek had connected the building of the dam to the USSR's commitment to internationalism and anti-colonialism. But in the first decade of construction, when the dam's fate remained uncertain, that promise seemed to have fallen by the wayside. In any case, a dusty field of tents and temporary housing peopled by drunken and diseased workers building a dam no one sure would be completed was hardly good propaganda material. By 1968–1969 officials again started talking about the project's importance for demonstrating internationalism, both among the peoples of the Soviet Union and working people the world over. Nurek became a site where one could find the "results of cooperation between workers, engineers, and technicians of different nationalities." In addition, from 1968 groups of Middle Eastern, Asian, Latin American, and African students attending the Patrice Lumumba University in Moscow began coming to Nurek to gain experience in their professions.[67]

FIGURE 5.4.   A postcard from Nurek showing the central square and the "Friendship" fountain, 1970s. From the author's personal collection.

Nurek also became a destination for domestic and foreign tourists, part of an itinerary that might include the ancient cities of Bukhara and Samarkand in neighboring Uzbekistan, a trip by train to Dushanbe, and then by bus to visit the site of the dam. Pamphlets in Russian, English, French, and German touted a city of "bright, comfortable apartment houses" had replaced an "old kishlak with its rickety huts" where "Tajiks and Russians, Uzbeks and Georgians, Evenks and Latvians, as well as representatives of many other nationalities and peoples of the Soviet Union live and work . . . as a large and well-knitted family." The Soviet tourist agency Intourist invited visitors to take in the city after dark and "admire a sea of lights which opens to view from the mountain ridge surrounding the city."[68] Bringing foreign students and tourists from across the world to observe and experience the reality of Soviet domestic internationalism helped demonstrate the Soviet commitment to anti-colonialism and its suitability as a model development for Third World nations.

As Nurek city became a showcase for Soviet internationalism and modernity, officials were under even more pressure to make it habitable and beautiful. In May 1968, Alexei Kosygin, the chairman of the Council of Ministers, visited the site and the city, instructing local officials to start taking the city's appearance seriously and encouraging them to make it as impressive as possible.[69] A new plan for improving the town's appearance, including the facades along the main street, the construction of a main plaza with a fountain, and the greening of the city, was drawn up in 1968.[70] "The face of the city of dam builders needs to become exemplary," said B. Shukurov, chairman of the city executive committee, "a great task has been set before us—next to the unique dam, rightly called the diamond of the Vakhsh, to build the city of communism's tomorrow, a source of pride for all the residents of Nurek and their guests."[71]

The identification of Nurek with internationalism was further strengthened in the 1970s, when the magazine *Druzhba Narodov* (Friendship of the peoples) assumed patronage over the dam and the city. The magazine promoted internationalism through literature, and it published writers from across the USSR and hosted debates about socialist art. *Druzhba Narodov* organized several round-tables on Nurek and published accounts by its managers and workers. Its biggest contribution, perhaps, was organizing a book drive for Nurek's library. Famous authors from across the world were invited to send autographed copies of their works to the magazine, which would then pass them on to the library.[72]

City and Village

Writers certainly took up Kalizhniuk's challenge to write about the city. Yet while both Russian and Tajik writers were willing to celebrate the dam and the new city, they also found much to lament. Mukhiddin Khojaev's *Voda k dobru snitsa,* first published in 1977, begins with a scene of chaos, as local residents saw their lives turned upside down: "For centuries the residents of Nurek had surrounded their yards with tall clay walls, and now these walls along with their way of life was crumbling to dust. . . . Some, like ants, tried to build new walls, others abandoned their homes and made their way back to remote mountain villages."[73] Khojaev's villagers experience the start of construction as an assault, whereas most propaganda pieces portrayed residents welcoming construction. Moreover, Khojaev's empathy for the villagers stands in sharp contrast to the view of the recently arrived engineers, who found that there was "practically nothing" at the site. Yet Khojaev's novel was hardly a rejection of the dam, of the kind pioneered by Khojaev's contemporary Valentin Rasputin in *Proschanie s matyoroy* (Farewell to Matyora), about the submersion of a village in the Angara river. In Khojaev's novel, acknowledging the disruption and pain caused by the dam's construction is a strategic device. If the dam was really meant to benefit Tajikistan, as claimed in propaganda, what about the Tajiks who lived in its vicinity? This question arose in the daily interactions between managers and workers, party officials and local residents.

Nurek had made the transition from construction site to city over the course of a decade, but the city was inhabited mostly by outsiders. Urban officials strove to eliminate traces of village life within the city's boundaries, and by the late 1960s there was a clear dividing line between the city and its satellite villages. As urban conditions improved, local workers and party members began to voice discontent regarding the situation in their own villages, forcing party organizations and construction agencies to expand the borders of their work.

Marx had advocated bridging the gap in living standards and culture between the countryside and the city, and Soviet planners like Miliutin had worked toward this goal. It was only in the Brezhnev years that sufficient resources were allocated to make this goal a reality on a wide scale. New agencies were created at the all-Union and republic levels to bring the benefits of Soviet modernity to rural residents.[74] This development, in turn, spurred a renewed interest in designing "model kishlaks" that would facilitate the cultural transformation of Central Asians. Planners and architects in Kyrgyzstan envisioned model villages where houses did not have the customary walls separating the yard from the street; removing the walls was supposed to make the village more social and integrate families.[75] Tajikistani archives similarly contain dozens of plans for "ideal villages" of various kinds, with the usual combination of modernized housing, cultural and medical facilities, and schools.[76] Nurek's satellite villages were not built on the basis of such plans; rather, elements of "modern" living entered villages through the demands of locals or insistence of party activists based in Nurek. As with the demands and expectations of workers from outside the republic, the demands of villagers were channeled through formal institutions like the village councils (*kishlachnyi sovet*), election meetings, and party organizations, as well as through informal ties between prominent workers from a village and manage-rial elites. The extension of infrastructure and services, in turn, led the state to increase its interventions in the lives of people. The city's party organization and its construction organizations would become responsible for modernizing the villages.[77]

The construction of the Nurek Dam made the city, previously of little ad-ministrative or economic importance, the nucleus of party activity. According to Pavel Gorbachev, Nurek's first party secretary, early in the dam's construction the villages that made up the city's periphery were already delimited as being part of the city's authority, and were to receive the same attention the city itself received. In 1962, Gorbachev claims, he arranged for Petr Stepanovich Neporozhniy, the USSR minister of Energy and Electrification, to visit Kibil at the invitation of one of the elders in the kishlak. During his tour of the village, the elder asked the minister:

> You've come to us from the heart of our Motherland—Moscow—a beautiful city with tall buildings. Thank you for finding the time to visit us. People say that Nurek will also become a beautiful city, of a kind not yet seen in the republic. In its new houses there will be electricity, the housewife will no longer have to cook soup on an open fire, because there will be gas stoves, and water will reach each kitchen. This is very good. But what does the great minister think about those kishlaks where there is no electricity, where people have to walk half a kilometer to draw water on the banks of the Vakhsh? Nor is there a good school or medical clinic, or asphalt roads or sidewalks.[78]

According to Gorbachev, Neporozhniy turned to him and said: "Take a compass, and make a circle around Nurek with a radius of fifty kilometers, and give elec-tricity to all the kishlaks [that fall within it]."[79]

The story may or may not be true, but it does point to the way the project transformed local geographies, and the role of the city as a civilizing agent and carrier of the Soviet welfare state. At first, the transformation of Nurek from a construction site to a city also accelerated the separation of European workers and locals. Concerns about disease pushed officials to speed up the construction of housing, improve infrastructure, and build health facilities. They also sharp-ened the divide between the city of Nurek and the surrounding countryside. At this point the older residents of Nurek were still living in their family homes, the settlements that would be absorbed into the city interspersed with tents, the quickly assembled wooden apartment blocks, and the more solid brick buildings in early stages of construction. Like most villagers they kept animals that helped supplement the family diet. But sanitation officials believed that these animals caused disease and made it clear that there was no room for farm animals in a city: "The residents of the city of Nurek, and of Saary-bolo and Dissabur keep animals (chickens, cows, pigs, geese, ducks, and many dogs). Keeping animals in the city and the unsatisfactory sanitation leads to a large number of flies, which are carriers of disease."[80] In the following years, these people would be resettled in surrounding villages, along with the barnyard animals. The only "farming" that was allowed within the city was the cultivation of small garden plots attached to some of the two-floor apartment blocks. Building cities of the future always required erasing something first.

The emerging city was primarily settled by European families, as well as Tajikistani professionals from other parts of the republic. Local families continued to live in the villages. This was largely a matter of preference; the villages provided more space and families could expand their dwellings as people were born or married into family.[81] In the early 1960s laborers from outside Nurek lived in squalid conditions, unlikely to inspire jealousy among local residents. A decade later that was no longer the case. Now the city had both light and running water, new schools and hospitals. The same could not be said for the villages. Officials noted that "in the majority of the kishlaks, located within the borders of the city, there is no running water, electric lighting, or radio. There are no pharmacies, medical centers (*medpunkty*) or libraries. There is no regular bus service between the kishlaks."[82] Resentment began to set in when it became clear that resources were mostly directed toward the city, while the villages were getting left behind in terms of access to electricity, running water, quality of construction materials for houses, roads, and schools.

On January 13, 1968, Sedykh, Nurek's representative in the Supreme Soviet, was meeting with voters from Kibil, New Tutkaul, and Karatay. Two communists who were present, Ahmedov, a laborer working on the dam, and Rahmonov, the head teacher at the Kibil school, complained about the state of their village. According to a report on the meeting, "they rudely blamed the executive committee (Ispolkom) of the City Soviet of Worker's Deputies and the deputy of the Supreme Soviet comrade E. K. Sedykh, who supposedly did not care about the conditions and services (*blagoustroistva*) in Kibil, which still does not have water, there is no bus stop, and the school is in a bad building." Ahmedov's real transgression was making it about nationality—he complained that if "Russians" lived in his village, surely it would already have all the things that had been promised before. It seems that a high degree of dissatisfaction led to the emotionally charged meeting: "despite the fact that in the course of this meeting the chair of the city executive committee sharply corrected these orators, nevertheless the communist comrades Ahmedov and Rahmonov continued to be rude and untactful." Their behavior was censured.[83]

By connecting the problem of running water, transportation, and schooling to nationality, Ahmedov and Rahmonov were appealing to the promises of internationalism, equality, and social welfare, calling out senior officials when these promises were not met. Ahmedov and Rahmonov's protest did get the attention of city authorities. It was one of the first issues Gorbachev brought up at his address to the party conference at the end of the month, placing the extension of services to the surrounding kishlaks on the top of the agenda for the party organization.[84] He also personally criticized officials who had failed to organize bussing for students from Karatash and the new school building for Tutkaul.[85] Increasingly, as the 1960s became the 1970s, the physical condition of the satellite villages as well as general social welfare there came under the purview of city organizations. Ahmedov and Rahmonov's complaint—and their claim that internationalist norms were being violated—had evidently been heard. The incident revealed a pattern, although one that usually played out in a quieter fashion, of local activists holding party and state authorities to account.

If ethnic inequality was one source of complaint, another was that residents were not being properly compensated for the dislocation caused by the dam. Although thousands of families would be resettled to work the cotton fields irrigated by Nurek, the dam itself required relatively little resettlement. One exception was the village of Tutkaul, which would be submerged as the reservoir rose, as well as some of the households that occupied what ultimately became the city of Nurek. As chapter 4 notes, both fictional and journalistic accounts spoke sympathetically of the special bond that locals had with the river and their ancestral villages; their relocation was justified not just by Nurek's economic importance, but also by promises of a better life for the residents and their descendants in a new village nearby. Tutkaul was indeed resettled nearby; just as Nurek was becoming a model city, New Tutkaul was supposed to serve as a model village, with a rational layout and modern conveniences. A publication from the 1970s boasted that New Tutkaul was a vast improvement over the original: "new everyday life is evident everywhere. In the so-called kishlak you have all the urban conveniences: electricity, radio, television, and refrigerators."[86] In fact, residents would have to wait for years before they got running water and electricity, though it does appear to have become one of the more well-serviced villages in the area by the late 1970s.[87]

By that time, it was taken for granted that the dam, the city, and its satellite villages constituted one whole as far as issues such as construction and the provision of welfare were concerned. The kishlak and city soviets became channels for directing the demands of villagers for roads, electrification, and housing. Officials who worked for the soviets were responsible for meeting with residents and party members to ascertain the needs of the different villages.[88] They would then bring their demands to the city party and construction organizations and coordinate the implementation of different projects. As elsewhere in the Soviet Union, formal and informal approaches were necessary to see a project through, and an effective chairman had to have good relations not just with the city party bureau but the various construction and supply organizations in the city and on the dam.[89] Besides the usual demands for paved roads or running water, people also asked for clubhouses, which were constructed in almost all of the satellite villages in the 1970s and 1980s. These clubs often doubled as mosques, with the full knowledge of the party organization. City authorities took responsibility for the cultural life of satellite villages, haranguing officials to meet the Soviet standards of cultural life as well as the demands of residents, such as showing Tajik language movies in village cinemas.[90] Party officials chided subordinates when they failed to follow through on the demands of village residents.[91]

The village and city councils were important for channeling the demands of residents but also organizing them to carry out some of the beautification and infrastructural work of on weekends. Such mobilization, known throughout the Soviet Union as *subbotniki* ("Saturdays," the day when such initiatives took place), were often referred to informally and in official documents as *hashar*, harking back to older Central Asian traditions of communal labor. Thus, while residents could use the institution of the kishlak and city soviets to demand housing materials, infrastructure, or schools, these same institutions were used to organize them for labor along communal lines, helping overcome the deficiencies in labor of local construction organizations.[92]

As the commitment of city authorities to the welfare of surrounding villages increased, so did the ambition of its reach into people's lives. Officials made sure schools were built but also put pressure on families to send their children to those schools. Activists on the village soviet visited families to make sure their children, especially their daughters, were attending school, and to convince them to send their children for further education. In some cases, there was a kind of quid pro quo—officials would win the trust of village elders by helping them expand their house or build a new club/mosque, but they would then expect them to support girls going to school. Officials were even expected to use their position to intervene in cases where families were not providing proper support for their children's studies.[93] Similar strategies were used to convince families to let wives and daughters join the workforce, especially the garment factory.[94]

As the capacity of party and state agencies to monitor and intervene in the lives of the rural population increased, so did resistance. Nurek's hospital, finally completed in the early 1970s, became the center of a kind of rural health network, with clinics and outposts in the satellite villages. Although it was activists from the villages themselves who often requested new clinics or schools, most villagers avoided interventions, especially when they related to childbirth and women's health. As elsewhere, many rural residents distrusted medical professionals, especially if they were male and not Muslim. This did not mean that they avoided biomedical interventions or services altogether, but rather that they were very selective in how they used them, often choosing to turn to "traditional" healers for some problems and to professional doctors for others.[95] Now that the infrastructure was there, officials were confronted with the disparity in medical practices between the urban and rural population. For local officials, the practice of delivering children at home and without professional assistance was evidence of dangerous traditionalism.[96] These concerns were sometimes brought up in articles or speeches about "internationalism," thus reaffirming the link between welfare, social transformation, and commitment to equality between Soviet nationalities.

Health care was part of the broader transformation of life and attitudes that Nurek-based agencies were supposed to oversee in the villages. By the end of the 1970s, officials boasted that with infrastructure and services now extending deeper into the villages, they were producing new Tajik men and women, noting: "Electricity and gas have become a part of everyday life, water supply has been improved, all of the kishlaks have a midwife-nursing stations, almost every family has a television, radio receiver, and each family gets three copies of newspapers and magazines." Soviet rituals, such as the day of the agricultural worker, Nowruz, and Komsomol weddings, had "firmly entered people's consciousness." Officials were nevertheless worried that they were still failing to bring women into "socially useful work," and found that in one village "120 young women are neither studying nor working." They found that the battle against the "antipodes of the socialist way of life" was weak, and that "backward traditions, habits, views are still common among a certain part of the workers of the sovkhoz."[97] The point is not that these phenomena were more widely present than they had been twenty years earlier, but rather that the capacity of local organization to measure them and attempt to act on them had grown along with the city and the social goods the state had brought into the villages. This was one of the paradoxes of the welfare state: residents and activists complained about its absence outside of the city; yet its growth and its involvement in the most intimate aspects of family life was passively resisted, setting up a potential confrontation between state agencies and local residents.

Locals could also use the resources of the construction project to create spaces that were not envisioned in Soviet ideas of urban planning. An interesting example of negotiation between the party's priorities and that of local villages is the case of clubs and prayer spaces. Clubs were supposed be a key institution in providing "cultured" rest and relaxation for workers, as well as a venue for socializing, reading newspapers, party meetings, and entertainment in the form of amateur theater groups or visiting performers. Clubs, in other words, were supposed to play an important role in the socialization of peasants as Soviet citizens.[98] Wealthier collective farms were sometimes able to build lavish "palaces of culture" that rivaled the more impressive urban constructions, but even poorer farms and individual villages usually constructed their own. Yet their actual role in people's lives was more complicated. In a context where many mosques had been destroyed, repurposed, or converted into clubs, the clubs themselves became a site for prayer. This did not mean that they completely stopped serving their intended function. The archives abound with complaints by officials that the clubs were not being active enough in promoting atheism or organizing cultural events; at the same time, the clubs served as a meeting space with party representatives, as sites for celebrations of (Soviet) holidays, and even just as reading rooms.

In Nurek, such clubs were constructed with the help of the local party and construction organizations. One party activist described how he had been put in charge of building a "club" in a village near Nurek. He was there when the construction markers were initially laid out, but when he came back a week later he found that they had been moved. He reset them back to their initial positions, but a week later the same thing happened. Eventually one of the older men who had petitioned for the club told him "maybe it's better if you leave it like this." Later he understood the men were hoping to use the clubhouse for prayer, and were reorienting the building to make it easier to pray facing Mecca.[99]

Consider the following example: in 1967 a new club was constructed on the outskirts of Nurek. Its initiators were a local representative in the Supreme Soviet of Tajikistan and several communists in local party and municipal organs. The materials were provided by the city executive committee, presumably from the resources allocated for housing construction, and the building itself was erected by volunteers. Activists organized a library with 4,500 books and quickly registered 256 readers. The club included a stage and audience hall, and hosted amateur theater and musical performances, patriotic gatherings, and lectures on atheism. Several years later, an article in *Kommunist Tadzhikistana,* titled "A Club or a Prayer Hall?," alleged that it was in fact being used for prayer. An inspection followed, and officials reported that there was no evidence that the club was being used for religious purposes.[100] In reality, it almost certainly served a double function, with people of different ages using it in different ways.

Although Nurek and its satellite villages were supposed to form one whole, the imaginary boundary between them never disappeared. Certain rituals did bring the two populations together—for example, each village hosting celebrations for one day during the Nowruz holiday, or weekly dances that attracted at least some young men from the villages. Screenings of Indian films in particular were popular with the Tajik population. The worksite itself, of course, was where "Europeans" and many "locals" interacted daily, and some of the more prominent workers like Muhabbat Sharipov hosted gatherings of Tajik and European workers in their own homes. On the whole, families from the villages were reluctant to let their young men—let alone young women—attend the discotheques and other social events organized within Nurek. Such events were set up to provide "cultured" relaxation for young workers to keep them from getting drunk in their dormitories and public spaces, but they were far from the notion of proper sociability as understood by local villagers.

The sense that the city was for "Russians" and the villages for Tajiks remained, as did complaints about inequality in the level of services in each. At a party conference in 1988, a teacher and party member pointed out: "The social problem in our city is not being solved at the proper level, especially in the kishlaks." Complaining about the state of schools, telephone access, and the failure to protect the villages from mudslides, he noted "these questions have been raised numerous times at plenums of the city party committee and sessions of the city's executive committee but have found no solution."[101]

These shortcomings should not obscure the fact in their interactions, local residents, managers, and party activists tried to find a way to make reality approximate stated ideals of Soviet equality and welfare. On the one hand, just as the typical problems of disease, boredom, and labor turnover convinced managers of the wisdom of investing in better facilities and housing for workers in Nurek, so did complaints from villagers lead those same officials to invest in infrastructure and facilities for the surrounding countryside. On the other hand, the way that these individuals approached both sets of problems reveals the powerful hold of utopian ideals of equality, internationalism, and urban and rural life.

The Local Politics Machine

Mass housing in the Khrushchev era and beyond created many neighborhoods and towns that looked indistinguishable from one another, as satirized in movies like Eldar Riazanov's film *The Irony of Fate*. Nurek, too, was a city built largely from prefabricated components—an assembly of available building designs, layouts, and materials. Yet in their assembly the city became something unique, precisely because of the myriad minor adjustments and negotiations between individuals, party officials, and planners. Most of my interviewees—both those who lived in the city and those who were in the villages—insisted on the uniqueness of the project of which they had been a part and recognized its place in a larger Soviet story. Although Nurek shares a great deal with other postwar Soviet company towns, its residents are not wrong to think that it was exceptional. Internationalism was a professed goal throughout the Soviet Union, but at sites like Nurek that ideal gained an additional importance as a way to prove Soviet commitment to anti-colonialism. Understanding the history of the city and its satellite villages requires looking beyond the dreams of planners and the goals of party leaders to see how these interacted with the engagement and resistance of workers and locals. It was not just the architectural shape of the city that emerged from these complex interactions, but the entire set of obligations between the state, the workers, and the villages surrounding Nurek; in other words, the local manifestation of the postwar Soviet welfare state.

The story of Nurek also challenges a familiar dichotomy that sees dreams of revolutionary transformation fading after the Khrushchev era.[102] It is true that utopian visions or internationalist ideals were sometimes obscured by the everyday needs of construction; however, it is equally true that that the commitment to these ideals, in terms of both physical resources and individual mobilization, only increased in the 1970s. It was in this period that resources became available to "bridge the gap between the city and the village" throughout the USSR, and the effects of this policy are dramatically visible in the relations between Nurek and its satellites. The ideological commitment of party activists, the mobilization of local residents, and the availability of resources all point to the fact that instead of stagnation, the period saw rapid movement and transformation.

To put it another way, in the late 1960s and 1970s the distance between present-day reality and the promise of socialism shrunk considerably. Stalinism offered the promise of communism in a distant future in exchange for suffering today; Khrushchev shrunk the time horizon to twenty years and eliminated the worst of the repressive apparatus. In the Brezhnev era, it was possible not only to demand paradise, or a version of it, immediately, but also to get it. One could no longer ask people to give up their ancestral villages for the promise of a modern Tajikistan decades later; their compensation, in the form of a new and improved home, had to be ready right away. Whether or not it did—or could—live up to expectations is a different story.

More broadly, the discussion of welfare and equality at Nurek forces us to revisit one of the fundamental critiques about development projects articulated by James Ferguson and frequently cited since. Ferguson found that the failure of development projects rarely led to their abandonment; on the contrary, it led to new initiatives that only increased the footprint of the state. At the same time, development had the effect of "depoliticizing both poverty and the state"—it was an anti-politics machine.[103] The evidence presented above suggests that the picture is more complicated. The footprint of the state grew, but the shape it took was determined by a constant negotiation between different actors. The project itself and the party and state institutions that grew in its wake had the opposite effect of the one Ferguson discovered. As people were encouraged to think of themselves as agents in the transformation of themselves and their community, they also learned to use those institutions to raise questions about poverty and inequality.

SHEPHERDS INTO BUILDERS

On one of my first trips to Nurek, I was met by Nurullo Shulashov, the town's former mayor. I acquired his contact information through the Dushanbe head-quarters of the Communist Party, of which Shulashov is still a proud member. The man who picked me up at Nurek's "bus station"—which has not seen any buses in a long time, but is rather the gathering place for private drivers picking up fares to Dushanbe—seemed less like a communist and more like a successful en-trepreneur. In his new Toyota SUV with the air conditioner turned up (a rarity in Tajikistan), he was more "new" Tajik than "old" Soviet. Nevertheless, he began our conversation with a suspicious "you probably think everything about the Soviet Union was bad." When I assured him that was not the case, he relaxed a little. As he drove me around town, Shulashov talked at length about the dam and his own life story. A local boy, he had gone to work on the construction site, becoming the personal driver of Yurii Sevenard, the chief engineer, then being licensed to drive a Belaz, the large yellow dump trucks from Belarus that circled the construction site around the clock in convoys. Eventually Shulashov became a brigade leader, studied engineering, and moved through a number of management positions. He remained a communist during the civil war (1992–1997), when he served as Nurek's mayor.[1] Shulashov took me through the access tunnels that were crucial to the dam's construction and through which he had himself driven countless times; at the top of the dam he patiently explained the construction process as we looked over the still water of the reservoir. Then he took me to the easternmost edge of the dam's top, where a yellow Belaz truck sat on a pedestal, an elderly Ger-man shepherd resting in the shade under its motor. It was the truck he himself had driven, Shulashov explained to me, and he had installed it there to commemorate the drivers and their machines. Shulashov also took credit for keeping the town's Lenin statue in place after the Civil War. When a new mayor wanted the statue removed, Shulashov mobilized people to protest in the central square.

Shulashov spoke with great pride about the dam, his own work, and his path from modest beginnings to accomplished manager (he even served as general director of Rogun in 2008–2010). He also talked about the creation of the city of Nurek, and the transformation of the town and villages that surrounded it. Many of the things he said were familiar from Soviet biographies of hero workers across the union—the narrative of the village boy turned leader, the recitation of nationalities that had taken part in the dam's construction, the transformations the dam had made possible for himself, for the area, for the republic as a whole. Shulashov also boasted of using his proximity to people like Sevenard to finally bring running water to the village of New Tutkaul. By the time I met Shulashov, I had heard versions of the narrative many times and had read it newspapers and various other publications about the dam. Yet it was clear that the man who was taking me around saw the narrative very much as his own. The dam—and by extension, the Soviet Union as a whole—helped him transform himself, and he in turn helped build the dam and transform his community, contributing to the larger goal of building a new world in the process. I would hear variations of this narrative many times over the coming months.

Life-stories like Shulashov's give us a window into the way that individual and collective lives were transformed by the dam. As we saw in chapter 4, development theorists in the East and West believed that large-scale infrastructure projects such as the Tennessee Valley Authority or the irrigation schemes in Afghanistan's Helmand Valley could mold the new subjects required for an industrial economy and modern nation-state. These social scientists expected industrialization to transform attitudes about everything from politics and religion to family life, and were confounded by the reluctance of rural Central Asians to enter the industrial workforce. Looking more closely at the life stories of workers in Nurek, we can get a better appreciation of what it took to draw workers into construction in the first place, what their experiences were like when they got there, and ways that participation affected their standing in their families, villages, and within the work site itself.

Development and the Making of Soviet Subjects

Soviet leaders believed that large construction projects (*udarnye stroiki*) shaped new Soviet individuals even as they shaped a new economy and state. The party promoted Stalin-era projects like Magnitogorsk, with their free and unfree labor, as opportunities for class enemies or those who had fallen under the sway of dangerous ideologies to redeem themselves. The big projects of the 1950s and 1960s tried to revive the spirit of personal transformation, but without the threat of the terror. Thousands of young workers went to build dams in Siberia and turn the "virgin lands" of Kazakhstan into a new breadbasket for the USSR. The opportunity to test one's mettle in an exotic and forbidden locale, to prove oneself as an individual and as a leader of a group enticed many young people, including recent graduates and demobilized soldiers. Yet, according to Mikhail Rozhansky, who studied the experience of workers in Siberian new cities of the 1960s, these projects also forced young people to "identify the fundamental contradictions of Soviet idealism, and ideals came face to face with idiocracy."[2] Confronted with poor management, sloganeering, and hypocrisy, young people became disillusioned and their energy was sapped.

Nurek, similarly, drew thousands of young men and women from across the USSR with the promise of adventure and career advancement in an exotic locale. As the high turnover rates discussed in chapter 4 suggest, many quickly became disillusioned and left. Their departure encouraged officials to focus on another transformational goal: that of making socialist workers and citizens out of the local population. As one party official boasted in 1969: "In this period many of the local builders (*binokoroni mahalli*), which in the past knew no vocation besides shepherd and farmer, have now improved themselves (*be kamol rasidand*) and today are the pride of the great collective of builders (*iftihorii kollektivi kaloni binokorom meboshand*)."[3] Young men and women, especially those from the surrounding districts, were encouraged to work on the dam and become a vanguard of their own societies and of all the formerly oppressed peoples of the world. Although drawing locals into labor was always problematic, the dam's construction did offer numerous opportunities for Tajiks to become skilled workers, engineers, and even managers. Social scientists and party leaders believed that these new workers would have to make a psychological break. The move from farm to industrial labor required adjusting to new work rhythms, labor discipline, patterns of speech and ways of comportment.[4] Potentially, it came with benefits that went beyond the relatively high salary offered to workers. Those workers who received official recognition—for their productivity, for particular feats at the work site, or for being the first "local" to take on a certain profession, gained capital that translated into more influence within their communities, on the one hand, and within the local party organization, on the other.

The stories of workers at Nurek provide a fascinating window into the question of subjectivity in the post-Stalin years, as well as the link between subjectivity and development more broadly. In his study of Magnitogorsk, the center of the steel industry in the Soviet Union and one of the grand industrialization projects of the 1930s, Stephen Kotkin noted the way workers learned to become Soviet subjects by adopting and deploying the language of the party—"life in Magnitogorsk taught one how to identify oneself and speak in the acceptable terms."[5] Other historians, most notably Jochen Hellbeck and Igal Halfin, suggested a different approach of Soviet subject formation, focusing instead on how the individual is inspired to break with a pre-existing identity and transform him or herself to "finally accede to a harmonious and integrated being."[6] These two visions of Soviet subjectivity are not irreconcilable—people did "speak Bolshevik" (in Kotkin's formulation) to achieve strategic goals. Yet they also reflected on their own experience and transformation in a way that emphasized self-realization within a new context.

It helps to step outside Soviet historiography and consider the place of subjectivity in the broader history of development in the twentieth century. As we saw in chapter 3, it was not just Soviet ideologists and social scientists who were interested in the link between individual (self-)formation and economic development. The individual who believed in his or her own ability to self-fashion and worked toward that goal was considered as a necessary precondition for capitalist development; only when the subject set out on the path of self-transformation would he or she break free of the ties of family and community and seek success in a wider world, contributing to the prosperity of the wider nation in the process.[7] It was only when the subject undertook to transform the whole physical, social, and moral environment that she could transform herself.[8] These notions linked socialist and capitalist development and the subject's role within them. In both cases, the transformation of self, environment, and social world are intertwined, and the first serves as a precondition for the others.[9]

Although Soviet propaganda often spoke of a complete break between the "feudal" past and inward-looking village life and the new world of individual development, class-based solidarity, and socialization into new forms of community, most individuals did not have to make a complete break with the networks and communities in which they grew up. Most workers recruited locally continued to live in their home villages, and even those that did not maintained ties with their extended family there. These workers built up important forms of capital that could be used across the worlds that they inhabited. A celebrated local worker like Shulashov, even if he or she had no formal party or government role, could use their position to bargain for resources with local leaders and agencies. Their ability to deliver goods such as running water or building materials, in turn, raised their standing within their own community. The Soviet system promised to take the marginalized and make them empowered members of the larger collective. But the very process threatened to marginalize the individual in their original community. In many cases, though, the system's flexibility and the ability of these individuals to help their communities enabled them to build a bridge between the two worlds.

Modeling Workers

One way to teach workers was to provide them with models. In the 1930s, the party celebrated Alexey Stakhanov, a supposedly record-breaking miner, to boost morale and productivity.[10] In the post-Stalin era, biographies of hero workers were also used to inspire and set higher standards of production, although with more modest ambitions. Such biographies and autobiographies were heavily promoted in the Khrushchev era, particularly in youth-oriented publications like *Komsomol'skaia Pravda*. Unlike the Stakhanovite heroes of the 1930s, Khrushchev era narratives tended to focus more on ordinary individuals who could serve as an example for others to follow. The stories of young people who went to build the great Siberian dam at Bratsk or till the virgin lands followed a twofold narrative leap: first, the decision to leave one's home and go on the adventure, and then, maturation and self-realization in the process of overcoming the difficulties of construction.[11]

The Nurek biographies were similar, but the transformation was mostly mental rather than spatial.[12] First came the subject's emergence from his or her environment—the decision to go from "shepherd" to "worker." There followed a period of apprenticeship, when one of the Russian workers, or, particularly in the latter period, one of the Tajik workers who had already "made it" acted as an "elder brother" or "elder sister" to someone just beginning on the journey. In many cases the subject went beyond his or her initial occupation, either acquiring additional technical training or becoming a party activist. Finally, there was some kind of "return"—a newfound appreciation by his or her family, village, and so on. Many official biographies appeared in Russian and Tajik, either in the local newspaper, *Norak*, or separately as pamphlets or short books. These publications served two purposes: they helped propagate the image of Nurek as an internationalist project, but even more crucially they celebrated local heroes and the transformations they had undergone as a result of participating in construction, with the ultimate goal of enjoining others to follow their path.

As presented in these biographies, the model dam builder was not just a good worker—he was ambitious, always seeking self-improvement; he was politicized, in the sense that he understood the larger significance of the task he undertook; and he was a leader to others. One such worker was Safar Rakhimov, a "young man from Tutkaul," the village where many workers initially settled with local families in the early 1960s but which would ultimately be submerged when the Dam was completed. According to an article that appeared in *Norak* in 1967, Safar, still a boy when the construction was first getting underway, fell in love with the machinery that began arriving in his village. Whenever Safar saw other young men behind the wheel of one of the excavators, his heart filled with longing to be one of them. Nisor Ne'matov, one of the young men that Safar saw every day, encouraged him to study, which he did. After a year at a technical school in Kurgan-Tyube (Qurghonteppa), he returned to Nurek and worked under Nisor. Eventually he became not only a model worker (overfulfilling his work plan by 120–150 percent and taking good care of the machinery) but he had trained other young men who were now helping to build the Nurek dam.[13]

Yet these qualities were not enough—workers were expected to have a nobility of spirit that was reflected in their home lives and their relations with their friends, their colleagues, and the city. In one article, Rem Fedorovich Yulaev, a communist and manager on the construction site, talked about his colleague Safarali Khukumov. Khukumov, Yulaev said, lost his father at a young age, and did not have the chance to study. While serving in the armed forces he learned carpentry, and then went to work on the Golovnaia Dam. When Khukumov heard about Nurek the young builder decided to go there. Besides being a skillful and

FIGURE 6.1.   Jabbor Rasulov awarding medals to dam builders, 1979.
Courtesy of the Russian State Archive of Photo and Video Documentation.

conscientious worker, he was raising four children—two of his own, and two he adopted after they lost their parents. Nor did he think that this was anything special—after all, he was a "Soviet person." Yulaev concluded "That's our Safarali Khukumov, a private in the army of Soviet workers . . . proud to carry the title of Soviet worker, a title he cherishes."[14]

Some biographies emphasized how workers combined what they saw as their traditional calling as Tajiks with the possibilities offered by modern technology in a Soviet context. Nosir Nigmatov, from Dangara district, explained his decision to become an excavator operator by referring to older traditions of irrigation: "There is no work more honorable for a Tajik than giving land water. That is why, after graduating from school, I chose the profession of excavator (*ekskavatorshchik*)." He spent several years working on irrigation projects in a kolkhoz, but, hearing about the construction Nurek of the Nurek dam, he decided to go work there "I thought about it and decided—my place is there where the work is harder."[15]

Other biographies emphasized how workers were intent on not being left behind by the times. Tagay Sobirov was born before the revolution in Tukmazur, four kilometers from Nurek. As he explained in a first-person narrative published in 1962, the construction of the dam woke up the sleepy valley. In just a few years everything had changed:

> Our life today is nothing like the old, too calm and rather too lazy one. This is a life whose pulse, if one can put it this way, is full of blood and precise. In the mountains you hear the ceaseless explosions. Bulldozers, excavators, and other machines are stubbornly attacking the mountains and cliffs. It is as if the area has woken up! And how can one sit still, when nearby such enormous and interesting construction is taking place, when people are coming to us from all the farthest corners of the country! Especially since while people of different nationalities are building it, it is, first of all a new construction (*novostroika*) of the Tajik people.[16]

For Sobirov, who was at least in his forties by the time the dam construction got underway, it was a wake-up call: "I couldn't stand it anymore, and, though I was no longer young, and it seems, it was too late to change one's life, I went to the construction site." When asked what he had done previously, Sobirov answered "kolkhoznik" and was offered a job in the Nurek Sovkhoz—a state farm that was supposed to provide the builders with food. Sobirov refused. "I want to build the dam with my own hands," he told them. He was assigned to pour concrete, and rose to become a brigade leader.[17]

These published biographies left an imprint. When I visited in 2013 and 2015, everyone in Nurek seemed to be familiar with the biographies of local hero workers, and often tried to present their own life stories according to similar templates. For locals who went to work on the dam, the biographies provided a model for self-representation, but also for self-understanding. They helped these new workers contextualize their experience. The biographies also played a role in recruitment, albeit an indirect one. It is unlikely that the biographies themselves were heavily read in Nurek's satellite villages, at least in the first decade of construction. But they gave workers already at the site stories they could tell back home. These biographies served as a model for the party activists and other recruiters who went out into the villages to encourage potential workers. And finally, the published biographies established their subjects as local heroes, which, as we will see, had important consequences for their relationship with party organs as well as their home villages.

Family Life

In the 1978 Tajikfilm production *A schast'e riadom* (Happiness is nearby), a forty-one-year-old brigade leader known to everyone as Usto (master craftsman) looks to find a new bride so he can start a family. A childless widower, he seeks the help of Rano, a dispatcher and a widow with three children who moonlights as a matchmaker. Usto is enchanted by a road engineer who grew up in Leningrad with a Tajik father and a Russian mother, but after spending a day with her and her "cultured" friends in Dushanbe he realizes the distance between them. He returns to Nurek and finds Rano in tears because her daughter has a fever, and one of the last shots of the film is him asleep at the foot of Rano's daughter's bed, a grateful Rano softly kissing him on the cheek.

The movie is remarkable in several ways—although it celebrates internationalism and the romance of dam construction, it avoids many of the clichés such movies carry. For example, there is no Russian "elder brother" in the film who inspires or teaches the main character—the only major Russian character is a kindly but partially handicapped war veteran who is Usto's roommate on the construction site and dies trying to save Rano's son from the Vakhsh River. In its portrayal of internationalism, the movie does not seek to make everyone uniformly "modern." At one point, Usto sees his bearded father, in a turban and *chopon* (a kind of robe), herding sheep and abandons the construction site to run after him and get his advice on marriage. As independent people who have gained recognition as workers and are fully integrated into the multiethnic community of the dam, Usto and Rano are avatars of the ideal projected in Soviet publications; at the same time, both are traditional and local in their own way—Usto in his relationship to his father and his ultimate rejection of the cosmopolitan road engineer, and Rano in her activities as a matchmaker.

On the surface, the film is about the building of the Nurek Dam, with the usual scenes of heavy machinery, imposing nature, and large groups of workers overcoming seemingly insurmountable obstacles. Mostly, though, the movie is about the different meanings of family. The film opens with a wedding of a couple Rano has brought together. Although many of the male characters are single, they all agree that having a family would be better. Usto's Tajik and non-Tajik friends encourage him to just marry Rano and be a father to her children. At the same time, the movie celebrates the other kinds of families that are formed in the process of a project like Nurek—Usto may be single and childless, but he is shown as a father figure within his brigade (composed of a Tajik, a Russian, a Kyrgyz, and an Armenian), demanding but also protective. The movie shows how a project like Nurek can transform individual lives, allowing men and women to develop and fulfill themselves. It also underlines the extent to which they can only complete their growth once they have grounded themselves and accepted their place in several overlapping family formations.

The movie thus reflects another central concern of development scholars, as well as the authors of worker biographies: the family and its place in the wider socialist order. As elsewhere in the Soviet Union, officials in Nurek promoted certain ideals of the Soviet family—where both the husband and wife worked and supported each other in their ambitions for further study, career advancement, and so on. If they were of different nationalities, so much the better, since it demonstrated the gradual erosion of national distinctions in favor of a Soviet identity. Officials also intervened in family life, actively encouraging girls to avoid arranged marriages and helping them get an education and join the workforce. Although such interventions were not unique to Nurek, they were shaped by the particular challenges of labor recruitment and the project's importance as a demonstration for Soviet successes in internationalism and modernization. Soviet officials both targeted the institution of the rural family and simultaneously sought to co-opt it for the cause of development.

Officials recognized that family relations could also help recruit local workers for the dam. Once the decision was taken to draw more locals into the workforce, officials had to find a way to overcome problems of language, attitudes, as well as inexperience with heavy machinery in use at the work site. Although published biographies usually featured young men, local officials saw the need to start with older family members. As the hero of Mukhiddin Khodzhaev's novel *Voda k dobru snitsia* explains, "If even one of these 'old men' accepts my invitation [to work on the dam], tomorrow you'll have ten new workers."[18] My interviews suggest that this did, in fact, become a part of local practice. For example, in recruiting drivers for the Belaz dump truck (a dangerous job—the trucks circulated around the clock along a treacherous precipice) managers found that if they could train one worker, he could then take a younger brother or cousin for a ride-along, and eventually convince him to train to be a driver himself.[19] As a result, working in Nurek often became a family affair, with many members of extended families working on the site, sometimes in one brigade.

Similar strategies were used to convince families to let wives and daughters join the workforce, especially the Nurek garment factory. As hard as it was to recruit young Tajik men into industry, it was almost impossible to recruit rural women. Getting girls into school and work was important from both an ideological perspective—working outside the home was a crucial step in women's emancipation—and an economic one—in a system with perpetual labor shortages, women were needed in the service as well as the industrial sector. The garment factory was originally conceived to provide employment for women who came to Nurek from elsewhere in the USSR to join husbands working on the dam—part of an emerging Soviet-wide practice where plants unconnected to the city's main industry were built to provide employment.[20] By the time the factory started production in the 1970s local officials saw it as a place where Tajik women could be more easily encouraged to enter the workforce, presumably because the collective would be almost entirely female and the work was closer to traditional crafts. Yet finding local women willing to work in the plant proved difficult, and by 1978 the factory had only half the workers it needed.

Again, there was a recognition that change had to start with the family. Activists from the plant and local party organization went into the villages to speak to male heads of families.[21] One activist recalled that she and her colleagues would target the most influential men in the village, men whose children were already grown. The activists could usually convince them to let their wives go at first, but after some time the men might let their daughters go or encourage others in the village to do so. Activists organized a bus that picked up female workers and brought them home after each shift.[22] Getting the approval of husbands and fathers was a concession to the patriarchal authority the activists were trying to undermine, but in their view it was a worthwhile one that made it possible to change attitudes in the long term.[23] Officials held out hope that the garment factory could serve as an intermediate step for women's emancipation—over time, women would acquire the habits of being part of the workforce, join the Komsomol and party, and even begin to accustom themselves to taking leadership roles and managing others, pulling their "sisters" along the same path.[24]

The construction project also encouraged people to think about the meaning of family in different ways. Thus, members of a brigade were supposed to think about their mutual obligations to each other, not just on the worksite but also in their daily lives. The model brigade family was international, with Russians, Tajiks, and people of other nationalities working alongside each other. The "head" of this family—the brigade leader—could be a local. In other situations, a more familiar kind of internationalism prevailed—a Russian man or woman would act as the elder brother or sister to a young Tajik man or woman, teaching them a specific craft and introducing them to their new life.

The (biological) family could also help promote productivity at the workplace by discouraging behaviors like drinking, carousing, and gambling, and encouraging "cultured" rest and relaxation, which included focus on family duties, the education of children, and personal improvement.[25] The domestic lives of local Tajiks and Europeans were frequently discussed at party meetings and in the local paper, although the focus varied. If the issues regarding Tajik families were usually connected to lack of support for girls to attend school or join the workforce, practices of early marriage or bride-price, discussion relating to European families tended to center on problems of alcoholism, absenteeism, and other forms of "immoral" behavior.

Mikhail Rozhansky, in his studies of the great Siberian construction projects, writes that in its drive to overcome marginalization and integrate the marginalized, the Soviet Union also engaged in the continuous marginalization of individuals because it "split natural human connections—family, neighbor, friend. . . . Only relations with the state were confirmed as being beyond suspicion."[26] This depiction may be true for the height of the terror, but it fails to capture the nuances of the period that followed. In the case of Central Asia, we see that the family posed a particular danger for authorities, because it was the institution that served to replicate practices that were antithetical to the Soviet vision of the future and its immediate goal for economic development. At the same time, Soviet officials recognized that the family could also transmit new values. In propaganda, as well as in practice, officials therefore sought a reconciliation.

In what remains of this chapter, I look in more detail at the life stories and biographies of workers and their families, shifting the focus from the official biographies published in the Soviet and post-Soviet periods to the first-person accounts provided by the subjects themselves. Because most of these workers did not keep diaries—at least I was not able to track any down—these life stories do not allow us to engage directly in the subjectivity debate as it has developed within Soviet historiography. Conducting interviews two decades after the Soviet collapse, in a place that had seen a bloody civil war, presents particular problems—the tendency to view the past as preferable to what came after, especially for those who benefited materially during the Soviet period, is strong. What was striking about these interviews were not the comparisons between the present and the past, but rather the way that these individuals sought to deliver a coherent narrative of their life story, placing themselves within the history of the larger dam project and that of the Soviet Union as a whole, even as their narratives sometimes departed in substantial ways from the orthodox Soviet ones.[27]

Beyond demonstrating the power of published biographies to inspires people's narrations of their own lives, these first-person accounts allow us to do three things. First, they show how ideals of individual behavior and family life were transmitted and enacted. Second, reading "official" biographies against first-person narratives available through contemporaneous party meetings and later oral histories, we can consider the forms of fashioning and self-fashioning that took place. Finally, by setting these stories against the bigger picture of what went on at Nurek, we begin to see how individual transformations affected power relations in the city and its satellites, and how these transformations brought these two worlds together and pushed them apart.

Women's Work: Cranes, Motorcycles, and a Komsomol Wedding

The emancipation of women—their ability to act as independent subjects, participate in political, economic, and social life, and pursue an education, was a central tenet of the revolution. Yet as with other forms of intervention in family life, campaigns for emancipation often sparked the most resistance. As long as women did not take part in economic and social life, the Soviet Union could not claim to have radically transformed its southern regions. But interventions of the kind attempted during the unveiling campaign (known as the *Hujum*, or assault) in the late 1920s would threaten to upset the stability of the post-Stalin years, undermining whatever progress had been made in integrating local men.[28] As we saw in the case of the garment factory, authorities preferred compromise—bringing women into the workforce slowly, while allaying the concerns of husbands and fathers regarding the women's exposure to other men. For this reason, authorities also sought out models from the local population that other women could emulate. Educated Tajik women and party activists came to work in and around the dam site, but to the local population they were somewhat foreign as well. The two women whose stories are relayed below were particularly interesting because they were truly local, and because of the way they embraced their roles as "elder sisters" for other women in their communities.

A profile on Jumagul Nazarova, Nurek's first female crane operator, began with a couplet from the Soviet-Tajik poet Mirsaid Mirshakar: "Life without a wish was not sweet/A wish was what made life sweet." The title of the article, which ran in September 1971, was "A wish that came true."[29] Jumagul, the article said, had dreamed as a schoolgirl of gaining a technical profession, and so after she finished the eight-year school in her native village of Dakhan she went to her local Komsomol secretary, who sent her to a technical college in Tashkent. Later she was trained by Lida Shubalina, a Russian woman. Now, according to the article, she was a model worker in her own right, not just fulfilling but overfulfilling her work plan by 25–30 percent. As a crane operator she had taken part in the transformation of Nurek into a city: "I am proud that with this profession, that I took part in the building of schools, the movie theatre 'Vakhsh,' the medical clinic and other buildings," Jumagul told the newspaper. A picture that ran with article showed a confident, smiling young woman wearing a traditional skullcap and what looks like a button-down blouse made from a pattern usually found in local dresses.

In 2013, Jumagul was running a small clothing shop in Nurek's market, but was still locally famous as the first Tajik woman to operate a crane, and also the first local girl to be married in a Komsomol ceremony. In fact, in the version of her life Jumagul presented, the love story and the professional story were inseparable. She began by saying that she had always wanted to study and to work in some sort of construction capacity. During our interview she kept returning to the theme that it was her "husband" who had inspired her: "From my childhood I dreamt of going to school, of studying, of working on a construction site. When I was studying I met my husband, he was not my husband then, but he told me what it was like to work, he worked as a crane operator. He worked there until his death. And he explained to me, he said [this is what is like] and so from my childhood I had a dream that I would work and live like a free woman and be useful for society." Similarly, she insisted that it was her attraction to the Komsomol from a young age that had made her want to become a "socially useful" and independent person. "When I was studying I was always . . . a *komsomolka* [member of the communist youth movement]. But I had my girlfriends keep the Komsomol ticket for me, so that my parents would not see it. And so being the active komsomolka, and this connection, and my [future] husband telling me about the work . . . [made me want to work on the dam]."

According to the published accounts of Jumagul's life and her own telling of the story in 2013, one thing stood in the way of both these personal and professional goals—Jumagul's parents had already arranged a marriage for her, which was to take place once she graduated from the eighth grade. At the time that the wedding was supposed to take place the man that she actually wanted to marry was in Novosibirsk. Jumagul's "liberation" would involve the mobilization of party, law enforcement, and even construction officials.

> I did not know at the time where the Komsomol, or hukumat [city government office], or the police was. And [my future husband] made a

map for me and said if anything happens, give this note and this map
to Habib Ashurov, [a classmate of Jumagul and a cousin of the man
she intended to marry] and he will know where to take it and who to
turn to. . . . And so the day that the wedding was supposed to take place
I was locked up in a room and they did not let me go anywhere. Well,
my younger sister came and said that someone has come to see you.
I had given the note beforehand. And so the whole management of his
department, and people from the police, the hukumat, from the central
committee of the Komsomol . . . they took me, and they told the parents
that they would take me away, that they [my parents] could not give me
away [in marriage]. And so they took me straight from the hukumat to
Dushanbe to a dormitory.

Several months later Jumagul married her beloved and started her own career
in Nurek. The young couple lived in a dormitory, and later in their own apartment. In the meantime she also enrolled in a teacher's college, studying history
and social sciences.[30] After graduating in 1975 she worked for ten years in the human resources division of the new garment factory and then as a teacher until her
retirement. Her parents shunned her for some time, but eventually accepted her
new life and her new family: "they came to visit us and we went to visit them."[31]

Jumagul's escape from her family and her decision to join the dam took out-
size importance for local party authorities who were struggling to recruit local
women. Marat Khakel, an engineer who was also on the committee that had to
certify Jumagul as a crane operator, recalled being under enormous pressure:
"Phone calls kept coming to me as the chairman of the examining committee to examine her and let her work independently. And I was constantly told
that I did not understand the importance of nationality politics in this question. She passed the exam only after I had left Nurek, and several years later
I read about the famous crane operator J. Nazarova in the local press."[32] Why
would the party go to such lengths just to make sure one local girl fulfilled an
important but nevertheless not particularly prominent task? As Makhram,[33] a
former secretary of ideology explained, the reason was self-evident: "A Tajik
girl became a crane operator!" The fact that a girl who was about to be married
and presumably confined to the domestic sphere instead married a man of her
choosing, acquired professional skills, and became a worker was a demonstration of what the Soviet Union made possible: "When [in history] would it have
been possible for a Tajik girl to operate a crane?!"[34] Officials like Makhram had
a hand in creating Jumagul's biography, from her "liberation" to her licensing as
a crane operator. This was not just about showing to the outside world that Tajik
girls were becoming Soviet women, but also to inspire other local girls. In fact

several women we interviewed in 2013 referred to her as an "older sister" and as an influence.

Jumagul's transformation was made possible by party members who took active measures to bring her into the work site and then help her excel. By the 1970s, there were many such activists on the work site. Some were members of the Komsomol or party organization and explicitly charged with finding potential workers, convincing them to join, and guiding the behavior and life-choices of those already employed. Of these, some were Russian, whereas others were Tajiks from other districts, and still others were local. Their motivations varied but as a whole they tended to have a commitment to the idea of social transformation and economic improvement, through education and the provision of basic social goods such as water, sanitation, and health care. By the time I began interviewing them in 2013, some of those that had been party members did not shy away from saying that they had joined the party to help advance their careers. At the same time, they spoke passionately about their jobs and their role in the construction of Nurek and the transformation of its satellite villages. Perhaps the most effective were those who had completed the path themselves. Such workers were informal activists who recruited from their own immediate and extended families, and sometimes they became party officials responsible for labor recruitment or worked in human resources departments. Their personal biographies then served as a starting point for their recruitment efforts. Nazarova not only inspired girls to join the dam's construction force; after 1975 she became head of personnel at the sewing factory, taking charge of recruiting women into the workforce. Part of her own personal transformation was taking charge of the transformation of others.

Jumagul's story points to the complicated gender politics of Soviet development. As long as it was mostly European workers building the dam, it did not matter so much whether local women took part. Yet once recruiting locals became a stated goal, the local party organization could no longer tolerate the lack of women among Tajik workers, because it was a glaring reminder of the limits to the party's attempts to effect social transformation. From the party's point of view, it was important to have a skilled woman on the dam—even if she was still poorly qualified—to demonstrate to others that they were not limited to "traditional" gender roles, but could carry out the same jobs as Tajik or even Russian men. Yet her story also emphasized more traditional gender roles. It was her husband-to-be who played a crucial role in her "liberation" and in her integration into a new, Soviet family, and becoming a worker did not mean abandoning her duties as a wife and mother. Jumagul and her husband formed a new but still recognizable kind of family.

If Jumagul Nazarova had to escape her family to marry the man she loved and pursue a career, for Shiringul Aezova things were a bit simpler. She came of age in the 1970s, when the construction of Nurek had been underway for over a decade, and her family had already been drawn into the "new" world being created by the dam. Still, her education and her career required intervention from the Komsomol and party officials, including the Komsomol activist and later secretary for ideology, Makhram:

> I wanted to work, I wanted to study, and when my father went to work [on the dam] my brother and I, my brother also studied in the evening, and I also studied "underground" . . . without my father's permission. . . . I was young and inexperienced. There was a classmate, Davlat Zamon, I think he said Shiringul, why don't you come and we'll find you good work. Well, I agreed, and then Makhram [a party activist] had to go to my father, and when my father saw my papers, that I had good marks, he said, OK, let her study, let her work, and I went to the technical college in the evenings.

Like Jumagul, she married a fellow worker, a man named Omar, rather than someone selected by her parents. Unlike Jumagul, Shiringul seems to have avoided a break with her parents. On the contrary, Shiringul was proud to be working alongside her father and her brother. "[My father] was a bulldozer operator, he was here on the bulldozer and I was there on the crane. He'd prepare the gravel and I'd pick it up, I had a twenty-seven cubic meter crane, I'd pick it up and drop it by the factory, whatever they needed . . . and my father was not against it, he was a hard worker too. And my brother [also supported me], my family was a worker's family."

Shiringul and her husband decided to live in the city rather than the stay in the village, first sharing a room and then eventually exchanging it for a three-room apartment. She appreciated life as it was organized in the city—"I liked living close to work, the kindergarten was close, school was close, the bazaar was close, the bread factory was close. And [there was] hot water!" She embraced the life of a "modern" woman—working for the party, serving on committees and comrades courts, raising her children in the Soviet way, taking full advantage of child-care facilities provided by the state.

Although her immediate family seems to have been supportive of her, Shiringul recounted several incidents that hinted at why, convenience aside, she may have preferred to live in the city. Not everyone accepted her life choices, or her style. Among other things, she was the first woman to ride a motorcycle, which did not sit well with her in-laws: "I used to keep the motorcycle near the crane, and as soon as we had an hour break I'd take off. . . . Then [my brother in law] would say, hey, you're my sister in law, how can you ride a motorcycle? It's shameful for us." At the same time, Shiringul's role as an activist and local celebrity (she received her share of newspaper coverage and public commendations) gave her political and social capital that not only compensated for such incidents, but even made it possible to face down her accusers from a position of power:

> I used to wear a uniform. . . . I would go back home for lunch and I did not feel like changing and so I went in trousers and there were two men who worked there with their sons, and they called me . . . well, they called me names. Rukia Atoevna, who was the first secretary of the city Komsomol, saw me and said why are you crying? Well I told her that they called me this and this. Some time passed and I was working in a people's control commission and there had been a landslide and they sent us to go to the villages and to check on these people, how their life is, what help they need. And I saw this guy and I said "aren't you ashamed? You said such bad words to me. I could not sleep for a week because of your words." I said, "I've never done anything bad, I worked, I had a good family, two sons, they were small then, how could you?" And he was begging me, "forgive me, *apa* [sister] Shiringul, forgive me, forgive me."

For Shiringul and Jumagul, the initial social and personal dislocation caused by entering the workforce was worth it. Not only did they speak with obvious pride about their personal transformation during our meetings, but they also pointed to the ways that their new positions made them role models to others in their immediate family and beyond. Their importance as role models meant that they received support from the party and from their work organizations, as well as extra attention when it came to questions of housing or other practical matters. They could then use their political or social capital to marshal resources for themselves, or for their village.[35]

Soviet institutions like the Komsomol had a hand in creating Shiringul's biography, but her own willingness to undergo the transformation was crucial.[36] In her own telling, she embraced her role, and encouraged others to do the same. The anthropologist Malika Bahovadinova and I interviewed Shiringul together with her sisters and other relatives for whom she now served as a matriarch. Both of her sisters, who used to babysit Shiringul's children while she was at party meetings when they were younger, also went to school beyond the mandatory eight years and still work at the dam.[37]

Shiringul's biography was also ideal for Soviet authorities because her immediate family, at least, was supportive. Officials were particularly critical of men who worked on the construction site but were unwilling to accept a "modern" approach to other aspects of their lives, especially their treatment of wives and daughters.[38] In practice, officials usually sought a compromise that would draw women into the workforce with their fathers' and husbands' support. As we saw with the case of the garment factory, activists went to great pains to secure the support of village elders. Jumagul Nazarova had to be torn from her family, and her story was not the best propaganda—it would create more suspicion than support in the village, and it is not surprising that the whole episode of her "liberation" is left out of her profile in *Norak*. Shiringul Aezova, by contrast, worked alongside her father, her brother, and her husband. It was a much more harmonious vision, closer to the milder ideal of social transformation of the post-Stalin era.

Being Soviet and Muslim

Jumagul and Shiringul's stories show how those who joined the dam and became prominent workers were able to gain authority and degrees of autonomy they probably would not have achieved otherwise. In other cases, such workers were also able to shape cultural practices on the dam site itself. This included issues such as prayer and fasting during the month of Ramadan, both of which were anathema to Soviet ideology. In shaping such practices from their position as model workers they also continued their own self-fashioning as Soviet subjects.

Safar Samiev was born in Kibil, a village across the river from Nurek, and was still living there in the summer of 2013, when Malika and I went to interview him. He received us in his yard, while grandchildren played nearby. Samiev was a Soviet man before Nurek—he had been made one by the orphanage where he spent five years after his parents died, and by the Great Patriotic War, where he served as an officer. On September 18, 1941, Samiev said, he responded to Stalin's call for Tajikistan's sons to join the war effort. After officer training in Ashakabad he went to the front, fighting across Belorussia, Poland, and into Germany.

Samiev joined the party at the front. Speaking in 2013, he complained that people now criticized the party and did not respect it; in his view it was the lack of a strong party leadership that was the cause of Tajikistan's present problems. He explained his decision to join in terms of his experience as a soldier. "Look, ten people smoke one cigarette, is that not friendship? Ten people drink from one glass of tea. A whole division drinks from the same Samovar. Is that not friendship? Tajikistan, Uzbekistan, Kazakhstan—sixteen [*sic*] republics were giving fraternal help." Samiev returned to Nurek in 1947, and after several years was given the opportunity to work for the party. He attended party school in Dushanbe and then in Tashkent, working among resettled cotton farmers near Qurghonteppa. When construction began at Nurek the party called him back. Samiev spent the rest of his career working on the dam until he retired in 1982.

Samiev saw the "internationalism" at Nurek as a continuation of what he experienced in the war: "I worked side by side with the Russians at the front, and at the construction site, and there were the [volunteers and trainees] from the Lumumba university. . . . Everyone worked, everyone studied, hand in hand." He insisted several times on the party's importance, going as far as to say "it's a shame nobody respects the party anymore." His statement should not be read as simple nostalgia. In the stories he recounted, the party had a kind of sacred authority that had to be honored and that could be invoked to ensure that things worked properly. In Samiev's view, it was his role as a party activist that made it possible to ensure the quality of construction, but he also felt that he had to interject against those who sullied its name. As an example, Samiev described a conflict he had with a worker from Ukraine who was not following proper protocols, and pouring concrete without proper insulation. The worker, a certain Vitokhin, wanted to rush the job. Samiev decided to confront the sloppy worker, telling him "Dogs run fast (*pobystrei sobaka bezhit*). We do it more slowly, but we do quality work. He said, 'fuck your mother.' I threatened to write to the party. He said, 'fuck your party.' I said I'll write to the central committee, and so on. Finally we went to the chief engineer's office, everyone gathered, ten to twelve communists . . . and I said, tell them what you said, say it among these people." The sanctity of the party, Samiev explained, and the moral oversight it provided in questions of industrial production, was why in the Soviet Union you could build a dam made to withstand high magnitude earthquakes. Samiev's story also underlines how the party made it possible to erase ethnic difference. It did not matter that the worker Samiev challenged was a European, because, in Samiev's narrative, the party believed that what mattered was the quality of the work and the values of the worker, not his ethnic origin.

Samiev's standing—as a war veteran, an experienced party organizer, and as a respected worker at the dam site—allowed him to negotiate room for practices that were forbidden by Soviet ideology. In 1962, during a trip to Moscow, he bought an Arabic dictionary and grammar book and taught himself the language in the evenings. He was proud of the fact that he continued to pray, and that it was possible to pray at work: "We prayed," he said, "anyone who wanted to. Even at work. We always prayed at work." Workers like him did not have to pray in secret, he insisted; on the contrary, they could challenge superiors by pointing out that their practices as Muslims were compatible with their role as workers and party members. As an example, Samiev described an incident that took place one year during Ramadan. A Russian manager confronted workers who had been fasting during Ramadan, on the basis that they could not possibly have enough strength to carry out the difficult labor required. To prove that fasting did not weaken the

Tajik workers, one of them challenged the manager to a test of strength, and they wrestled until finally the manager gave up.

In this example, the manager tried to use a frequently cited argument—that fasting was unhealthy and led to physical weakness—against the Tajik workers. Yet the Tajik worker was able to use his physical strength to demonstrate that the manager was wrong. Such compromises were not unusual, although one will rarely find them in the archives or the printed literature. In Samiev's narrative, one could be a practicing Muslim, a good worker, and a good communist— you just had to be strong enough. This was not a case of evading rules; on the contrary, Samiev's story involved a confrontation and a resolution. Samiev's story was of transformation and realization—as both Soviet and Muslim.[39] As with the story about the worker who disrespected the party, Samiev emphasized how developing one's own moral strength as a party member and as a Muslim, and one's physical strength as a worker, gave one the power to shape oneself while also working to shape the physical and political environment which one inhabited.

Samiev's story was not unique. In Iusuf Akobirov's novel *Nurek,* written in the 1970s, a brigade leader is accused of fasting during Ramadan and encouraging others to do so. Anvar, a young Komsomol activist and the hero of the novel, goes to investigate; the brigade leader, it turns out, was not fasting, but he does defend some of the workers who are. They were "Former peasants on a collective farm. Tobacco growers. And now they've become tunnelers. They keep the fast openly, they don't try to hide it. Who can forbid it? A person who becomes a worker also knows their rights!"[40] Anvar is forced to agree. After all, he reflects, "yesterday's farmers, having come to Nurek, feel themselves to be full-fledged workers, free people."[41] Sure, anti-religious propaganda was important, but, for the moment, the fact that these former peasants had become workers and knew the Soviet constitution was something to celebrate. (Unlike in real life, in the novel communists and Komsomol members do not pray or fast, but they do follow certain other traditions, such as avoiding pork.)

The ability to combine these two worlds had its limits. Operating outside the formal guidelines, both managers and workers had to negotiate boundaries of acceptable practices and behavior. Managers may well have felt that they were fulfilling their ideological mandate by being flexible, since they were drawing in and promoting local workers. Yet they also operated from a position of pragmatism—flexibility was useful only as long as it helped achieve results. For example, while managers may have tolerated breaks for prayer or fasting during Ramadan, in their eyes it also disqualified local workers from certain jobs. Thus, they were sometimes reticent to hire locals for tunneling work, where they felt that by taking an unsanctioned break a worker could leave his comrades in danger. This in turn led some workers to feel that they were being discriminated against.[42]

The Sharipov Family

Perhaps the most storied laborer in the history of Nurek is *brigadir* (brigade leader) Muhabbat Sharipov. Handsome and photogenic, by the early 1970s he had become a minor media star, a local boy who had made the path from a childhood on a collective farm to leading a model brigade on the construction site. The story of Sharipov and his family allows us to explore in some more detail the meanings of local celebrity, of leadership, and of the importance of social ties that were formed as a result of construction.

One of Sharipov's first profiles appeared in *Norak* in December 1971, the year he graduated from the local technical college and was elected to the Supreme Soviet of the Tajik SSR. It begins: "A slim young man stood over a cliff and looked thoughtfully into the distance. Below him ran the Vakhsh, now tame. Muhabbat Sharipov remembers when it was different. Powerful and angry, it carried water far away, noisily rustling and rattling as it went. And now here it was—quiet and calm, tamed by the hand and mind of man. There was a lot of his own labor in

FIGURE 6.2.   Muhabbat Sharipov, 1970. Courtesy of the Tajikistan State Archive of Photo and Video Documentation.

that affair. And the heart of Muhabbat swells with pride for those who came here first." Thirteen years earlier, the article explained, Muhabbat saw the first expeditions studying the Vakhsh in preparation for the dam and offered to work for them. Then he became one of the first builders on the dam itself. His enthusiasm "infected others." Within two years he became a brigadir, but felt that his eight years of schooling were inadequate. So he went to the "school of young workers" and completed the final years of school he had been missing. In 1964 he was drafted into the army, but "dreamt of his native Nurek and the construction [of the dam]." Two years later he was back at work and studying in the newly opened technical college. He was raising his own family as well as his younger siblings, two of whom had already become workers. He was "growing together with his city which he helped build and was setting an example that attracted others."[43]

Sharipov's fame grew through the 1970s and 1980s. His wife and daughter, who received Malika and me in the family guest room, proudly showed us the relics of Sharipov's many travels, including commemorative watches from the 26th Party Congress. He eventually became part of the Central Committee of the Communist Party of Tajikistan, a representative in the republican parliament, and even a delegate to the 26th Party Congress of the CPSU.

As Sharipov explained, his whole life was tied up with the dam. As a teenager he had joined the geological expeditions of 1959/60 as a cook and scout, helping the engineers and scientists who were doing the final exploratory work necessary before construction could begin. It was during his army service that he first got a taste of leadership, being promoted to *starshina roty* (company sergeant). In Nurek, he became the first Tajik leader of a complex brigade—one that fulfilled a whole set of different tasks rather than focusing just on one, such as pouring concrete or installing fittings.[44] Being the only Tajik leader was not always easy, as not everyone in the management believed that he was up to the job. But his brigade showed good results, and he felt that soon he was able to prove himself: "because of my knowledge, my understanding, my professionalism no one could do anything to me." Like Samiev, he believed that the system allowed him to attain a position of leadership on the basis of his achievements and strengths.

Sharipov's fame and official recognition came with many tangible benefits for himself and his family. But it would be wrong to see Sharipov's participation in these various leadership roles as strictly instrumental. In his own reflections, Sharipov underlined the way that these organizations provided a moral compass, and the way they were put in a position to do more for one's own community. As a member of the village council, he also acted as a mediator between local authorities and residents of the villages that surrounded Nurek; as a hero worker who had frequent access to the top engineers and party leaders, he was, like Shulashov, in a unique position to secure resources for those villages. By negotiating with various agencies and laborers, he was ultimately able to get roads and electric lines to some of the more remote villages in the area: "I made this road, I made a road in the village, and I brought light."

In other words, Sharipov had completed the path from a target of development intervention to developer—not only was he building the dam with his own hands, but he was using his authority to transform the lives of people in his community. Naturally, he was held up as a model for others to emulate, and played a role in recruitment. Several of Sharipov's siblings followed his path, although none achieved the same level of fame. Among those we interviewed was his younger brother, Abdurahim. Abdurahim trained first as a carpenter. He took a job in Ordzhonikidzeabad, but, as he put it, yearned to get back to Nurek "where everything was just getting started." He came back and worked in a repair brigade fixing houses, but wanted to be involved with the dam itself. Along with Shulashov and some eighty others, he signed up for the Belaz driving courses and soon joined the ranks of drivers. After doing his army service in Kazakhstan, he came back and spent the rest of his career working on the dam or in various jobs around the city, picking up additional trades over the years. When we met him he was officially retired, but was working as a mechanic and instructor at a driving school.[45]

Just like his famous brother, Abdurahim was active in all sorts of party and civic organizations. Throughout the interview, he underlined his commitment to activism in organizations that worked to educate and mobilize the other people in the community. He volunteered in the "people's brigades" that were supposed to help keep order in the city and even for the local traffic police. He was insistent on his faithfulness to the party: "In 1963 I joined, well, now some people laugh at us. I joined the party, I was honest, conscientious. After this I did not join any other party. I keep my party card, I even keep my Komsomol card." He explained the importance of the party and his work in terms of the overall moral order that these organizations kept in the city. For Abdurahim, work in Komsomol and party organs gave his the opportunity lead a fulfilling life and do particular meaningful work, so much so that getting expelled from these organizations could understandably make one suicidal:

> Maybe my opinion is not correct, but the first thing I wanted was to be normal person. You know, the Komsomol, even the pioneers, the Komsomol, they kept a person from doing stupid things. At the technical college we had this incident, there was a Tatar named Shahid Umerov, he was a year or two older. I don't remember what he did, but in any case I remember at a Komsomol meeting we wanted to exclude him. You know what he said? I'm going to go throw myself under a car. You

know, these organizations they make you responsible. . . . All of this gives a person direction, it puts one on a path.

We can only speculate what Umerov's actual reasons for being so despondent were. Although being a Komsomol activist did come with perks, it is unlikely that the loss of privileges would be enough to make someone suicidal. For Abdurahim, the story illustrated how being in the Komsomol gave one a sense of being at the forefront of exciting changes, and getting expelled from the organization would separate one from the things that made it possible to be a "normal" person. Abdurahim's definition of "normal" included moral behavior, but also being open to the "wider world": the dam and its international workforce brought to Nurek. It was in this world that Abdurahim felt he had realized himself. With the beginning of construction, Abdurahim said, "our intellect was elevated, our world view became wider. Can you imagine, every day I met here a different person, and if you learn something bad from one person, you learn something good from someone else."

Not everyone was affected by the dam project in the same way. The recruitment of local women into the workforce and into positions of authority remained frustratingly difficult. An example from Sharipov's family shows how certain patterns and expectations about the role of women remained resistant to change, even as the transformations brought by the dam project created new possibilities and desires.

Sharipov raised not only his younger brothers, but also eleven children of his own. His sons and daughters all had at least some form of higher education. Yet, even in his family, it was not a foregone conclusion that the girls would continue their education beyond the state-mandated eight years. Sharipov's daughter Zebonissor explained that while her father was supportive of her desire to study and acquire a profession, her mother was against the girls in the family studying beyond the mandatory eight years: "Our father wanted us to study, to go to university, to institute, but mom—she was a little strict. She was from the kishlak, and you know, you have these conversations among neighbors, this girl does this, that . . . so she did not want [to let me study], but now she says that before she had not thought about it, but now [she says that] she would have let everyone go study."[46] According to Zebonissor, her father helped her eventually prevail over her mother, and she and her sisters all studied.

For Zebonissor, who came of age when the dam itself was mostly finished, there was clearly some special pride in continuing (in some way) her father's work. Like her uncle Abdurahim, she cherished her Komsomol participation, which she saw as helping her fulfill her potential, join something bigger, and open up a new world of opportunities: "I thought that those who joined the

Komsomol were different from others and so with studying and other events, anyway at school and at work also, I thought, that we in the Komsomol stood apart. And what else? We wanted to study." Every young person was expected to belong to the Komsomol. How was it that Zebonissor felt that it made her stand apart? One could hardly imagine a member of the Komsomol in Moscow or even Dushanbe in the late 1970s having similar sentiments.[47] And yet there was not a trace of irony or cynicism when Zebonissor spoke. "Now, when I open my suitcase, I see this [Komsomol] pin, the membership card, I see it and I remember how interesting it was at work and at school. . . . We were proud to be in the Komsomol."

Nostalgia for a past when the only barrier to studying was a conservative mother (rather than exorbitant fees or corrupt admissions officers) may partially explain her attitude. But Zebonissor associated the Komsomol with becoming her best possible self, and following in the footsteps of her father. In both her and her uncle's stories, the Komsomol emerges not as a replacement for the family, but as a kind of extension.

Zebonissor believed that it was her mother's attachment to "village" norms that made her reluctant to send her daughter to study or work. Yet it is also worth considering another possible, complementary explanation: Muhabbat was celebrated for achievements in the dam and for his exemplary family, but neither of these could be achieved without a partner who took on all the duties in the domestic sphere. Sharipov, after all, was raising his own children as well as various younger siblings and cousins. His status as hero worker meant, as Zebonissor herself put it, that there were always people coming over for lunch—often senior party officials and managers. Presumably the famous dam builder was not cooking the food for the guests himself. Even as Sharipov himself became a model Soviet Tajik, in other words, his heroism actually reproduced the very gender arrangement that such workers were supposed to help subvert.

The Trial of an Activist

For many years, Makhram was among the most important men in Nurek's party hierarchy. As secretary for ideology, he was responsible, among other things, for overseeing efforts to bring more Tajiks into construction and other aspects of Soviet life—the army, education, and politics. He had a hand in the recruitment and promotion of both Jumagul Nazarova and Shiringul Aezova. Alas, Makhram's career in Nurek ended ignobly. In 1988 he was the subject of a lengthy investigation by party authorities and faced his accusers at a plenum of the Nurek City party organization in August of that year.

The details of Makhram's alleged infractions are irrelevant—suffice it to say that they were not considered serious enough for the prosecutor to treat as a criminal matter, but important from the point of view of party discipline. The "party trial" is primarily of interest to us for two reasons. First, it brought together many of the people discussed in this chapter, and the minutes provide a fascinating look into the self-representation of Makhram and other communists during the Soviet period. Second, the investigation and subsequent discussion demonstrate how precisely status as a celebrity or hero worker translated into concrete benefits.

Makhram was born on a collective farm near Ordzhonikidzeabad, a small city about a third of the way between Dushanbe and Nurek where the road begins its ascent, during World War II.[48] In my interview with him, the former activist remembered the immediate postwar years as particularly difficult and hungry. His mother died when Makhram was young, leaving his father with three children. Still, Makhram managed to complete eleven years of schooling and even take top prize in a republic-wide physics competition. It seemed that this would be the end of his studies. As he explained, his father did not have the money for Makhram to go even as far as Dushanbe to take the university entrance exam, and in any case did not really see the point of studying. "My father was a religious man," Makhram told me. "My mother died young. I was twelve years old then. He said, you don't need to go to the institute, and there's no money. Why do you need to study? He said, no, go take the cow down to the river [i.e., become a cowherder], what do you need [studying] for? So I ran away from him."[49]

The Komsomol and a Russian friend made allowed Makhram to escape the limits set by his father. Nurek gave him the opportunity to complete a transformation:

> I had a Russian friend, a beekeeper named Ezhegonov, he used to bring bees to us. He asked me, why didn't you go to university? I said, well, I don't have the means. What means, he said? Well, for the road, and so on. And I'm already too late. He said, go to the Komsomol district office and get them to send you to Nurek. Well, I came there, and they said, what do you need? I said, I need to go to Nurek. They knew me, because I had won the competition [in physics]. Gladly, they said, and wrote me a *putevka* [a travel voucher]. [The Komsomol worker] gave me ten rubles and my Russian friend gave me ten rubles. Well, I got there, I had no trade, so I sat near the Komsomol and waited. On the fourth day they found work for me as a porter in the building of the dam. It was already 1963. And so I had a salary of 80 rubles a month, this was good money. I could support myself and save some money to get married, which I did, in 1965. And in 1964 I was accepted into the pedagogical institute.

Like many workers who enrolled in an institute or university, he studied in absentia—nonstop for forty days of the year, the rest of the time by correspondence. By 1968 he had graduated and began working as a teacher, simultaneously becoming more involved in the Komsomol. His rise up the career ladder was steep: he was promoted to party instructor, sent to party school in Tashkent for six months, quickly appointed a deputy head of department and finally a secretary of Nurek's party organization. During his "trial," Makhram used an up-by-the bootstraps narrative in his defense: "I am happy that the Komsomol sent me to the construction of the Nurek hydropower dam. All of these years I have worked honestly and hard. And the fact that I rose from being a porter to the position of second secretary of the city party organization is my own achievement. I had no one 'up high' to help me."[50]

During the plenum and our conversation in 2013, Makhram took pride in the personal role he was able to play in the lives of locals. For Makhram, the transformation meant that he could work for the kind of Tajik he had once been: "I was responsible for all of the political-enlightenment work. All of these questions, and schools, and social infrastructure. Education. It was good. For me, the son of a farmer (*dehkanin*), a shepherd. I came from the people and I served the people." It was a refrain to which Makhram returned many times.

But what did it mean to serve the people? Makhram spoke with great pride about all aspects of the city and especially the dam, explaining in detail the technical aspects of its construction. Just as important, if not more so, was the social transformation of the dam—and Makhram as the person in charge of overseeing that transformation—made possible, changing people's physical environment and their worldview at the same time: "If you have light," he explained "you have everything. You have heat and everything else. Thanks to Nurek, the people also developed. People began to interact with other nations and nationalities. And [they gained] an understanding of the economic condition of the country. And their worldview became different." His job, as he saw it, was to talk to people and make them see the need for change—the kind he himself had undergone. "There were so many such moments. A boy finishes school, he wants to study, but his father does not let him. Why study? These are the kind of things people would say. So you go, you talk, you explain. We always talked."

The transformation that Makhram and other activists were after was not just about internationalism and enlightenment, but the elevation of desires. Tagay Sobirov saw the old life as "too sleepy"; Makhram talked about the people who simple did not see the kind of life that was possible. These people "sat at home and did not work, they lacked understanding. The father works and finds some bread, some tea, some sugar, watches after the cow." Again and again, the narrative of transformation he was trying to engender sounded very much like the one he described for himself: "People were shepherds and became leaders. Public leaders. Their understanding became completely different. They came from all over . . . a porter, and then something else, and so forth. They became, good, educated (*gramotnymi*) people."

Makhram was proud of being an example to others, of his ability to connect with Tajiks and take them on the path he himself had taken. The theme of short-sighted parents and children who wanted a chance at a better life that Nurek and the Soviet Union as a whole offered them came up again and again. As for Makhram 's own father, he apparently came to appreciate what his son had become.

> Many years had passed [since Makhram left home]. Once he [Makhram's father] came on a day when I was receiving visitors from 9 [am] to 1 [pm]. After the last person came in around 1, I asked is there anyone else still waiting? They said, well there is one old man still sitting out there, in a turban and galoshes. I came out and saw that it was my father. I said, father, why are you sitting there, why don't you come in? I would have sent you [to my] home, you could rest. And he said, I didn't come here to rest. Why then? I saw that you had a visiting day that people are coming and going. I thought I would sit and listen, see what people say about you, if people are unhappy. Mostly they are happy, they say that when they cannot find some boss you solve their problems.
>
> I offered to take him to lunch, but he said I didn't come here to go to lunch. [So I asked,] "Why did you come here?" He showed me his torn Tajik robe. And his turban. And his galoshes. You see me? You came from someone like me. Now you have been given trust. If you come from people like this than you must serve such people . . . the people have trusted you, even though you are young, you are now a father to people. You have to be like a father to them. Otherwise it's a sin! You will serve people like me.

Makhram is particularly interesting because as a teacher, Komsomol activist, and party secretary he was tasked with shaping other people's lives. In this narrative, he fused his father's injunction to "serve" with the rhetoric he had learned and even reproduced. This reconciliation was possible because his father recognized that Makhram was now in a position to serve his community. Nurek was first and foremost a personal transformation for Makhram, and it was the possibility to multiply that transformation by enabling it for others—with his father's blessing—that completed Makhram's "self-realization."

Among Makhram's defenders at the August 1988 plenum were individuals who benefited from his active support, most notably Shiringul Aezova. Along with Jumagul Nazarova, Aezova was one of the first Tajik women to operate a crane on the Nurek site. At the plenum, she credited Makhram as her "teacher and mentor," saying "if it was not for him I would not have worked as a crane operator, I would have been a housewife. Thanks to him I graduated from our technical college."[51] Aezova, who had inspired others to take the steps she took and challenge the social role assigned by her extended family, gave Makhram credit for playing a transformative role in her life.

Within the broader discussion of Makhram's transgressions was a conflict between Makhram and Muhabbat Sharipov. The two should have been natural allies, but while they shared superficially similar life trajectories and were both committed to the dam and what it presented, their broader outlook and role in the community differed significantly. Makhram had been accusing Sharipov for several years of being religious, and thus engaging in behavior unbecoming of a communist. According to the plenum records, Makhram had insisted on removing Sharipov's portrait from a board where heroes of labor were honored.[52] During the plenum, Makhram emphasized his commitment to atheism.[53] It is significant to note that Sharipov did not explicitly deny being religious, and simply asked people to judge him on his record as a worker. Three years into perestroika, it no longer seemed necessary to demonstrate ideological purity on questions of faith. One of the people who defended Sharipov underlined this point, saying that while communists should not take part in religious holidays, the fight needs to be focused only on those who are "ardent enemies of our point of view."[54]

At the core of the dispute between Makhram and Sharipov was housing. Both lived in the city and had large families that had long outgrown their small apartments and were petitioning the authorities for larger spaces. Since housing in the city, as we saw, had largely been designed for small families, such spaces were hard to come by. In the 1980s, with the dam finished and senior engineers and managers departing for other projects, some of the larger apartments and private cottages constructed in the 1970s had become available. As senior communists and celebrated workers, both Makhram and Sharipov were candidates for one of these spaces. When Sharipov was awarded the cottage that had belonged to Semen Laschenov, the last chief of construction, Makhram felt short-changed and tried to convince Sharipov to turn it over.[55] It was Sharipov's refusal to do so that allegedly led Makhram to use his status as arbiter of ideological questions to put pressure on the celebrated worker.

It was an ugly dispute, and it is not surprising that none of the subjects I interviewed brought it up in our conversations. But it also points to how local politics had begun to change in subtle but important ways during the perestroika era. Despite the fact that Makhram was a Tajik, his doctrinaire attitude on atheism was now used against him, even within a party meeting. While Makhram may have been a senior party leader, it was Sharipov who clearly had greater sympathy among party members. Over three decades, Sharipov had been made a local and national hero on the basis of his accomplishments and leadership in the workplace. His reputation as a solid family man, and perhaps even the fact that he was known to be pious, was an asset that made him a fitting heir to the chief engineer's house.

The Experience of Development

Writing about the transformation of his native Bronx in the 1930s under the direction of the controversial city planner Robert Moses, Marshall Berman observed that the workers "seem to have been able to find meaning and excitement in work that was physically grueling and ill-paying because they had some vision of the work as a whole, and believed in its value to the community of which they were a part."[56] Nurek, for all of its many manpower problems, had a similar effect. Consider, again, Abdurahim's explanation for why he took part in the law and order brigades: "This was my city. I built it. Why shouldn't I keep order here? [Nurek] was my child (*detishche*), you could say. Everything good, bad happened here. Every little stone is valuable to me."

Development creates new subjects, but it also needs new subjects to be successful. Much ink has been spilled in western development thought explaining how shortages of human capital explain the failure of development efforts. Projects like Nurek made it possible to do both—create new human capital while erecting the infrastructure that would drive development. It was the very enormity of the task that drew people in, opened up a sense of radically new possibilities for their lives, and, as Abdurahim's comment suggests, gave them a sense of ownership over the result. The story of Nurek also underlines the immense investment of resources this kind of effort required, and shows why analogous projects rarely achieved similar results.

The Nurek subject was in one sense very particular, and it is hard to use what took place there as any kind of generalization for subjectivity in post-Stalin Tajikistan, let alone Central Asia as a whole. Yet it reminds us that there were many ways that the Soviet subject became local, or as Sergey Abashin put it "even though the 'Soviet subject'—the reflecting and acting Homo Sovieticus—had a fair share of recognizable generic traits, that same subject in Central Asia was still endowed with the capacity to have, and the ability to shape, his or her particular desires, interests, and qualities, including those of the Muslim kind."[57]

We should not underestimate the importance of these changes for many people, not least of all the heroes of labor described above. In subtle and not so subtle ways, these interventions did change attitudes, both of men and women, and introduced new ways of thinking about the family. It is no accident that women like Jumagul Nazarova or Shiringul Aezova spoke of those who mentored them as "mothers," and their fellow workers as "sisters." These individuals valued the freedom and opportunities opened up by the intervention of the state, but they were also proud of their ability to reconnect with their families, to use their political and social capital to help their kin, and to form new family connections. The fact that their self-transformation was embodied in material goods (motorcycle, house, road, electricity) is hardly a sign that this transformation was "only" tactical. The goal of development, and of Soviet development, was to raise the material and the cultural level of the population. The material goods were concrete proof of that success.

Yet these stories also show the limits of that success. Not only were there far more women like Sharipov's wife than Jumagul or Shiringul, but the trial that pitted Sharipov against Makhram also showed the difficulty of supplying even the heroes of construction with rewards commensurate with their achievements, let alone delivering such benefits to the population at large.

THE COUNTRYSIDE ELECTRIFIED

One freezing Friday afternoon February 2013 I found myself in the foyer of an imposing building in central Moscow. A few weeks earlier I had come across some fascinating perestroika-era documents signed by one Mamlakat, of the Congress of People's Deputies.[1] I had never heard of her, but a quick Google search revealed that she lived in Moscow and her home phone number. To my surprise, the information was accurate—Mamlakat herself picked up the phone when I called. I explained who I was and she quickly agreed to a meeting. And so, several days later, we met at the end of her workday. I waited while she put on her fur coat, and then we set out to her apartment by metro. The crowds heading home to start the weekend made it difficult to talk, and when we got out Mamlakat insisted that we first go on a mini-hike, through a park and up a hill where skiers and children on sleds were enjoying the snow. Finally, we went to her one-bedroom apartment, in a complex built for government officials in the 1980s. While Mamlakat began preparing dinner, I told her more about my research and how I had come across her information. Over the next four hours she told me her life story.

Mamlakat was born on a collective farm outside of Ordzhonikidzeabad, a half-hour drive south from Dushanbe. Her father was a teacher in the local school and had worked for the party on education issues. He encouraged her to read and to study. According to Mamlakat, her mother resisted the idea of her going to a university or a technical school, but what made it impossible in the eyes of both her parents was the murder of a girl (Mamlakat's cousin) who had been the first from their village to go to university. Instead Mamlakat was

married off and proceeded to have children and work on the farm. Her brothers, by contrast, became doctors, engineers, and party officials. At some point,
Mamlakat's brigade needed a new leader, and Mamlakat was chosen, with the
support of the farm's chairman. Although some of the men resisted taking orders
from her and even called her names, she insists that she was able to establish her
authority, in at least one case by physically confronting a man who refused to
do the tasks she assigned him. She began taking part in meetings of the farm's
management and followed correspondence courses at the agricultural university,
eventually getting her degree. She was later elected to her local council, served as
a delegate to the 26th party congress, and ultimately sat in the USSR Council of
People's Deputies convened under Gorbachev. All of her children—including her
daughter—graduated from university.

In subsequent months I would make several trips to the farm where Mamlakat grew up. I had long conversations with her extended family there and in
Dushanbe. I learned more about her family history, the fate of individual family members, and where they fit into the broader history of the farm. One of
Mamlakat's brothers, a former party official (and still a committed communist)
claimed that he had been responsible for the launch of her political career, rec-
ommending his sister when higher-ups in Dushanbe pressed local officials to
find a woman to represent the area. If true, it is an important detail that points
to the way officials strove to present a certain image of equality for the consumption of more senior officials and the broader public. I learned also that her initial
promotion to brigade leader had to do in part with an effort to sideline ethnic
Uzbeks who had held many management positions in the farm throughout the
1960s and 1970s. Although these stories certainly qualified the more individual-
istic narrative that Mamlakat had initially relayed in Moscow and that dominates
her memoir, they did not make her story any less fascinating, at least to me. What
they did do was help situate Mamlakat's experience in the broader context of
personal and group relations, farm and party politics, and the realities of cotton
farming in the late Soviet period.

Mamlakat's story captures many of the possibilities, limitations, and contradictions of the Soviet experience in rural Tajikistan. On the one hand, the
cotton economy shaped her family's life and limited opportunities; on the other
hand, the expansion of education, health care, and an avowed commitment
to gender equality clearly provided opportunities which were appreciated and
cherished. For Soviet planners, the situation in the countryside was of particular interest, since it held the key to all of the hopes pinned on the post-Stalin
industrialization project in the republic. As we saw in the chapter on Central
Asian economists, the failure of men and women from the countryside to join
the industrial workforce, pursue technical education, and generally to leave the

farm upended development plans. Yet as Mamlakat's story suggests, the binaries of "success" and "failure" are as unhelpful as "modernity" and "tradition." To understand what happened in the Central Asian countryside in the postwar era, and what that meant for broader visions of social and economic transformation, we need to think about the interaction between several different interventions and the consequences they unleashed.

The Soviet Union had an ambitious program to transform peasant life, combining economic goals (increased agricultural production) with social ones (enlightenment, the introduction of a welfare state). Though they rarely achieved the ideals professed by party visionaries or touted in propaganda, and brought immense misery to the Soviet peasantry, the collective farms (kolkhozy) set up in from the late 1920s were supposed to fulfill both missions.[2] From the Khrushchev era on, the Soviet Union invested increasingly greater resources to bring the welfare state to the countryside. Simultaneously, and like many other industrialized countries, the Soviet Union saw a mass exodus of people from the countryside to the cities, as mechanization freed up labor and people sought the opportunities afforded by education and urban living.[3] The exception to this pattern was the Soviet South—Central Asia and part of the Caucasus. Western scholars trying to understand the lack of rural outmigration in Central Asia focused on either political explanations (mechanization was limited because political leaders feared the instability caused by masses of migrants)[4] or cultural ones, such as the importance of family networks, religious belief, and attitudes about gender.[5] In this reading, the Soviet state undertook a project of massive social engineering that included mass resettlement, collectivization, and the intervention of the state into family life, and people turned to tradition to shield themselves from these disruptive forces.

Soviet officials—both in Moscow and in Dushanbe—believed that they could greatly expand cotton production while simultaneously transforming the lives of Central Asian peasants, drawing them into industry and making life for those who stayed on the farm more "modern." Yet problems with how technologies were introduced meant that while cotton output expanded, it required increasing amount of labor. This stimulated a kind of "involution" on the collective farms, where managers had to find ways to keep labor on the farm.[6] To do so, they could offer cash rewards, building materials, and access to private land and fertilizer. They also relied on kinship networks and figures of respect within the community, in turn helping shield them from persecution for pursuing religious traditions. Resettlement, too, was shaped by competition for labor between districts and farm managers. Increasingly, in the Brezhnev era, resettlement also came to be seen as an easier way to fulfill the modernizing imperative and the commitments of the welfare state. Under pressure to ensure access to schools and medical services, officials found it easier to move villages to areas where such services could be more easily provided. My point is not to deny the importance of cultural factors in establishing patterns of work and migration, but rather to consider the way that the introduction of technologies that should have been transformative promoted or reinforced certain tendencies, and the kinds of possibilities for engagement and resistance they (inadvertently) created.

Envisioning the Modern Tajik Village: The Cotton Economy and the Transformation of Rural Life

Central Asian cotton had become particularly important during the industrialization of the 1930s, and its production received a new push after Khrushchev came to power. Expanding cotton production involved opening up new lands through irrigation, but it also meant pushing out other crops and planting cotton season after season, a practice that depleted the soil and required increasing amounts of chemical fertilizer further down the line. But it would be simplistic to think of this as a case of central directives overriding local interests. Central Asian party leaders as well as district leaders and farm managers had an interest in meeting targets and promising more, because doing so bought them the political capital to pursue other goals. In the 1950s and 1960s, Central Asian leaders tried to balance between meeting ever-greater targets and pushing back when they felt the amounts expected by Moscow were unreasonable, or the negative effects too egregious.[7] At the same time, Moscow's willingness to raise prices for cotton—while subsidizing other agricultural goods, many of which had to be imported into the republic—meant that farm managers and ordinary peasants actually had a good incentive to participate in the cotton economy. Until 1963, Moscow had tried to depress cotton prices to stimulate mechanization, but this only led to stagnation in production. From 1963 on prices were raised repeatedly, and the wages of farm workers climbed as well.[8] As a result, the cost of production rose considerably through the 1970s.[9]

Soviet officials believed that they could reconcile their broader revolutionary goals with the massive expansion of cotton production. In effect, they envisioned that cotton production would become the job of land and machines, with minimal manual labor—as it had in the American south. Mechanization would free up people to join the industrial labor force, while access to schooling medical care, electricity, and comfortable housing would raise standards of living in the Central Asian countryside. In reality, Soviet cotton agriculture was so labor intensive that managers resorted to pulling children out of school during harvest season. The practice seems to have begun as a temporary measure in the 1950s, but gradually became institutionalized.[10]

Yet there is little doubt that many Soviet officials believed doggedly, even passionately, about changing this state of affairs. Khrushchev, for example, was impatient with party leaders who were slow to catch on with the program and had become used to meeting targets primarily through the limitless mobilization of manual labor. This was one of his complaints against Uzbekistan's first secretary, Usman Yusupov.[11] And when Yusupov's successor, Sabir Kamalov, was removed in 1959, one of the charges against him was that he too had failed to do anything to mechanize cotton and instead allowed the mobilization of manual labor to get further out of hand.[12]

Khrushchev believed, not without reason, that the quickest way to transform the republics was to change life on the collective farms, and he not was alone in feeling that life on the farms was lagging behind other accomplishments of Soviet modernization. Tursun Uljaboev, the Tajik first secretary, also complained that the way people lived on kolkhozes seemed to have changed little since the coming of Soviet power. Too many people were still living "in their grandfather's huts, with dirt floors . . . without electricity or radio."[13] In his memoirs, Khrushchev wrote that after visiting Uzbekistan, he "proposed that urban type settlements be constructed, with buildings of three and four stories, and all the conveniences: a public water supply, sewage system, gas lines to the houses, radios, a telephone system, paved roads, and sidewalks. Bakeries, restaurants, kindergartens, and child care centers began to go up." All of these seemingly mundane proposals—which drew on utopian visions that dated back to the earliest years of Russian revolutionary thought—were part of a larger vision for the transformation of individual and collective lives and outlooks. Economic transformation was just one component of a broader transformation of collective lives and individual mind-sets to be achieved through education, architecture, and patterns of work and relaxation. And as we saw in Chapter 3, some Central Asian social scientists urged investment in such facilities, precisely because they believed that peasants were more likely to become modern workers if they were first socialized into Soviet modernity within their own villages.

Central Asian peasants and farm managers were constantly encouraged to strive for the ideal of "cultured" life on the farm. The monthly journal *Sel'skoe Khoziastvo Tadzhikistana,* which had a Russian and a Tajik edition and was intended for farm managers and specialists, featured short articles by scholars and news items about particularly successful farms. One can find quite frank discussions about problems relating to mechanization, the use of labor, and other issues. Yet each issue had photographs placed throughout that showed new schools, houses of culture, health clinics, and other "cultural" facilities. Considering that this

СЕЛЬСКОЕ
ХОЗЯЙСТВО
ТАДЖИКИСТАНА

6

ИЮНЬ 1967

FIGURE 7.1. The cover of a 1967 issue of *Sel'skoe Khoziastvo Tadzhikistana* focused on mechanization.

magazine was primarily for internal consumption, one can interpret the placement of these images not just as propaganda of what had been accomplished but
admonishment to the farm managers and specialists to aspire towards the same.[14]

Khrushchev claimed satisfaction about what he found when he came back to
the region later in his tenure, where the new states farms had "municipal services
of the kind that people need in the modern world: schools, hospitals, cultural
centers, movie theaters and so forth."[15] Khrushchev boasted that "the young
women of Uzbekistan were now sitting at the wheels of the tractors and cotton-
harvesting combines. This was a battle not just for cotton but also for a higher
level of culture in the work process, alleviating the burden for women workers in
the cotton fields."[16] But making these proposals a reality on a large scale proved
difficult.[17] Many farms either lacked resources to fulfill projects, or tried to shift
the costs to republic and union-level agencies and ministries. Such problems
were endemic and affected everything from water distribution to electrification,
housing, and health care facilities. The Soviet Union threw extensive resources
at the mechanization and electrification of Tajikistan's countryside through the
1960s, 1970s, and 1980s, hoping to change how people worked and lived. Various bottlenecks—some related to the way the distribution of technology was
organized, others to the priorities of farm mangers—limited the effect of both
initiatives.

Electrification and Mechanization

In an issue devoted to electrification in Tajikistan that appeared on February 5,
1956, *Kommunist Tadzhikistana* printed a letter from N. Salimova who complained that her new, two-story apartment building still did not have electricity.
This caused a number of difficulties: "In each family we have schoolchildren,
and in a few [college] students, and they are forced to work by kerosene lamp.
Because of the absence of electricity we do not have the opportunity to use radio
receivers and listen to programs." Studying by kerosene lamp was probably not
that uncommon in other provincial towns of the USSR in the 1950s, but the
letter pointed to a crucial contradiction: a modern, Soviet building, where the
residents were not able to properly participate in Soviet life. Lack of electricity
made the other elements of Soviet modernity, especially urban modernity, difficult to accomplish.

As the historian Thomas P. Hughes argued, "power systems are cultural ar-
tifacts [that] embody the physical, intellectual, and symbolic resources of the
society that constructs them."[18] In Soviet Central Asia, the shape of the electricity
network reflected the particular economic priorities of the 1950s and 1960s, the

changing relationship between overlapping state agencies and state and collective farms, and the social, political, and cultural significance assigned to electrification by Soviet authorities. With the postwar recovery underway, officials renewed the USSR's commitment to bringing electricity to the masses. Publicists and propagandists revived Lenin's famous equation, "Communism = Soviet Power + Electrification," and hailed the achievements of the State Committee for the Electrification of Russia (GOELRO), set up at the tail end of the Civil War in 1920. Lenin had hoped to win over the Russian peasants with technology that would lighten their load and turn them away from superstition. Electrification was a "metaphor for overcoming backwardness," in the words of Susan Buck Morss, that would make Russia a modern, cultured society, on par with Western Europe.[19] In similar ways, the electrification of the Central Asian countryside in the postwar decades was presented as the first step in that region's finally catching up with the European USSR. Newspapers and pamphlets trumpeted the transformative nature of electricity for economic and social life and the role of the Soviet state in making its use widespread. Electrification was the "key node of fundamental social and cultural changes in a society free from all sorts of exploitation and oppression" and was supposed to play "a great role in solving not only economic, but social problems—the liquidation of manual and difficult physical labor."[20]

Yet producing electricity was easier than electrifying the countryside. Many neighborhoods and collective farms were not using electricity long after electricity had become available in the area. The reason was often that the grid had not been completed, or that buildings had not been connected to it—in fact, this was behind the complaint of N. Salimova cited earlier. Rural communities were, as expected, the furthest behind. In 1960, only nine of the thirty-one collective farms that were supposed to be connected to the grid that year had actually been connected; only 53 percent of collective farms in the republic were "considered to be" connected to the grid, but of those only 35 percent were actually using electricity.[21] The engineer Yakov Fligelman complained: "us builders are getting the impression that we are building high voltage lines to decorate collective farms, cotton fields, and the mountain landscape."[22] As we saw in chapter 5, electrification (and running water) arrived only in the late 1970s and early 1980s even in some of the villages around Nurek, which were supposed to become a showpiece of Soviet modernity in the countryside. At the end of the 1970s, Tajikistan had among the lowest rates of electrification in the country, even as it boasted one of the world most powerful hydroelectric dams.[23]

Understanding why farms might not connect to electricity grids helps us make sense of the broader difficulties with the introduction of technology into the Central Asian countryside, and the social effects it did and did not have on the people living there. It was state agencies that hung the high voltage lines from dams and power plants through individual districts, but farms were expected to pay for the costs of connecting to the grid, which they were often unable or unwilling to do. Poorly performing farms could petition to have the state pay for electrification. There was thus an incentive to hold off on investing in electrification until the cost could be shifted back to the republic-level government and away from the farm.[24] Further, many of the farms had small hydroelectric dams and generators installed over previous decades. Almost a third of electrified farms were using their own small power stations as of 1965. These were unreliable and insufficient for full electrification and mechanization, but they may have been sufficient for the basic needs of administration and services.[25] Inspectors found that many of these were out of order, suggesting that the number of farms that were actually electrified may have been lower than official figures suggested.[26]

It is ironic, though perhaps not surprising, that the electrification program in Central Asia replicated the mistakes of the 1920s. By relying on a centralized system and neglecting small-scale electricity production, the program actually slowed the spread of electricity into people's homes.[27] The GOELRO engineers eventually learned their lesson and made room for local initiatives and small-scale electricity production in the Russian countryside, contracting with smaller firms and cooperatives. Their compromise reflected the overall flexibility of the New Economic Policy (NEP) era. The engineers organizing electrification in Tajikistan in the postwar era seem to have been more single-minded in their pursuit of a centralized grid. Officials at the republic level refused to invest in the repair of existing small power stations or the construction of new ones, expecting the Vakhsh dams to cover all electricity needs.[28]

The electrification campaign thus enjoyed only mixed success. By the 1970s, the share of collective farms without access to electricity had shrunk from 49 to 16 percent.[29] Yet these figures belie the relatively small impact of electrification within the farms themselves. Many more households now had access to electricity for personal use—according to 1965 statistic, 64 percent of all households, compared to 27 percent in 1958. Still, even within farms that had access to electricity, 29 percent of households were not connected to the grid.[30] The impact of electrification on the actual production process was small even on those farms where electricity was available.[31]

If electrification was supposed to transform labor in the production process and in the home, and thus people's lives and outlooks, its absence, as Salimova noted in her letter, retarded any other kind of progress. On the farms, absence of electricity was one of the factors limiting refrigeration and thus to spoilage of fruits and vegetables while they awaited transportation. In the home, lack of electrification placed additional burdens on women, who participated in the work of the collective farm and on personal plots, but had no access to household devices to lessen the burden of their chores there. Since entry into the workforce, in formal or informal ways, did not liberate women from their household obligations, they faced a "double burden"—much like their counterparts in other parts of the Soviet Union, but with even less access to consumer technology and social services to lighten the load.

Similar problems plagued the program to mechanize the cotton growing cycle. In the immediate postwar years, officials predicted a full mechanization of all stages of the cotton production process: planting, harvesting, cleaning, and drying. The establishment of the Tashkent Agricultural Machinery plant in 1948 was to make this vision possible by providing the region with the necessary tools.[32] Over a decade later, the June 1959 Central Committee plenum made the mechanization of cotton picking an official priority, and in the following months the local party organizations tried to follow through on the campaign.[33] As the decades passed cotton production continued to rely on manual labor—including child labor—especially during the fall harvest. The problem was not lack of machinery. Rather, it was at the farm level that managers chose either not to acquire technology or not to use the machinery they did have. For managers, as the economist Richard Pomfret argued, using labor was simply cheaper than using machinery.[34]

But why would this be the case? And why would farm managers be so obstinate in using manual labor, when they were constantly being reminded that doing so was backward? One way to answer this question is to look at what was happening within the institutions responsible for perfecting and distributing these tools in the countryside. The materials these agencies left behind show the frustration of republic level officials with the failure of mechanization to transform labor on state and collective farms, and they also point to the reasons that managers and brigade leaders might shy away from using the technology available to them. Consider the following examples: a report from September 1966 noted that of seventy-three cotton-drying machines inspected that summer, only thirty, or less than one-half, could easily be brought into operation. The rest needed fundamental repairs.[35] Inspectors found torn wires, missing switches, motors that had been removed and stores in sheds, and in some cases parts that could not be accounted for. Mostly the problems seemed relatively easy to address, providing the materials and personnel could be found. Many of the reports noted that ongoing maintenance work had not been carried out.[36] In at least one district, tractors were not being used to full capacity, and inspectors recommended buying the tractors back from collective farms and organizing stations to lend them back to farms as needed—effectively reviving the Machine Tractor Stations of an earlier era.[37] In Shartuz some 80 percent of automobile transport was not functioning in part because there was nowhere to buy spare parts in the district.[38] Meanwhile, retail agencies apparently found it difficult to sell agricultural equipment to farms. Farm managers were reluctant to use state bank credits to purchase machinery, and as a result the retailers continued to release products with understanding that repayment would come later, absorbing the difference in their own balance sheets. Even still, their warehouses accumulated spare parts and equipment that no one seemed to want, even as new models appeared making the older stock obsolete.[39] Farms were asking state agencies to buy back machinery.

Technology is useful as long as it reduces costs and helps free up labor. But machinery, especially complicated machinery, needs skills to maintain it and spare parts to keep it functioning after heavy use. If there were not enough specialists available to maintain the machinery, nor easily accessible spare parts, machines became a burden rather than a help,[40] and if they proved unreliable during any stage of the production process it made more sense to leave them idling and rely on labor instead.[41] As of the mid-1960s, most harvesting machines produced in the USSR were unsuited for the long-staple cotton grown in parts of Tajikistan, including the Vakhsh Valley, and which commanded higher prices. Lower quality bolls tended to mix in with the long-staple ones, prompting angry letters from processing plants that bought the crop.[42] In addition, the machines failed to perform consistently on farms with rolling terrain.[43] Ministry and party officials had only limited means to get farms to mechanize, and even when officials effectively forced machines on the farms they often sat idle. Officials could resort to assigning quotas, but this too had limited effect—when they insisted that farm managers demonstrate that they were adopting mechanization, the latter sometimes responded by falsifying reports—passing off cotton harvested and processed manually as having been picked and processed by machines.[44]

The situation did not improve significantly in subsequent years. Since the demand for cotton grew faster than the ability to mechanize production, the demand for labor grew as well. Besides the regular collective farm laborers and the local school children used for the harvest, 12,000 "nonagricultural" workers had to be hired in 1965 and 18,000 in 1967, at a cost of 5.2 and 7 million rubles, respectively.[45] In that same year, only 14 percent of cotton in Tajikistan was harvested mechanically. This number rose to a high of only 36 percent in 1980 before sliding down substantially until 1984 and then rising again after 1985, when perestroika-era exposés in the press drew attention to the problem of manual labor, especially child labor, in the cotton complex.[46] Tajikistan was last even among the Central Asian republics, presumably because access to spare parts and specialists to help maintain the machinery was greater in the other four. At the same time, the stock of harvesters kept growing—by 1980, Tajikistan had roughly the number of harvesters that officials said would be necessary for eliminating the use of school-age children and hiring of nonagricultural labor to bring in the cotton.[47]

Resettlement, Labor, and the Welfare State

Mamlakat's family was originally from Fayzabad in the Rasht Valley, but in the 1950s they were resettled outside of Ordzhonikidzeabad, about a thirty-minute drive east of Dushanbe, to help with cotton farming there. With cotton planting expanding so rapidly and mechanization proceeding so slowly, demand for manual labor grew. Resettlement was one way to meet this demand. All Soviet republics employed some sort of resettlement for the purpose of "rationalizing" the use of labor and land, to make room for hydroelectric dams or new industries, or to deliver social welfare goods more efficiently. The labor-intensive cotton economy created particularly heavy demand for new labor. Tajikistan, where the majority of the population at the dawn of the Soviet era lived in mountainous areas poorly suited for cotton farming, saw the most intense resettlement program of the post-Stalin era.

By the early 1960s, social scientists and planners were already talking about surplus labor in the Central Asian countryside—yet the resettlements continued. Beyond labor demand, then, two other factors motivated resettlement and shaped the way it was carried out. First, resettlement offered the possibility of transforming not just where people lived but how—the kinds of houses they occupied, the kind of schooling they received, what they did in their spare time—more easily than in remote mountain villages. Second, as the commitments of the Soviet welfare state grew throughout the 1960s and 1970s, the costs of delivering these goods to mountain villages grew as well, as did concern for those villages located in seismic or otherwise vulnerable areas. Resettlement was thus not just a way to solve a labor problem, but also and perhaps more important a way to bring people into modernity and operate the welfare state more efficiently. These transfers are usually portrayed as resulting from a central decision or directive. An examination of the evidence suggests a more complicated dynamic, where local officials and managers petitioned and lobbied for labor.

Labor hoarding was a feature of the socialist economy. All sectors suffered from irregularities in supply of inputs, meaning that factories or construction sites might have to operate at a fraction of capacity one month and then quickly try to catch up the next. With Soviet labor law making it difficult to fire workers or hire temporary ones, managers instead sought to keep them on the books so that the extra hands would be available when needed.[48] In the case of cotton agriculture, farm managers, as we saw, preferred to rely on manual labor than bother with machines, which in turn led them to lobby for resettlements to their farms. Resettlement began on a substantial scale in the 1920s. Between 1925 and 1939, some 400,000 people were resettled from Gharm, Panjikent, and Ura-Tyube, as well as the Ferghana Valley, in the Vakhsh Valley and in the Surkhan Darya. After the war, the emphasis shifted from resettling individual families and brigades to moving entire farms; further, rather than targeting all densely populated districts, populations were now supposed to come primarily from the mountain areas.[49]

As more and more land was irrigated in the 1960s, the need for manpower grew. Officials from the committee on labor would visit farms to enquire where labor was needed, where there might be too many hands, and who had the facilities to accept migrants. During these visits, managers of cotton growing farms, especially those with newly irrigated lands, would ask for settlers and promise to find housing and land for them.[50] Occasionally, farm managers might appeal directly to the Council of Ministers to help speed up resettlement. As one manager of a state farm in the Vakhsh Valley complained in 1967, he had 400 new hectares of irrigated land, but if he did not get 100 families promised to him the farm would not be able to make use of it.[51] The following year, the head of the resettlement committee explained that all the new land being opened up made an enormous expansion of cotton farming possible, but "the availability of labor resources is not sufficient for solving the problem of irrigating and development of unutilized lands. The only way to provide these farms [with sufficient labor] is to resettle the population of the mountains and foothills areas, as well as the densely populated cities and districts of the Hissar district and the northern group of districts."[52]

If lowland farm managers wanted the state to send them manpower through resettlement, managers of the highland farms often resisted letting go of labor. Besides arguing with officials and trying to change resettlement targets, they defied resettlement orders by simply not doing their part, which was to agitate among farmers and encourage them to leave.[53] It is impossible to speak with any certainty about their reasons—perhaps they were championing families who had no desire to move, and who may have formed part of an extended kinship network, perhaps they feared what would happen to their own authority if the farm emptied out—but the reason they gave to visiting officials and inspectors was that they needed the labor force themselves.[54]

District- and state-level party authorities received targets and were supposed to agitate among families to find volunteers for resettlement. At meetings with households, they highlighted the importance of farming the newly irrigated land and the benefits they would receive upon arrival. Once a group of families agreed to move, they nominated representatives who traveled to their new farms to make final arrangements. Relocation was supposed to be voluntary. Unlike the Stalin period, it appears that force was not used to get families to move, though it is likely that some intimidation or coercion did take place. The most basic way to encourage reluctant peasants to move was to dissolve the administrative unit, which oversaw the area and thus cut services. Oral histories conducted after the

Soviet period showed that shutting down local stores could put peasants in a particularly difficult situation in the late winter, when the previous year's supply ran low.[55]

In theory, resettled families were supposed to find land plots and houses waiting for them, or at the very least have temporary housing and materials for the construction of permanent dwellings, credit for buying livestock, and of course access to schools, stores, running water, and electricity. In addition their transportation costs were covered and they were given some start-up funds. In practice, newly arrived families often found only temporary housing, with inadequate or non-existing school and medical facilities and no running water. The problems extended to all districts and farms; inefficiencies in the construction firms and shortages of materials were part of the problem. The settlers themselves complained about indifference on the part of farm managers. These problems were endemic in the late 1950s, as reports from almost every district where households were resettled indicate.[56] The situation was only marginally better in the late 1960s and early 1970s. As a result, many families left to return to their home villages. Sometimes, they petitioned officials for permission to return, citing failure to adapt to the new climate or the lack of facilities. In other cases they seem to have simply left. There were incidents of families convincing drivers who had been paid to take them to their new kolkhoz to take them elsewhere—presumably because they had heard bad things about the place where they were expected and preferred to try their luck on another farm.[57] The fact that farm managers apparently accepted such families rather than reporting them and forcing them to move to farms where they were expected again points to the way labor needs encouraged hoarding among managers and also provided peasants with the means to escape state coercion.[58]

Families who chose to return to their place of origin often found an ally in local officials and farm managers there. Managers from farms with a large number of resettled families even complained that officials and managers from highland districts were actively campaigning for these families to return. The director of a farm in Shartuz—in the south of the republic, close to the border with Afghanistan—protested that managers from several farms in Jirgital district were "agitating the households of our collective farm, saying that it's supposedly hot in Shaartuz, move to Jirgital, and in this way they lure farmers away . . . these households are given land plots, have houses built, they reorganize brigades, stores and schools."[59] The competition for labor thus created opportunities for families that wanted to escape resettlement.

If labor needs were the primary motive for cotton farm managers to lobby for resettlement, state officials had another: namely, bringing people to Soviet modernity. As officials explained, highland villagers often lived in primitive conditions and made few contributions to the national economy; at the same time they had no access to what was understood as "culture:"

> The resettlement of people who live in small villages far away from each other in mountainous and foothill regions has a political as well as national-economic importance. The population of these villages that is capable of work is engaged in rain-fed agriculture and animal husbandry and as a rule spends 70–110 labor days per year in collective work, and the rest of the time on their own personal plots. Women are mostly engaged in household work.
>
> The majority of small villages consists of three to twenty households and are cut off from any foci of culture, there are no middle schools, hospitals, or clubs, as a result of which children are denied the opportunity to advance their education in eight year and general education schools, there is insufficient medical care, and no films are shown.[60]

It followed that since bringing schooling, medical care, electricity, and cultural institutions to these remote mountain villages was difficult, it made more sense to move the villages to where they could be integrated into an expanding network of educational, cultural, and welfare facilities.

Sometimes, the net effect of resettlement was precisely the opposite of what officials intended in terms of binding peasants closer to the state. As many as 20 percent of resettled families returned to their points of origin, which in some cases had been substantially "emptied out" not just of other families but also of state or party institutions. They could now farm and raise animals as they chose, and live largely free of any state interference. For example, in the early 1960s thousands of families had been settled from Matcha, in the Zarafshan highlands, to a valley that was then renamed "New Matcha."[61] An inspection in 1968 found that 100 families had returned to the highlands and joined the roughly 318 other families that had stayed behind and engaged mostly in sheepherding. The result was a network of sparsely settled villages, some consisting of just one household.[62] These families acquired relatively large flocks of sheep and cattle. Although the lands in the area technically belonged to a collective farm, "the distance of these lands from the new district (360 kilometers over the Shahristan Pass and 710 kilometers through Samarkand) makes it very difficult for farm management or for village Soviets to maintain constant control over land." Thus, locals were using from ".3 to .6" hectares as personal plots, at a time when the republic average was closer to .122. Most of the returnees were not involved in any work for the collective farm.[63]

For officials, the refusal of returnees to take part in collective labor was only part of the problem. The families lived largely out of reach of the welfare state as well. Inspectors found that the district had one functioning eight-year school and twenty-five temporary classrooms housing 640 students. All of these were mudbrick houses, lacked floors or finished ceilings, and were in poor conditions. Some 73 percent of school-age children did not go to school. The few medical facilities lacked equipment, stores were empty, there was not a single functioning club or library, and not a single movie had been shown since the district was dissolved in 1965. Marriages and births went unregistered, and the registry for military service was out of date.[64] A similar situation developed in other areas where families resettled from mountain districts returned to their places of origin.[65] Dealing with returnees was a major concern of the Committee every year, and persisted at least into the 1970s.[66] The problem was sufficiently widespread that officials devised a standard letter, with only the name of a district and the local committee chairman to be filled in, alerting local officials of the problem and urging them to see through the returnees' re-resettlement.[67]

In the late 1960s, some officials shifted their thinking. Perhaps if these people did not want to move, it made more sense to extend the (welfare) state's reach into the mountains rather than forcing people to move. Thus, in the case of the returnees in Matcha, a senior official in the Council of Ministers recommended organizing a local council to "improve cultural and medical services for the population, increase control over the proper use of land and other natural resources ... and also to improve the work of schools, stores, medical and cultural-educational facilities."[68] This approach was consistent with what some Tajikistani economists began urging around this time—rather than resettling people, planners should think about redistributing services and developing industries and agriculture which could employ people in these more remote areas.

For the most part, though, officials still preferred to move people to the welfare state than bring the welfare state to the people. In the early 1970s we see for the first time resettlement plans that seem to be motivated entirely by this impulse and have no mention of labor needs. Some geographers urged the resettlement of people into more densely packed villages to help stimulate industrialization and improve the population's access to services.[69] Thus, in 1972 the executive committee (Ispolkom) of the Fayzobod District Workers' Council resolved to move families from ten isolated villages, noting that the residents "do not work anywhere ... their children do not study anywhere, and as a result of this in recent years the district plan for education of children could not be fulfilled. Because of the villages' remoteness no cultural-education events take place."[70] Although the resolution mentions labor and advises that these families be resettled to cotton-sowing areas, the document's phrasing suggests that officials also turned to resettlement out of frustration with the difficulty of bringing Soviet modernity to such remote villages.[71]

Finally, in the 1970s Tajikistani officials also undertook resettlement of people from geologically unstable areas. The files of the USSR Council of Ministers in Moscow are filled with requests from Dushanbe to help respond to natural disasters—usually landslides, floods, or minor earthquakes. Such requests seem to have come on a yearly basis; unlike other requests for economic subsidies or investment, these were granted without much debate or discussion. By the 1970s, it seems, officials had come to the conclusion that it was better to proactively move people from unstable areas rather than wait for a natural disaster and then undertake recovery operations. Among the groups moved in this period were the Yagnobi people in northwest Tajikistan. Although the primary concern seems to have been the vulnerability of the Yagnob villages, their labor was still in demand—collective farms in the lowlands lobbied to receive the new villagers.[72] Nevertheless, their resettlement faced all the same problems as the ones of the 1950s and 1960s—the conditions at their destination were poor, their houses were unfinished, they had no access to cooking fuel, no space to keep their animals, and so on.[73] During perestroika, the resettlement of the Yagnobis galvanized some intellectuals to campaign for them to be allowed to return to their place of origin.[74]

Whether families were moved to fulfill an economic need, to be closer to the welfare state, or to be protected from earthquakes and landslides, resettlement was often a traumatic experience. Changes in climate and lack of housing were only part of the problem. Resettlement meant abandoning homes and lands that had been farmed for generations and abandoning familiar sacred geographies. Cemeteries, local shrines, and sacred streams with their purported healing powers were left behind. Such trauma is not captured in official documents that focus almost exclusively on material concerns. Nevertheless, at least some officials seem to have been aware of the broader psychological dislocation caused by resettlement. Rafiq Nishanov, the Uzbek communist party's central committee secretary for ideology in the late 1960s, spoke of having two chief regrets from his time in the republic's leadership. One was failing to limit students' participation in the harvest. The other was his part in an initiative to resettle people from small and distant villages: "I insisted that remote villages be liquidated as quickly as possible. Some of them had only five-six families. . . . It genuinely seemed to me that people from such forgotten places would be better off in centrally located houses of collective and state farms. Health clinic, club, school, library—civilization! People listened to me, and [in two regions] people were resettled. God, how they resisted leaving, how they struggled, finding themselves far from their homes and roots . . . soon this local experiment was recognized as a failure."[75]

Gender, Child Labor, and the Limits of State Power

We have seen how the expansion of cotton farming, combined with a failure to mechanize agriculture, led to a competition for labor, which in turn helped stimulate the mass resettlement of peasants from the highlands to the valleys. Yet resettlement did not solve the labor problem. In fact, the use of child labor, students, conscripts, and even industrial workers and professionals to help bring in the harvest continued. Despite hoarding labor, farm managers still needed more hands to bring in the harvest quickly. Even if a significant portion of that labor was arguably surplus, as economists insisted, it still made sense, from the managers' point of view, to keep it around for the times of the year when it was necessary. As an incentive, they could offer additional land for personal plots, access to irrigation, fertilizer, and tools, through formal and informal mechanisms.[76] Rising income also encouraged people to stay on the farm, even while officials in Moscow and Dushanbe scratched their heads trying to figure out how to get them out of the village and into the factory. All of these factors reinforced a cultural conservatism that encouraged young people to stay put.

Officials at the republic level felt helpless when dealing with what was happening on the farm. In effect, while they needed farm managers to meet cotton and other quotas, they had little influence on how the managers would get there. We saw earlier their frustration over the misuse of irrigation systems, the resistance to mechanization, and the way state agencies became tools in the competition for labor. They felt similarly helpless when it came to stopping what was perhaps the most pernicious effect of the cotton economy, the use of child labor. A party member from Leninobod complained in 1961:

> It is bitter to acknowledge that the production of cotton carries a high cost for the state. With each year the conditions surrounding the harvesting of cotton becomes more difficult, more and more school pupils and workers from the cities are brought to the collective farms and state farms. This year all the students from grades five through ten have been mobilized to harvest cotton. Despite the cold and snow, children are still continuing to work in the fields from morning to the late evening without any days off, and the cotton harvesting machines in many collective farms are not being used.[77]

This was one of many such letters that reached the Central Committee in Moscow; a collective letter from farmers in Matcha similarly complained that "the mobilization of students for the cotton harvest has brought about a situation where the school year is only four–five months long, and therefore many children

even in the fifth grade cannot read or write well."[78] Officials in the central committee noted that "these kind of letters are received by the CC CPSU every year,
but local party and Soviet organs are not drawing any conclusions from this."[79]

One reason was that collective farm life tended to create new forms of patri-
archy even as it drew women into the labor force. Men tended to find the work
demeaning and tried to secure jobs in administration or elsewhere on the farm
to avoid being sent to the fields; the job fell instead on women, children, and ir-
regular labor.[80] The economist Rano Ubaidullaeva, who investigated collective
farm life in the countryside around Tashkent for her dissertation in 1964, found
that all too often even those women who qualified for technical or management
roles ended up performing manual labor, while all of the more advanced jobs
were done by men—something she concluded could only be explained by the
survival of "feudal" attitudes.[81] Mamlakat also recalled her struggles as a brigade
leader trying to get men to do their part—while the women picked cotton, the
men insisted that their job was drying it, a much easier task.[82]

Central and republic organs had difficulty regulating how labor was actually used. One illustration of this comes from a discussion that took placing in
1974, among members of a committee within the USSR Supreme Soviet who
were in the process of amending the law on education. One of the issues that
came up was the problem of child labor in Central Asia. A committee member complained that when he and his colleagues had traveled to Uzbekistan "the
machines were standing there, and children were picking the cotton. This was
simpler."[83] The committee wanted to introduce a new article making managers
liable for the use of child labor. As another committee member explained, "We
are not talking about the normal involvement [of nonagricultural workers] in
labor in accordance with the decisions of party and state organs. We are talking
about the systemic violation of the regime on the part of particular industrial and
local organs. This involvement in [agricultural] labor is completely without basis
and is backbreaking for young people and occasionally serves to cover up for the
inactivity of managers."[84]

Not everyone supported this proposal. Rajab Nurov, the head of the legal department of the Presidium of Tajikistan's Supreme Soviet, worried that such an
article might be unenforceable, and thus make the state look weak. "We won't
send students from lower grades or from the first year of university to pick cotton, tobacco, and so on. But we have resolutions of the Council of Ministers of
the republic, coordinated with the Central Committee of the party, and nobody
will be against it. It happens as an exception: they send students from the institutions of higher education, and mothers send their children, so that they'll earn
some money picking cotton and tea. In recent years we have studied the problem
of mobilizing children to grow tobacco and have found that infants sometimes

lay next to a pile of tobacco that a mother with other, school-age children, is processing. What is to be done? If we write it down in the Law, but are unable to enforce the unquestioning compliance and fulfillment of this norm, it will be even worse. Still, if we can get schools not to send children from the lower three grades to work, that will already be good."[85] Further, he warned: "If you write down such a statute, I am afraid that it will exist only on paper."[86] Officials knew the situation and recognized how problematic it was, but seemed to have lost faith that there was much they could do.

Rural Construction and the Welfare State

Mechanization, modernization, and the development of Soviet cultural institutions may have lagged behind irrigation and the expansion of the country crop, but that is not to say that it had ceased to be part of the Soviet project. On the contrary, the 1960s and especially the 1970s saw unprecedented investment in the countryside, while the profits earned by farms also made it possible to invest in facilities. At the March 1965 plenum, about six months after the ouster of Khrushchev, his successors tried to undo many of his reforms but made new commitments to raising the quality of life in the countryside. Among other things, the plenum reduced prices on agricultural goods, canceled 35–40 percent of collective farm debt to the state, increased the funds available for investment in agriculture, and created a pension system for collective farm workers.[87]

In the wake of the March 1965 CPSU plenum, Tajikistan organized a Ministry of Rural Construction. This was a typical Soviet bureaucratic solution, but it is nevertheless significant for several reasons. First, it demonstrated the extent to which the state was making a commitment to improved livelihood in the countryside. Second, it created an authority able to organize not just construction brigades but also the procurement and delivery of materials, a crucial issue in Tajikistan. The ministry oversaw the expansion of brick factories and units for mixing cement and other materials. It faced some of the same difficulties that plagued the smaller organizations it had replaced or subsumed, including shortages of qualified workers. Ministry officials also complained about farm managers being unwilling to settle debts with their construction brigades, or trying to shift construction costs on to other organizations. Nevertheless, it is clear that construction expanded rapidly. The money spent on rural construction nearly tripled from 10,000,000 to 28,000,000 rubles between 1964 and 1967.[88] In 1967 alone the ministry's brigades had constructed seventy-eight schools, twenty preschools, as well as warehouses, clubs, movie theaters, hospitals, and other facilities.[89] The resources invested in rural construction continued to increase year on year.[90] In the 1970s, Mamlakat's farm received a new hospital and prophylactic treatment center, built by construction firms and brigades under the ministry's control, and as part of its broader mandate to build facilities to "service the cultural needs of the population."[91]

The state and the party promised housing, schools, and medical facilities to peasants, and people came to expect them. At a January 1970 meeting of the local council in Ayni, for example, peasants and deputies complained that "many *kishloks* [villages] are in need of residential housing. But they do not have the opportunity to build because construction brigades are never seen in the district."[92] Many such requests and complaints were addressed to the Minister of Rural Construction. Some came from individuals, others from groups of peasants, still others from managers or local officials writing on behalf of individuals, in Russian, Tajik, and Uzbek. The requests varied—one group of peasants asked for a bus to take them from their village to their fields; others complained about the state of the irrigation system on their farm, building materials for their houses, and telephone lines. Some of these are authored by farm managers and thus leave doubt as to whether they reflected the requests of actual peasants, whereas others clearly reflect individual needs and desires. This was most often evident in the case of requests for construction materials. Such requests were also frequently expressed in larger meetings: "Tadzihkpotrebsoiuz" [the organization in charge of distributing products to retail chains] was reproached for failing to provide the retail network with construction materials, and especially saw-wood and slate . . . those who spoke asked for an increase in materials for construction in collective farms, especially of residential houses."[93]

These requests cannot be taken as evidence that Soviet modernity was being adopted wholesale. But the aspiration and demand for these "modern" materials should not be overlooked. In my interviews in the villages around Nurek, residents pointed to the availability of materials that came with the dam's construction as one of its most welcome features. Despite the fact that their houses had presumably been adequate, their aspirations were changing. Needless to say, the desire for a new house did not mean a completely transforming one's way of life. Still, like the parents who complained that their children were being sent to pick cotton rather than to school, these petitioners were taking the claims of the Soviet development project seriously, and calling out officials for failing to deliver.

Life in the countryside was being transformed, though perhaps not in the way officials envisioned. People came to expect the state to deliver services and help them build "modern" houses. When the state failed to fulfill its promises—as it inevitably did—they used formal institutions like the Supreme Soviet, meetings with district representatives, and the party to have their demands met, as well as informal networks that operated through those same institutions, much as elsewhere in the USSR. At each level, individuals negotiated their engagement with Soviet modernity and its various avatars—the school, the farm management, the construction brigade, the retail sector, and so on.

When I asked Mamlakat what accomplishments she was proud of as head of her brigade, she began to tell me about initiatives she took to bring enlightenment to her fellow workers—taking them to Dushanbe to attend museums and the theater, or to visit the Nurek GES, and encouraging them to read. She was also proud that in her tenure as brigade leader she was able to arrange for a club to be constructed. In fact, it had been a mosque that had been closed (at least officially) and had fallen into disrepair. During the winter of 1981 she obtained the support of the farm leadership and organized some of the workers from her brigade to fix the mosque so it could be used as a club. Soon after, she organized a celebration of Nowruz at the new club. At the time, Nowruz was becoming an officially sanctioned holiday; in Nurek and the surrounding villages it became an annual tradition for a different village to host a celebration for all of the dam's builders and workers each day of the week-long holiday. The club was a place where the workers could gather and relax in a cultured way, she explained. When I pressed her further she admitted that it was also a gathering place for prayer—"but only for the older men, so they would have a place to pray in the evening."[94]

Interviews I conducted with former local and district officials suggest that the initiative for new clubs often came precisely from those people who wanted to organize a prayer space.[95] Ismoil Tolbakov, who worked in the Sovetskii Raion near Kulab and then in the Kulab party organization in the 1980s explained that the construction of houses, schools, clubs, mosques, and other facilities fit into the work of local party officials:

> So [a man] would come to the Jamoat [the Soviet] and say, we need to build this or that, here we have a shortage of this, or in this village there is a school or a hospital but not in that one. We need you to build it from your budget . . . so we would suggest building a school in this village and a local hospital in that one, and here a new road, or somewhere else you need to build a bridge over a river, or a club, so they would bring these proposals to us and we would see how much we could help from our own budget and the rest we would ask the district. And when we put all this together it would be reviewed at a session of the Council of People's Deputies. They would support some of it, elsewhere they would say use your own funds. And then you would have a case where some old men would come and say we need to build a mosque, the government doesn't give money for that, but if you like you can put the money together and build it, and we would give them a plot of land, legally, and they would

find the money, and in this way some twenty-five to thirty mosques were built in my time. And we would also actively participate [helping them get materials] and now these mosques are still active.[96]

Talbakov may have exaggerated the number of mosques, or perhaps included those built during perestroika, when construction of mosques became easier. Still, the process he describes is interesting. As Talbakov explained, it also involved pushing village elders and religious figures on issues that were important for some of the party's goals, including encouraging girls to attend school or at the very least not interfering. Officials—or even prominent workers, like Mamlakat, whose status as one of the few female brigade leaders gave her a kind of political capital—could use their access to materials, supply chains, and planning agencies to secure the things that mattered to influential figures in their communities, but they could also use these tools to extract concessions from those figures and gain at least some support for their own goals.

When Mamlakat talked about her accomplishments as brigade leader in the 20th Party Congress collective farm, she talked about the kind of things one would expect from a brigade leader—how she earned the respect of her team, the challenges and successes they faced in their work, the organization of communal labor to build a club, and so on. But she also mentioned her role in bringing together a couple who had grown up on the farm. A boy and a girl from neighboring families had both grown up with some mental disabilities. Their parents had assumed that they would never be able to marry. But Mamlakat intervened and convinced the two families that the children (now in their late teenage years) should marry each other. When the two failed to consummate their marriage, she went further, having her physician brother examine the young man and taking the bride to a Russian gynecologist she knew. The fact that she played matchmaker to her neighbors is in and of itself not particularly surprising, but the fact that she saw this as part of her duties as brigade leader tells us something about the intersection of different kinds of authority and social capital, some related to a formal position in a state-recognized hierarchy, and others from the "informal" setting of the family, extended kinship network, or *mahalla*.

Our initial meeting had taken place in Moscow. Mamlakat had not hesitated to take me to her one-bedroom apartment in a Moscow *mikroraion* (residential complex). When I first visited her sons who still lived on the farm, we sat in exclusively male company. A black and white photograph of a young Mamlakat hung on the wall. When I met Mamlakat again in Dushanbe, at her son's house in a Soviet-era apartment, we sat in a room typically reserved for hosting guests. Her daughter was also present, but seemed intent on serving the food and quickly leaving, as would have been the custom. Mamlakat told her firmly that she should stay, and the four of us ate dinner together. Later, visiting the farm again during a large gathering of the extended family, men and women again gathered separately. Yet when Mamlakat came in to greet her relatives, she took a seat at the head of the table. Leaning back, she seemed poised to chair a meeting of the farm management. It seemed that all the men present—her brothers and her sons—deferred to her.

Throughout the 1960s and 1970s, the Soviet Union invested ever more resources to raise the standard of living in the countryside, building schools and hospitals, raising agricultural wages, and setting up construction agencies to help people improve residential housing. Paradoxically, these investments had the effect of actually encouraging people to stay in the countryside, which in turn limited some of the social changes elites had hoped to see among the region's peasantry. Some, like Mamlakat, were a testament to what the system could achieve in terms of moving people from the margins to full participation in political and economic life. However, many more experienced only displacement and the drudgery of labor, alleviated somewhat from the late 1960s and 1980s by what assistance the state could provide in terms of material goods. Even as they tried to achieve the social goals of revolution in the Central Asian countryside, officials consistently undermined them as they tried to reconcile utopian visions, economic imperatives, and the demands created by local conditions. Cotton demand alone cannot explain the social upheaval caused in Soviet Tajikistan through resettlement. Rather, it was evolving ideas about what constituted progress in the Central Asian countryside and how it could be achieved that affected how Soviet planners, agency officials, and farm managers responded to problems of labor, production, and the making of a welfare state for the Tajik countryside.

"A TORCH LIGHTING THE WAY TO PROGRESS AND CIVILIZATION"

In September 1961 Morocco's first ambassador to the USSR, Abdel Keir Al Fasil, came to the Soviet Republic of Tajikistan. Like many diplomats from the postcolonial world, Al Fasil was invited to tour the republics of Central Asia soon after his appointment to Moscow. The sites he visited in Tajikistan included the state library, industrial enterprises, and active mosques. At an official banquet during his visit, he said, "We are awed by the achievements of the Soviet people, and especially the fraternal Tajik people, in the field of science and education." Later, at an event with Mirzo Rakhmatov, the chairman of Tajikistan's parliament, Al Fasil once again praised his hosts: "Tajikistan is a republic whose example we need to follow. And in the near future we will do everything in our power to catch up with you, no matter how quickly you move forward."[1]

Rakhmatov welcomed Al Fasil's challenge, but pointed out that with the building of the Nurek Dam under way, Morocco might have a hard time catching up. Al Fasil replied that Morocco already had a station that produced so much power it fed not only Morocco's electricity grid, but that of neighboring countries as well. Alas, it was still owned by the imperial power, France, that had controlled Morocco until 1955. Al Fasil found this state of affairs unacceptable: how could all the electricity produced in the country be owned by a foreign company? What, he asked Rakhmatov, would the Tajiks do if they were in the same situation?

It is not surprising that Rakhmatov evaded the question, saying that although the Soviet Union supported Morocco's independence it did not want to interfere in the country's internal affairs. For even as Al Fasil seemed to suggest that the cases of Morocco and Tajikistan were fundamentally different, his question also pointed to a potential contradiction: would the Nurek dam and everything it brought really be Tajikistan's, or would it belong to a foreign power? Was Tajikistan truly free within the Soviet Union, or was its situation similar to countries like Morocco, which found themselves in colonial or neocolonial relationships? Was Soviet Central Asia a model for the Third World, or itself a colony?

Soviet engagement with the Third World changed the politics of development during the Khrushchev era, allowing Central Asian political elites to renegotiate their republics' economic and cultural role within the union. It also gave rise to the idea of a Central Asian model for developing countries. Briefly considered as an actual program that could be derived from a study of Soviet Central Asia's economic history, the idea of a "model" quickly gave way to the use of Central Asia as an exhibition of Soviet achievement. Within this paradigm, Tajikistan was supposed to focus on relations with India and Afghanistan,[2] though as the example of Al Fasil's visit suggests, its actual remit extended to the entire Muslim world and even the Third World generally. Afghanistan and other Soviet allies were brought to witness modernity and cultural tradition existing side by side, and Central Asian specialists were sent abroad to provide technical aid and act as traveling exhibits themselves. Meanwhile, Soviet development failed to live up to its promise of greater social and economic equality, creating a primarily European industrial elite surrounded by a native population engaged overwhelmingly in agriculture. In the late 1980s, some Tajikistani economists and other intellectuals began to see Central Asia as itself a colony rather than a model for others—an argument they formed at least in part through their experiences acting as representatives of the Soviet Union in the Third World.[3]

A Soviet Central Asian Model for Development?

Bolshevik leaders had proclaimed Central Asia a model for the colonial world in the Soviet Union's first years. Stalin had famously called on Tajikistan to be a model for its backward and oppressed neighbors back in 1924, when former territories of the Bukharan emir were declared an Autonomous Soviet Socialist Republic; it became a Soviet Socialist Republic five years later, in 1929. But as the USSR turned inward, such ideas were largely forgotten. They were revived in the 1950s along with Nikita Khrushchev's push to the Third World. Tashkent, Dushanbe, and Nurek all became destinations for visitors from the Third World, especially from Afghanistan and India. There is no doubt that Soviet leaders in this period saw Central Asia as having enormous propaganda value, a view shared by many Central Asian elites themselves. But to what extent did they really believe that the republics could serve as a model? And to what extent did they apply lessons from Central Asia to their projects abroad?

Some of the most detailed studies of Central Asia and the "Soviet south" as a development model were actually written by Western scholars in the 1960s. Alec Nove and J. A. Newith, in their 1966 study, noted that on most development indicators Soviet Central Asia and the Caucasus compared favorably to Turkey and Iran.[4] Charles K. Wilber was similarly impressed with Soviet achievements in Central Asia, citing in particular the benefits of capital investment and the emphasis on Soviet capital formation.[5] Whether or not the Soviet development experience in Central Asia was applicable was a different question than whether the Soviet experience as a whole was appropriate for developing countries to follow.[6] The beauty of a Soviet Central Asian model, or a "Soviet Middle East" (Central Asia plus the Caucasus) model was that it showcased the internationalism of Moscow's development strategy. The lateness of the region's industrialization made it possible to avoid discussing the violence of the first five year plan.

Already in the late 1950s plans put together by the State Committee on Economic Cooperation—the agency charged with coordinating Soviet foreign aid programs—explicitly included references to learning from the Central Asian experience in the mechanization of agriculture and industrialization.[7] In 1965, the Soviet Academy of Sciences instructed its affiliates to study the Central Asian experience of development to see what lessons might be drawn for less developed countries and Soviet projects abroad.[8] This theme was taken up by economists working in the republics. In a 1965 article published in the Bulletin of the Academy of Sciences of the Tajik SSR, G. Kurtzer pointed, not surprisingly, to the advantages of socialist development over capitalist development for recently liberated countries, and the importance of outside aid in this process. Engaging a debate among Soviet economists, he argued that developing countries needed to focus on heavy industry to stimulate their overall economy. Here he took Central Asia as a model. Focusing on light industry and agriculture in the 1930s had been a mistake, he pointed out, one that arose from a poor understanding of the republics' natural resources. Had their resources been properly surveyed, it would have been clear that these republics would have made good targets for investment in heavy industry. In the mid-1950s Central Asia finally began developing heavy industry.[9] One of the article's conclusions was that primary commodity exporting countries like Cuba, with its export of sugar, should follow the pattern of the Central Asian republics in moving from cotton to industrialization.

The mid-1960s turned out to be the high point for an idea of a "Central Asian model." In 1965, an international economic seminar was held in Tashkent whose purpose was to discuss "the experience in socialist construction of union republics of Central Asia and Kazakhstan, the experience of forming and developing industrial complexes, territorial-production and sectoral complexes." Guests came from Asia, Africa, and Latin America, to learn about the Soviet Central Asian experience from economists, planners, and industrial managers. An economics professor from Tashkent boasted that the foreign delegates praised the "colossal technical progress," and "industrialization" of the Central Asian republics, and asked the representatives of the Central Asian states to "disclose how they managed to achieve [this]; which methods were employed to create the great industrial complexes in Kazakhstan, Tajikistan, Kirgizstan, and elsewhere?; how did you make this happen?; where did you start?" He, too, encouraged his colleagues to produce more literature that could be of use to the Soviet Union's friends.[10]

Yet the idea of Central Asia being a model was quietly abandoned, for reasons that had little to do with Central Asia and more with changing ideas about the USSR's own role in international development. By the mid-1960s Soviet development economists and policymakers had largely given up the promotion of a "socialist" path to development in favor of a "noncapitalist" path. As David Engerman has shown, the interaction of Soviet economists with their Indian counterparts led them to appreciate approaches that were not closely modeled on the Soviet experience in Central Asia or elsewhere.[11] The goal of Soviet policy was to "help underdeveloped countries ensure their economic independence, to more quickly stand on their own two feet, [and] to create a modern national industry."[12] Central Asia, which after all was part of the Soviet Union and thus protected from the capitalist world, was not necessarily the best model. As Sh. Tursumatov, a Tajik analyst, explained in a 1978 article: "The noncapitalist path of development at this stage and the noncapitalist path followed by the countries of the Soviet East have similar characteristics. This is the fight against foreign imperialism and the beginnings of capitalist relations in the economy, a socialist outlook, a deep unity of people (*narodnost'*) and an accelerated path of development." Yet there were also some very important differences: "The revolutionary movement in the Soviet Union developed as part of an all-Russian revolutionary movement, and it joined the socialist revolution in the central districts of the country. . . . The newly liberated countries are carrying out the transition to a non-capitalist path of development without escaping from the global capitalist economy."[13]

By the mid-1960s, the optimism of the previous decade was fading away and the challenges of industrialization and social transformation in Central Asia were becoming clear. Although it was costly enough to fund industrialization and a welfare state within the Soviet Union, suggesting that countries in Africa or South Asia should follow the Central Asian path could raise expectations that Moscow would invest similarly there as well. By the early 1960s some Soviet officials were already skeptical about the benefits of Soviet aid to the developing world. And in 1966, no less a champion of Soviet involvement in the Third World than Bobojon Gafurov complained in a letter to Brezhnev: "economic, technical, and military aid to countries in Asia and Africa over the last ten years has cost our motherland many billions. And yet not once have the heads of the international departments of the CC CPSU directed scholars to sum up the social-economic and political result of this aid, find out its effectiveness, and figure out its consequences for us, socialist cooperation, and progressive forces in the world."[14] Soviet aid to the Third World would continue and even grow, of course. As Gafurov's complaint about the party's international department suggested, there was a strong lobby that believed that such aid was ultimately in Soviet interests, even if the aid did not achieve desired results.[15]

Central Asian Expertise and the Presentation of Modernity

The idea of a Central Asian model of development as something that could be studied and reproduced thus fell away by the late 1960s. But Central Asia's importance for the Soviet Union's relationship with the developing world only grew. Even if the Central Asian experience could not be modeled, certain skills and techniques perfected in Central Asia—dam building, irrigation, the production of certain kinds of crops, could still be exported. More important, the idea of a Central Asia that could be held up as an inspiration became a crucial part of Soviet relations with the Third World, with important consequences for the Central Asians themselves.

India and Afghanistan had a particularly important place in Tajikistan's international outreach efforts. Both were neutral countries that were sympathetic to the USSR, and were seen as part of a cultural sphere that emerged from a shared Persian and even pre-Islamic heritage. These links were promoted in the works of Bobojon Gafurov and through various joint research projects and seminars, such as the 1968 conference on the Kushan epoch hosted in Dushanbe, with guests from Afghanistan, India, Iran, and Pakistan.[16] Soviet officials believed that Oriental studies, broadly understood as scholarship of languages, literature, culture, and history of "eastern" countries could be a useful tool in the broader anti-imperial struggle waged by the USSR, particularly when it could be shown to come from within the Soviet Union's east. As the Afghanistan specialist Iurii Gankovskii noted with satisfaction in 1972, "one could cite many examples that prove that the flowering of Oriental science (*vostokovednaia nauka*) in Tajikistan is attracting the sympathy of the foreign progressive intelligentsia in Iran, in Afghanistan, in India, in Pakistan, as well as in Arab countries, in Bangladesh, [arousing sympathy] toward those social, cultural, economic and political conditions that make such research possible [in the Soviet republics of Central Asia]."[17] In other words, the development of Oriental studies, even in its most classical forms of historical and philological analysis, was already proving to be a victory in public diplomacy for the USSR, even without engaging within more "immediate" problems of economics and politics.[18]

These cultural links were not an end in themselves, but formed a base for broader cooperation and especially development aid, which is arguably what Afghan and Indian elites were particularly interested in. Scientific exchanges between Tajikistan and Afghanistan took off in the early 1960s. Aside from the usual propaganda program—showing off Tajikistan's universities, schools, laboratories, and factories—the visits also served to establish direct links and cooperation on projects. These included joint projects to investigate flora and fauna, seismic conditions, and natural resources on both sides of the border. Afghanistan's planners, economists, and public health officials were brought to Tajikistan to witness the Soviet republic's success in "gastroenterology, infectious diseases, neurology, the development of mountain pastures, in the battle against diseases affecting cotton plants, irrigation, etc."[19] Teachers from the universities and institutes were also dispatched to Kabul to teach courses at Kabul University and the Technical College built by the Soviet Union.[20]

Soviet aid to Afghanistan increased after Mohammed Daoud overthrew his cousin King Zahir Shah and proclaimed a republic in 1973. Tajikistan and Central Asia's role in aiding Afghanistan's development increased as well. In 1974 Tajikistan's Academy of Sciences, the Ministry of Water, and the Ministry of Agriculture were all tasked with helping conduct research on and implement the irrigation of new lands, as well as establishing "government control over the national economy." Tajikistani seismologists were also involved in researching seismic conditions and designing buildings and dams that could withstand even the most serious disturbances.[21]

Numerous Soviet aid projects were carried out by agencies based in Central Asia. Thus, the same organization that had helped design the Nurek Dam also worked on the hydroelectric station at Pul-i-Khumri, while Uzbekistan's Ministry of Water Resources provided supplies for irrigation projects.[22] Tajikistani specialists built electric lines in Afghanistan's cities and across its countryside.[23] Soviet Central Asian aid to Afghanistan also included the development of broadcast radio, musical recording technology, and even theatrical expertise.[24] Just as the path to modernity within the USSR included not just industries and dams but theaters and even opera, Soviet aid abroad carried the tools that could help create new men and women along with the technologies that would help them live in prosperity.

In all of these cases, Central Asians were stepping in to the role of "elder brother" for the developing world previously played for them by the Russians. These exchanges were usually presented as arising from technical similarities: similar seismic conditions, similar climate, soil, development needs, and so on. Clearly, the propaganda value of having Central Asians act as development workers was just as important. Already in the 1950s, the journalist Georgii Zhukov, who also led the State Committee on Cultural Ties with Foreign Countries, urged senior officials to engage the many "wonderful [Central Asian and Caucasian] writers, economists, historians, philosophers" in outreach to Asia and Africa.[25] Young communists from countries like Afghanistan, Bangladesh, Nepal, India, Namibia, and Ethiopia would train at the Komsomol school in Tashkent.[26] Even tourism became a part of Soviet outreach—Tajik writers and other intellectuals were invited for subsidized trips to countries like Mali, Guinea, and the Ivory Coast where they could "speak about the Soviet Union and our republic and establish contacts with leading members of society."[27]

Promoting the Soviet Union as a modernizing state that preserved cultural heritage was an integral part of Soviet aid. Gafurov's call to invest in Central Asian studies paid off because it allowed Soviet representatives to claim that the study of cultural heritage was blossoming within Soviet borders. Successful cultural figures used their performances to underline the shared heritage of Soviet Central Asian culture and that of their host country, while at the same time showcasing achievements made under Soviet rule. Thus the actor Mahmud Vahidov, part of a delegation sent in 1966, recited classic Persian poetry by Rudaki, Hofiz, and Jomi, along with contemporary Tajik poets such as Mirzo Tursunzoda and Loiq Sherali.[28] H. K. Rahimzoda, the deputy head of the Persian language department at Tajik State University, was sent to represent the USSR at an exhibition of Tajikistan's achievements in education presented in Kabul in 1965. His job included fielding questions from visitors, and when he was asked whether the Arabic script had really been forbidden, he explained the advantage of shifting away from that script for the purposes of achieving universal literacy, then showed him "a textbook for fifth and sixth grades, through which our students study the Arabic script," and added that "in the faculties of humanities studying the Arabic script was mandatory. Therefore in our republic there are hundred times more people that know the Arabic script than there were in the pre-revolutionary period and many more than there are in Afghanistan today."[29] Even better if this exhibition of Soviet cultural politics could be combined with a demonstration of Soviet technical capabilities. The archives contain the record of an exchange that took place between Afghan officials and an irrigation engineer from Soviet Central Asia working on the Jalalabad irrigation canal:

> Abdul Hakim Khan (chairman of the construction of the canal): In 1967 I was in the Soviet Union and saw with my own eyes how they work there. In a short time the Hungry Steppe was transformed. Instead of ancient medieval cities modern cities have appeared in Uzbekistan.
>
> Shah Vali Khan (the king's uncle, marshal in the Afghan armed forces): Have the historical buildings constructed in Samarkand at the time of Tamurlane been preserved?
>
> Mukhitdinov: In the Soviet Union a lot of attention is paid to the preservation of historical monuments. They have been restored everywhere and they are being restored now. These monuments act as a historical museum showcasing the ancient culture of the peoples of the USSR.
>
> Abdul Hakim Khan: I was in Samarkand and I saw these buildings. It's true that they are being maintained in exemplary condition.[30]

The great value of such exchanges, for Soviet propaganda, was how seamlessly they wove together Soviet technical achievements and its anti-colonial promises: a Soviet Uzbek engineer, helping a neighboring country develop its economy, while also testifying to the cultural heritage that lived on in the USSR and continued to link it with Afghanistan.

Central Asians were often Moscow's preferred representatives at anti-imperialist conferences. Sharof Rashidov, for example, kept up his globe-trotting activity long after he took over the Communist Party of Uzbekistan. In 1966 he delivered an impassioned speech to the Tri-Continental Congress in Havana, telling an audience of Asian, African, and Latin American politicians and activists that the Soviet delegation "represented the different nationalities inhabiting the Union of Soviet Socialist Republics." At an Asian-African People's Solidarity Conference in 1963, the Soviet Union had tried to limit Chinese influence and cool the anti-imperialist militancy of the Cuban delegation. The result was a defeat for the Soviets, who admitted that the conference was "very difficult."[31] Now Rashidov underlined Soviet support for freedom struggles everywhere, emphasizing that although the Soviet Union fought for world peace, there could be "no peaceful coexistence between the oppressed people and their oppressors . . . between the imperialist aggressors and their victims." He pointed out that "with its might the Soviet Union [is] tying down the main forces of imperialist power . . . making it much easier for all peoples to struggle for freedom, independent development, and social progress."[32] It was stronger language than the USSR usually used with regard to Third World issues, and it is hardly surprising that a Central Asian was chosen to underline Moscow's solidarity with the freedom struggle.

From the 1950s, Central Asians also began to fill important diplomatic posts. Jabbor Rasulov served as ambassador to Togo several years before assuming the leadership of the Communist Party of Tajikistan. Nuritdin Mukhitdinov would spend a decade as Moscow's ambassador in Syria. Dozens of Central Asians would take up such posts, primarily in the Third World, during the Cold War era. Though they were never more than a tiny minority of the professional diplomatic corps, which drew heavily on the children of the Moscow elite, Central Asians played a highly visible role in diplomacy. Many of them served in high-priority countries at points when the USSR's influence was vulnerable. Mukhitdinov was sent as ambassador to Syria from the time of that country's 1967 defeat to Israeli forces, a major blow to Soviet interests in the region. Another Uzbek politician, Rafiq Nishanov, helped mediate talks between India and Pakistan in Tashkent after those countries went to war in 1965. Dispatched with a delegation to Egypt after the 1967 war, Nishanov met with senior leaders, including Nasser and his Vice-President Anwar Sadat, and the Palestinian leader Yasser Arafat.[33] Nishanov then served as ambassador to Sri Lanka for many years. After Egypt, once a Soviet ally, signed the U.S.-sponsored Camp David accords with Israel, he was dispatched as ambassador to Jordan. As the Soviet foreign minister Andrei Gromyko explained to Nishanov, Moscow needed someone in Amman who could make sure that Washington did not completely dominate the region.[34]

The career of Mirzo Rakhmatov provides a good example of the special role Central Asian diplomats played in forging ties with the developing world. Born in Gharm in 1914, he joined the Komsomol in 1933, rose through its ranks, and eventually joined the party in his home region. After the war he was transferred to the central committee in Stalinabad, where he must have performed well because by 1948 he was sent for further training to the Higher Party School in Moscow. He held a series of positions including chairman of the Presidium of the Supreme Soviet of the Tajik SSR, minister of culture, and member of the all-Union party's *revizionnaia kommissia* (audit committee). (He was also a leading contender to replace Tursun Uljaboev as first secretary when the latter was ousted in 1961.) Along with Mukhitdinov and Alexei Kosygin, Rakhmatov accompanied Nasser on his tour of the Soviet Union in 1958.[35] Rakhmatov's actual diplomatic career began relatively late in life, when, at the age of fifty-two, he was appointed ambassador to Yemen, then in the midst of Civil War.[36]

Rakhmatov published a memoir about his diplomatic service in 1991. Despite being written at the apex of perestroika, it is remarkably doctrinaire in its views on Soviet foreign policy—whose great strength, according to Rakhmatov, is its Marxist-Leninist foundation—and its anti-American and generally anti-Western tone. Nevertheless, what stands out for a student of Soviet foreign policy is how Rakhmatov used his particular experience and background. Rakhmatov was well aware that he was not in Yemen simply to cut ribbons on Soviet aid projects or negotiate the details of Moscow's relations with Sana. He was there as living proof that the Soviet Union was a genuinely anti-colonial power, committed to the defeat of imperialism and the progress of formerly oppressed people.

According to Rakhmatov, he frequently had to defend the Soviet Union against the charge that it oppressed Muslims, a sentiment exploited by Western powers like the United States. Once, Rakhmatov explains, he brought wonder to the face of an interlocutor by bringing up Lenin's address to the Laboring Muslims of Russia and the East. The interlocutor, presumably a Yemeni, could not believe that Lenin actually called on Muslims to kick out Russians. Rakhmatov explained that Lenin was calling on Muslims to kick out all colonizers, meaning "those who came not as friends and helpers, but rather those who wanted to use their lands in their own selfish goals, interfered in their social and cultural development, mock faith, customs, and traditions, and treated people only as cheap labor." Did that really mean that one could live "as Allah willed?" the Yemeni asked. "If they wanted, they could live according to the sharia," Rakhmatov explained "but progress destroys insularity, and even purely economic motives require the broad interaction between different nations and people, and this in turn changes much in people's preconceptions and habits, in their psychology."[37]

As ambassador, Rakhmatov also helped oversee Soviet aid in Yemen, including the work of engineers who were trying to irrigate new lands, some of which would be used to grow cotton. "I often remembered how the spaces of the Vakhsh Valley and Hungry Steppe, Dalverzin and others placed in my homeland were reborn and transformed thanks to artificial irrigation. Now—I would think with pride—we transfer our experience to others, we bring water, and that means new life into the barren deserts of Arabia, wishing with all of our hearts that this part of the earth will become a land of plenty and true happiness."[38] Here, too, Rakhmatov says, he had to face the skepticism and derision of Western diplomats and experts who claimed that growing cotton in the Wadi Surdud was impossible. Rakhmatov again relied on his own background, reminding these westerners that their countrymen had said the same thing about Soviet irrigation and cotton-growing plans in Tajikistan.[39]

Potemkin Villages?

For critics, tours of industrial facilities and model collective farms organized for visitors from abroad and particularly the developing world had all the hallmarks of Catherine the Great touring the Potemkin villages—facades of model villages created for the empress to behold as she toured her empire. Yet as Michael

David-Fox writes, Potemkin villages, in the sense that the term is popularly understood—hastily constructed temporary facades erected to create an illusion—simply did not exist. Rather, the villages had been decorated in advance of Catherine's visit. The trope of Potemkin villages was born out of diplomatic strife and revived by the USSR's enemies in the twentieth century as a way to disparage Moscow's presentation of its achievements to the outside world.[40] More important for our case is David-Fox's insight that what was demonstrated to outsiders was meant for domestic as well as external consumption. Thus, "there was hardly a single model shown to outsiders that did not have its own important role for insiders. It was as if Potemkin's decorated villages had been designated not for diplomatic elites but instead had been promulgated on a mass scale to inspire Russian peasants throughout the land."[41] Similarly, presentations of Central Asian achievements were not just aimed at foreign audiences; they were meant to inspire Central Asians themselves, and also served to remind party and state officials of the broader social and political promises of promises of Soviet development.

The poems and articles of Mirso Tursunzoda, who served as head of the writer's union and chaired the Soviet Committee of Solidarity with Asian and African Countries; his endless public appearances and reports of his travels to India and other newly decolonized countries, the rallies of the Solidarity Committee and the Committee of Peace organized in Dushanbe, Tashkent, and other Central Asian cities—all of these drew locals, particularly university-age Komsomol members, into the romance of revolution.[42] The idea that they stood at the vanguard of this revolutionary world flattered them. Those who went to work abroad as specialists, advisors, or translators, were likewise informed of their special role in aiding their less fortunate cousins, or serve the cause of peace and understanding.[43] Meanwhile, comments by visitors praising the republic were frequently repeated at party meetings and in the press.

Tursunzoda was the most famous of the figures who took part in delegations and wrote about their experiences in poetry and prose, but he was far from alone. Writers, artists, and party members all took part in extensive junkets and returned home to write about their experiences in newspaper articles, brochures, and books. Mirzo Rakhmatov, for example, wrote a book about Africa that was published in 1961.[44] Abdullahad Kakhorov, who spent many years working in planning and served as Chairman of the Council of Ministers between 1964 and 1974, coauthored a book, published in Tajik in 1959 called *Economic and Technical Cooperation of the USSR with a the Poorly Developed Countries of the East*, which included a chapter highlighting how Tajikistan and the other Central Asian republics compared favorably to the countries of South and Southeast Asia, and "set an example for the weakly developed countries. . . . The Republics of the Soviet east will be torches lighting the way to progress and civilization for less developed countries."[45] Kakhorov later traveled to South and Southeast Asia and parts of Africa and wrote about his experiences in a series of pamphlets published in Dushanbe, all of them in Tajik.[46]

Such publications differed in details but followed similar arcs: the writer described the suffering of these countries under colonialism and their struggle for freedom, supplementing facts gleaned primarily from Soviet publications with eyewitness accounts. Inevitably, the writer also pointed to the yearning he or she found for friendship with the Soviet Union, and Moscow's willingness to extend a helping hand. Often, as with Rakhmatov's memoir, they also included comparisons with the author's own republic or home district. Sometimes, in more private settings, the accounts of Central Asian travelers took on a more overtly paternalistic and Orientalist tone. Thus the Tajik poet Mirzo Tursunzoda, the chairman of the Soviet Afro-Asian Solidarity Committee, told his colleague that Guinea was "full of natural gifts, pineapples, bananas, coconuts, but with illiterate people [who were] simply big kids." Now that they were free from colonialism they were "out in the streets, singing and dancing." It was up to the Soviet Union, nevertheless, to "give them correct education and enlightenment, so that their country takes the right path."[47]

FIGURE 8.1. Abdullahad Kakhorov meeting with Afghanistan's prime minister Mohammed Hashim in Dushanbe, 1966. Courtesy of Ria Novosti.

Foreign Encounters of a Different Kind

If Central Asians' enthusiasm for such demonstrations of Soviet modernity and anti-colonialism were genuine, they were hardly as one-sided as pamphlets like Kakhorov's might suggest. The interactions between Central Asians and locals, especially in places of "shared cultural heritage" like Iran, Afghanistan, and India, sometimes led intellectuals to question both premises of the Soviet engagement with the Third World: that the Soviet Union was a genuine anti-colonial force that protected native cultures, and that it possessed the keys to economic and technical progress for people whose development had been stymied by colonialism. Many came to see their own situation as similarly colonial, something reflected in their later creative and scholarly work.[48]

Hudoĭnazar Asozoda, a literary historian, first went to Afghanistan as a translator in 1971 and stayed until 1973 working with a team of geologists. He witnessed, among other things, the overthrow of the monarch in 1973 and the creation of the republic by the king's cousin, Mohammed Daoud Khan. He returned after Daoud was in turn overthrown in 1978 by the members of the People's Democratic Party of Afghanistan and their sympathizers in the military. In Kabul, he was shocked by the bazaars, which seemed to spring forth from every street, and the sound of music coming out of every corner. "For someone coming from the environment of the Soviet Union to Kabul," he wrote, "everything was new and astonishing."[49] The most interesting pages of his detailed memoirs, which are based on diaries he kept at the time, relate his interactions with Afghanistanis. Asozoda found that most Afghanistanis had little information about what life in the USSR was really like, and tended to repeat what they heard from "foreign radio." At the same time, he admitted it was not always easy to refute some of the critiques posed to him. For example, Tohir Badahshi, who was involved with a leftist (most likely Maoist) party, insisted to Asozoda that groups like the Tajiks had little real autonomy in the Soviet Union. Badahshi introduced him to other cultural figures, who also challenged him in similar ways. Asozoda knew that both Soviet and Afghan services were probably keeping an eye on him, and so he could not really engage in such discussions. Still, he noted "the views [of his interlocutors] were not without effect on my worldview."[50]

For others, travel abroad, even to the Third World, showed how far behind the USSR was in material terms. Amirkul Erov was one of those who had started as a laborer at Nurek but eventually trained as an engineer and held various management positions. In the 1980s he was selected to do several tours abroad, one in Libya and one in Iraq, along with other specialists from Tajikistan, Uzbekistan, and elsewhere in the USSR. Like many Soviet citizens abroad, he was fascinated by the abundance of consumer products, even in a relatively poor place like Libya.

> There were very many cars, cars that had been in accidents, with broken windows, or a door was broken, there was a whole [lot] the size of half of Nurek . . . you look and no one is even taking a radio [from any of the cars] And then our guys asked, what is this? And they say this is "scrap, scrap" meaning it's a scrap yard. And our guys, joking, ask "what do you mean, its scrap?" This is abandoned? Yes, they say, you can take it. We couldn't believe it. Why? Because we didn't have this kind of abundance . . . and then they joked and said why should we work here? We'll just each take a car and bring it back to the Soviet Union.

Looking back from the vantage point of contemporary Tajikistan, Erov reflected that perhaps there was good reason that such abundance did not exist in the Soviet Union, where the focus instead was on making inexpensive food widely available. Nevertheless, he could not help but be awed: "A second impression: I go to the store, and I see they have cars, this was just in 1981 and there in Libya on the first floor there is just a store where they sell cars. We saw this and could not believe it. How could it be that you could buy a car without waiting in line? Just pay money and go. And then you have another store for carpets, and there also you don't have to wait in line."

In his travels, Erov also heard about how dams were constructed elsewhere. He learned that in France, engineers had constructed a series of dams along a major river that were less powerful than Nurek but, because they were run of river dams that did not obstruct the water's natural flow, they also caused less flooding than Nurek, which had submerged several villages and many acres of farmland. Erov was impressed by how technologically advanced the operation of the entire cascade was compared with the Vakhsh dams, relying more on technology to signal problems and thus requiring far fewer workers to keep the dams in operation. Erov's tone as he spoke about this was not angry, but rather reflective: like the other workers on the dam he had been told that he was part of the fairest society that also happened to be the most advanced in technology and science, and yet he saw evidence abroad that other systems seemed to be fulfilling certain promises better than his own.

For some Central Asian economists, the opportunity to engage with foreign colleagues and travel abroad encouraged a more critical approach to their own research regarding the Soviet Union. Hojamamat Umarov was still a relatively young researcher when he was asked to present at a seminar in Tashkent on the achievements of socialist agriculture with specialists from India. Umarov had completed a dissertation on the problems of Central Asian villages and felt embarrassed by the way his colleagues seemed to be repeating slogans about the achievements of Soviet agriculture rather than engaging in actual problems.

According to Umarov, a Russian colleague approached him after the first day and asked if he was planning to present in the same vein. Umarov promised he would not, and delivered a talk that actually engaged with some of the problems of mechanization and living standards he had found in his own research.

Umarov's interactions with Indian colleagues at that seminar led to a series of exchanges, and in the 1980s he would be invited to present at events in India. India was one of the few countries that withheld from criticizing the Soviet Union's invasion of Afghanistan in 1979, and as a result Moscow tried to do everything to further cement its alliance with New Delhi. Again, these tours were meant to highlight Soviet achievements. During his 1982 trip, Umarov and his colleague Kh. M. Saidmuradov gave a series of lectures on topics like "Central Asia: A Model of Social and Economic Development" and "The Central Asian Economic Region: History, Present, and Perspectives for Social-Economic Development." Saidmuradov also coauthored a book with R. G. Gidadhubli, an Indian specialist on the Soviet economy, titled *Central Asia: A Model for Social-Economic Development.*[51]

At least some of the economists came back from these interactions with a new willingness to challenge their own earlier conceptions about development. Umarov was particularly impressed with the way his Indian colleagues studied

FIGURE 8.2. The economists Hojamamat Umarov and Kh. M. Saidmuradov, 1987. Courtesy of H. Umarov.

poverty, an indicator that Soviet social scientists had avoided. He made this a focus of his second doctoral dissertation during perestroika, although it was still considered a sufficiently controversial topic that the defense was closed and the thesis marked "for official use only."[52] Drawing on his interactions with Indian colleagues and his reading of Club of Rome materials, Umarov also became a proponent of family planning within Tajikistan as a path to greater prosperity—a highly controversial position which earned him the enmity of some nationalists as well as economists who held fast to the idea that a booming population was Tajikistan's best argument for greater investments from the center.[53]

The Central Asian Model at War

The biggest test of the "Central Asian Model" would come after the Soviet intervention in Afghanistan.[54] Central Asians had been taking part in Soviet aid projects in that country since at least the 1960s, but the Soviet intervention in December 1979 thrust them onto the front line of Soviet foreign policy in an entirely new way. First, the United States, the Soviet Union's main adversary, began to see Central Asia as a soft spot that could be targeted to undermine internal Soviet stability. The CIA developed programs to infiltrate anti-Soviet propaganda into Central Asia, and even supported a few (albeit half-hearted) armed operations on the Soviet-Afghan border.[55] Second, and more consequential, was Moscow's reliance on Central Asians for the war effort.

As the intervention turned into an open-ended occupation, the Soviets tried to combine military counterinsurgency with economic aid and state building, hoping that development would legitimize the communist government in Kabul and drain the insurgency of support. Central Asians were mobilized and sent as soldiers, translators, engineers, party activists, and university teachers. Once again, they were expected not only to do their regular job, but also to demonstrate the ability of the system they represented to combine respect for national culture with progress and equality. Some of these individuals mobilized came to question key elements of belonging in the Soviet Union: that their system represented the best path to modernity, that it was genuinely anti-colonial, and that internationalism truly defined their relations with other Soviet nationalities. All of these premises had been questioned before 1979, of course, but for some the war experience sharpened doubts.

Central Asians had been serving as translators on Soviet projects in Afghanistan since at least the 1960s, but once Soviet troops were in Afghanistan, the need for translators grew exponentially. Most Soviet officers and commanders did not speak any of the local languages, and only some of the Afghan officers were fluent

in Russian. Translators were required from the most senior government functions and all the way down to unit level.[56] The translators were recruited once
they were already in university. Their motivation for signing up varied. Some
genuinely believed in the mission, and saw themselves as playing a role in helping
to modernize Afghanistan and protect it from imperialists. The valorization of
veterans of the Great Patriotic War, which included the grandparents of some of
these translators, helped create a sense that they were defending the Soviet Union
while helping less fortunate people under attack from reactionary forces. Some
went because they saw the mission as an adventure. But material reward was also
a powerful motivator. A translator could potentially earn many times the salary
of someone with a comparable level of education within the Soviet Union, and
return to purchase an apartment or a car.[57] Compared to the pre-intervention
period, translators had relatively little freedom to move or interact independently
with Afghans. Their Central Asian background did not prevent them from being
attacked as Soviets by insurgents. Security officials also tried to keep interaction
to a minimum.

Translators and other Central Asian advisers were expected to project a positive image of Soviet life to the soldiers and civilians with whom they interacted.
This was especially true of the CPSU or Komsomol members who happened to
be serving as translators, and was probably especially important in the case of
Uzbeks, Tajiks, and other Soviet Muslims. Some of the translators were explicitly
designated as propaganda workers, and briefed by a Central Committee member
in Moscow before being sent on their assignment.[58]

The case of Abdurashid Samadov provides an interesting illustration of how
the role of translators changed as a result of the intervention, and the subtle
transformation in attitudes toward the Soviet Union and one's place in it that
the experience engendered. Abdurashid was first introduced in chapter 2, as one
of the students taking active part in Dushanbe's literary scene in the 1960s. He
went to Afghanistan in the 1970s, where he worked on translations for the Ministry of Justice, helping Soviet specialists advise on legal reforms. In his spare
time, Abdurashid worked in the archives and collected manuscripts relating to
twelfth-century Dari poetry, ultimately writing a monograph on the topic. One
of these manuscripts was lent to him by a villager from outside Kabul, a fact
that points to the relative freedom enjoyed by Soviet specialists prior to the intervention. Although he stayed on for five years after the war, the old freedom
to interact was gone, and he also became more aware of corruption among his
Soviet colleagues. There were various ways to earn money "on the side," primarily
through the resale of Western goods but also through promotions and even arms
sales.[59] Although he had gone to Afghanistan intending to join the party upon
his return, seeing party members behave in this way turned Abdurashid off from

the idea, and when he returned to Dushanbe he did not try to join. He did use the money he had saved abroad to purchase an apartment in a new *mikroraion* (residential complex), a car, and a dacha.[60]

Tajiks and other Central Asians were not just translators and soldiers in Afghanistan—many were advisers in their own right, and others came to work as teachers in Afghan universities. One of the more dramatic stories was that of Muhammedali Khait, a translator who also served as an adviser with the Main Intelligence Agency (Glavnoe Ravedyvatel'noe Upravlenie; GRU). Khait had grown up on a collective farm outside of Dushanbe and gone on to study at Leningrad State University, earning a degree in Oriental studies focusing on Iranian languages and literature in 1980. Thus far his life represented the kind of social mobility that the Soviet Union was supposed to make possible for all. Although he had been planning to continue with graduate work, the military needed him in Afghanistan, and he was soon assigned as a translator to work with Afghan military trainees at a training center in Kyrgyzstan. Eventually, he was sent to Afghanistan, where he observed what could only be described as war crimes.[61]

> There was a report that in one of the districts there was a group under the command of Said Jargann, from the Islamic Party. And at the start of the operation the group went to the mountains using underground irrigation channels. So [the group] left and [Soviet forces] started killing ordinary people. They gathered some fifty people, farmers, various traders, women and children, and they wanted to prove that the operation was successful. Well I insisted and they let almost everyone go except for ten people. The ten best farmers, stall-keepers, they were supposed to serve as proof that the operation was successful and that there were trophies. Both biological and material ones, you could say. So they brought these ten people to Kabul and kept them on one of the Soviet bases. I managed to get them released. But after this something changed in my soul and in my mind . . . and when I talked to the commander of the army, and with others, I insisted that one could not solve the Afghan problem through military means, that this would lead to consequences.

Khait got his chance to "solve the Afghanistan problem" another way when he was brought into a GRU group that was trying to negotiate with the Afghan-Tajik leader Ahmad Shah Massoud. Over the course of the war, the Soviet military negotiated several such cease-fire with Massoud, and even tried to broker a deal between him and the communist regime in Kabul. At the same time, Khait and some of his colleagues, both Russians and Central Asians, were becoming aware of corruption on the one hand and false reporting on the other. Presumably serving in military intelligence gave them particular insight into the differences between what actually happened during a battle and what was reported afterwards. They decided to write a report, which according to Khait, amounted to forty-eight pages and was discussed even at the Politburo level.

The report also drew the ire of some of the GRU's rivals in the KGB. The two intelligence agencies had a long-standing rivalry that became particularly poisonous during the war in Afghanistan. Khait was arrested and questioned on suspicion of selling secrets to Massoud. After several months he was transferred to Tajikistan and was further questioned there, but ultimately released. For some time he was unable to find work, but eventually found a job as a deputy director of a polytechnic. It is difficult to verify Khait's story—the relevant documents are unlikely to become available for decades. But Khait has denied that there was anything to the charges against him, and his story fits what we know about the KGB-GRU rivalry in Afghanistan—it often played out in such ugly ways. But when Khait talked about his time in Afghanistan he emphasized how the experience of war transformed his own thinking:

> You see, both as a person and as a specialist I learned a great deal. Both about Soviet reality, and about my own life. Everything changed for me after Afghanistan. After I got into this situation, I changed. In a different direction. It's not that I hated the Soviet Union. I was just repulsed. Starting from 1985, and later when I worked in a technical college, where I was a deputy principal, and later when I worked in radio and television. My views were different from those of people who had developed here. And even from those who had taken part in military activities [in Afghanistan]. I thought differently; I had developed a nonconformist way of thinking (*inakomyslie*) compared with others.

Khait believed that the Afghanistan experience and the transformation he underwent as a result shaped his political path in the perestroika years and after independence, when he joined first the secular opposition movement Rastokhez and later the Islamic Renaissance Party.

Khait's experience was not typical—extensive oral histories by different scholars have shown that the paths of veterans ranged widely. Some came back full of patriotic fervor, proud of the role they had played.[62] Many reported seeing in Afghanistan the backwardness and poverty that would have been Tajikistan's fate if it had not become part of the Soviet Union. Others, like Abdurashid, were disappointed by some of the things they saw during the war but did not undergo a wholesale personal transformation of the kind Khait described.

Development, Disappointment, and Anti-Colonialism

By the late 1970s, the optimistic Soviet vision of development for the Third World had begun to crumble. Soviet leadership was challenged by several concurrent developments: Chinese assertion of a global role on the one hand, and the emergence of "dependency theory" and a new international politics that emphasized the divide between the North and the South rather than the East and the West.[63] At the same time, Soviet scholars and politicians were confronted with the poor results of their aid programs over the previous decades. They also found that, contrary to their predictions, "traditionalism" was making a revival in many parts of the Third World, particularly in Muslim countries, and that religion was proving a more potent mobilizing force than class-consciousness or even nationalism.[64] The Soviet response was not so much to change policy but rather to double down the commitment to the Third World, adjusting theory and positions as necessary.[65]

Nevertheless, in the late 1970s and early 1980s Soviet scholars of the Third World, including economists, theorists in the party's international department, and specialists in the Institute of Oriental Studies, were trying to understand why these countries had failed to develop along the lines predicted by the Soviets. Among the issues they confronted was the population boom and unemployment, the failure to create a progressive working class, and the persistence (or revival) of traditionalist politics.[66] Similar critiques already helped break apart the development consensus in the United States and Europe during the 1970s.[67] What is noticeably absent in the Soviet critiques is any comparison with the problems in Central Asia. Naturally, such a comparison would have been extremely problematic. True, Central Asian economists and planners had been alerting Moscow to many similar problems in their own republics. But their arguments did not challenge the system as a whole, nor the relationship between the center and the periphery. All of this would change in the perestroika era.

THE POOREST REPUBLIC

By the early 1980s state-led development and international aid had been under pressure for over a decade. Donor countries increasingly questioned the value of their aid, suspicious that it was being eaten up by bureaucracies. A new orthodoxy, often referred to as "neoliberalism," attacked the Keynesian state in developed countries and insisted that the solution for poorer countries was to pull the state back and allow private enterprise to flourish. Countries that had relied on commodity exports to fuel domestic investments found themselves in debt when prices plummeted. Governments in the Middle East, Africa, and Latin America were forced to cut back on social programs and lay off workers to pay off debts accrued in previous decades. But the development project was also under sustained attack from the left—for the environmental damage it caused, the destruction of indigenous habitats and livelihoods, and the way it seemed to entrench state power.[1]

Within the USSR, too, the wisdom and rationale of the two related development projects—aid abroad and industrialization in the poorer republics—was increasingly subject to debate. Scholars and planners working in Moscow criticized the wastefulness of Soviet projects at a time when the country was facing growing economic problems; some intellectuals in the republics were growing concerned about the environmental and social costs of economic development. Until the perestroika era (1985–1991) these criticisms were raised primarily in closed-door forums or in specialist journals. After Mikhail Gorbachev came to power and liberalized the press these debates spilled out onto the pages of the periodical press.

We have seen throughout this book how the tension between the promises of Soviet anti-colonialism, internationalism, and economic progress, on the one

hand, and shortcomings in these areas, on the other, animated the way politicians, intellectuals, and ordinary people engaged in cultural and economic politics. Even the most critical individuals seemed willing to work through Soviet
institutions; compared to areas like Georgia, the Baltic Republics, or even Russia,
there was virtually no separatism or what could properly be described as a "dis-
sident" movement in Central Asia. During perestroika this would rapidly change.
Although support for maintaining the union remained higher in Central Asia
than elsewhere in the USSR right until its dissolution, new forms of critique and
mobilization challenged the very premise of the Soviet project, not just the gap
between promises and reality.

Scholars looking at perestroika in Central Asia have focused on the role of
nationalist mobilization, corruption scandals, and the "return" of religion. In the
case of Tajikistan in particular, perestroika is often treated as a pre-history of the
civil war that wracked that country between 1992 and 1997. This chapter focuses
on the way the entire model of Soviet development came under question—both
within and outside the republic. Several trends came together at the same time.
First, many members of the intelligentsia began to see inequality not as a temporary aberration but as endemic to the system. Some linked the republic's economic, social, and environmental problems after six decades of socialism with a
critique that emphasized the cultural loss of the Soviet era. These ideas were not
reached in isolation, but were developed through this elite's interaction with the
postcolonial world as well as counterparts throughout the Soviet Union. Second,
thanks to Gorbachev's policy of *glasnost* (openness), these ideas received a wider
airing than they could have previously. Third, these centrifugal forces were catalyzed by changing attitudes in the center.

Ultimately, perestroika proved tragic—and not just because of the violence unleashed as the Soviet Union fell apart. Gorbachev's reforms provided an opportunity for the first time to really debate fundamental issues about development, to
reconsider the premises of an earlier era and make future decision-making more
democratic. Instead, important discussions about the environment, demography, cultural heritage and economic policy quickly devolved into competing nationalist discourses. Within Central Asia, this new nationalism also undermined
the possibility of cooperation, while within Tajikistan itself it helped set different
regions against each other, contributing eventually to the outbreak of civil war.

The Politics of Difference

Jabbor Rasulov, Tajikistan's long serving first secretary, died on April 4, 1982.
Leonid Brezhnev passed away later that year, and his generation was passing

along with him—Uzbekistan's first secretary Sharof Rashidov, in office since 1959, died in 1983. Rashidov's death was followed by an investigation into corruption in the republic and a wholesale purge of cadres, whereas no immediate aftershocks followed Rasulov's death. Nevertheless, Gorbachev was intent on removing cadres who might stand in the way of reform plans. In Tajikistan, he replaced Rahmon Nabiyev, a former planning official who had been promoted to first secretary on Rasulov's death, with Qahor Mahkamov, an engineer by training who, like Nabiyev, had come up through the planning organs. In an attempt to break through established patronage networks, Mahkamov pushed through the retirement of many local cadres, often replacing the departing officials with those from different districts. Mahkamov himself did not have much of a power base, and his background as a technocrat was poor preparation for the politics of the perestroika era.

The "cotton affair" had consequences that went far beyond Uzbekistan. It originally surfaced when the CPSU was led by Yuri Andropov, who made the investigation part of his anti-corruption drive. In sum, officials at every level overreported cotton production, and used the payments received to line their own pockets and for patronage. Yet the investigation also alienated the local elite, who felt that a long-established practice, in which Moscow officials had clearly also been implicated, was now suddenly labeled illegal and pinned squarely and unfairly on them. Uzbekistani officials and intellectuals became suspicious of Moscow, and officials in other republics realized that they too might fall under the thumb of eager anti-corruption crusaders from the center. Under Gorbachev, the investigation continued, and in the context of glasnost, the new policy of openness, received increasing coverage in the press. Newspapers like *Komsomol'skaia Pravda, Moskovskie Novosti,* and the magazine *Ogonek* carried stories on corruption, and on other failures of Soviet development, including the environmental and social effects of cotton monoculture.[2]

None of this was news to Central Asians themselves, who not only knew of these problems but sought ways to solve them. Yet the fact that these stories were now being carried in the central press, and that the Central Asian republics were being portrayed as exotic and backward places where corruption and exploitation were culturally rooted, served to distance the local elite from Moscow. These reports fed a growing narrative in the center that continued investment in industrialization for these republics was useless. Such views had already taken hold among some scholars, advisers, and planners by the early 1980s.

The view that some ethnicities were profoundly different and not well suited to industrialization received a prominent airing in a series of articles by the ethnographer Yulian Bromlei. Bromlei, a historian by training, was a specialist on the southern Slavic peoples and had led the Institute of Ethnography since 1966.[3]

In the 1970s and 1980s Bromlei focused on questions of ethnogenesis and the definition of ethnos. His writing resonated with that of a rival, the Eurasianist scholar Lev Gumilev, in that both saw ethnicity as having a biological component, and both were skeptical of the notion that the various Soviet nationalities would merge to form one people.[4] In a piece coauthored with Ovsei Shkaratan, a fellow ethnographer, and published in *Sovetskoe Gosudarstvo i Pravo*, Bromlei engaged the issue of labor and the problem of industrialization in Central Asia and the Caucasus.[5] The article contained a thinly veiled critique of the entire Soviet development approach and a direct critique of Soviet economists. The construction of factories and technical colleges failed to draw the local population into the work force, the authors pointed out. The problem, they felt, was the failure to take account of national traditions in determining industrial policy. As a result, people did not take up job created for them, and were inefficient even when they did so. The details of the argument are less important than the authors' insistence that populations will be drawn only into those industries that reflect their own traditions. The authors did not offer a solution (in fact, they stated that they did not have one), but rather articulated a research agenda. Their article explicitly linked the challenges facing the USSR internally with those of the developing world. Finally, it pointed to the success of Western anthropologists in studying native traditions in countries where the capitalist mode of development was being promoted.[6] It is not clear how influential the article was, but it seems that at least someone in the leadership agreed with its views. Bromlei and Shkaratan made a similar argument in *Voprosy Ekonomiki* only a few months later, and Bromlei published yet another piece in *Kommunist*—the party's key theoretical journal—in May 1983, which echoed similar themes.[7]

The ideas these articles contained were dangerous—they undermined the concept that there was a developmental path open to all peoples. Earlier attempts to learn more about "local conditions" by, for example, bringing ethnography and sociology into economic planning, assumed that knowledge to be gained from such research could help find the best path to an end-point that looked more or less similar for everyone. Bromlei and his supporters dismissed this reasoning, simultaneously challenging the Marxist notion that economic conditions determined culture.

The idea that Central Asians were too different had also taken hold in planning offices. As one economist who was also a senior official in Tajikistan's Gosplan complained in 1981, "We need to overcome this psychological barrier in ministries, offices, and research organizations, where they think that in Central Asia people do not want to work and the industrial enterprises are idle and people are idle."[8] A 1984 memo on economic reform prepared for Gorbachev noted the futility of investing in the kind of industry Central Asian planners requested, since the local population was interested only in "traditional production" and refused to join the industrial workforce.[9] Meanwhile, some Russian economists clearly felt that attention to problems in Central Asia was detracting from problems within Russia itself. At a SOPS (Council for the Study of Productive Forces) meeting in 1983, one Russian economist complained that while issues like child mortality and standards of living in Central Asia were getting attention, those in Russia were being ignored.[10] The fact that discussions in a technocratic body like the SOPS could become emotionally charged and take on a nationalist tone did not bode well for Soviet ethnic relations.

The struggle over cottage labor versus industrial employment was not just about central Soviet ministries and decision-making bodies trying to shed responsibility for unprofitable investments in the periphery; rather, the calls for using cottage labor presaged a more profound shift in Soviet thinking. During perestroika, the Soviet Union began to promote individual and cooperative enterprise as a way to make the economy more dynamic.[11] The debate about cottage labor in Central Asia had broader implications. While industrial labor was supposed to shape the socialist individual, the idea of cottage labor presumed the idea of the individual as an entrepreneur who would develop him or herself. The turn toward encouraging cottage labor among Central Asians was also premised on an idea of profound cultural difference that made some ethnic groups better suited for work outside of socialist industrial production; in the Soviet context, where so much social welfare provision was tied to the workplace, it also presumed a new and more targeted investment in the individuals and groups who would no longer be expected to play a part in socialized production.

In the early 1980s, these ideas were still fairly new and controversial, but by the end of the decade they would come to play an important role in how established elites and critics of the Soviet system in Moscow argued for economic reform and for looser ties between the republics. In May 1989, the journal *Kommunist,* together with party newspapers in all of the Central Asian republics, organized a roundtable with leading planners and scholars. By this point, Gorbachev had already introduced principles of self-financing for republics and enterprises, but the implication for redistribution between wealthier and poorer republics were as yet unclear. The journal noted that over the past two decades, the production of national income of the Central Asian republics had fallen further and further below the union average, and that production per capita was now half of the USSR as a whole.[12] The speakers and their positions were predictable. Shkaratan once again emphasized the folly of industrialization for societies that were "on the threshold of traditional and urban-industrial culture."[13] He went further than he did in his earlier articles in urging planners to avoid trying to achieve equality in republics that were so different. Rather, the point was to try to get republics and enterprises to compete with each other: "Relations of redistribution, the paternalism of the center, the pursuit of unified economic growth bring only harm, [are] an obstacle in the way of true competitiveness on the basis of [republics' own] resource potential."[14]

Notable was the participation Georgy Mirsky, a specialist on the developing world who had been critical of state-led industrialization since the 1970s. He explained that in the 1950s and 1960s, postcolonial states had sought rapid industrialization because they believed that was the only path to equality with the nations that had previously colonized them. At the time, "those who were against building factories and resettling the majority of the population in cities were [considered to be] in favor of backwardness and ultimately facilitators of neocolonialism." Ultimately this modern industry proved counterproductive to human development goals—being capital rather than labor intensive, it employed too few people, and it usually proved uncompetitive. Finally, Mirsky said that while he did not want to make a direct analogy between the situation of developing countries and that of Central Asia, it was clear to him that the lessons were obvious and needed to be taken into account. Further, he noted, it was a dangerous time to push for urbanization. If the experience of the Third World showed anything, he said, it was that rapid urbanization combined with unmet expectations produced a dangerous mix, and could easily lead to uncontrolled social unrest.[15]

Glasnost and Local Criticism of Soviet Development

As elsewhere in the Soviet Union, the press began to write more freely in the second half of the 1980s—particularly local papers like *Paemi Dushanbe* and primarily "cultural" ones like *Sadoi Sharq* and *Adabiat va San'at*. Similarly, new instructions about party relations with local councils began to have a very real effect on how problems were voiced and discussed.[16] This is not to suggest that in the 1970s officials ignored all the concerns of their "constituents," but problems were usually solved through informal negotiations. Now officials had to register and discuss discontent, which in turn emboldened people to voice their unhappiness more assertively. From 1987, environmental issues began receiving increasing coverage in local newspapers. In addition, social and natural scientists gave voice to doubts they previously shared only with colleagues or in memos circulated within their institutes. These included not just concerns about air pollution, but the broader environmental effects of the developmental strategy pursued since the 1950s: the construction of giant dams to power heavy industry and irrigate cotton lands.

In responding to growing mobilization on environmental and social issues, republican leaders had limited room to maneuver. Officials had been aware of environmental problems since the 1960s and had taken measures, along the lines of those pursued in other republics, to mitigate the effects of pollution by tightening control over emission and waste standards. In the perestroika period, these issues became part of public discussion. The era saw some key demands of Tajikistani planners finally being met: new labor-intensive plants were being placed in regions where reserves were concentrated, rather where it was hoped that people would move; grape and vegetable harvests were beginning to replace cotton production, and people from mountain villages who had been resettled to farm cotton in the lowlands were being allowed, in some cases, to return to their native homes.[17] Yet concerns about pollution now turned local residents against some of the new industrial enterprises. Such was the case with the Kulob Battery Factory. It was precisely the kind of plant that Tajik economists had been pushing for since the 1960s. But the very public discussions about environmental pollution made even this project difficult. Protests in Kulob, sparked by concern over the plant's environmental effects, forced construction to be shut down. The resources allocated were directed to the already more prosperous and industrialized Khojand province.[18]

The air quality in Dushanbe was getting worse every year and taking a toll on people's health, and the giant cement plant was one of the main culprits. Concerns about the cement plant were not new—they emerged almost as soon as the plant was built.[19] What had changed was the way that problems were discussed. Now there were calls to shut the plant down. At the same time, the republic was facing a housing crisis, and one of the main complaints being leveled against the republic was the failure to provide housing for the growing Tajik population. "We cannot simply liquidate the cement plant right this minute, as some people are demanding," First Secretary Mahkamov pleaded in 1988. "Shutting down the factory means stopping all construction."[20]

One of the most interesting discussions at the meeting on Central Asian development organized by *Kommunist* had to do with demographic policy. Soviet leaders had been reluctant to promote family planning in earlier decades. Soviet officials pointed to Central Asia as proof that population growth and economic wellbeing went together.[21] The USSR also used its anti-Malthusian position to demonstrate its solidarity with developing countries. At the 1974 World Population Congress in Bucharest, the USSR, along with other socialist states, rejected the link between family planning and development. Instead, they backed those developing countries that emphasized redistribution from rich countries to poorer ones.[22] At the same time, there were dissenting voices, including that of the demographer Boris Urlanis.[23] In the following years, the USSR continued to engage with the UN on population issues, and by the 1980s family planning had gained substantial support among planners and scholars studying the Third World.

In Central Asia, family planning was controversial for a different reason. Large families were considered an important part of local tradition, and limiting their size was an unacceptable intrusion into what had come to be seen as part of "national" identity. Some Russian and Central Asian specialists had suggested promoting family planning among the rural population as far back as 1974, but the idea did not get much traction.[24] By the 1980s, however, the idea of promoting family planning was increasingly attractive to Moscow and also won the support of important Central Asian specialists.[25] As was discussed in the previous chapter, the economist Hojamamat Umarov had come around to the idea after having learned about similar efforts in India. One of its most vocal proponents in Tajikistan was Sa'diniso Hakimova, a specialist on women's health. She had begun her medical training before the Second World War, and eventually went on to earn a research degree and found an institute focused on maternal and child health. While economists like Umarov believed that raising standards of living was impossible with existing birth rates, Hakimova argued that advances in women and children's health were impossible without family planning.[26]

In 1987 and 1988, a debate raged in the republican press, especially the Tajik-language *Tojikiston Soveti*. The opponents of family planning argued that the policy would be instituted by "command-administrative" methods, that is, the kind of top-down directives being criticized in the perestroika era. Some of the opponents of family planning were also part of the emerging nationalist opposition.[27] Others argued that when taking the demographic situation in the USSR as a whole, limiting family size in Tajikistan and the other Central Asian republics was not wise.[28] Family planning's proponents insisted that it would always be voluntary, that it would take into account "national traditions" and habits, and was absolutely necessary if there was ever going to be a chance to raise standards of living in the republic.[29] Similar debates were taking place in the other Central Asian republics, with similar fault lines.[30] At the May 1989 roundtable organized by *Kommunist*, Hakimova raised the issue again, noting that she cursed the day she decided to become a gynecologist because she felt unable to help the women whose health was being destroyed by frequent childbirth and poor living conditions.[31]

Evident in all of these debates was a changing understanding of the role of the state in economic development and social welfare. The consensus of the 1950s held that cheap energy and a large labor force made the region a good setting for industrialization, which in turn would raise standards of living, promote modern attitudes, and help raise levels of social welfare. This vision assumed that people were more or less similar—a Tajik or an Uzbek could just as easily be a factory worker, an engineer, or a scientist as a Russian or a Latvian. Now every part of this vision was under scrutiny. If the universalist vision was invalid then what was the

FIGURE 9.1.   The physician Sa'diniso Hakimova photographed here drinking tea with her family in their Dushanbe apartment—the idealized image of the Tajik-Soviet middle class, 1970s. Courtesy of the Russian State Archive of Photo and Video Documentation.

role and purpose of the Soviet Union? Analysts like Shkaratan believed that the center would continue to invest in the republics, but mostly to fund social welfare and education. But how politically feasible was such an arrangement when it was no longer clear that all Soviet people were following the same historical progression?

Cultural Development and Anti-Colonial Critique

The sociologist Georgi Derluguian has argued that those mobilizing against Soviet rule in the late 1980s and early 1990s were very often the people who had benefited from the system and the social mobility it offered.[32] It was not just the technical intelligentsia that rebelled; rather, the cultural and technical elite developed overlapping critiques of Soviet economic and cultural policy, which in turn echoed and helped shape the broader discourses emerging across the USSR, from the Baltics to the Caucasus and Central Asia. Poets and scholars who came of age in the 1960s, like Loiq Sherali and Gulruhsor Safieva, became frustrated at what they saw as Russian dominance in the arts, and at the same time were forced to revisit earlier assumptions about the status of culture in countries like India, Pakistan, Afghanistan, and Iran, for whom they were supposed to be the guiding light. In one of Sherali's more famous poems, a lament addressed to his mother, he complains about living in a society where no one speaks his language— a barely hidden critique of the republic's political leadership that seemed more comfortable in Russian than Tajik.[33] In the perestroika era, Sherali became a leading figure among those who sought to elevate the status of the Tajik language, a campaign that culminated in a 1989 law.

One issue around which the Tajik intelligentsia mobilized was the fate of Tajik speakers in Uzbekistan.[34] The Tajik elite well into the 1950s had been drawn from Bukhara and Samarkand, long the cultural and intellectual centers of the region. The two cities continued to be seen as the proper capitals of Tajik cultural life even for elites that had no family connection to them. In the perestroika period some began to openly question the justice of the 1924 national delimitation that had given those cities to Uzbekistan.[35] New freedoms afforded by perestroika made it possible to organize new Tajik language schools in Uzbekistan. Concerns over the fate of the Tajik language were at least partially channeled into supporting these schools through book drives and other initiatives.[36] As in other republics, institutions devoted to literary history and cultural heritage became the focal points where the intelligentsia worked out its emerging anti-colonial critiques of the Soviet Union.

Intellectuals from different republics developed these emerging critiques through a great deal of interaction and mutual influence across the entire union. Serguei Oushakine argued that Soviet dissidents employed a kind of "mimetic resistance," copying the language and frameworks of the Soviet government to critique it.[37] The emerging nationalist intellectuals of the 1980s were also employing a kind of "mimetic resistance," but in different ways. They developed their arguments on the basis of Soviet claims about equality and national culture, using official discourse and ideological texts to show that Soviet principles were constantly being violated. At the same time, they used memes that were being shared across the Soviet space.

One meme emerged from Chingiz Aitmatov's *The Day Lasts Longer Than a Hundred Years,* a novel whose impact extended far beyond the author's native Kyrgyzstan. The novel has parallel plotlines that, together, spell out virtually the

whole Soviet era. The novel's greatest resonance comes from the legend of a tor-
ture technique supposedly employed by certain Mongol warriors. The warriors,
so the legend goes, would stretch a skin over the head of a captive, then leave him
without food or water in the hot sun. As the skin dried, it shrank on the captive's
head, putting immense pressure on his skull. The captive, if he survived, was
spiritually broken. Completely subservient to his captors, the *mankurt*, as he was
called, also lacked any memory of his past. At the novel's emotional peak, the
main character shouts "mankurt!" as an epithet against members of the younger
generation who seem to have lost touch with their traditions.

The novel also touches on themes of ecological degradation and thus echoes
the "village prose" pioneered by Russian writers in the thaw and developed in
the 1970s and 1980s. This genre often set up an idealized rural Russia against
a corrupt urban modernity and economic development that brought ecological and social disaster. The most prominent example is the novel "Farewell to
Matyora" by the writer Valentin Rasputin, which describe the last months of a
village about to be submerged because of a new dam on the Angara River. Yet the
village prose movement was focused on the damage done to the Russian nation,
and served to inspire the nationalist Russian intelligentsia.[38] Aitmatov's novel
carried a more universalist message which resonated across the USSR and was
popular with the liberal Russian intelligentsia who found the village prose writers' nationalist tendencies suspicious.[39] It had particular resonance, of course,
in Central Asia. The writer Juma Odinaev's daughter recalled that immediately
after reading it as a teenager she asked her father if she, too, was a mankurt, since
she attended a Russian school and had no particular ties to Tajik culture.[40] The
anxiety about becoming mankurts permeated the political discussion in the late
1980s and early 1990s.

Equally important for developing an anti-colonial stance with regard to the
Soviet Union were the networks that Tajikistani intellectuals had built up inside
and outside the USSR. As was discussed in chapter 8, their travels in postcolonial
countries had exposed them to anti-colonial politics as well as skepticism toward
the USSR's claims of equality. The cultural elite also had become well integrated
into Soviet institutions in the postwar decades, and through them came into
close contact not only with staunch defenders of official orthodoxy but also those
who, while working within the system, began to articulate fundamental critiques.

Consider, for example, the case of Muhammadjon Shukurov (Shukuri)
(1926–2012). Born in Bukhara, he was the son of Sadri Ziyo (1867–1932), a Qazi
(judge) in the Bukharan emirate in the years before revolution who managed to
make a career of sorts under the Soviet regime before perishing in the purges.
Although born in Bukhara, Muhammadjon studied in Stalinabad (Dushanbe), at
the pedagogical institute, graduating in 1945. After earning a graduate degree he

spent most of his career in the Academy of Sciences. In his memoirs, Shukurov recalls that in the early perestroika era he heard people from different republics complaining about the poor state of "national" culture in the USSR at meetings with cultural figures in Moscow. Among the speakers who made an impression on Shukurov was Aitmatov, who complained that there was only one Kyrgyz-language school in the Kyrgyz SSR's capital of Frunze (Bishkek) and that only the least able students were sent to study there; a Moldovan deputy who complained about the switch to Cyrillic from Latin script; and even the Academician Dmitry Likhachov, the Russian historian and cultural preservationist.[41] Their speeches inspired Shukurov to write a series of articles on the state of national languages in the republic. One of the first, after some difficulty, came out in Moscow in *Literaturnaia Gazeta*. Once again, his networks and integration into the Soviet literary world made it possible for him to argue a position that was at the core of the emerging nationalist movement.[42]

The problem of language ran up against the problem of economic development. Russian "chauvinism" may have been a factor in keeping Russian as the primary language of government across the USSR, but there were also practical reasons—among them that in a centrally planned economy allowing each republic to use its own language would be tedious and expensive at best, chaotic at worst. At the same time, the inability to master Russian kept potential students, particularly rural ones, from technical colleges. The solution called for was usually to increase Russian language training in the rural areas, itself not an easy task. But focusing on the Tajik language threatened to make the problem worse—less attention to Russian language training meant even fewer young people would be ready for technical colleges, while the chances that the entire Soviet Union would find a way to accommodate dozens of languages in its economic life were almost nil. Mahkamov supported the language initiatives as long they concerned primarily the cultural sphere, but he drew the line at switching alphabets. Those who wanted to could study it, but actually replacing Cyrillic was out of the question: "Wouldn't such a reform set our development back several years? There is every reason to think that it would," he said at a party conference in December 1988, not long after Shukurov's articles initiated a vibrant discussion in the republic and the first calls for making Tajik the official government language.[43]

Mahkamov's points were reasonable. The problem was that the intelligentsia were no longer convinced that Tajikistan was so developed, culturally or otherwise. Mahkamov was out of step with the times. Like many engineers of his generation, he had a single-minded commitment to the industrialization of Tajikistan, a goal he had pursued while working in the republic planning committee (Gosplan) and in the Council of Ministers.[44] Yet the urban intelligentsia's understanding of the republic's problems was in its own ways limited to their own experiences. Although closer to its rural roots than the Moscow or Leningrad intelligentsia of the same period, a lifetime in the republic's centers, the union's institutions, and even international forums gave them a particular view of the challenges in their own republic. Malika Jurabekova, an actress who had toured abroad, complained "Why do we, Tajiks, speak only Russian at home? One needs to know Russian, it is necessary, this is a language of communication, of world culture. That's not what I am speaking about, but rather that we do not know our own language. This is our misfortune, that we don't know our language, our history, or our own culture."[45] In fact, surveys showed that even in the late 1980s only 30 percent of Tajiks were fluent in Russian, and very few spoke it as their primary language.[46] Complaints by Sherali and others that the leadership could not speak Tajik were also exaggerated—the problem was not that they could not speak Tajik, but that their professional language had become Russian, although they were perfectly comfortable speaking Tajik at home or in their home region.

First in the Third World or Last among the First?

Like anti-colonial activists of earlier decades who had mobilized against European empires, the Central Asian intelligentsia developed their critiques of the Soviet system as part of what Robert J. C. Young calls a "national internationalism."[47] Although their networks within the USSR were important, their ideas were also shaped by their encounters with the postcolonial world beyond the USSR.

For decades, Central Asian intellectuals had taken part in presenting their republics to the Third World as examples of enlightened development. Economists played a particularly important role. With the coming of perestroika, some Tajik economists began to articulate a more direct comparison between their own situation and the problems of the Third World. By 1989, the economist Umarov had emerged as a strong critic of Soviet economic policy within Central Asia, and within Tajikistan in particular. In an article published that year, he argued that economic relations in the union were inconsistent with claims to equality between nationalities: "According to the constitution of the USSR, one of the political foundations of Soviet society is that it is a federation of nations and nationalities, and the friendship between them. It was believed that between them there were not and could not be any conflict (*protivorechie*). When such conflicts did appear, they were hushed up."[48]

Umarov's specific complaints were not much different from what other Tajik economists had been saying for some time. Like them, he decried the spread of cotton monoculture and low levels of industrialization. Referring presumably to the aluminum plant discussed in chapter 4, Umarov argued that to the extent that industry had been constructed in the republic, it had done little for the native population, and effectively extended Tajikistan's role as a producer of raw materials. What changed was how he articulated the problem. Not only was Umarov's language more forceful than what was typical for his fellow economists, but he explicitly compared Central Asia to other less developed countries:

> Many social-economic and demographic problems of the Central Asian republics are analogous to the problems facing developing countries in the East. The majority of them are the result of the fast population growth. . . . This is the contradiction between the growth of the size of the average family and the growth of the demographic load on the working members of the family, between the fast pace of natural population growth and the shrinking availability of land per person. No less serious is the contradiction between the excess labor resources and the insufficient number of qualified working cadres and specialists, the necessity of providing for full employment and the insufficiency of productive reserves. . . .[49]

Umarov did not see this simply as a problem of mistakes in planning, but rather as a more fundamental issue resulting from the relationship between the center and the periphery: "It seems that this situation is explained by the strict regulation of regional development from a single center, which infringes local and regional interests, suppresses initiative and enterprise from the population and territorial organs, sharply decreases interest in a more complete and effective involvement of the productive resources of the region."[50]

Center-periphery relations were thus becoming politicized in a way that they had not been since the Khrushchev period. If leaders like Uljaboev, Rashidov, and Rasulov had employed anti-colonial arguments largely to mobilize their own elite and populations and to push leaders in Moscow to fulfill the promise of the revolution, these arguments now re-emerged as a more fundamental critique of the system.

Umarov was a relative moderate, but his views were echoed by another economist of that generation, Tohir Abdujabbor. Their biographies overlapped: both came of age in the 1960s, studied in Moscow in the 1970s, and worked abroad for part of the 1980s. Abdujabbor had started his career conducting research on development-related issues. As a graduate student at the Institute of Oriental Studies, he wrote a thesis titled "Northwest Frontier Province of Pakistan: Social-Economic Features," a survey of climate, natural resources, and labor reserves intended to serve as a further guideline for development strategy.[51] Curiously, many of the issues Abdujabbor raised were ones that Tajikistani economists were

debating with regard to their own republic: the shortcomings of industrialization, the problem of excess labor, the difficulty in balancing heavy and light
industry, and so forth. Still, it remains a fairly conventional work for the time
period—very much the kind of scholarship encouraged among Central Asian
intellectuals, geared toward Soviet-led development. After defending his dissertation, Abdujabbor went to Afghanistan as an economic adviser and translator.
Abdujabbor worked there for four years, and then again from 1983 to 1985.[52]

Abdujabbor's transition from Soviet intellectual to opposition figure seems
to have begun during that second period in Afghanistan. In the late 1980s he
became one of the founders of Rastohez (Revival)—a perestroika-era group that
pushed for the revival of the Tajik language and its use at the government level.
Beyond the cultural and linguistic argument that became so central to Rastohez's
campaigns, there were also more concrete economic complaints. In his articles
and speeches, Abdujabbor criticized the cotton monoculture imposed on Tajikistan for the benefit of the center while degrading the soil and harming the health
of farmers. He also rejected the notion that Tajikistan was backward until the
Russian Revolution. On the contrary, Abdujabbor wrote, the region had a vibrant
agriculture.[53] Comparing industrial production levels to 1913 might show a great
transformation, he said, but that failed to account for the fact that half the working population was engaged in farming, and that the standard of living was the
lowest in the Soviet Union.[54]

Although as an activist Abdujabbor spoke and wrote more on language and
culture than on economic questions, he saw the two as linked. Industrial development and the modern cities built in the Soviet period had failed to attract the
Tajiks, he insisted, because they were built with Russians in mind. The culture of
the Tajiks and their needs had not been taken into account when building cities,
and a strict regime of residence permits made it hard for them to settle there even
if they did want to. "It is no accident that today after more than seventy years have
passed since the foundation of the Soviet Union the number of Tajiks in the cities and especially among workers and specialist cadres in industrial factories and
construction is very insignificant. This is not without influence on the progress
and advancement of the nation, language, and culture."[55] These ideas were at the
core of the economy and ecology section of Rastohez's program, approved in
September 1989. Short on specifics, the program called for Tajikistan's "economic
independence": control over Tajik economic institutions, infrastructure, planning, and resources.[56]

Other intellectual and cultural figures also became outspoken critics of Soviet development, horrified by its effects on local populations and culture. Some
became campaigners for resettled groups, such as the Yaghnobi people, a small
group moved to the lowlands in the 1970s. The campaign succeeded in forcing

the authorities to let the Yaghnobi return home.[57] Perhaps the most prominent example of elite mobilization against Soviet development related to the Rogun Dam. The dam had been envisioned back in the 1950s as the largest and most powerful of the dams in the Vakhsh Cascade. Work on Rogun finally began in 1976, when the first turbines of Nurek were already operational. Yet the heyday of dam building had passed, and by the 1970s there were serious doubts about the broader industrialization program envisioned in the 1950s. Attracting funds from the center, especially after the late 1970s, was increasingly difficult. A large part of the workforce was from Nurek, and there was less need to engage the local population and fewer resources to do so.

For local activists, the biggest concerns related to the dam's social and environmental damage. The environmental consequences of water misuse in Central Asia had already become a public issue in the 1970s. Diversion and waste of water was drying out the Aral Sea, what was once a large lake that straddled Kazakhstan and Uzbekistan. The proposed response was audacious and frightening: to reverse the course of Siberian rivers through a series of subterranean atomic explosions. The idea had the support of the Kazakhstani party leadership and other Central Asian elites. Russian environmentalists rallied against it and the project was abandoned under Gorbachev.[58]

By 1987, Tajikistani intellectuals had also begun to doubt the wisdom of the Rogun Dam. Safieva, the poet, became a vocal opponent on the grounds that its construction would lead to the submergence of her birth village, among others. Her opposition to the dam, which she voiced in Moscow as a representative in the Council of People's Deputies, is often credited with stopping the dam's construction. Yet she was hardly alone in sounding the alarm. Otahon Latifi, a long-time correspondent for *Pravda* who had penned a number of upbeat reports about Nurek and Rogun in the 1970s and early 1980s, began to publish eloquent critiques of the Rogun project and related environmental issues. Following the collapse of a small dam in Dangara in 1987, which destroyed dozens of homes and killed a number of people, he noted that scientists had been warning about the dangers of constructing dams in seismic zones, especially large dams like Rogun.[59] A year later he published a lengthier article that took a much broader view of the problems that could be caused by Rogun, even if it did not collapse. Among other things, Latifi noted, it would contribute to the tragedy of the Aral Sea, destroy thousands of hectares of good farming and grazing land, and force the relocation of over twenty thousand people while simultaneously depriving them of their livelihood, since they would lose their fruit orchards, vineyards, and grazing land for their sheep.[60] These were precisely the kinds of consequences that had galvanized opinion elsewhere against large dam construction.

Nationalism and environmentalism often dovetailed in the late perestroika era. Some of the Russian opponents of river diversion from the Aral Sea focused on the fact that among the proponents were non-Russians, including the Tajik scientist P. A. Pulad-Zade. The "cosmopolitanism" of these scholars supposedly made them negligent of Russia's land.[61] Sa'diniso Hakimova also increasingly turned to explicitly nationalist arguments in discussing the damage done by economic policies and official negligence. In 1990 she wrote, "The health of the nation has been sacrificed for cotton. Our genetic fund has been completely destroyed. It must be [considered] a case of genocide."[62] The language again echoed that of Russian nationalists, who were making the same point about the Russian nation.

Social Mobilization and Urban Tensions

Zafar A. grew up in Nurek. His father had been one of those who had come to the city as a laborer and gradually worked his way up to become a senior official responsible for food procurement and distribution. Since Zafar's father worked in one of the city organizations, the family lived in the city rather than one of the surrounding villages, with other senior party members, engineers, and managers as neighbors. Zafar knew Tajik, but his friends were a multiethnic bunch who spoke Russian to each other. He recalled that as perestroika went on, something changed in the attitude of villagers toward the residents of Nurek city, on the one hand, and in the attitudes of local Russians toward Tajiks, on the other. It seemed to be a kind of sport, he recalled, for boys from the surrounding villages, who were generally tougher than their urban peers, to ride their bicycles into town and chase city boys. He attributed this hostility to jealousy on the part of the rural residents toward the urbanites who had better access to consumer goods and state-provided resources. At the same time, he recalled that it was in the late perestroika era that he heard a Russian call a Tajik *churka*—a derogatory term used in the Soviet era and post-Soviet Russia for all people from Central Asia and the Caucasus—for the first time.[63]

In the 1960s, the influx of Europeans into Nurek led to rising expectations from the local population, who demanded that they too share in the social goods the state was providing to the settlers. In the perestroika period, such inequalities were discussed more widely, even as expectations rose. Yet faith in the existing formal and informal institutions that served to negotiate such conflicts was disappearing, as discussion about the shortcomings of the system became public. Groups of underemployed young men—not integrated into the local industries or institutions—organized on the basis of village or mahalla. Similar groups seem to have organized within the city itself, sometimes based on neighborhood or school.[64] These kinds of "urban formations" were typical for rapidly growing Soviet cities of the late socialist period, but they also seem to have sprung up in smaller towns like Nurek, where the city/village boundary was more porous.[65] In Dushanbe, these groups often developed along regional as well as neighborhood (*mikraraion*) lines; just as university students sought out people from their own village or district within the republic and tried to share rooms, so working class youth from one region might band together and assert themselves by challenging those from another group.

Although the background of these confrontations is complex, one cause surely was frustration with the uneven distribution of economic development and a sense of exclusion among more recent arrivals to the city. It was contemplating these kinds of frustrations that led the economist Albert Hirschman to one of his more famous observations about economic development in the early 1970s. Hirschman used the metaphor of a traffic jam in a two-lane tunnel: if the adjacent lane starts to move, a driver still stuck will nevertheless be pleased because she will expect her own lane to start moving shortly after. When that fails to happen, the mood turns to one of frustration.[66] Hirschman's observation was not just meant to explain political attitudes, but also to identify possible sources of mobilization in societies undergoing rapid development. In some developing societies, Hirschman noted, the upwardly mobile might retain their sense of social justice, and thus grow disaffected if they did not see the promise of equality being fulfilled, regardless of how much they personally had benefited; if those who had not benefited were to lose hope that they ever would, then the result could well be revolution.[67] It was an answer of sorts to Samuel Huntington, whose *Political Order in Changing Societies* posited, controversially, that democracy and development were not linked, and that democracy was poorly equipped to handle the challenges of urbanization and rising (but unfulfilled) expectations.[68] Hirschman's article was a call to limit social unrest not by resorting to repression, but by mitigating inequality.

We have seen that Soviet social scientists were developing similar concerns. Georgy Mirsky, for example, warned his colleagues about the dangers of promoting urbanization and rapid social change in the context of democratization. Indeed, urban protests, sometimes slipping into violence against minority groups, took place throughout the USSR in the late 1980s. In 1986, students marched in Almaty, ostensibly to protest the appointment of a Russian as the party's first secretary.[69] In 1989, protesters took to the streets in Tbilisi against a proposal to restore the Abkhaz Soviet Republic that had briefly existed during the civil war in 1921. The crackdown carried out by the Soviet army resulted in a bloodbath and accelerated calls for independence. An analogous dispute promoted mobilization in Armenia and Azerbaijan (over the disputed Nagorno-Karabakh region).[70] The same year saw pogroms against Meskhetian Turks (Muslims from Georgia) in the Ferghana Valley.[71]

As of January 1990, Tajikistan had not seen anything similar. The most prominent political movements were those like Rastohez which, like the "Fronts" in the Baltic republics or the Birlik (unity) movement in Uzbekistan, positioned themselves as being pro-perestroika even as they articulated positions that were increasingly critical of the entire Soviet system.[72] Taking advantage of Gorbachev's call for local organization to solve immediate social and economic problems, members of the local intellectual and creative elite in some areas began to bypass the Communist Party completely. For example, a committee in Komsomolabad, consisting of local party members, village elders, and prominent individuals who lived outside the district, convened a protest against the Rogun Dam in August 1989.[73]

These new organizations also channeled feelings of discontent, which were often expressed in terms of relative deprivation. It became increasingly common for Tajik organizations to talk about the relative prosperity of Uzbeks, for Gharmis and Kulobis to talk about the political and economic dominance of the Leninobodis, and for Pamiris to complain about their relative poverty and lack of political institutions with respect to the rest of the republic. Not only was the region dealing with rural poverty, and a housing shortage, it also faced a worsening problem of underemployment. Studies found that many young men and women who had gone to the European USSR to learn a skilled trade under a program launched in 1981 were unable to find jobs in their profession upon returning home. Many of these young people had been recruited with the help of the Komsomol, whose activists had to convince reluctant parents to let their children go to a distant part of the country for training. Now these young specialists returned to their villages, where they grew frustrated, or joined the ranks of underemployed in the cities.[74]

On February 11, 1990, around 300 young men gathered outside the headquarters of the Tajik Communist Party on Prospekt Lenina and demanded to speak to First Secretary Mahkamov. The ostensible reason for the meeting was a rumor that Armenian refugees—fleeing violence in Azerbaijan—were to be given houses in the city, despite the fact that the waiting list for apartments in the city was tens of thousands names long. When the government refused to respond, more protesters arrived. The next day the protesters attacked the building of the Central Committee. An attempt to impose martial law was ineffective. The protests quickly turned violent—internal troops of the Ministry for Internal Affairs were called in, shots were fired, and rioting and looting broke out all over the city. A group of younger politicians, particularly those from southern districts, tried to use the crisis to solidify their own position with the party leadership. Acting as intermediaries, they secured the resignation of Mahkamov and several other senior officials, but these resignations were rejected at a party plenum held after the violence subsided.[75]

No objective investigation of the events has ever taken place—or could take place. Accounts and explanations of the events vary enormously.[76] It is clear that the housing shortage was at least one of the reasons that the rumors about Armenian refugees had such an effect. As Mahkamov admitted several weeks later: "Since 1986, the pace at which apartments are completed has increased by 34 percent compared with the period of the eleventh five-year plan. But still the problem of housing is acute. We have over 150,000 families waiting for housing. And that queue is moving very, very slowly."[77] Similar complaints contributed to other ethnic conflicts, such as the violence in the Kyrgyz city of Osh in June 1990.[78]

The violence and its aftermath also revealed the extent of regional discontent. In a sense, the complaints were the same everywhere—underemployment, a low standard of living, and shortage of housing. But in every region there was a sense that it was the locals who had been slighted. At the March 3 plenum, I. Khalimov, first secretary of Kurgan-Tyube Oblast, claimed that 36,000 people were unemployed in his district. "In every rural household there are two, three, and sometimes more families which need more living space. More than 20 percent have no cows. . . . Over 45,000 have no personal plot (*podsobnoe khoziastvo*). Where can our people turn if in our rural stores there are no meat products? No wonder that their dissatisfaction turns against the leaders who they see as responsible for all these failures." Sulton Mirzoshoev, a poet and former Komsomol leader who was now the first secretary of the Kulob region, pointed out that protests had also taken place in the city of Kulob and smaller regional towns. Again, the complaints were familiar: "If Tajikistan is last in the union, Kulob is last in the republic," he complained. "How can we have enterprises build housing, when [in] over seventy years all that we have built is one cotton factory and one butter factory, which uses ancient equipment? We're lying to the people. We're building small local branches of plants for forty to fifty people and calming down. This isn't going to solve our problems."[79] Tagoev, from Komsomolabad, still felt that his district was the worst off. In a city that was near the Rogun power plant, which should have been the pride of the republic, none of the promises made in previous decades had been realized, he complained. "Since 1971, twenty years have passed, and nothing has been built. . . . I showed a comrade from the Ministry of Education our best school and he said I saw one like this in a museum, and they were exhibiting it as the worst one. For twenty years nothing has been built. . . . There is really a difficult, tense feeling in our district. Four [protest] meetings have taken place recently. The reason—social-economic backwardness of the region."[80]

These complaints served two purposes. First, they absolved the oblast secretaries of responsibility for the February events. In the aftermath of the violence, various reports had cited the overwhelming representation of youth from one or another region among the protesters and hooligans. By pointing to the problems in their regions, the party secretaries laid the blame at the feet of those who had failed to deliver on earlier promises. At the same time, the oblast secretaries were trying to use the opportunity to attract attention and resources to deal with very real problems. It is significant that all three regions mentioned fell within the Southern Tajikistan Territorial Production Complex, which was supposed to bring development and higher standards of living to the region. More than twenty-five years after the complex's inception, many people felt that there was little to show for the effort. Though they probably had no intention of doing so, by defining these problems in local terms the delegates only deepened the sense of regional discontent that would prove so devastating in 1992. The violence and subsequent smaller protests highlighted yet again the distance between the generation of leaders who had made their careers in the 1950s and 1960s and the youth that had been born around that time.

Each Republic Miserable in Its Own Way

The open discussions about poverty and the problems of the command and control economy forced Tajikistani economists to rethink some of their long held assumptions about what it would take to raise the standard of living in the republic. The idea that industry, particularly labor-intensive industry, was the key to improving people's lives was still dominant, but some economists questioned this logic not just on the basis of environmental concerns but the very nature of how they had understood "excess labor" over the previous decades. As they pointed out, most of the unemployed (90%) were women, and many of those had five children or more. They were unlikely to join the work force, and even if they did it was questionable whether their participation would actually raise their family's standard of living.[81] The solution, then, was to increase the republic's overall income level and distribute it more evenly. Ideally, the transition to a regulated market system would allow them to earn more profits from agricultural production, keep more of the processing in the republic, and raise the overall income level by specializing in those fields that would bring the greatest profits. These optimistic economists and planners assumed that they would continue to have support from the center as they transitioned to a "regulated market" economy.[82]

It quickly became clear that the center's retreat was going to be much more rapid than anyone had envisioned.[83] Several documents illustrate this dilemma

particularly well. In the aftermath of the 1990 violence, Tajikistan's representatives in the Supreme Soviet asked for a parliamentary commission to examine the
cause of the violence and determine ways further outbursts could be prevented.
They echoed the new consensus that the "extreme situation in the republic [was]
caused by economic backwardness, the failure to solve economic and social problems of workers and the population of the republic, and the lowest standard
of living in the country."[84] Safieva followed ten days later with an impassioned
handwritten letter to Gorbachev. She too begged him to form a commission to
examine the situation and answer people who saw this as an example of "extrem-
ism" among Tajiks: "The pain of my people has not been meet with empathy on
your part, and that is tolerable, since it is possible to share happiness, but grief
stays with a person, on his soul. And that is what has happened with our grief.
The cause of the events in Dushanbe has not been evaluated!!! I am asking you, as
I promised people at a meeting on February 20 in Dushanbe: I promised [them]
that I would tell you about the situation of the people: *poverty, destitution, social
injustice, unemployment*—and so forth which has driven people to extremes."[85]

A parliamentary committee traveled to Tajikistan several months later and
included Davlat Khudonazarov, a filmmaker who became active in the democratic movement, and Mamlakat, whom we met in chapter 7. The committee
visited some of the more "backward" economic regions, including the Pamirs,
Ordzhonikidzeabad, Panjakent, and Ayni. They recited similar complaints about
poverty in the region, the effects of cotton monoculture in some areas and the
toxic effects of tobacco farming in others. In their recommendations they insisted
that the only way to deal with the underemployment problem was industrialization.[86] Even critical Tajikistani elites had a hard time abandoning industrialization as a solution to the republic's problems.

By this point no one in Moscow had much time for such appeals. The Soviet
Union was on its way to becoming a country that begged for aid, not one that
distributed it. Officials from state planning explained that the country was making a transition to the market and the republic's institutions would have to find
their own solutions. Mamlakat followed up with a private plea that echoed the
frustrations expressed by many Central Asians:

> It is natural that republics with different starting positions will be un-
> equal partners on the market. What kind of competitiveness can we
> talk about for Tajik cotton producers if the price of cotton is thirty-one
> times lower than the final product? The republic has been and remains,
> to our great shame, a natural resource appendage of the center. Discus-
> sions about the necessity of our consumers from the RSFSR, Ukraine,
> and Belarus constructing processing branches of their processing plants

has been just talk. And this problem (just like many others) cannot be simply referred to the "competence of the Council of Ministers of the Tajik SSR and local organs of power."[87]

All republics were suffering, but as the poorest republic Tajikistan was in a particularly difficult spot. The Soviet economy had been developed primarily for internal trade, and Tajikistan's products in particular were primarily destined for other Soviet republics. As the Soviet Union came apart and everyone sought foreign outlets for their goods, poorer republics were at a particular disadvantage. In a letter to Soviet prime minister Valentin Pavlov Mahkamov explained that the republic was in deep trouble because its trade with other Soviet republics had come to a near standstill. No one wanted what the republic had to offer. The result was that reserves were down to zero and "entire parts of the economy are in danger of paralysis, spring agricultural work was not getting underway, vehicular transport, which makes up the main (95%) of transport in the mountainous republic, was limited by the lack of fuel."[88] Republic leaders and enterprise managers had been given autonomy to establish their own links, but this had proved a disaster: "the attempt of enterprises to enter into direct relationships, sign contracts with the state committees of oil products in union republics, as well as production plants in Omsk, Achinsk, Orsk, Krasnovodsk, Ferghana, and Bashkiria have not been successful. The republic cannot satisfy the demands of the suppliers in barter, as it has only a small list of products and goods which are in demand, and there are not even enough of those for the republic's own needs."[89]

Tajikistan's problems were one part of a broader breakdown of internal economic links within the Soviet Union that was well on its way by 1991. As Safieva poignantly noted, everyone felt the misery in their own way. All Soviet republics experienced an economic shock as a result of the USSR's rapid disintegration, but those that were most dependent on subsidies from the center and whose production was geared toward trade within the union were dealt a particularly harsh blow.

Stumbling toward Independence

Throughout the Soviet period, Tajikistan, like the other southern republics, had been presented as a vanguard of the colonial and developing world. Soviet publications trumpeted the republic's progress in education, health care, and measurements like industrial output per person. Although economists and others had long understood the limitations of these claims, it was only in the perestroika period that a wholesale reassessment took place. It became common to talk about

Tajikistan as the poorest republic of the Soviet Union. If in the 1950s and 1960s politicians used Tajikistan's vanguard status to argue for the importance of development, poverty was now primarily used as complaint and critique, both within the republic and within the union as a whole.

The tragedy of perestroika was that while it created the possibilities for a radical rethinking of development in the Central Asian context, it led instead to increasingly violent mobilization on national, regional, and ideological lines. The critiques voiced by many actors in the 1980s provided an opportunity to keep the best features of the Soviet project—an emphasis on liberation, on equality, and on inclusion—while discarding the worst ones. Many had come to realize that the economic system did a poor job of serving women, and rural women in particular. For every Mamlakat, after all, the system also created thousands of women who were expected to raise large families, do backbreaking work picking cotton, and have little access to tertiary education or a fulfilling career. Hakimova and Umarov remained committed to including women in economic and social life outside of the family structure but wanted to do this through an expansion of welfare payments and family planning, doing away with an economic system that pushed them into low-paid work that was also dangerous for their health. Hakimova became a strident nationalist, seeing the failures of the system as a concerted attack by Uzbek and Central Party authorities against the Tajiks.

After the 1990 riots, Tajikistan remained mostly peaceful. The Communist Party's authority was steadily eroding. Although it won most of the seats in the first open elections to the republic's Supreme Soviet in February 1990, the party now had to contend with new political groups. Rastohez, which primarily represented the urbanized intelligentsia, had already become a political force in 1989, but by 1990 it had splintered, with some members going to the new Democratic Party of Tajikistan. In that same year a group of religious activists, who had maintained an underground network promoting the study of Islam since the early 1970s, announced the formation of the Islamic Renaissance Party of Tajikistan— as a branch of an all-Union party that had formed earlier that year. The Supreme Soviet refused to register the party and outlawed its activities. The leadership in Uzbekistan clamped down forcefully, arresting 400 members of the party there, whereas the regime in Tajikistan avoided a direct confrontation.[90]

The failed August 1991 putsch against Gorbachev put an end to Mahkamov's attempts to hold on to power and finished off the Communist Party as a political force. Like most republican organizations, the party in Tajikistan did not oppose the putsch, although there is no evidence it wholeheartedly supported it either. When the coup failed and the CPSU was discredited Makhkamov was forced to quit the party. Having no other base of support, he resigned as president, too.

Although Tajikistan's formal independence was celebrated by many members of the intelligentsia, their hopes for a cultural and economic resurgence were soon dashed. The tensions and debates of the late perestroika years had opened up ideological and regional fissures within Tajikistan. By May 1992 the newly independent Republic of Tajikistan was engulfed in civil war.

A DREAM DEFERRED

In 1932, the African-American poet Langston Hughes traveled through Soviet Central Asia or, as he called it, the "Soviet South." For Hughes, the Central Asian republics, like the American South, were cotton growing regions; more important, they were sites of exploitation by one race over another. He was curious to see if the Soviets had managed to overcome legacies of colonial rule. Hughes set down his thoughts in a pamphlet called "A Negro Looks at Soviet Central Asia," published in Moscow in 1934, and he devoted a large section of his 1956 memoir, *I Wonder as I Wonder* to the trip.[1] By the mid-1950s, many American communists had soured on the Soviet Union, dismayed by the crimes of Stalinism. Hughes, however, defended his earlier convictions on the basis of what he had found in Central Asia, which he thought was overcoming both its feudal past and the colonial era. "The overlords have fled, along with the Emirs, the Khans and the tsarist officers," he wrote. "Now it is the turn of those who in former days had to beg of the Cossacks, 'Please, master! No more lashes, please! White master, no more! Please!'"[2] For Hughes, Central Asia was a land that had been oppressed by its own rulers and then conquered by a European empire, but was now beginning to see truly radical progress which still seemed a long way off in his own south.

In effect, the Soviet period saw three postcolonial moments. The first was in the aftermath of the Russian Revolution, when a struggle broke out over the way forward for Central Asian societies. Those Central Asian reformers that ultimately chose to work with the Bolsheviks did so in the hopes of using the new states towards their own goals. That phase came to an end with Stalinism and the terror, which eliminated (as it did elsewhere) most of the political and intellectual leadership that had authority independent of the party, and of Stalin. The second phase began after Stalin's death, when the Cold War and domestic alliance politics led Khrushchev to empower local leaders, engaging them in international diplomacy and policy debates. The changes that took place under Khrushchev—institutional, political, cultural—had long lasting effects.

Most of this book has focused on that second phase. The preceding chapters have all dealt, in one way or another, with the attempt to overcome the legacies of colonialism and Stalinism in Central Asia. In economic terms, overcoming that legacy meant establishing industry, raising the standards of living, and developing a welfare state. In cultural terms, it meant giving artists, writers, and intellectuals not just the space but the resources to develop what they saw as their own culture and language, with relatively little interference from Moscow. The Soviet promise to deliver material improvement in people's lives was important within Russia and the other European republics, but it had a particular resonance in Central Asia because it became enmeshed in the anti-colonial struggle. That is, overcoming the legacy of colonialism meant overcoming economic backwardness. Those efforts were linked to Soviet Cold War foreign policy in the era of decolonization. Moscow needed to show it was overcoming colonialism at home to make its bid for leadership of the postcolonial world.

In the decades that followed Stalin's death, much changed. Health and schooling penetrated the most remote corners of the region. Central Asian politicians got more of a voice in central decision making and planning organs, and much more say in how their own republics were governed. State and party institutions at different levels took the wellbeing of the population seriously and tried to channel resources to meet those goals. The completion of the Nurek Dam helped extend electricity to all corners of the republic and link Tajikistan's hydropower to a Central Asian network. Thousands of students got access to higher education and went on to take jobs in a diverse range of professions. Many took pride in their status as Soviet professionals and their vanguard position in the global fight against colonialism.

All of these were real achievements. But they were accompanied by a number of contradictions. The industrialization drive foundered on the inability to draw peasants out of the countryside. Unsure of decent housing in industrial cities, young men preferred to stay close to home, supplementing farm income with personal plots or working in the grey economy. The need to produce cotton led authorities to resettle peasants from the mountains to the lowlands and kept them on collective farms. The cotton economy caused enormous ecological damage and did much harm to public health. Thus, although standards of living in Tajikistan arguably rose in absolute terms between the Second World War and the Soviet collapse, in relative terms the republic fell behind the rest of the union—something which was true for the region as a whole.

Those economic contradictions undermined Moscow's claim that it was possible to achieve anti-colonialism within a Soviet framework. The influx of European workers to the new industries created a new sense of inequality and injustice among locals. The seeming dominance of Europeans in Central Asian cities—with their concentration of social services and levers of power—accentuated the feeling that all of the development being undertaken in the name of Central Asians was actually being done for the benefit of Russians and others. Success in the new industries, and in politics, required the use of Russian, putting rural populations at a disadvantage. The dominance of Russian also alarmed intellectuals who had come to see themselves as responsible for the cultural and economic advancement of the Tajik nation—a responsibility they took very seriously. The second phase of "decolonization" did not end abruptly or violently; rather, a growing number of local elites began to lose faith that decolonization within a Soviet context was satisfactory. The third phase—the perestroika era—saw them question whether such decolonization was even possible or desirable.

It is impossible to understand the fate of Soviet development without looking at the inner workings of Soviet institutions. Moscow tried to maintain a centralized grip on power and ultimate control over ideology and culture; at the same time it created academies, ministries, cultural unions, and solidarity committees in every republic. These could and did challenge or reinterpret directions coming from the center. The more this infrastructure grew, the less Moscow could control how it was used. Up to a certain point, the system was just flexible enough—and offered enough resources—that intellectuals felt comfortable, empowered even, to work through their vision of culture and progress within it. Ultimately many grew frustrated by ideological restrictions, the rigidity of the economic system, and by the seeming dominance of Russian culture.

The political scientist James Scott believed that authoritarian states like the USSR were likely to display the worst features of "high modernism," because they lacked "working, representative institutions through which a resistant society could make its influence felt."[3] But these republic-level institutions, as well as the party and city organizations active on the ground, often played that very role. Those institutions involved in economic management stood mid-way between decision makers in Moscow and the daily reality of development. The knowledge required to assemble plans was produced locally; the knowledge required by local politicians to have their projects included in the plan was often provided by economists, social scientists, and engineers working in republic-level academic and government institutes. It was in these institutes that the rationale for industrialization was developed in the 1950s, and then revised and questioned in the decades that followed. Economists and other social scientists did not develop their ideas in isolation—they engaged colleagues across the USSR and beyond, sometimes drawing on ideas they encountered abroad. But their critique also emerged from an empirical understanding of the day-to-day reality of what was actually happening on the ground. Their work demonstrated to central planners and political leaders that society and the economy were indeed "too complex to be managed in detail," as Scott puts it, following Foucault.[4] That is, by creating an increasingly more nuanced understanding of the population and the ways it might or might not behave given certain conditions, the people working in these institutions forced a re-evaluation of initiatives dreamed up in Dushanbe, Tashkent, or Moscow. These findings in turn forced more flexible approaches on the ground, whether related to issues of gender, religion, or material provision.

Looking out at the Soviet Union from Central Asia also clarifies some issues regarding options for reform in the late 1980s. Debating why the Soviet Union did not follow the Chinese path to reform is a favorite pastime in Russia. Recently, historians such as Sergey Radchenko and Chris Miller have explored this question, trying to make sense of how assessments of Chinese reforms in the 1980s informed debates within the Soviet leadership.[5] The Communist Party of China retained control of power while liberalizing some sectors of the economy and opened special economic zones where export-oriented manufacturers could set up shop. Almost all of these were near port cities and had large concentrations of people. Soviet ports, by contrast, were located in areas that were already developed and experienced labor shortages. The greatest potential labor pool was located in Central Asia and had shown almost no interest in relocating. Whatever optimism planners had shown in the 1950s about employing Central Asians outside the region had long evaporated. Moreover, the Soviet Union in the 1980s was a middle-income country with a well-developed welfare state. Its citizens would not accept the relatively low wages and conditions on offer in the Chinese case. Only when the Soviet state collapsed did Central Asians begin to come to Russia's industrial sites in large numbers.

A central assertion of this book has been that schemes for improvement in the Soviet Union, and in particular in the Soviet periphery, were not only comparable to the efforts of postcolonial nation states but that they were linked—ideas circulated between the USSR, the Third World, and the "capitalist West"—and found their local adaptations. Ideas about what development constituted and how to make it happen tended to reflect trends far beyond the USSR. The same goes for development's problems, whether related to the way that workers resisted the industries that were built with them in mind, the mismatch between skills and available jobs, or the way technological innovations led to completely unexpected results. The imbalance between education and employment opportunity was typical for a number of countries attempting rapid modernization in the post–World War II period. Both Afghanistan and Iran, for example, confronted this problem in the 1960s and 1970s; in the former case, the government's solution was to rapidly expand its bureaucracy (which did not translate into a corresponding increase in the strength of the state overall); in the latter, Reza Shah's regime used oil income to combine the expansion of the bureaucracy with a major modernization program, the so-called white revolution, and a repressive state apparatus to limit dissent. Both countries saw a growth in corruption, while dissatisfied graduates flocked to either leftist groups or an emerging conservative opposition.[6]

In fact, some of the problems observed in the Central Asian case were not unlike the ones the Soviets were facing in Afghanistan, both before and after the intervention. Preparing specialists was considered one of the most important ways that the Soviet Union could help Third World countries—through education within the USSR, setting up institutes in the countries themselves, and providing on the job training. Yet drawing local labor into the workforce was a constant problem and had enormous long-term consequences.[7] Most of the Soviet enterprises were unprofitable, even as their construction, carried out on the basis of loans, added to Afghanistan's debt to Moscow (on top of the debt Afghanistan owed to the United States, the World Bank, and other countries and institutions). This debt was offset by Afghanistan's exports, of which only natural gas, extracted with Soviet help and exported to the USSR, made a serious dent. Throughout the 1980s, as Afghanistan's dependence on Soviet aid grew, it was largely natural gas that kept the budget balanced. Once Soviet troops and experts departed, it proved impossible to continue operating the gas fields.[8] In the case of Afghanistan and Iran, these issues were at the very center of the struggles that emerged in the late 1970s, carrying away Mohammed Daoud's republic and Reza Shah's monarchy.[9] Such problems were hardly limited to those two cases, but were endemic of development schemes in Asia, Africa, and Latin America. As a result, as David Ekbladh wrote, "the general consensus on development . . . emphasizing large-scale multipurpose technological programs to produce grand social and economic change, was under sustained attack."[10] Such problems could at least be papered over in the case of Soviet Central Asia, where the center continued to invest in medical and social services, subsidize housing and electricity, support large families, and look the other way at certain kinds of black market trade. These problems therefore remained depoliticized until the late 1980s.

It would be too simplistic to say that development "failed" in any of these cases, or in the Soviet one. Most individual projects met some goals but not others. They often had unintended consequences, some positive (as Hirschman hoped), others negative. The underlying problem, however, was that to achieve a broad social transformation alongside the economic one, developers needed to get people to believe in a future of continuous improvement. Communism and the developed society were always somewhere just beyond the horizon. Inevitably, the number of people whose expectations were raised was much higher than those who got to enjoy its fruits in the present. For many, development proved to be—to borrow a phrase from one of Hughes' most famous poems—a perpetual "dream deferred."

Scholars of development have noted how whatever the effects and failures of development intervention, development is notable for creating more development—a rationale for the expansion of expertise, institutional presence, and new projects to improve on failed ones. With each step, the reach of the state extends. Tanya Murray Li writes of "the persistence of the will to improve—its parasitic relationship to its own shortcomings and failures."[11] James Ferguson describes a "'development' apparatus [that] promotes a colonizing, expanding bureaucratic power, that . . . expands its reach and extends its distribution."[12] This certainly holds for the Soviet case, both at the level of all-Soviet and re-public-level politics, and on the ground, as was the case in Nurek. But what the Soviet case also shows is that the will to improve is not ever lasting. Social scientists in the republics and in the center effectively collaborated (unintentionally) to undermine the rationale of development schemes; planners in Moscow were increasingly unwilling to fund what they saw as irrational projects; and finally, nationalist sentiments portended a rebellion against any improvement scheme that was not directed inward. Soviet development—the attempt to improve the lives of the poorest citizens in the poorest republics—came to an end in 1991, or even a few years earlier.

The decline in support for developing the Soviet periphery has echoes in the fate of welfare politics in the First World since the 1970s. The social democracies that emerged from the wreckage of World War II in Western Europe and the New Deal order in the United States both came under more and more strain. On the one hand, governments found it increasingly difficult to meet obligations, leading them to experiment with new financial instruments and to try to shed some of the burdens of welfare programs.[13] On the other hand, public support for the welfare state dropped as different constituencies felt that the benefits were accruing to racial or immigrant others while the costs felt mostly on their own group. One of the criticisms of the New Deal in the United States was that its benefits accrued primarily to whites; while Lyndon Johnson's Great Society program expanded social programs and made them more inclusive, it also led to the white backlash against the welfare state.[14] Thus western welfare states, which were mostly designed with relatively homogenous populations in mind, suffered the same fate as the Soviet Union, which had made the equality of a diverse population an explicit goal.[15]

The notion of development has nevertheless proved durable internationally, and it has taken on new life in post-Soviet states. Post-Soviet governments in Central Asia have all made development a central part of their nation-building projects, even as they have taken on board some of the anti-colonial and nationalist rhetoric of the perestroika era.[16] No doubt, the promise of development serves to legitimate the power of post-Soviet leaders, and to help them avoid calls for democratization. But this is not the only reason that development has proved enduring. As Frederick Cooper notes: "However much validity there is in critiques of self-serving development institutions and ideologies, critiques do not bring piped water to people who lack it; they do not ease the burdens of women caught between rural patriarchies and urban exploitation; they do not distribute readily available antidotes to childhood diarrhea and malaria in areas of high infant mortality."[17] One of the persistent legacies of the Soviet past—which often frustrates neoliberal reformers—is people's expectations that the state provide goods and make an effort to improve their lives in material ways.[18] People's belief that the state could and should do things to make life better (provide decent healthcare, education, reliable and cheap electricity) shaped not only what they expected from officials today, but also how they viewed the Soviet legacy and contemporary aid donors.

Yet some of the biggest questions about development remain unsettled. How, ultimately, can one design a development program that actually helps the people it claims to serve? As Soviet scholars reflected on the failure of their models in the 1970s and 1980s, they were forced to rethink their assumptions about the rural population, its needs and desires. This led some of them to support forms of individual entrepreneurship. Just as the environmental degradation caused by the misuse of water in cotton farming led officials to consider a liberalization of pricing mechanisms, the failure of Soviet economic policies to fulfill social goals led some scholars to chip away at the planning system as a whole. The late Soviet era saw some fascinating debates and attempts to rethink the approach to welfare and equality. The Soviet collapse, ironically, interrupted this process of internal critique and reform rather than accelerating it.

It is not hard to imagine debates about development continuing along the lines that scholars of development have pursued elsewhere. Some countries have experimented with cash transfers as a welfare and development tool. Some have used conditional cash transfers to nudge people towards certain behaviors, such as school attendance.[19] Others have gone further, providing cash unconditionally to people in need. The idea satisfies the liberal economic critique of planning and development efforts, because, theoretically at least, it tackles poverty without disrupting the market's ability to allocate resources efficiently. The idea also satisfies a critique of the left, because rather than paternalistically presuming to know what people need, cash transfers allow individuals to make their own decisions.[20] Scholars and activists are even championing the idea of a universal basic income as the solution in a world where work is increasingly being automated, and citizens in rich and poor countries alike are finding it harder to count on paid work to guarantee a stable middle-class existence.

Would the USSR have gotten there as well? At first glance, such a turn of events is unlikely. One of the recurring arguments against basic income has been a moral one—that it deprives people of an incentive to work and lead a meaningful life. Considering how central labor was to Soviet ideology, it is hard to imagine the idea of simply giving people money gaining serious consideration. Nevertheless, it is not inconceivable. As far back as the early 1970s leading Central Asian economists were urging a focus on consumption rather than production in measuring the success of Soviet policies; by the 1980s others were beginning to focus on poverty and arguing that individuals should be given more control over how they can earn money. Considering the growing chorus of criticism regarding development's environmental costs, it is not inconceivable that Central Asian, and perhaps even Moscow-based planners, would reach the same conclusion that some western and developing world economists have arrived at: if you want to improve the lot of the poor, just give them money. Such an approach, though, would replace the social, economic, and personal transformation envisaged by Soviet development and replace it with more modest goals of economic well-being. Even in the relatively de-ideologized late Brezhnev era such a turn of events seems unlikely.

The Soviet experience also helps us reflect on another problem of changing development paradigms. In a most basic sense, broad based development, whether Soviet- or US-inspired, was difficult and costly. It was not enough to build a factory or a dam; one had to budget for roads and electricity lines, universities and schools, hire activists to argue with village elders and mobilize youth, open entire workshops just to employ people who could not or would not work in the industries that actually had an economic purpose. It is hardly surprising that, at a certain point, politicians and experts began to doubt the wisdom of such spending. The development field has only continued to grow; however, the focus over the last three decades has increasingly fallen on technical solutions that, proponents hope, will spur bigger social change. Thus, mosquito nets were supposed to eliminate malaria, get children to school, and lead to growing wealth; water pumps in African villages were to liberate girls from the drudgery of carrying water, setting off a virtuous cycle of change as those girls stayed in schools, pursued a professional education and opened businesses, and so on. The mosquito nets were often used for fishing; the water pumps broke down and gathered rust.[21] There has been no shortage of such initiatives and the disappointments that follow in their wake.

It is not surprising that the critique of development practice lately appears to have come full circle. A technical fix, whether in the form of a drug, a water source, or an injection of cash or credit, is entering a crowded ecosystem and does nothing about power imbalances, entrenched poverty, gender hierarchies, or endemic global inequality. The United Nations and other development actors have begun to rediscover holistic approaches to development, with a publication of the Economic and Social Council stating that the need for such an approach is "self-evident" and that "any successful development must take into account the social, cultural, economic, environmental, and geographic realities that shape the lives of people all over the world."[22] Perhaps, if one is serious about changing the world, it is not such a bad idea to go back to the dreams of Soviet planners in their more optimistic moments, and to "try to take everything into account." If such an approach does not offer a solution, perhaps it will give us the humility to think twice before promising to change the world.

Like most of the USSR, Tajikistan suffered a catastrophic economic collapse after 1991. Worse, in the spring of 1992, the country descended into a civil war that would not be resolved until 1997, with violence reappearing sporadically for several years afterward. In the capital city, political actors that had made their appearance in the perestroika era vied for power, with Islamists, nationalists, and "democrats" aligned against the old communist party elite; in the southern districts, fighting broke out between resettled peasants and locals. Regional identity and political loyalty overlapped, but not precisely. In a pattern repeated across the non-Slavic republics, Russians, Jews, ethnic Germans, and other non-Tajiks were already leaving for other republics or emigrating abroad before independence; the rest tried to get out before it was too late.[23] Many Tajik professionals also left the country. Some went to Russia, where their connections from earlier days helped them continue their careers; others tried their luck in Iran or further abroad. When the opposition forces were pushed out of Dushanbe in December 1992, many of their supporters took shelter in Afghanistan, where they were hosted by Ahmad Shah Massoud, an ethnic Tajik commander who had spent many years fighting the communist government and Soviet troops.

Against this background, the welfare state that had been constructed over the previous fifty years nearly collapsed. Doctors and nurses, engineers and economists were rapidly leaving the country. Just enough stayed behind to keep things from collapsing completely. In Dushanbe, those economists who stuck around and were trying to help the new country formulate an economic policy kept showing up to work at their institute, and even organized a self-defense brigade to protect the various computers and other equipment the institute had managed to acquire in preceding decades. The city of Nurek changed hands several times between pro-regime and opposition forces, but the dam kept working and feeding electricity into the grid. Residents often came close to starvation, as roads were cut off by multiple checkpoints and fighters seized food. As always in such tragic situations people also proved their resourcefulness and resilience. Muhabbat Sharipov got access to land in the nearby kolkhoz and used it to keep his large extended family alive, also sharing with his less fortunate neighbors.

It was during the war that Tajikistan became the target of new development interventions and humanitarian aid, this time coming primarily from western donors. Organizations like Doctors Without Borders and Save the Children began operating during the fighting, and the United Nations played an important role in securing the peace. As Tajikistan began to rebuild, other actors entered the field, more directly concerned with "development" rather than humanitarian aid, as they were doing throughout the former USSR. They included international financial institutions such as the World Bank, the Asian Development Bank, and the European Bank for Reconstruction and Development, as well as various nongovernmental organizations, which focused on particular issues, such as legal reform, education, or women's rights. Many of these institutions pursued goals that had been part of the Soviet development project, such as education, but they also worked with paradigms that had become dominant since the 1980s. There was a great deal of emphasis on markets and entrepreneurship, with many programs geared to helping local producers find outlets for their products.[24] Although the emphasis on markets and entrepreneurship is something closely associated with the so-called Washington Consensus, regarding development that emerged among western donors and institutions in the late 1980s, we have seen that many Soviet scholars and planners were already thinking along similar lines, at least when it came to Central Asia.

The government of independent Tajikistan, meanwhile, has stubbornly maintained an adherence to some of the projects outlined in the 1950s. It has resurrected the Rogun Dam, although its construction proceeds in fits and starts due to lack of funding and opposition from Uzbekistan, its downstream neighbor. Nevertheless, the construction of the dam remains a point of pride and central to the regime's self-portrayal and claims to legitimacy.[25] The semi-privatized aluminum plant, while operating at a fraction of its peak capacity, remains one of the country's main exporters.[26] Yet if the old symbols of development remain, their social function has mostly evaporated. No one is envisioning a "city of the future" around Rogun, or investing in a social transformation of the peasantry that will be affected by it. Instead, Tajikistani citizens were forced to buy shares to fund the dam's construction; if Nurek's builders were encouraged to claim ownership of the project based on their participation, now ownership was paid for by hard earned cash and symbolized with a piece of paper.[27]

The foreign donor that has come closest to replacing the Soviet Union as a source of resources for development in Tajikistan (and to an extent in the other Central Asian states) is China. It is primarily Chinese firms that are building or refurbishing the roads that stitch the country together; Chinese funds that are building new power plants and other industrial facilities; and Chinese firms that are bringing old mining facilities back online. China's pursuit of hydrocarbon resources has led it to invest in exploration within Tajikistan, and more importantly into the construction of a pipeline that would carry gas from Turkmenistan over Tajikistani territory and on to China. The economist Branko Milanovic recently noted that the Chinese approach in Eurasia "brings us back to a philosophy that prevailed in development lending before the 1980s. Development does not happen by itself and it is not just a matter of having the right prices, lowering taxes, and deregulating everything. For development to happen, you need "hard" stuff: you need roads for farmers to bring their goods, you need fast railroads, bridges to cross the rivers, tunnels to link communities living at different ends of a mountain."[28] Chinese aid certainly focuses on the "hard" stuff, but evidence that this aid aims to actually improve people's lives is harder to find. Such projects help prop up the state budget, although their effect on citizens' welfare is limited at best.[29] Although testaments to Chinese-Tajik friendship are inscribed on public buses in Dushanbe, echoing the internationalism of the previous century, Chinese development today has little in common with its Soviet predecessor. There is no vision of inclusion or social transformation. Chinese aid is about Beijing's economic interests and its desire for stability in the region.

The real improvements in living standards over the last fifteen years have not come from any foreign investment or aid program but from another development that some Soviet planners encouraged in the 1970s: migration. Migrants began traveling to Russia for seasonal labor in the 1990s, when Tajikistan was in civil war, but their numbers really grew after 2000, when Russia's own economy picked up steam. Many went to work in Moscow or Petersburg, but others went to provincial cities or even to Siberian sites. Such migration naturally brought its own problems, but it also meant millions of dollars in remittances that funded consumption at home and allowed thousands of families to climb out of poverty. At their peak, remittances from labor migrants were estimated to equal more than half of Tajikistan's gross domestic product. Although remittances have proved important as a lifeline, their impact on development in the longer term is limited. For one thing, very little of the money seems to go toward investment; almost all of it is used for consumption. More important, the fact that over 90 percent of migrants head to Russia means that Tajikistan and, to a lesser extent, Kyrgyzstan and Uzbekistan are highly vulnerable to shocks in the Russian economy, as was proven after the crises in 2008 and 2014.[30] Against this background, the relationship between Chinese aid and labor migration is a puzzling one. The present government has at least partially staked its legitimacy on development, and frequently says that projects like Rogun are needed to provide jobs for Tajiks. Yet Chinese companies working in Tajikistan, as elsewhere, rarely hire Tajik workers, preferring instead to bring in their own labor.

The Soviets proceeded from the notion that progress was universal and available to everyone regardless of ethnic origin. Today we tend to scoff at such claims, because we see them as reproducing a Eurocentric and historically contingent vision of being in the world. Perhaps we should not be so dismissive. The Soviet Union found ways to accommodate quite a bit of diversity, both formally and informally, as it sought a path to material prosperity and equality. Without those universal claims, there was nothing binding different groups toward a shared future. We should not be so quick to assume, as some critics of development do, that what is local is necessarily liberating—on the contrary, it can often be oppressive and limiting. As Cooper puts it, "it is not clear that celebrations of 'indigeneity' or hope that 'social movements' will provide local answers where top-down developments projects have failed address the range of problems that impoverished societies face. They do not address the possibility that indigenous social structures and social movements—not just external colonialism and global capitalism—can be oppressive and reactionary as well as liberatory."[31]

This is not to suggest that the Soviet experience shows the best way forward. The environmental damage caused by dam building and heavy industry alone (although hardly unique to the Soviet Union) is already enough to suggest that humanity will need to think of radically different approaches as it faces the challenges of poverty, inequality, and global warming in the twenty-first century. Yet it is unlikely that it will be able to do so without the ideals of solidarity and universality that were at the heart of the Soviet project.

A Note on Sources

The research in this book is based on Russian and Tajikistani archival sources, memoirs, and extensive oral histories. Each one of these sources presents its own unique challenges.

I began collecting material for this project in 2009, initially working through the collections of Soviet documents housed at the British Library, the Hoover Institution at Stanford University, and the Lamont Library at Harvard University. (For the sake of simplicity and consistency I have provided the original Russian archival citations for all documents obtained there.) I continued working through party and state materials in Moscow and Dushanbe.

In Dushanbe, I was fortunate to get access to the Archives of the Communist Party as well as the Central State Archive of Tajikistan. The former is housed in the Institute of Party History—which once had a staff of fifty and now has only one full-time employee and a part-time archivist—which holds the records of republic-level and local party organizations, including protocols from buro meetings, stenographic accounts of plenums and conferences, and other correspondence from the Central Committee and its various departments. All of these are found in fond 3. I also made extensive use of fond 56, which contains the files of the Nurek party organization. I was able to gain access to this archive on two occasions: first in the summer of 2011, and then again in the spring of 2013. My time in the archive was limited, and I had to be selective in my focus. I do not believe that any materials were hidden from me, although of course I cannot know for sure. The greatest value of these materials is that the documents generated at the republic level and those at the district level reveal how party institutions functioned; how they sought to discipline and mobilize workers, managers, and activists; and the role they played in economic debates, planning, and local oversight.

The state archives contain a wealth of materials from various state agencies, including the republic-level Council of Ministers and various ministries, as well as files related to local representative bodies. These materials were of particular value for understanding the inner workings of production organizations and state agencies, their relationship with the local population and labor, and connections between Dushanbe and Moscow. As is usually the case with Soviet archives, there is some overlap between the materials in the party and state archives. Again, I do not believe any materials were actively hidden from me, but in certain instances the staff was unable to find materials I requested, and in others it appeared that the materials had never been properly indexed.

I was able to work in these archives in 2011, 2012, and 2013. Although gaining access was never immediate or straightforward, it generally required little more than patience, persistence, and letters of introduction and affiliation. When I returned in 2015, the political situation had grown much more tense, and working in the archives was nearly impossible. In the nearly six months I spent in Dushanbe that year I was able to get access to only one archive—at the Institute of Literature—and even there my access lasted all of one day.

In Moscow I worked in a range of archives, including the Russian State Archive of Contemporary History, where the files on party work (fond 5, opis 30) and those dealing with relevant departments were of particular interest. The State Archive of the Russian Federation (GARF), and particularly the files of the Council of Ministers (fond P-5446), which include correspondence between republic-level councils and the all-Union one in Moscow, allowed me to trace many of the debates on investment and other economic issues. The Russian State Archive of Economy (RGAE) was a particularly important resource, as it contained relevant files across various collections, including the Council of Productive Forces (SOPS, fond 399), the State Construction agency (Gosstroy, fond 339), state planning (fond 4372), and agencies involved in electrification and dam construction (including fonds 7954, 9572, and 7964). The Russian State Archive of Social and Political History, RGASPI, had many interesting files in Fond M-1, opis 8, related to the Komsomol and various large construction projects in the USSR, including Nurek. RGASPI also replicates some of the buro and plenum records found in republican party archives (fond 17). Finally, the archives of the Russian Academy of Sciences (ARAN) proved immensely valuable for studying the formation of academic institutions throughout the Soviet Union, tracing debates on issues of economic and demographic policy, and compiling biographical materials on various scholars.

I undertook shorter research trips to Uzbekistan and Kazakhstan. In Uzbekistan I did not succeed in getting into the archives, but the ability to meet local scholars and explore the book markets proved valuable. In Kazakhstan the archives were remarkably efficient, but the material collected there did not ultimately make it into this work, although it did help me understand regional debates.

Memoirs

Memoirs in Russian and Tajik are cited extensively throughout the book. For the most part, memoirs were written by public officials and intellectuals. They naturally reflect the biases of their authors. Officials who were active in the highly controversial late-perestroika period or during the civil war in particular wrote memoirs to explain or justify their position. Some memoirs are particularly valuable for their insight into certain institutions, or certain aspects of the writer's life; some are collections of anecdotes about famous people that the author knew. Even these can be useful for tracing connections and associations through formal institutions and informal networks. As a rule, intellectuals active in the humanities wrote their memoirs in Tajik, while social scientists and engineers did so in Russian. A few were published with the aid of the Iranian embassy and were rendered in the Persian script.

Unfortunately, there was no systematic way to collect these memoirs. Many were produced in very small print runs of 100, 250, or 500 copies, and then distributed to friends and family. I usually learned about the existence of a memoir from a local scholar, a mention in the Tajikistani press, or from the author or author's family. Only a few were available in libraries. The rest I acquired in secondhand bookstalls, or through acquaintances. Some memoirs that were published in Khujand were unavailable in Dushanbe and vice versa. I can thus make no claim to having acquired a complete collection of available memoirs, but I believe the several dozen memoirs I did collect have helped me gain a much better sense of how individuals experienced the period under discussion, as well as the networks and institutions they moved in.

Oral History

One of the most important sources for this study was oral history. The first interviews were conducted in 2009 in London, the last in New York in 2016. The bulk of interviews were conducted between 2011 and 2015 in Tajikistan. I interviewed former politicians, intellectuals, and government officials, as well as workers and peasants. I had interviewed diplomats, politicians, and military officers for my first book on the Soviet war in Afghanistan, but the experience was quite different. Back then I knew that my time with these individuals was limited, and I came prepared to ask fairly specific and pointed questions on the basis of what I had found in the archives, memoirs, and secondary literature. Although I conducted some similar interviews for this project, most were much more open-ended oral histories. I encouraged people to tell me about their lives, reflect on their path and choices, as well as to provide broader family histories where possible. Some interviews lasted as long as five hours, and often led to repeat invitations and conversations. The most valuable were those where I was able to meet multiple members of one family and get different perspectives on the same set of events.

Among the most interesting and problematic were the interviews conducted in Nurek and its satellite villages. The Communist Party in Dushanbe provided contacts that served as my first interviewees and guides, often accompanying me and making introductions but never interfering in the interviews themselves. Many of the people involved in the dam's construction or otherwise affected by it still live in Nurek and the surrounding villages and agreed to be interviewed and share their experiences. Sometimes the interviews were short, but often they stretched on for several hours and involved family members (children, spouses, siblings) who shared their own memories.

On many of these interviews I was joined by Malika Bahovaclinova, an anthropologist studying the way that state and international organizations manage migrant flows. We asked people to recount their life histories before and after the start of construction, their reasons for following the course that they did, their relationships with family members and coworkers. Nurek was the subject of much media attention while it was still under construction. As a result, people were generally quite open to being interviewed; at the same time, it sometimes seemed as if their narratives were very close to that presented in the Soviet press decades earlier. Repeat visits and interviews with extended family were thus particularly important to gain a more nuanced understanding and hear different perspectives.

A common issue for both sets of oral history conducted in the course of my research is the attitude towards the Soviet past. Some of the people I interviewed had become harsh critics of the Soviet system and either sought to explain their work within the Soviet system or else to accentuate ways that they worked against the system or maintained resistance in their daily lives. Others, on the contrary, felt that the Soviet period was being unfairly maligned and sought to convince me of that system's superiority. Still others had worked within the system, emerged as critics in the late 1980s, and become passionate defenders later in life. Such problems are endemic to the entire post-Soviet space, of course, but in Tajikistan they are accentuated by the legacy of civil war (1992–1997) and the particularly sharp drop in standards of living that followed the Soviet collapse.

My own positioning in the field no doubt affected how people related to me. As an ex-Soviet Russian-American with a PhD from the UK, employed in the Netherlands, who spoke Tajik with (I was told) an Iranian accent, I often inspired confusion. Some of those who saw me as first and foremost a westerner felt the need to lecture me on the benefits of the socialist system I could not understand; others, on the contrary, sought to underline their commitment to liberal democratic values. In Nurek, Malika and I were often initially greeted as the latest in a long line of journalists who had come for sound bites about the glories of dam building. Occasionally, I had to reach into my own family history to build up trust. The ability to relate the stories of revolutionaries on my mother's side of the family often helped break the ice with communists; the fact that a great-uncle was a fairly well-known economist and was fondly remembered by those who had studied in Moscow helped in my research into the economics profession.

The interviews with political figures, planners, and social scientists were relatively straightforward. The information they told me could be cross-referenced with public and archival records. With the Nurek interviews, as well as those that were used in chapter 2, I took a different approach, using the life histories to establish patterns in life and career trajectories, while also leaving room for individual experiences. Rather than shutting out everything that might be contemporary reflection, I have tried to foreground the complexity of the choices people made as well as their interpretation of them. I have also tried to make sense of how these memories, even if constructed, reflect the power of what happened in the past.[1]

Almost everyone who agreed to speak to me was comfortable with the conversation being recorded and no one asked me to hide their identity. Nevertheless, I decided to anonymize individuals who might in any way be negatively affected by the publication of this book. In some cases I identify people only by first name; in a few instances I have changed names completely. In other cases this was impractical, either because I was discussing people who published frequently, had been well known public figures, or were frequently mentioned in the press. This is the case, for example, with some of the individuals discussed in chapter 6. Although they are not well-known beyond Nurek, even the most basic elements of their life story would make them easily identifiable to people in the area.

Notes

INTRODUCTION

1. See, for example, David Engerman, "The Romance of Economic Development and New Histories of the Cold War," *Diplomatic History* 28, no. 1 (2004): 23–54; David Engerman and Corinna Unger, "Towards a Global History of Modernization," *Diplomatic History* 33, no. 3 (2009): 375–385. The literature has become quite vast. Among the works that have informed my thinking are: Odd Arne Westad, *The Global Cold War: Third World Interventions and the Making of Our Times* (New York: Cambridge University Press, 2005); Nick Cullather, *The Hungry World: America's Cold War Battle against Poverty in Asia* (Cambridge: Harvard University Press, 2010); Michael E. Latham, *Modernization as Ideology: American Social Science and "Nation Building" in the Kennedy Era* (Chapel Hill: University of North Carolina Press, 2000); Latham, *The Right Kind of Revolution: Modernization, Development, and U.S. Foreign Policy from the Cold War to the Present* (Ithaca: Cornell University Press, 2011); David Ekbladh, *The Great American Mission: Modernization and the Construction of an American World Order* (Princeton: Princeton University Press, 2011); Nils Gilman, *Mandarins of the Future: Modernization Theory in Cold War America* (Baltimore: John Hopkins University Press, 2007); Michael Adas, *Dominance by Design: Technological Imperatives and America's Civilizing Mission* (Cambridge, MA: Harvard University Press, 2010); Daniel Immerwahr, *Thinking Small: The United States and the Lure of Community Development* (Cambridge, MA: Harvard University Press, 2015); Vanni Pettina, "Global Horizons: Mexico, the Third World, and the Non-Aligned Movement at the time of the 1961 Belgrade Conference," *International History Review* 38, no. 4 (2016): 741–764. See also the excellent two-part article by Joseph Hodge, "Writing the History of Development (The First Wave)," *Humanity* 6, no. 3 (Winter 2015): 429–463; "Writing the History of Development (Part 2: Longer, Deeper, Wider)," *Humanity* 7, no. 1 (Spring 2016): 125–174.

2. David Engerman, "The Second World's Third World," *Kritika: Explorations in Russian and Eurasian History* 12, no. 1 (Winter 2011): 183–211. Jeremy Friedman, *Shadow Cold War: The Sino-Soviet Competition for the Third World* (Chapel Hill: University of North Carolina Press, 2015); Natalia Telepneva, "Our Sacred Duty: The Soviet Union, the Liberation Movements in the Portuguese Colonies, and the Cold War, 1961–1975" (PhD diss., London School of Economics, 2014); Alessandro Iandolo, "Imbalance of Power: The Soviet Union and the Congo Crisis, 1960–1961," *Journal of Cold War Studies* 16, no. 2 (Spring 2014): 32–55; Iandolo, "The Rise and Fall of the Soviet Model of Development in West Africa, 1957–1964," *Cold War History*, 12, no. 4 (November 2012): 683–704.

3. Daniel Lerner, *The Passing of Traditional Society: Modernizing the Middle East* (New York: Free Press, 1958).

4. Frederick Cooper and Randall Packard, *International Development and the Social Sciences: Essays on the History and Politics of Knowledge* (Berkeley: University of California Press, 1997), 5–6.

5. Martha Finnemore, "Redefining Development at the World Bank," in Cooper and Packard, *International Development and the Social Sciences*, 203–227.

6. See, for example, Arturo Escobar, *Encountering Development: The Making and Unmaking of the Third World* (Princeton: Princeton University Press, 2011).

7. James Ferguson, *The Anti-Politics Machine: Development, Depoliticization, and Bureaucratic Power in Lesotho* (Cambridge: Cambridge University Press, 1990).

8. James Scott, *Seeing Like a State: How Certain Schemes to Improve the Human Condition Have Failed* (New Haven: Yale University Press, 1999); Cooper, *Colonialism in Question*, 113–152.

9. Frederick Cooper, *Colonialism in Question*, 148; Engerman and Unger, "Towards a Global History of Modernization," 376.

10. Sergei Poliakov, *Everyday Islam: Religion and Tradition in Rural Central Asia* (London: Routledge, 1992). On the context of Poliakov's work and its implication for contemporary study of the Soviet era, see Sergey Abashin, *Sovetskii kishlak: Mezhdu kolonializmom i modernizatsiei* (Moscow: Novoe Literaturnoi Obozrenie, 2015), 16–20.

11. See, for example, N. I. Lychagina and A. S. Chamkin, "Vliianie kul'turnykh traditsii vostoka na khozaistvennuiu deiatel'nost'," *Sotsiologicheskie issledovaniia*, no. 4 (1990): 13–17.

12. See, for example, William Fierman, ed., *Soviet Central Asia: The Failed Transformation* (Boulder, CO: Westview Press, 1991); Boris Rumer, *Soviet Central Asia: A Tragic Experiment* (London: Routledge, 1989).

13. Cooper, *Colonialism in Question*, 114.

14. See Michael David-Fox, *Crossing Borders: Modernity, Ideology, and Culture in Russia and the Soviet Union* (Pittsburgh: Pittsburgh University Press, 2015), 21–47.

15. See, for example, Adeeb Khalid, *Making Uzbekistan: Nation, Empire, and Revolution in the Early USSR* (Ithaca: Cornell University Press, 2015); Adeeb Khalid, *The Politics of Muslim Cultural Reform: Jadidism in Central Asia* (Berkeley: University of California Press, 1998).

16. Vadim Volkov, "The Soviet Concept of Kul'turnost': Notes on the Stalinist Civilizing Process," in *Stalinism: New Directions*, ed. Sheila Fitzpatrick (London: Routledge, 2000), 216.

17. See, for example, David Hoffman, *Peasant Metropolis: Social Identities in Moscow, 1929–1941* (Ithaca: Cornell University Press, 2000).

18. On the importance of examining the struggles that lead to the formation of welfare states rather than assuming an already formed "rationality" that guides these states, see Dennis Sweeney, "'Modernity' and the Making of Social Order in Twentieth-Century Europe." *Contemporary European History* 23, no. 2 (2014): 209–224. See also Mortiz Follmer and Mark B. Smith, "Urban Societies in Europe since 1945: Towards a Historical Interpretation," *Contemporary European History* 24, no. 4 (2015): 486–487; Mark B. Smith, "Faded Red Paradise: Welfare and the Soviet City after 1953," *Contemporary European History* 24, no. 4 (2015): 597–615; Konrad Jarausch, "Care and Coercion: The GDR as Welfare Dictatorship," in *Dictatorship as Experience: Towards a Sociocultural History of the GDR*, ed. Konrad H. Jarausch (NY: Bergahn Books, 1999), 47–72.

19. See, for example, Jennifer Johnson, *The Battle for Algeria: Sovereignty, Health Care, and Humanitarianism* (Philadelphia: University of Pennsylvania Press, 2016).

20. The model for writing about the intersection of culture, politics, economics, and social welfare in Soviet history remains Stephen Kotkin's magisterial *Magnetic Mountain*, a study of industrialization in the Urals. Kotkin's research focused on the everyday practices of Soviet industrialization—how people lived and worked, how they adopted the Communist Party's language to their own ends, and how utopian ideals were instrumentalized. As Kotkin says, the focus needs to be not just on the limits imposed by Soviet rule, but "what the party and its programs . . . made possible, intentionally and unintentionally." Stephen Kotkin, *Magnetic Mountain: Stalinism as Civilization* (Berkeley: University of California Press, 1995), 22–23. *Magnetic Mountain* has inspired a host of other works on infrastructure and industrialization projects in the Stalin era and beyond, but none have

really combined the study of Soviet institutions and political economy with examination of discourse and subjectivity as Kotkin was able to do. Some of these later works examine their projects through the binary of success and failure, usually emphasizing the latter, particularly when dealing with the Brezhnev era. See, for example, Christopher J. Ward, *Brezhnev's Folly: The Building of BAM and Late Soviet Socialism* (Pittsburgh: University of Pittsburgh Press, 2009).

21. Nathan J. Citino, *Envisioning the Arab Future: Modernization in the Middle East* (Cambridge: Cambridge University Press, 2017), 8.

22. Note Timothy Mitchell's observation, in a different but analogous context, that "the narrative of 'change,' focusing on initiatives from the center and abstracting them into a story of development, inevitably tends to overlook the concrete political struggles in which political and economic control is contested or reaffirmed, as well as the forms of coercion and violence this involves. Power is not simply a centralized force seeking local allies as it extends out from the political center but is constructed locally, whatever the wider connections involved." Mitchell is criticizing the way social scientists write the story of modernity according to abstractions created by distant authorities (in his case, the Egyptian state), ignoring the local struggles involved in implementing, challenging, adopting, and redefining such initiatives. Timothy Mitchell, *Rule of Experts: Egypt, Techno-Politics, Modernity* (Berkeley: University of California Press, 2002), 169.

23. Terry Martin, *The Affirmative Action Empire: Nations and Nationalism in the Soviet Union, 1923–1939* (Ithaca: Cornell University Press, 2001).

24. This was a highly politicized question in western scholarship during the Cold War. See Artemy M. Kalinovsky, "Encouraging Resistance: Paul Henze, the Bennigsen School, and the Crisis of Détente" in *Reassessing Orientalism: Interlocking Orientologies during the Cold War,* ed. Michael Kemper and Artemy M. Kalinovsky (London: Routledge, 2015), 211–232.

25. See, for example, Alec Nove and J. A. Newith, *The Soviet Middle East: A Communist Model for Development* (New York: Frederick A. Praeger, 1966); Charles K. Wilber, *The Soviet Model and Underdeveloped Countries* (Durham: University of North Carolina Press, 1969); Norton Dodge and Charles K. Wilber, "The Relevance of Soviet Industrial Experience for Less Developed Economies," *Soviet Studies* 21, no. 3 (January 1970): 330–349. See also Teresa Rakowska-Harmstone, "Soviet Central Asia: A Model of Non-Capitalist Development for the Third World," in *The USSR and the Muslim World,* ed. Yaacov Ro'I (London: George Allen & Unwin, 1984), 181–205.

26. Gregory J. Massell, "Modernization and National Policy in Soviet Central Asia," in *The Dynamics of Soviet Politics,* ed. Paul Cocks, Robert Daniels, and Nancy Whittier Heer (Cambridge: Cambridge University Press, 1976), 265–290.

27. See Adeeb Khalid's introduction to a special issue on this topic, "Locating the (Post-) Colonial in Soviet History," *Central Asian Survey* 26, no. 4 (2007): 465–473; Nazif Shahrani, "Soviet Central Asia and the Challenge of the Soviet Legacy," *Central Asian Survey* 12, no. 2 (1993): 123–135. See also Deniz Kandiyoti, "Modernization without the Market? The Case of the 'Soviet East,'" *Economy and Society* 25, no. 4 (2006): 529–554; Douglas Northrop, *Veiled Empire: Gender and Power in Stalinist Central Asia* (Ithaca: Cornell University Press, 2003); Paula Michaels, *Curative Powers: Medicine and Empire in Stalin's Central Asia* (Pittsburgh: Pittsburgh University Press, 2003).

28. See, for example, Marianne Kamp, *The New Woman in Uzbekistan: Islam, Modernity, and Unveiling under Communism* (Seattle: University of Washington Press, 2006); Adeeb Khalid, "The Soviet Union as Imperial Formation: A View from Central Asia," in *Imperial Formations,* ed. Ann Laura Stoler, Carole McGranahan, and Peter C. Perdue (Santa Fe, NM: SAR Press, 2007), 113–139.

29. See the discussion in Dominic Lieven, *Empire: The Russian Empire and Its Rivals* (New Haven: Yale University Press, 2002), 288–342.

30. Botakoz Kassymbekova and Christian Teichmann, "The Red Man's Burden: Soviet European Officials in Central Asia in the 1920s and 1930s," in *Helpless Imperialists Imperial Failure, Fear and Radicalization*, ed. Maurus Reinkowski and Gregor Thum (Freiburg: Vandenhoeck & Ruprecht, 2012), 173–186.

31. Bruce Grant, *The Captive and the Gift: Cultural Histories of Sovereignty in Russia and the Caucasus*. (Ithaca: Cornell University Press, 2009).

32. I agree with Matthew Connelly that it is important to take off the "Cold War lens" when considering histories of decolonization. Mathew Connelly, "Taking Off the Cold War Lens: Visions of North-South Conflict during the Algerian War for Independence," *American Historical Review* 105, no. 3 (June 2000), 739–769. However, I found the Cold War played a role in areas I did not expect to find it. On intersections between the Cold War and decolonization, see also Jeffrey James Byrne, *Mecca of Revolution: Algeria, Decolonization, and the Third World Order* (Oxford: Oxford University Press, 2016); Leslie James and Elisabeth Leake, *Decolonization and the Cold War: Negotiating Independence* (London: Bloomsbury Academic, 2015); Robert J. McMahon, ed., *The Cold War in the Third World* (Oxford: Oxford University Press, 2013).

33. David-Fox, *Crossing Borders*, 79.

34. See Patryk Babiracki and Austin Jersild, "Editor's Introduction," *in Socialist Internationalism in the Cold War: Exploring the Second World*, ed. Babiracki and Jersild (London: Palgrave Macmillan, 2016), 1–16.

35. Tanya Murray Li, *The Will to Improve: Governmentality, Development, and The Practice of Politics* (Durham, NC: Duke University Press, 2007), 4.

36. Johanna Bockman, *Markets in the Name of Socialism: The Left-Wing Origins of Neoliberalism* (Stanford: Stanford University Press, 2013); Johanna Bockman and Gil Eyal, "Eastern Europe as a Laboratory for Economic Knowledge: The Transnational Roots of Neoliberalism," *American Journal of Sociology* 108, no. 2 (2002): 310–352. See also Raewyn Connell and Nour Dados, "Where in the World Does Neoliberalism Come From?" *Theory and Society* 43, no. 2 (2014): 117–138.

37. See Michel Foucault, *Security, Territory, Population: Lectures at the Collège de France 1977–1978* (New York: Picador, 2009) and *The Birth of Biopolitics: Lectures at the Collège de France, 1978–1979* (New York: Picador, 2010); Stephen Collier, *Post-Soviet Social: Neoliberalism, Social Modernity, Biopolitics* (Princeton: Princeton University Press, 2011). As Collier notes on page 17: "All modern governments are concerned with managing the biological, social, and economic life of their subjects. What is most interesting in Foucault's work is an analysis of the successive formations of biopolitical government, and of the different ways that biopolitics has been problematized."

38. In addition to the key works already cited, see Flora Julia Roberts, "Old Elites under Communism: Soviet Rule in Leninobod" (PhD diss., Chicago University, 2016); Patryk Reid, "Managing Nature, Constructing the State: The Material Foundation of Soviet Empire in Tajikistan, 1917–1937" (PhD diss., University of Illinois at Urbana-Champaign, 2016); Maya Peterson, "Technologies of Rule: Empire, Water and the Modernization of Central Asia, 1867–1941" (PhD diss., Harvard University, 2011); Benjamin Loring, "Building Socialism in Kyrgyzstan: Nation-Making, Rural Development, and Social Change, 1921–1932" (PhD diss., Chicago University, 2008); Botakoz Kassymbekova, "Helpless Imperialists: European State Workers in Soviet Central Asia in the 1920s and 1930," *Central Asian Survey*, 30 (2011): 21–37; Ali Igmen, *Speaking Soviet with an Accent: Culture and Power in Kyrgyzstan* (Pittsburgh: Pittsburgh University Press, 2012); Botakoz Kassymbekova, *Despite Cultures: Early Soviet Rule in Tajikistan* (Pittsburgh: Pittsburgh University Press, 2016). See also Botakoz Kassymbekova, ed., *Stalinism and Central Asia: Actors, Projects and Governance Central Asia Survey*, 36, no. 1 (March 2017).

39. See Alexander Morrison, "Introduction: Killing the Cotton Canard and Getting Rid of the Great Game: Rewriting the Russian Conquest of Central Asia, 1814–1895," *Central Asian Survey* 33, no. 2 (2014): 131–142.

40. Khalid, *Making Uzbekistan*, 276–277.

41. Kirill Nourzhanov and Christian Bleuer, *Tajikistan: A Political and Social History* (Canberra: ANU Press, 2013), 77–84.

42. Stephane A. Dudoignon, "From Revival to Mutation: The Religious Personnel of Islam in Tajikistan from De-Stalinization to Independence (1955–91)," *Central Asian Survey* 30, no. 1 (2011): 53–80.

43. Roberts, *Old Elites*, 1–2.

44. Abashin, *Sovetskii kishlak*, 333–347.

CHAPTER 1. DECOLONIZATION, DE-STALINIZATION, AND DEVELOPMENT

1. Westad, *Global Cold War*, 1–72.

2. For example, Mary L. Dudziak, *Cold War Civil Rights: Race and the Image of American Democracy* (Princeton, NJ: Princeton University Press, 2000); Thomas Borstelmann, *The Cold War and the Color Line: American Race Relations in the Global Arena* (Cambridge, MA: Harvard University Press, 2003). Ellen D. Wu argues that the changing status and image of Japanese and Chinese Americans were "tied directly to the national identity politics of World War II and the Cold War . . . Cold Warriors encountered the dilemma of differentiating their own imperium from the personae non grata of the European empire." Ellen D. Wu, *The Color of Success: Asian Americans and the Origins of the Model Minority* (Princeton: Princeton University Press, 2014), 4–5.

3. See Khalid, *Politics of Muslim Cultural Reform*, 286–289, 299–300.

4. Note that the use of the term in this way is contested on the grounds that the jadids were hardly a coherent group, and there was often less dividing them from their opponents on issues of religious and educational reform than is sometimes attested in the historiography. See Paolo Sartori, "Ijtihād in Bukhara: Central Asian Jadidism and Local Genealogies of Cultural Change," *Journal of the Social and Economic History of the Orient* 59, nos. 1–2 (2016): 193–236; Jeff Eden, Paolo Sartori, and Dewin DeWeese, Moving Beyond Modernism: Rethinking Cultural Change in Muslim Eurasia (19th–20th Centuries)," *Journal of the Social and Economic History of the Orient* 59, nos. 1–2 (2016): 1–36. For our purposes, here and in the following chapter, the key point is that there was a group of intellectuals in the late nineteenth and early twentieth centuries who saw themselves as campaigning for a broad transformation of their societies, and that some of these ultimately worked with the Bolsheviks in part because the latter seemed willing and able to create the conditions for some of these reforms, which by 1917 included the creation of a state of settled Turkic speakers. These connections are convincingly laid out in Khalid, *Making Uzbekistan*. Moreover, Soviet intellectuals of a later generation would look back to the jadids as role models.

5. Khalid, *Jadidism in Central Asia*, 299.

6. Adeeb Khalid, "The Fascination of Revolution: Central Asian Intellectuals, 1917–1927," in *Empire, Islam, and Politics in Central Eurasia*, ed. Uyama Tomohiko (Sapporo, Japan: Slavic Research Center, 2007), 137–152; Khalid, *Making Uzbekistan*, 371–378, 384–388.

7. Donald S. Carlisle, "The Uzbek Power Elite: Politburo and Secretariat (1938–83)," *Central Asian Survey* 6 (1986): 100.

8. Ibid., 101–102.

9. Another was that he was speaking out against corn as "food for poor people" just as Khrushchev was beginning his campaign, which would turn into an obsession, to plant

NOTES TO PAGES 21–24

more corn throughout the USSR. Documents on Yusupov case, Russian State Archive of Contemporary History (RGANI), fond 5, opis 31, delo 12, 148–149.

10. See Iurii Aksiutin, "Popular Responses to Khrushchev," in *Nikita Khrushchev,* ed. William Taubman, Sergei Khrushchev, and Abbott Gleason (New Haven: Yale University Press, 2000), 185–194.

11. Rasul Khodizoda, *Khudoe va hudro bishinosam* (Dushanbe: Devashtich, 2006), 4.

12. Bobodzhan Gafurovich Gafurov, *Istoriia Tadzhikskogo naroda v kratkom izlozhenii* (Moscow: Gospolitizdat,1949). The book was expanded many times and published in a number of languages. I am indebted to Hanna Jansen at the University of Amsterdam, who is writing a dissertation on the Institute of Oriental Studies in Moscow, for opening the fascinating world of Gafurov studies to me. On Gafurov's career and influence, see also Lisa Yountchi, "The Politics of Scholarship and the Scholarship of Politics: Imperial, Soviet, and Post-Soviet Scholars Studying Tajikistan," in *The Legacy of Soviet Oriental Studies,* ed. Michael Kemper and Stephan Connerman (Abingdon: Routledge, 2011), 217–240. Marlene Laruelle, "The Return of the Aryan Myth: Tajikistan in Search of a Secularized National Ideology," *Nationalities Papers* 35, no. 1 (2007): 51–70.

13. See the correspondence on the creation of a university in Dushanbe and other matters related to education and culture from February–March 1947 in State Archive of the Russian Federation (GARF), fond P 5446, opis 49a, delo 3649.

14. Teresa Rakowska-Harmstone, *Russia and Nationalism in Central Asia: The Case of Tadzhikistan* (Baltimore: Johns Hopkins University Press, 1970).

15. Ibid., 159–160. See also my discussion of the June 1957 plenum in this chapter.

16. Archives of the Communist Party of Tajikistan (ACPT), fond 3, opis 101, delo 118. Masha Kirasirova suggests that Gafurov's career suffered after a setback after Khrushchev took the side of the Persian émigré poet Abolqāsem Lahūtī in a dispute between the two men. This does not seem to be the reason for Gafurov's eventual move to Moscow, though. See Masha Kirasirova, "My Enemy's Enemy: Consequences of the CIA Operation against Abulqasim Lahuti, 1953–54," *Iranian Studies* (2017), DOI: 10.1080/00210862.2017.1292817.

17. Gafforov, *Uljaboev,* 30–42. Rakowska-Harmstone, *Tadzhkistan,* 161.

18. Carlisle, "Uzbek Power Elite," 107. For a close analysis of cadre shifts in Uzbekistan in this period, see Claus Bech Hansen, "The Ambivalent Empire Soviet Rule in the Uzbek Soviet Socialist Republic, 1945–1964" (PhD diss., European University Institute, 2016).

19. Mukhitdinov, *Gody provedennye v Kremle,* 312.

20. Ibid., 237.

21. Carlisle, "Uzbek Power Elite," 109. Shirinsho Shotemur, one of the Tajik leaders who perished in the purges, was not rehabilitated until the early 1960s.

22. RGALI, fond 2077, opis 1, delo1207, 148–206; B.A. Antonenko et al., *Iz istorii kul'turnogo stroitel'stv v Tadzhikistane* (Irfon: Dushanbe, 1972), 383–385.

23. Central State Archives of the Republic of Tajikistan (TsGART), fond 1505, opis 1, delo 148.

24. RGANI, fond 5, opis 39, delo 29. It appears that Dehoti was criticized for the latter proposal. On language and indigenization, see Bergne, *Birth of Tajikistan,* 82–83.

25. Mukhitdinov, *Gody, provedennye v Kremle,* 243. This was part of a wider problem of "nationalism" emerging during "de-Stalinization," although the specifics varied widely form republic to republic. See Jeremy Smith, "Leadership and Nationalism in the Soviet Republics, 1951–1959," in *Khrushchev in the Kremlin: Policy and Government in the Soviet Union, 1953–1964,* ed. Jeremy Smith and Melanie Ilic (London: Routledge, 2011), 79–93.

26. Lowell Tillet, *The Great Friendship: Soviet Historians on Non-Russian Nationalities* (Chapel Hill: University of North Carolina Press, 1969), esp. 222–273.

27. See, for example, Moritz Florin, "What Is Russia to Us?: Making Sense of Stalinism, Colonialism and Soviet Modernity in Kyrgyzstan, 1956–1965," *Ab Imperio* 3 (2016): 165–189.

28. *Perviy s"ezd uzbekskoii inteligentsii* (Tashkent, 1957), 10.

29. Mukhitdinov, *Gody, provedennye v Kremle*, 243.

30. On the Bandung Conference, see Christopher J. Lee, "Introduction," in *Making a World after Empire: The Bandung Moment and Its Political Afterlives* (Athens: Ohio University Press, 2010), 1–42; Westad, *Global Cold War*, 97–109.

31. Richard Wright, *The Colour Curtain: A Report on the Bandung Conference* (London: Dennis Dobson, 1955), 134.

32. Ibid., 141.

33. Friedman, *Shadow Cold War*, 27, 66–67.

34. Rakowska-Harmstone, *Tadzhikistan*, 73.

35. Although some foreign travelers were taken to Tashkent and other parts of Soviet Central Asia to show off Soviet achievements. See Langston Hughes, *A Negro Looks at Soviet Central Asia* (Moscow: Cooperative Publishing House, 1936) and Hughes, *I Wonder as I Wander* (New York: Rhinehart, 1956).

36. There were some exceptions during the Stalin years. When the USSR occupied Iran during World War II, for example, it used the Persian heritage of Central Asia from propaganda purposes. James Pickett, "Soviet Civilization through a Persian Lens: Iranian Intellectuals, Cultural Diplomacy and Socialist Modernity 1941–55," *Iranian Studies* 48, no. 5 (September 2015): 805–826.

37. Kirasirova, "Sons of Muslims."

38. Quoted in Hanna Jansen, "Soviet Orientalists during the Thaw and the Encounter between a 'Spiritual' and a 'Material' Asia," in *Alternative Encounters,* ed. James Mark, Steffi Marung, and Artemy M. Kalinovsky (Indiana University Press, forthcoming).

39. Rafiq Nishanov, Marina Zavade, Yurii Kulikov, *Derev'ia zeleneiut do metelei* (Moscow: Molodaia Gvardiia, 2012), 76. It is not clear which trip Nishanov is referring to. Nishanov mentions Bulganin and Khrushchev arriving in Tashkent from Indonesia, but Khrushchev did not go to Indonesia until 1960, by which point Bulganin had already been deposed.

40. Mukhitdinov, *Gody, provedennye v Kremle*, 257.

41. On the changing culture of regional party networks in the Khrushchev and Brezhnev era, see Oleg Khlevniuk, "Regional'naia vlast' SSSR v 1953–kontse 1950-kh godov: Ustoichivost' i konflikty," *Otechestvennaia istoriia*, no. 3 (2007): 31–49; Yoram Gorlizki, "Too Much Trust: Regional Party Leaders and Local Political Networks under Brezhnev," *Slavic Review* 69, no. 3 (2010): 676–700.

42. Khlevniuk et al., eds., *Regional'naia politika Khrushcheva* (Moscow: Rosspen, 2009), 10.

43. Memo to N.A. Mukhitdinov, date not provided, but mostly likely late 1955 or early 1956 in S. Rizaev, *Sharaf Rashidov: Shtrikh k portretu* (Tashkent: Yozuvchi-Nur, 1992). The book is an attempt to defend Rashidov against many of the charges against him that had emerged during perestroika. The book's greatest value is that a number of documents from the Uzbek party archives, which are almost completely closed to researchers, are provided in full.

44. Ibid.

45. CC Uzbek CP resolution, based on Rashidov's proposals, in Rizaev, *Sharaf Rashidov*, 26–28.

46. Among them the Institute of History of the Academy of Sciences of the Republic of Tajikistan. B.I. Iskandarov identifies this period with the institute's expansion as well as its internationalization in terms of hosting scholars and sending its researchers abroad. B. I. Iskandarov, *Trudnyi put' k znaniiu*, (Moscow: Izdatel'stvo Moskovskogo Universiteta, 1999), 95–113.

47. Alfrid Bustanov, *Settling the Past: Soviet Oriental Projects in Leningrad and Alma-Ata* (PhD diss., University of Amsterdam, 2013), 314–320.

48. Eren Tasar, "Soviet Policies towards Islam: Domestic and International Considerations," in *Religion and the Cold War: A Global Perspective,* ed. Phillip Muehlenbeck (Nashville: Vanderbilt University Press, 2012), 168–169.

49. One of the reasons Rashidov highlighted these travels was to point out that he was in good health following some heart problems the previous year.

50. RGANI, fond 5, opis 31, delo 84, 15.

51. The minutes of the meeting are reproduced in Rizaev, *Sharaf Rashidov,* 31–45. Unfortunately, the archives in Moscow contain only the protocols of party buro meetings, not the full minutes. For the minutes of the plenum where Kamalov was removed and replaced by Rashidov, see RGASPI, fond 17, opis 89, delo 649.

52. Tillet, *The Great Friendship.* As in the Soviet period, historical writing today is used in various contests between the independent republics. See Mohira Suyarkulova, "Statehood as Dialogue: Conflicting Historical Narratives of Tajikistan and Uzbekistan," in *The Transformation of Tajikistan: The Sources of Statehood,* ed. John Heathershaw and Edmund Herzig (London: Routledge, 2013), 161–176.

53. RGANI, fond 5, opis 35, delo 118, 38.

54. RGANI, fond 5, opis 35, delo 78, 1–7.

55. Babadzhan Gafurov, "Uspekhi national'noi politiki KPSS i nekotorye voprosy internatsional'nogo vospitaniia," *Kommunist,* August 1958, 10–24. For more on the way the Soviet Union employed the cultural heritage of Central Asia in its relationship with the Middle East, see Masha Kirasirova, "Sons of Muslims," in "Moscow: Soviet Central Asian Mediators to the Foreign East, 1955–1962," *Ab Imperio* 4 (2011): 106–132.

56. GARF, fond 5, opis 1, delo 50. For more on the development of the SKSAA, see Kirasirova, "Sons of Muslims."

57. M. Tursunzoda, "Nash velikii drug i sosed," *Kommunist Tadzhikistana,* January 26, 1956.

58. Ibid.

59. Quoted in Gerhard Simon, *Nationalism and Policy toward the Nationalities in the Soviet Union: From Totalitarian Dictatorship to Post-Stalinist Society* (Boulder, CO: Westview Press, 1991), 106.

60. On Vakhshstroi, see Maya Peterson, "Technologies of Rule: Empire, Water and the Modernization of Central Asia, 1867–1941" (PhD diss., Harvard University, 2011).

61. Quoted in Simon, *Nationalism and Policy,* 106.

62. Quoted in Jeffrey James Byrne, "Our Own Special Brand of Socialism: Algeria and the Contest of Modernities in the 1960s," *Diplomatic History* 33, no. 3 (June 2009): 429.

63. Cullather, *The Hungry World,* 134–135.

64. See Nick Cullather, "Damming Afghanistan: Modernization in a Buffer State," *Journal of American History* 89, no. 2 (2002): 512–537. Antonio Giustozzi, Artemy Kalinovsky, et al., *Missionaries of Modernity: Advisory Missions and the Struggle for Hegemony in Afghanistan and Beyond* (New York: Hurst, 2016); Timothy Nunan, *Humanitarian Invasion: Global Development in Cold War Afghanistan* (Cambridge: Cambridge University Press, 2016).

65. Or as Timothy Mitchell so aptly puts it, "Dams were unique in the scope and manner in which they altered the distribution of resources across space and time, among entire communities and ecosystems. They offered more than just a promise of agricultural development or technical progress. For many postcolonial governments, this ability to rearrange the natural and social environment became a means to demonstrate the strength of the modern state as a techno-economic power." Mitchell, *Rule of Experts,* 21.

66. Frederick Cooper, "Writing the History of Development," *Journal of Modern European History* 8, no. 1 (2010): 5–23; Joseph Hodge, "British Colonial Expertise,

Post-Colonial Careering and the Early History of International Development," *Journal of Modern European History* 8, no. 1 (2010): 24–46.

67. Westad, *Global Cold War,* 91. In the case of India in the 1950s, US officials wanted to focus on agricultural modernization and were skeptical about the prospects for industrialization, but Indian leaders used US food aid to subsidize their industrialization program. Calluther, *The Hungry World*. The United States would also eventually support the Volta River project. See Thomas J. Noer, "The New Frontier and African Neutralism: Kennedy, Nkrumah, and the Volta River Project," *Diplomatic History* 8, no. 1 (1984): 61–79; Stephan F. Miescher, "'Nkrumah's Baby': The Akosombo Dam and the Dream of Development in Ghana, 1952–1966," *Water History* 6 (2014): 341–366.

68. On comparisons between US and Soviet dam building and their effects on the natural environments, see Paul R. Josephson, *Industrialized Nature: Brute Force Technology and the Transformation of the Natural World* (Washington, DC: Shearwater Books, 2002).

69. A. Tursunov, *Torzhestvo Leninskoi idei elektrifikatsii v respublikakh Srednei Azii.* (Dushanbe: Irfon, 1972).

70. TsGART, fond 282, opis 5, delo 5, 19–20.

71. See Peterson, "Technologies of Rule."

72. See Oscar Sanchez-Sibony, *Red Globalization: The Political Economy of the Soviet Union from Stalin to Khrushchev* (Cambridge: Cambridge University Press, 2014).

73. Benjamin Loring, "'Colonizers with Party Cards': Soviet Internal Colonialism in Central Asia, 1917–39," *Kritika* 15, no. 1 (Winter 2014: 77–102; Christian Teichman "Canals, Cotton, and the Limits of De-colonization in Soviet Uzbekistan, 1924–1941," *Central Asian Survey* 26, no. 4 (December 2007): 499–519.

74. Peterson, "Technologies of Rule"; Christian Teichmann, "Wildscapes in Ballyhooland," *Cahiers du monde russe* 57, no. 1 (2016), 221–245.

75. On coalition building and dam construction, see Marc Elie, "Coping with the 'Black Dragon': Mudflow Hazards and the Controversy over the Medeo Dam in Kazakhstan, 1958–66," *Kritika* 14, no. 2 (Spring 2013): 313–342.

76. "Zaklucheniia," RGAE, fond 339, opis 6, delo 3368, 130–131.

77. Flora Roberts, "A Controversial Soviet Dam," *Ab Imperio Quarterly* (forthcoming).

78. Moriz Florin, "Emptying Lakes, Filling Up Seas: Hydroelectric Dams and the Ambivalences of Postwar Development in Soviet Central Asia," *Ab Imperio Quarterly* (forthcoming).

79. The most extensive study of the politics behind big Soviet construction projects, including dams, in this period is Klaus Gestwa, *Die Stalinschen Grossbauten des Kommunismus* (Munich: De Gruyter Oldenbourg, 2010).

80. GARF, fond P-5446, opis 81, delo 4242.

81. Grey Hodnett, "Technology and Social Change in Central Asia: The Politics of Cotton Growing," in *Soviet Politics and Society in the 1970s,* ed. Henry W. Morton and Rudolf Tokes (London: Free Press, 1974), 65–66.

82. Throughout the 1960s, at least, we find Central Asian leaders asking to lower their cotton targets, often with some success. See RGANI, fond 5, opis 45, delo 12, 45–48. See also Rashidov's complaints about the damage caused by chemicals in Aleksey Krasnopivtsev, *Zhazhda spravedlivosti: Politicheskie memuary* (Moscow: Algoritm, 2013), I: 109.

83. Alessandro Iandolo, "The Rise and Fall of the 'Soviet Model of Development' in West Africa, 1957–64," *Cold War History* 12, no. 4 (2012): 683–704.

84. B. V. Iunusov, *Elektroenergetika Tadzhikistana* (Dushanbe: Irfon, 1975), 79.

85. XXI (vneocherednoi) s"ezd KPSS, 1959 (Moscow, 1959), 170.

86. Usmonjon Gafforov, *Tursun Uljaboev* (Dushanbe: Sharqi ozod, 1999), 75–82; "Obodi kardem . . . ," *Adabiët va san'at,* November 1, 1990.

87. Nazorsho Dodhudoev, *Vlast' vremeni* (Almaty: Daĭk press, 2001), 33–35. See also "Norakro u oghoz," *Sadoi mardum,* December 20, 1997; "Dar pai sharaf . . . ," *Adabiët va san'at,* January 31, 1991.

88. Arne Haugen, *The Establishment of National Republics in Soviet Central Asia* (New York: Palgrave Macmillan, 2004); Paul Bergne, *The Birth of Tajikistan: National Identity and the Origins of the Republic* (London: I.B. Tauris, 2007).

89. Mukhitdinov, *Gody, provedennye v Kremle*, 312.

90. Gafforov, *Tursun Uljaboev*, 46; "In qofilai umr ajab miguzorad . . . ," *Sadoi mardum,* October 11, 1995.

91. RGANI, fond 5, opis 35, delo 29, 74–75.

92. June 1963 Plenum of the Central Committee of the Communist Party of Tajikistan, ACPT, fond 3, opis 177, delo 41, 18–19.

93. GARF, fond 5, opis 1, delo 50.

94. Dispatch from the Embassy in the Soviet Union to the Department of State, June 26, 1959, Conversation between N. S. Khrushchev and Governor Harriman, June 23, 1959, *Foreign Relations of the Unites States, 1958–1960. Eastern Europe Region, Soviet Union, Cyprus (1958–1960)*, 278.

95. This was claimed by Uljaboev's daughters, author's interview, Dushanbe, Tajikistan, July 2011.

96. William Taubman, *Khrushchev: The Man and His Era*, (New York: W.W. Norton, 2004), 318–319.

97. Ibid.

98. There was no record of the presidium meeting, but when the plenum began, Suslov and others several times mentioned Mukhitdinov as one of the Presidium members who rejected Molotov, Kaganovich, and Malenkov's attempts to have the issue decided without convening a plenum. Aleksandr Yakovlev et al., eds. *Molotov, Malenkov, Kaganovich 1957: Dokumenty* (Moscow: Demokratiia, 1998), 26–27.

99. Mukhitdinov, *Gody, provedennye v Kremle*, 268–269.

100. Yakovlev et al., *1957*, 259–261.

101. Ibid., 261.

102. Uljaboev's speech at June 1957 plenum, cited in Yakovlev et al., *1957*, 434–435.

103. Ibid. This claim in particular needs to be taken with a grain of salt, but the point here is how Uljaboev chose to defend Khrushchev and his policies in the republics.

104. Gafurov did not speak at the plenum but he did submit a statement in support of Khrushchev. Yakovlev et al., *1957*, 601.

105. See Oleg Khlevniuk, "The Economy of Illusions: The Phenomena of Data Inflation in the Khrushchev Era," in Smith and Ilic, eds., *Khrushchev in the Kremlin*, 171–189.

106. ACPT, fond 3, opis 157, delo 49, 2–3.

107. Ibid., 10.

108. RGANI, fond 5, opis 30, delo 345, 20–27.

109. Sulton Mirzoshoev, *Arzi Dil,* 14–15.

110. ACPT, fond 3, opis 157, delo 49, 20. Halfway through the plenum, Kozlov was called away to take a call from Moscow and returned to tell the assembled delegates that Yuri Gagarin had become the first man to travel to space.

111. ACPT, fond 3, opis 157, delo 49, 105.

112. Ibid. According to Sulton Mirzoshoev, who was head of the republic's Komsomol at the time, Uljaboev's trouble began earlier in the year when he refused to replace Obnosov. Mirzoshoev, *Arzi dil,* 14–15.

113. ACPT fond 3, opis 157, delo 49, 141.

114. Author interview with Uljaboev daughters, Dushanbe, June 2011.

115. ACPT, fond 3, opis 157, delo 49, 7–8.

116. ACPT, fond 3, opis 157, delo 49, 12–13.

117. Khrushchev's note to the Presidium of the CC CPSU in connection with a trip to Turkmenistan, September 29, 1962, cited in *Nikita Sergeevich Khrushchev: Dva tsveta vremeni,* ed. in N. G. Tomilina et al. (Moscow: Demokratiia, 2009), 686–687.

118. Resolution of the CC CPSU on the creation of a Central Asian Bureau of the CC CPSU, cited in Khlevniuk et al., *Regional'naia politika Khrushcheva,* 484–487.

119. Nishanov, *Derev'ia zeleneiut do metelei,* 79–80.

120. Kh.M. Saidmuradov, *Vidnyi uchennyi-ekonomist Sredneii Azii (k 70-letiu so dnia rozhdeniia I.K. Narzikulova* (Dushanbe: Irfon, 1981), 26.

121. Mukhitdinov, *Gody prevedennye v Kremle;* Jeremy Smith, *Red Nations: The Nationalities Experience in and after the USSR* (Cambridge: Cambridge University Press, 2013), 213-215, 219.

122. Nishanov, *Derev'ia zeleneiut do metelei,* 78.

123. Andrei Artizov, ed., *Nikita Khrushchev, 1964: Stenogrammy plenuma TsK KPSS i drugie dokumenty* (Moscow: Demokratiia, 2007), 223.

124. See Gregory J. Massell's discussion of the possible destabilizing effects of Soviet modernization for Central Asia, including the elevation of expectations that the elite have about their own role: Gregory J. Massell, "Modernization and National Policy in Soviet Central Asia," in *The Dynamics of Soviet Politics,* ed. Paul Cocks et al. (Cambridge, MA: Harvard University Press, 1976), 265–290.

125. Artizov, *Nikita Khrushchev,* 201.

CHAPTER 2. AYNI'S CHILDREN, OR MAKING A TAJIK-SOVIET INTELLIGENTSIA

1. See Vladislav Zubok, *Zhivago's Children: The Last Soviet Intelligentsia* (Cambridge, MA: Belknap Press, 2009).

2. Donald Raleigh, *Soviet Baby Boomers: An Oral History of Russia's Cold War Generation.* (Oxford: Oxford University Press, 2012).

3. Raleigh, *Soviet Baby Boomers,* 33.

4. Massell, "Modernization and Nationality Politics."

5. Georgi M. Derluguian, *Bourdieu's Secret Admirer in the Caucasus: A World-System Biography* (University of Chicago Press, 2005), 287.

6. See also Benjamin Tromly, *Making the Soviet Intelligentsia: Universities and Intellectual Life under Stalin and Khrushchev* (Cambridge: Cambridge University Press, 2014), 8–9.

7. Stuart Finkel, *On the Ideological Front: The Russian Intelligentsia and the Soviet Public Sphere* (New Haven: Yale University Press, 2007), 3.

8. On higher education in the early Soviet Union, see Michael David-Fox, *Revolution of the Mind: Higher Learning among the Bolsheviks, 1918–1929* (Ithaca: Cornell University Press, 1997). There was no direct translation of this term in Persian, for example, but in the twentieth century the group of intellectuals who campaigned for major social and political reforms were referred to as *raushanfikr* (roughly, enlightened thinkers.) See Ali Gheissari, *Iranian Intellectuals in the Twentieth Century* (Austin: University of Texas Press, 1997). The term that has become common in Tajik, primarily since perestroika, is *ziyonyon.* In my interviews and conversations, people used the term "intelligentsia" sometimes to indicate the more narrow idea of an intellectual elite somewhat apart from state and society (and carrying the values of *intelegentnost'*) and sometimes in the broader sense meaning an educated professional elite.

9. Roberts, *Old Elites under Communism.*

10. See for example the writer Ikromī's description of being "recruited" for work in Tajikistan in 1930. Ikromī, *On chī az sar guzasht* (Dushanbe: no publisher listed, 2009). For a discussion of how one chose to become a "Tajik" or an "Uzbek," see Gero Fedtke,

"How Bukharans Turned into Uzbeks and Tajiks: Soviet Nationalities Policy in the Light of a Personal Rivalry" in *Patterns of Transformation in and around Uzbekistan*, ed. Paolo Sartori and Tommaso Trevisani (Reggio Emilia: Diabasis, 2007), 9–39.

11. See, for example, Ikromī, *On chīaz sar guzasht*, and the memoirs of Ikromī's son, Jonon Ikromi, *Jalol Ikromi: Neizvestnye stranitsy* (Dushanbe: Sharqi ozod, 2010).

12. Munira Shahidi interview, 2013. Lahūtī's own relationship with local authorities, and Bobojon Gafurov in particular, was difficult. See Kirasirova, "My Enemy's Enemy."

13. See Hursheda Otahonova, *Dil mehokhad, ki gūiamu giram* (Dushanbe: Irfon, 2011), 61–63, 75–76.

14. Hudoīnazar Asozoda, *Dostoni Zindagī* (Dushanbe: Devashtich, 2006), I:31.

15. Asozoda, *Dostoni Zindagī*, I:88–89.

16. See Amir Weiner, *Making Sense of War: The Second World War and the Fate of the Bolshevik Revolution* (Princeton: Princeton University Press, 2001); Elena Zubkova, *Russia After the War: Hopes, Illusions, and Disappointments. 1945–1957* (Armonk, NY: M. E. Sharpe, 1998)

17. Eren Murat Tasar, "Islamically Informed Soviet Patriotism in Postwar Kyrgyzstan," *Cahiers du Monde Russe* 52, no. 2 (2011): 387–404; Moritz Florin, "Becoming Soviet through War: The Kyrgyz and the Great Fatherland War," *Kritika* 17, no. 3 (2016): 495–516; Charles Shaw, "Soldiers' Letters to Inobatxon and O'g'ulxon: Gender and Nationality in the Birth of a Soviet Romantic Culture," *Kritika* 17, no. 3 (2016): 517–552; Flora Roberts, "A Time for Feasting? Autarky in the Tajik Ferghana Valley at War, 1941–45," *Central Asian Survey* (2016), DOI: 10.1080/02634937.2016.1202193.

18. Kamp, *The New Woman in Uzbekistan*.

19. Alex Calvo, "The Second World War in Central Asia," in *Social and Cultural Change in Central Asia: The Soviet Legacy,* ed. Sevket Akyildiz and Richard Carlson (London: Routledge, 2014), 99–110. See also Rebecca Manley, *To the Tashkent Station: Evacuation and Survival in the Soviet Union at War* (Ithaca: Cornell University Press, 2009) and Paul Stronski, *Tashkent: Forging a Soviet City* (Pittsburgh: Pittsburgh University Press, 2010), 72–144.

20. Aslamsho interview, Dushanbe, June 2013.

21. The World War II victory is still celebrated in Tajikistan, and books devoted to the war experience continue to appear periodically. Primarily these are "books of memory," containing the biographies or short reminiscences of veterans, as well as collections of materials published in the Soviet period. For example, Hussein Mirzoev, *Kitobi xotira (shahri Norak)* (Dushanbe: Sharqi Ozod, 2010); O. I. Obidov, ed., *Tojikpisari afsonavi: Zindaginomai Teshaboy Odilov* (Dushanbe: Irfon, 2005).

22. Osimī, *Ёdnomai ustod Osimī*, 41–42.

23. Ikromī, *On chīaz sar guzhast*

24. Haydarov, *Zhizn' v isskustve* (Dushanbe: published by the family, 2001), 59–60.

25. Ibid., 106.

26. I am grateful to his daughter Lola Haydarova for providing this information.

27. Oleg Budnitskii, "The Intelligentsia Meets the Enemy: Educated Soviet Officers in Defeated Germany, 1945," *Kritika* 10, no. 3 (2009): 629–82; Vladislav M. Zubok, *Zhivago's Children: the Last Soviet Intelligentsia* (Cambridge, MA: Belknap Press, 2009).

28. Khodizoda, *Khudoe, hudro bishinosam,* 5–6.

29. Munira Shahidi interview, Dushanbe, 2013.

30. Muhammad Turbati, *Az Tehran to Stalinabad* (Berkeley, CA: Nogtuch, 2000).

31. Shahidi interview.

32. Jura L. interview, Dushanbe, April 2013.

33. Roberts, *Old Elites*.

34. On the elimination of jadids and other early Bolshevik allies in Central Asia, see Khalid, *Making Uzbekistan*; William Fierman, *Language Planning and National Development: The Uzbek Experience* (New York: Mouton de Gruyter, 1991), 243–251; Bergne, *Birth of Tajikistan*, 66–74.

35. See, for example, the discussion of Ayni's relationship with Khodizoda in this chapter. See also Mohammad Osimī's lengthy essay on Ayni's influence in his own life and that of others in his generation. *Ēdnomai ustod Osimī* (Khojand: Nuri ma'rifat, 2005), 8–51.

36. It is not clear if she is referring to a daughter of Jan Gamarnik, who was sentenced to death in 1937.

37. Munira Shahidi interview, 2013.

38. Lewis H. Siegelbaum and Leslie Page Moch, "Transnationalism in One Country? Seeing and Not Seeing Cross-Border Migration within the Soviet Union," *Slavic Review* 75, no. 4 (2016): 970–986.

39. Khodizoda, *Khudoe, hudro bishinosam*, 80.

40. Tromly, *Making the Soviet intelligentsia*, 2.

41. Tim Harper, "The Tools of Transition: Education and Development in Modern Southeast Asian History," in *History, Historians and Development Policy: A Necessary Dialogue*, ed. C.A. Bayle, Vijayendra Rao, Simon Szreter, and Michael Woolcock (Manchester: Manchester University Press, 2011), 194. For the imperial Russian case, consider the goals of the jadids in education versus those of Russian native schools. See Khalid, *Jadidism in Central Asia* and *Making Uzbekistan*; Robert Geraci, *Window on the East: National and Imperial Identities in Late Tsarist Russia* (Ithaca, NY: Cornell University Press, 2001).

42. Artemy M. Kalinovsky and Antonio Giustozzi "The Professional Middle Class in Afghanistan: From Pivot of Development to Political Marginality," *Humanity: An International Journal of Human Rights, Humanitarianism, and Development* 8, no. 2 (2017): 355–378. See also Corinna Unger, "The United States, Decolonization, and the Education of Third World Elites," and Andreas Hilger, "Building a Socialist Elite? Khrushchev's Soviet Union and Elite Formation in India," in *Elites and Decolonization in the Twentieth Century*, ed. Jost Dülffer and Marc Frey (Basingstoke: PalgraveMacmillan, 2011), 241–286.

43. GARF, fond 5446, opis 49, delo 3649.

44. Khodizoda, *Khudoe, hudro bishinosam*, 157.

45. Ibid., 158.

46. Hursheda Otahonova, "Jam' chun homush gardad, doghi mahfil meshavad" in Davronov, *Ēdi ēri mehrubon*, 25–26.

47. Aslamsho interview.

48. Aslamsho interview.

49. Consider this report on a dormitory constructed for students of the preparatory division in 1977: "The dormitory is designed for 660 people, has six floors, and was approved for use in February 1977. At the moment the entire fourth floor is undergoing repairs. Common rooms, the Red corner, and the kitchen are all occupied by residents from the fourth floor. The trash chute and elevator are out of order . . . order and cleanliness are not maintained, the showers are broken and out of order, and there is no lighting in the corridors, toilets and showers. The cafeteria is designed for forty seats and works from two in the afternoon to eleven at night. The students have no opportunity to eat in the morning." GARF, fond 9606, opis 1, delo 8234.

50. See Vadim Volkov, "The Concept of Kul'turnost': Notes on the Stalinist Civilizing Process" in Fitzpatrick, ed., *Stalinism*, 210–230.

51. R. K. Rakhimov, *O proshlom, s gordost'iu, o buduschem s optimizmom* (Dushanbe: NPITsentr, 1997), 8–9.

52. Shukur Sultonov, *Ēddoshtho, fehristi osor, va andeshaho* (Khujand: Khuroson, 2012), 69.

53. Manzar interview.

54. Jura L. interview.

55. Olimjon H. interview, Leninobod, June 2013.

56. Z.Z. Bogumanova, "Pomoshch' bratskikh respublik Tadzhikistanu v podgotovke kadrov vyshchei kvlaifikatsii (1959–1970)," *Izvestiia Akademii Nauk Tadzhikskoi SSR* [*Bulletin of the Academy of Sciences of the Tajik SSR* hereafter *BAST*] 1 (1974), 14; P. V.

Boiarshchikov, "O roli tekhnicheskoi intelligentsia Tadzhikistana v reshenii narodnokho-zaistvennykh zadach semiletki (1959–1965)," *BAST,* 1967, 42.

57. GARF, fond 9606, opis 1, delo 6726, 3–5.

58. Ibid. See also M. G. Buglenko, "Podgotovka i rost chislennosti nauchnykh i nauchno-pedagogicheskikh kadrov," *BAST* 1, 1975, 16–23.

59. GARF, fond 9606, opis 1, delo 3568, 6–7.

60. GARF, fond 9606, opis 1, delo 8234, 1.

61. Bogumanova, "Pomoshch' bratskikh respublik Tadzhikistanu," 16

62. Ibid., 7.

63. GARF, fond 9606, opis 1, delo 8234, 23.

64. For more on Osimī, see Roberts, *Old Elites under Communism.*

65. Jura L. interview; Osimī's influence is also discussed in Naim Iakubov, *Dorogu osilit iduschi* (Dushanbe: no publisher listed, 2004), 71–85.

66. Ibrohim K. interview

67. GARF, fond 9606, opis 1, delo 5667.

68. Ibid.

69. Asozoda, *Dostoni Zindagī,* I:351–354.

70. Hudoĭnazar Asozoda, *Ta'rihi Adabieti Tojik* (Dushanbe: Maorif va Farhang, 2014), 462–463.

71. Abdurashid Samadov interview.

72. Kamoli Sūfiën, *Taqdir: khotira va ëddoshtho* (Dushanbe: Adib, 2011), 26; See also M.K. Gafforova, *Maktabi Man* (Dushanbe: Irfon, 2014), 46–57. Gafforova worked in the Leninobod Komsomol and in the Central Committee Tajikistan's Komsomol during the war and in the immediate postwar years.

73. Shukur Sultonov, *Ëddoshtho, fehristi osor, va andeshakho* (Khujand: Khuroson, 2012), 69.

74. On Central Asians in the Soviet military in this era, see Ellen Jones, *Red Army and Society: A Sociology of the Soviet Military* (Boston: Allen & Unwin, 1985), 180–209.

75. Kamoli Sufiën, *Taqdir* (Dushanbe: Adib, 2011), 35–36.

76. Interviews with Kholmahmad M., Dushanbe, April 2013; Olimjon H., Khojand, June 2013.

77. Interview with Olimjon H., Khojand, June 2013.

78. Bogumanova, "Pomoshch' bratskikh respublik Tadzhikistanu," 15.

79. Khodizoda, *Khudoe, hudro bishinosam,* 196–197.

80. Iakubov, *Dorogu osilit iduschii,* 42.

81. "Kahhor Mahkamov, besedy s pervym prezidentom," *AsiaPlus,* April 18, 2016.

82. Khodizoda, *Khudoe, hudro bishinosam,* 202–203.

83. I. P. Gurshumov and R. L. Kogay, "Podgotovka rabochikh kadrov za predelami Tadzhikistana—metod upravlenkia mobilnost'iu," *BAST,* December 1984, 40–41.

84. Iakubov, *Dorogu osilit iduschii,* 46–47; Rakhimov, *O proshlom s gordost'iu*; Gafforova, *Maktabi man,* 84–94.

85. Sahadeo, "Soviet Blacks,'" 343.

86. Sahadeo, "Soviet 'Blacks,'" 344–45, 358.

87. Khodizoda, *Khudoe va hudro beshinosam,* 227.

88. Interviews with Odinaev family, January 3–4, 2015, New York.

89. TsGART, fond 1505, opis 1, delo 86.

90. RGANI, fond 5, opis 58, delo 3. Since the late perestroika era, and especially Tajiki-stan's civil war, when resentment and competition between regional groups ultimately led to armed conflict, Rasulov has been maligned as someone who entrenched the Lenino-bodi elite at the expense of other regional groups. This charge may be somewhat unfair, as it seems that he did try to fight the pattern, at least early in his tenure as first secretary. ACPT, fond 3, opis 177, delo 41.

91. RGANI, fond 5, opis 35, delo 61, 46.

92. Manzar interview.

93. Ibrohim K. interview.

94. Asozoda, *Dostoni Zindagī*, I;73, 151.

95. Miriam Dobson, *Khrushchev's Cold Summer*; Robert Hornsby, *Protest, Reform and Repression in Khrushchev's Soviet Union* (Cambridge: Cambridge University Press, 2014).

96. See also Florin, "What Is Russia to Us?"

97. Sherali in particular was supported by Tursunzoda, who introduced him and some of the other writers to Russian audiences and protected them from ideological critics. Yusufi Akbarzoda, "Turfa shogirde, ki dar xairat kunad ustodro," in *Risolati shoir va she'r*, 36–53.

98. Salimi Aiubzod, *Tojikon dar Qarni Bistum* (Prague: Post Skriptum Imprimatur, 2002), 212–218. See Zubok, *Zhivago's Children*; Mirzoi Salimpur "Buriniso Berdieva—Kakhramoni Nawruz," Radio Ozodi, March 18, 2011, http://www.ozodi.org/content/article/2341996.html.

99. See Zubok, *Zhivago's Children*; Geoffrey Hosking, *Victims and Rulers*; Yitzhak M. Brudny, *Reinventing Russia Russian Nationalism and the Soviet State, 1953–1991* (Cambridge: Harvard University Press, 2000).

100. ACPT, fond 3, opis 177, delo 41, 15.

CHAPTER 3. DEFINING DEVELOPMENT

1. Marion Fourcade, *Economists and Societies: Discipline and Profession in the United States, Britain, & France: 1890s to 1990s* (Princeton: Princeton University Press, 2009); Mitchell, *Rule of Experts.*

2. See, for example Sarah Babb, *Managing Mexico: Economists from Nationalism to Neoliberalism* (Princeton: Princeton University Press, 2001); Alden Young, "African Bureaucrats and the Exhaustion of the Developmental State: Lessons from the Pages of the Sudanese Economist," *Humanity* 8, no. 1 (2017): 49–75. See also George Rosen, *Western Economists and Eastern Societies : Agents of Change in South Asia, 1950–1970* (Baltimore: Johns Hopkins University Press, 1985).

3. Thus the Nobel Prize winning economist Arthur Lewis, originally from Saint Lucia, worked as an adviser in Ghana, while the Argentinean Raul Prebisch became known for his work on the Economic Commission for Latin America and later as the secretary general of the United Nations Conference on Trade and Development. See Robert L. Tignor, *W. Arthurs Lewis and the Birth of Development Economics* (Princeton: Princeton University Press, 2005); Edgar J. Dosman, *The Life and Times of Raul Prebisch, 1901–1986* (Montreal: McGill-Queen's University Press, 2008).

4. See James R. Harris, *The Great Urals: Regionalism and the Evolution of the Soviet System* (Ithaca: Cornell University Press, 1999); Jan Ake Dellebrant, *The Soviet Regional Dilemma* (Armonk, NY: M. E. Sharpe, 1986); I. S. Koropeckyj, "Equalization of Regional Development in Socialist Countries: An Empirical Study," *Economic Development and Cultural Change* 21, no. 1 (October 1972): 68–86; Jonathan R. Schiffer, "Interpretation of the Issue of Inequality in Soviet Regional Disputes," 508–532; Leslie Dienes, "Investment Priorities in Soviet Regions," *Annals of the Association of American Geographers* 62, no. 3 (September 1972): 437–454; Donna Lynn Bahry and Carol Nechemias, "Half-Full or Half-Empty? The Debate over Soviet Regional Equality," *Slavic Review* 3 (1981): 366–371.

5. Nataliya Kibita, *Soviet Economic Management under Khrushchev: The Sovnarkhoz Reform* (London: Routledge, 2013); Peter Rutland, *The Politics of Economic Stagnation in the Soviet Union: The Role of Local Party Organs in Economic Management* (Cambridge: Cambridge University Press, 1992).

6. RGANI, fond 5, opis 35, delo 115, 11–16.

7. Archive of the Russian Academy of Sciences (ARAN), fond 591, opis 1, delo 1073, pp. 6–10; ARAN, fond 1877, opis 8, delo 394, 45.

8. Ana Maria Bianchi, "Visiting Economists through Hirschman's Eyes," *European Journal of the History of Economic Thought* 18, no. 2 (2011): 217–242.

9. H. M. Saidmuradov, *Vidnyi uchennyi-ekonomist Srednii Azii (k 70-letiiu so dnia rozhdenia I. K. Narzikulova)* (Dushanbe: Donish, 1981).

10. ARAN, fond 591, opis 1, delo 1073, 81.

11. Nekrasov's obituary in the *Bulletin of the USSR Academy of Sciences*, no. 7 (1984), 101.

12. RGAE F. 399 op.3 d.420.

13. Bianchi, "Visiting Economists through Hirschman's Eyes."

14. N. Batova, "Novoe v razmeschenii proizvodstvennykh sil," *Voprosy Ekonomiki,* no. 11 (1967), 158–160.

15. Saidmuradov, *Vidnyii uchennyi-ekonomist*, 19.

16. I. K. Narzikulov, ed., *Narodno-khoziastvennoe znachenie Nurekskoi GES* (Dushanbe: Irfon, 1964).

17. Some of his works were collected posthumously into a book on the Southern Tajikistan Territorial Production Complex. See I. K. Narzikulov, *Problemy razvitiia proizvodstevnnykh sil Tadzhikistana i formirovanie Iuzhno-Tadzhikskogo Territorial'no-Proizvodstvennogo Kompleksa* (Dushanbe: Donish, 1975).

18. I. Narzikulov and Kirill Stanukevich, *Atlas Tadzhikskoi SSR* (Moscow: Main Directorate of Geography of the USSR Council of Ministers, 1968).

19. I. Narzikulov, *V. I. Lenin i razvitie proizvodstvennykh sil Sovetskogo Gosudarstva* (Dushanbe: Donish, 1969).

20. Author's interview with Rashid Rakhimov, Dushanbe, May 2015. Karimov was the only one of the Tajik economists to write a memoir: see R. K. Rakhimov, *O proshlom s gordost'iu, o budushchem s optimizmom* (Dushanbe: NPITsenter, 1997).

21. Author's interview with Nazarali Khonaliev, Dushanbe, March 2013.

22. For a useful discussion on the professional status of economists within the nation state, see Babb, *Managing Mexico,* 24–47.

23. One criticism from colleagues at the Academy of Sciences in Moscow was that Tajik economists were so drawn into planning debates they had little time for more theoretical research. ARAN, fond 1731, opis 1, delo 56, 81.

24. Just among the scholars discussed so far, all of whom were in favor of developing Southern Tajikistan, Rakhimov was from Khujand, Khonaliev was a Pamiri, and Narzikulov was originally from Samarkand.

25. Robert C. Allen, *Farm to Factory: A Reinterpretation of the Soviet Industrial Revolution* (Princeton: Princeton University Press, 2003), 47–60.

26. See Mathew J. Connelly, *Fatal Misconception: The Struggle to Control World Population* (Cambridge, MA: Harvard University Press, 2008).

27. Arthur Lewis, "Economic Development with Unlimited Supplies of Labor," *Manchester School of Economic and Social Studies* 22 (1954): 139–191; Gustav Ranis, "Arthur Lewis' Contribution to Development Thinking and Policy," Discussion Paper no. 81, Economic Grow Center, Yale University, August 2004, http://www.econ.yale.edu/growth_pdf/cdp891.pdf.

28. Gerald M. Meier and Dudley Seers, *Pioneers in Development* (New York: Oxford University Press, 1984), 178, 186.

29. See Cynthia Weber and Ann Goodman, "The Demographic Policy Debate in the USSR," *Population and Development Review* 7, no. 2 (June 1981): 279–295; David M. Heer, "Three Issues in Soviet Population Policy," *Population and Development Review* 3, no. 3 (September 1977): 229–252;

30. A view replicated by contemporary Western observers. See Delenbrant, *The Soviet Regional Dilemma*, 13.

31. "Energy and Questions of the Central Asian Economy," in Narzikulov, *Narodno-khoziaistvennoe znachenie Nurekskoi GES*, 16–17.

32. See Sugata Bose, "Instruments and Idioms of Colonial and National Development: India's Historical Experience in Comparative Perspective," in Cooper and Packard, *International Development and the Social Sciences*, 45–63; Artemy M. Kalinovsky and Vanni Pettina, "From Countryside to Factory: Industrialisation, Social Mobility, and Neoliberalism in Soviet Central Asia and Mexico" *Journal für Entwicklungspolitik*, 33, no. 3 (2017), 91-117.

33. See Martha Finnemore, "Redefining Development at the World Bank," in Cooper and Packard, *International Development and the Social Sciences*, 203–227.

34. Michele Alacevich, "Visualizing Uncertainties, or How Albert Hirschman and the World Bank Disagreed on Project Appraisal and What This Says about the End of 'High Development Theory.'" *Journal of the History of Economic Thought* 36, no. 2 (2014): 141.

35. See, for example, Yu. I. Ishakov, Sh. M. Solomonov, and B. V. Iunusov, *K probleme vyravnivaniia urovnei ekonomicheskogo razvitia Soiuznykh respublik na primere Tadzhikskoi SSR* (Dushanbe: V. I. Lenin State University of Tajikistan, 1968) and especially B. V. Iunusov, "Rol' energeticheskogo faktora v vyravnivanii ekonomicheskogo urovnia soiuznykh respublik," in ibid., 41–54; B. G. Schiy, "Vyravnivanie urovnii ekonomicheskogo razvitia Tadzhikskoi SSR s drugimi respublikami strany," 1967–1968, research project summarized in GARF, fond 9606, opis 1, delo 3456.

36. B. G. Schiy, "O zakonnomernosti vyravnivaniia urovnei ekonomicheskogo razvitia natsional'nikh respublik," in *Sbornik trudov kafedry politekonomii*, ed. R. Yusufbekov (Dushanbe: V. I. Lenin State University of Tajikistan, 1970), 51–52. The issue of regional equality was also the focus of a similar volume published by the faculty in 1968.

37. See, for example, Sara Lorenzini, "Comecon and the South in the Years of Détente: A Study on East-South Economic Relations," *European Review of History: Revue européenne d'histoire* 21, no. 2 (2014): 183–199.

38. Ia. T. Bronshtein and R. K. Rakhimov, "Nekotorye voprosy razvitia ekonomiki Tadzhikistana," *BAST,* no. 4 (1972): 3–12. The bulletin was circulated within other Soviet institutions and would have been available to economists and planners throughout the union. Although we cannot know how widely any particular article was read, the points raised in these publications were sometimes popularized in more widely read newspapers. The same points outlined here found their way into the demands and claims of Tajik planners and were debated often in Moscow. Regardless of how widely the journals actual readership may have been, it serves as a useful guide to how the priorities and thought of social scientists evolved between the 1950s and 1991.

39. Bronshtein and Rakhimov, "Nekotorye voprosy razvitia ekonomiki Tadzhikistana," 8.

40. They also sought to preempt any criticism that in a period of intensive growth the Soviet Union should not be focusing on areas, like Tajikistan, where extensive growth was required, by arguing that these could proceed simultaneously. Ibid., 6–7.

41. Ibid.

42. As Nancy Lubin noted in her survey of Uzbek labor and education debates, the introduction of PTUs largely replicated the urban/rural and Uzbek/European divide within the republic—Uzbeks overwhelmingly attended those PTUs located in the countryside and focused on agriculture, while the urban PTUs preparing cadres for the industrial workforce primarily attracted Europeans. Lubin, *Labour and Nationality,* 120–130.

43. ACPT, fond 3, opis 259, delo 162.

44. AAOS, fond 1731, opis 1, delo 96,

280   NOTES TO PAGES 78–83

45. Ibid., 57–58.
46. Boris Firsov, *Istoriia sovetskoi sotsiologii, 1950–1980-e gody* (St. Petersburg: European University of St. Petersburg, 2012), 112–118. See also Elizabeth A. Weinberg, *Sociology in the Soviet Union and Beyond: Social Enquiry and Social Change* (London: Ashgate, 2004).
47. Amsler, *Politics of Knowledge*, 51–60.
48. "Regarding the condition of sociological research within the republic," CC CPT resolution, September 6, 1973, ACPT, fond 3, opis 268, delo 22.
49. R. Galetskaia, "Demograficheskaia situatsiia i trudovye resursy SSSR," *Voprosy Ekonomiki,* 1973, no. 10, 155-159. Fifty thousand families were surveyed.
50. Similar studies had already begun appearing elsewhere in the USSR. See, for example, V. I. Staroverov, *Gorod ili derevniia* (Moscow: Politizdat, 1972).
51. Sh. Shoismatullaev, "Professional'noe opredelenie molodezhi v Tadzhikskoi SSR," *BAST,* no. 1 (1976): 32–38. Even among those who did only two-thirds of young men (18.3% of all graduates) and one-half of young women (8.5%) follow through with plans to go to technical college and even fewer attended PTUs.
52. I am grateful to Professor Shoismatullaev for providing me with information regarding the history of sociology in Tajikistan during our meeting in February 2015.
53. Khonaliev interview; Juraev interview.
54. Russian State Archive of the Economy (RGAE), fond 399, opis 1, delo 1771, 316.
55. Arthur Lewis, "Economic Development with Unlimited Supplies of Labour," *Manchester School of Economic and Social Studies* 22 (1954): 139–191.
56. Clark Kerr, J. Dunlop, F. Harbison, and C. Myers, *Industrialism and Industrial Man* (Cambridge, MA: Harvard University Press, 1960), 79. The exception was cases where extended families pulled capital for investment.
57. I. K. Narzikulov and I. M. Kleandarov, "O perspektivakh razvitia sel'skogo khoziastva gornykh raionakh Tadzhikistana," *BAST,* no. 4 (1972): 27–32.
58. A. Majidov, "Razmeshchenie naselenie i ispol'zovnia trudovykh resursov," *BAST,* no. 4 (1972): 72–76. See also Nazarali Khonaliev, "Razmeshchenie promyshlennosti i problemy effektivnogo ispol′zovaniia trudovykh resursov Tadzhikskoi SSR" (PhD diss., Academy of Sciences of the Kazakh SSR, 1976).
59. Ester Boserup, *Woman's Role in Economic Development* (New York: St. Martin's Press, 1970).
60. Boserup, *Woman's Role in Economic Development,* 106–118.
61. Escobar, *Encountering Development,* 183. See also Irene Tinker, Michile Bo Bramsen, and Mara Buvinic, *Women and World Development* (New York: Praeger, 1976).
62. R. A. Ubaidullaeva, *Zhenskii trud v kolkhozakh Uzbekistana* (Tashkent: Institute of Economics, 1964); see also R. A. Ubaidullaeva, ed., *Sotsial'no-ekonomicheskie problemy ispol'zovaniia zhenskogo truda v Uzbekskoi SSR* (Tashkent: Fan, 1980).
63. Frederick A. Leedy, "Producers' Cooperatives in the Soviet Union," *Monthly Labor Review,* no. 80 (1957): 1064–1068.
64. Sergey Abashin, in his detailed study of Oshoba, an Uzbek-speaking northern village in northern Tajikistan, demonstrated that collectivization initially had little influence on the daily life of the villagers, who put in minimal work for the collective farm and otherwise continued their usual economic activities. Abashin, *Sovetskii kishlak.* My own interviews with residents of Dushanbe as well as families from the vicinity of the Nurek Dam similarly revealed that various forms of domestic production played an important role in family income in the postwar decades.
65. RGASPI, fond 17, opis 89, delo 649.
66. See, for example, L. Chizhova and L. Lagutin, "Ekonomisty o zhenskom trude," *Voprosy ekonomiki* no. 2, (1967): 153–155. See also *Sotsial-no-ekonomicheskie problemy isspolzovanie zhenskogo truda v Uzbekskoi SSR,* ed. R. A. Ubaidullaeva (Tashkent: Fan,

1980), 114–129; Joel C. Moses, "The Politics of Female Labor in the Soviet Union," (Ithaca, NY: Cornell University Center for International Studies, 1978).

67. RGAE, fond. 399, opis 1, delo 1989, 43

68. Author's interview with Rashid Rakhimov, Dushanbe, May 2015.

69. Meeting of the research board of the Council for the Study of Productive Forces, September 10, 1981, 43.

70. Janice Peterson and Margaret Lewis, *The Elgar Companion to Feminist Economics* (Cheltenham, UK: Edward Elgar, 1999), 95–107.

71. Mahkamov, who served as the chairman of the Tajik Gosplan in the 1960s and 1970s, described this ritual to journalist Salomiddin Mirzorahmat: Salomiddin Mirzorahmat, "Mahkamov: ia toropilsia, no ne uspel," *Asia Plus,* January 31, 2013 http://news.tj/ru/news/makhkamov-ya-toropilsya-no-ne-uspel.

72. V. Kornaukhov, who worked in the Central Committee in the 1970s and 1980s, told me that while Uzbek first secretary Sharof Rashidov, a candidate Politburo member and a close friend of Brezhnev, could go "straight to the top" when he wanted to lobby for something, while the Tajiks usually had to work their way through formal structures. Author's interview, Moscow, February 2013.

73. ACPT, fond 3, opis 185, delo 49.

74. Ibid., 31, 33.

75. It also tied the issue of industrialization to living standards, although in a limited way, by using the example of Gorno-Badakshan Autonomous Oblast—with its limited agricultural potential, the only solution for further development was industrialization. Ibid, 32.

76. Narzikulov, *Problemy razvitiia proizvodstvennykh sil Tadzhikistana,* 83. The term itself appears to have originated at a meeting of the Central Asia Committee in Dushanbe in 1963, although it was called the "Southern Tajikistan National Economic Complex."

77. As Dellenbrant notes, "a major aim in establishing TPCs was to enable economic activity to proceed without the administrative obstructions experienced under the sectoral and ministerial systems." See Dellenbrant, *Soviet Regional Dilemma,* 79–81. For a broader history, see Richard E. Lonsdale, "The Soviet Concept of the Territorial Production Complex," *Slavic Review* 24, no. 3 (1965): 466–478. A key theorist of the concept was N. N. Kolosovskij. See N. N. Kolosovskij, "The Territorial-Production Combination (Complex) in Soviet Economic Geography," in *Geographical Perspective in the Soviet Union: A Selection of Readings,* ed. George J. Demko and Roland J. Fuchs (Columbus: Ohio State University Press, 1974), 105–138. For further development of the concept, and debates about what factors were to be considered in the shaping of a complex, see Ia. G. Feygin, et al., *Osobennosti i faktory razmeshchenia otraslei narodnogo khoziastva SSSR,* (Moscow: Izdatel'stvo Akademii Nauk SSSR, 1960).

78. GARF, fond 5446, opis 101, delo 574.

79. Usmonjon Gafforov, *Abdulakhad Kakhorov* (Dushanbe: Adib, 2009), 65–68.

80. At the very least, there is no obvious reason for Mahkamov to have lied about this, considering that in retrospect that construction of the plant led to environmental problems and was of questionable benefit to the Tajiks, issues that had exploded during the late perestroika period and become a source of opposition to the communist party.

81. This would be consistent with Narzikulov's writings, which called for the simultaneous development of giants like the aluminum plant as well as a more diversified range of industrial plants that could serve local and national needs and while drawing on local labor.

82. RGAE, fond 99, opis 2, delo 341.

83. GARF, fond 5446, opis 108, delo 291. Forwarded to N. K. Baibakov, chairman of Gosplan, on September 30, 1974 with the note "Review in conjunction with the plan for 1976–1980," A. Kosygin.

84. ACPT, fond 3, opis 347, delo 19, 4.

85. Ibid. Between 1978 and 1979 alone the number of unskilled workers of local nationality declined from 71.4 percent to 57.8 percent, while the number of those doing more complicated tasks involving machinery rose from 26.8 percent to 43.9 percent.

CHAPTER 4. PLANS, GIFTS, AND OBLIGATIONS

1. Sūfiën, *Taqdir,* 26–27.

2. M. Faizulloev, *Field Notebook Tajikistan, Norak 1974,* no. 5, http://www.asia-europe.uni-heidelberg.de/en/research/heidelberg-research-architecture/projects/the-m-faizulloev-collection/field-notebooks.html, 27–28.

3. In some of the earlier planning documents it is referred to as "a dam at Tutkaul," i.e., the village that would eventually be submerged at the bottom of the dam reservoir.

4. See, for example, Mitchell, *Rule of Experts*; Ramachandra Guha, *India after Gandhi: The History of the World's Largest Democracy* (New York: HarperCollins, 2007), 209–232. For similar arguments about the Rogun Dam, see Filippo Menga, "Building a Nation through a Dam: The Case of Rogun in Tajikistan," *Nationalities Papers* 43, no. 3 (2015): 479–494; Mohira Suyarkulova, "Between National Idea and International Conflict: The Roghun HHP as an Anti-Colonial Endeavor, Body of the Nation, and National Wealth," *Water History* 6 (2014): 367–383.

5. Iusuf Akobirov, *Nurek,* trans. Olga Markova (Moscow: Sovetskii pisatel', 1980), 13–14.

6. L. A. Korobova, *Proshchai Tutkaul* (Dushanbe: Irfon, 1968).

7. Grant, *The Captive and the Gift,* 157.

8. Albert O. Hirschman, "The Principle of the Hiding Hand," *National Affairs,* no. 6 (1967): 10–23.

9. Michele Alacevic, "Visualising Uncertainties, or How Albert Hirschman and the World Bank Disagreed on Project Appraisal," *Journal of the History of Economic Thought* 36, no. 2 (June 2014): 151. The World Bank was unhappy with Hirschman's conclusions and largely ignored them—his emphasis on uncertainty did not sit well with the bank's culture.

10. Ira Katznelson, *Fear Itself: The New Deal and the Origins of Our Time* (New York: W. W. Norton, 2013), 254–255. See also Kiran Klaus Patel, *The New Deal: A Global History* (Princeton: Princeton University Press, 2016), 97–103; Erwin C. Hargrove, *Prisoners of Myth: The Leadership of the Tennessee Valley Authority, 1993–1990* (Princeton: Princeton University press, 1994), 19–41.

11. Quoted in Ekbladh, "Mr. TVA," 352.

12. Katznelson, *Fear Itself,* 254–255. See also Nancy L. Grant, *The TVA and Black Americans: Planning for the Status Quo* (Philadelphia: Temple University Press, 1990).

13. Christian Teichmann, "Wildscapes in Ballyhooland," *Cahiers du monde russe* 57, no. 1 (2016): 223.

14. Daniel Klingensmith, *One Valley and a Thousand: Dams, Nationalism, and Development* (New Delhi: Oxford University Press, 2007); Hargrove, *Prisoners of Myth.*

15. Paul S. Jones, *Afghanistan Venture: Discovering the Afghan People—The Life, Contacts and Adventures of an American Civil Engineer during His Two Year Sojourn in the Kingdom of Afghanistan* (San Antonio, TX: Naylor Company, 1956), 112.

16. Cullather, "Damming Afghanistan," 523.

17. US Ambassador William Dreyfus to Secretary of State, September 19, 1949, *Foreign Relations of the United States 1949: The Near East, South Asia, and Africa, 1778,* vol. 6 (1949).

18. Çullather, "Damming Afghanistan," 527.

19. Memorandum of Discussion of the 228th Meeting of the National Security Council, December 9, 1954, *Foreign Relations of the United States, 1952–1954: Africa and South Asia, vol. 11,* pt. 2 (1952–1954), 1150.

20. Cullather, "Damming Afghanistan."

21. Corinna Unger, "Toward Global Equilibrium: American Foundations and Indian Modernization, 1950s to 1970s," *Journal of Global History* 6, no. 1, (2011): 121–142.

22. Kalizhniuk is touchingly fictionalized as Anton Grigorevich Karpov in Akobirov, *Nurek.*

23. Author's interview with Nikolai Savchenkov, Moscow, May 2014.

24. TsGART, fond 1501, opis 1, delo 179, 20.

25. Ibid., 21. Kalizhniuk would not live to see his project completed. He died of natural causes in 1962; at that point his work was continued by another experienced engineer, Konstantin Sevenard. Sevenard was joined by his son, Yuri (b. 1935), who would work at Nurek until 1980, leaving only for a three-year stint at the Aswan Dam in Egypt. Yuri would take over as head of construction in 1969.

26. RGAE, fond 339, opis 6, delo 3372.

27. RGAE, fond 339, opis 6, delo 3372, 118–139.

28. RGAE, fond 339, opis 6, delo 3373, 324–340.

29. Gorbachev, *Plotina*; "Iunomu gorodu dostoinyi oblik," *Norak,* May 17, 1968; "Plany i fakty," *Norak,* September 19, 1968; Vladislav Ianelis, "Goriachii polius Nureka," *Smena,* May 1981, 2.

30. On planning and negotiation under socialism, see Katherine Verdery, *What Was Socialism and What Comes Next* (Princeton: Princeton University Press, 1996); Michael Ellman, *Socialist Planning,* 3rd ed. (Cambridge: Cambridge University Press, 2014); Peter Rutland, *The Politics of Economic Stagnation in the Soviet Union: The Role of Local Party Organs in Economic Management* (Cambridge: Cambridge University Press, 1992); Jerry Hough, *The Soviet Prefects: The Local Party Organs in Industrial Decision-making* (Cambridge, MA: Harvard University Press, 1969).

31. See Kalizhniuk's letters from 1962 in RGAE, fond 9572, opis 1, delo 1930, 2–3; RGAE, fond 9572, opis 1, delo 1928, esp. 140–141; and RGAE, fond 7964, opis 15, delo 4629, 115, which show that NurekGesStroy ended up taking over many of the drafting and planning functions. Kalizhniuk was simultaneously fighting against what he saw as incompetent management on the part of the directorate of the whole project. See ibid., 149–157.

32. Hirschman, "Hiding Hand," 11.

33. Interviews. This is also evident in the yearly reports cited throughout this chapter, which note both the "arrhythmic" nature of work caused by the late arrival of key materials as well as waste of materials that do arrive.

34. See Kalinovsky, "Tractors, Power Lines, and the Welfare State: The Contradictions of Soviet Development in Post-World War II Tajikistan," *Asiatische Studien* 69, no. 3 (2015): 563–592, and chapter 7 of this book.

35. Interviews; wastefulness with regard to materials is often mentioned in the yearly reports.

36. On transport, see Patryk Reid, "Managing Nature, Constructing the State."

37. RGAE, fond 7964, opis 15, d 957, annual report for 1968.

38. Interview with Abdullaev, who was in charge of provisioning for the city. On Moscow provisioning see Madeleine Reeves, *Border Work: Spatial Lives of the State in Rural Central Asia* (Ithaca, NY: Cornell University Press, 2014), 111–119; Till Mostowlansky, *Azan on the Moon: Entangling Modernity along Tajikistan's Pamir Highway* (Pittsburgh: University of Pittsburgh Press, 2017), 42.

39. ACPT, fond 3, opis 264, delo 201, 82.

40. ACPT, fond 3, opis 264, delo 201, 81–82.

41. ACPT, fond 56, opis 7, delo 13, 20.

42. Ibid., 21.

43. Z. Shokirov, "Ba sokhtmon beshtar kadrhoi mahalli zarurand," *Norak,* March 14, 1969.

44. Protocol of the 2nd Plenum of the Nurek City Committee (Gorkom) of the Communist Party of Tajikistan, July 20, 1966, 21.

45. TsGART, fond 378, opis 1, delo 55.

46. Ibid.

47. In itself this is a major difference from how international development and industrial projects were run, both then and now—it is usually taken for granted that expatriate workers will earn more than locals, even if they are performing the same kind of work. See, for example, Robert Vitalis, *America's Kingdom: Mythmaking on the Saudi Oil Frontier* (Stanford, CA: Stanford University Press, 1996); Isaacman and Isaacman, *Dams, Displacement, and the Delusion of Development,* 73–89.

48. See, for example, RGAE, fond 7964, opis 15, delo 5801 and 5804. Bonuses were often used for labor retention in other construction projects, of course. See, for example, the Hungry Steppe case, in Olbertreis, *Imperial Desert Dreams.*

49. Annual audits conducted by officials from Moscow show a consistent pattern of "bonuses" paid out to workers at all levels, as well as lax attitude to absenteeism. Despite chiding from central ministries, the pattern does not seem to change. These figures do not tell us if Central Asian workers were rewarded as regularly as European ones, but the oral histories I conducted suggest that both groups benefited from the system. RGAE, fond 7964, opis 16, delo 5933.

50. Ibid., 7.

51. The condition of schools within the villages around Nurek was increasingly discussed in party meetings from the late 1960s. The director of a school in Kibil also related how Sevenard's support had been crucial for getting a new school built in the early 1970s.

52. "Sila druzhby," *Norak*, November 16, 1972. For more on Sharipov, see chapter 6.

53. As one official proclaimed at a party meeting in 1974: "Labor collectives play an enormous role in internationalist education, where in the production process relationships are formed that are based on strict [mutual] demands, mutual aid, and paternal concern. It is in such collectives, where a healthy moral-psychological climate has been created, that the formation and assertion of a person as an individual (*lichnost'*), a citizen, and worker takes place." "Vyshe znamia internatsionalizma," *Norak,* May 24, 1974.

54. Marat Ianovich Khakel, *Unesennoe vetrom*, ch. 19.

55. Khakel, also Falaleev interview.

56. This was particularly noticeable when I talked to the engineer Nikolai Savchenkov.

57. RGASPI, fond M-1, opis 35, delo 494.

58. ACPT, fond 3, opis 300, delo 325, 33–34.

59. Many works have addressed the issue of internationalism on large construction sites in the USSR, usually noting the gap between promise of equality and reality of ethnic tension and discrimination. See, for example, Mathew Payne, *Stalin's Railroad: Turksib and the Building of Socialism* (Pittsburgh: University of Pittsburgh Press, 2001). Even more stark in this regard is the comparison offered in Christopher Ward, *Brezhnev's Folly: The Building of BAM and Late Soviet Socialism* (Pittsburgh: University of Pittsburgh Press, 2009).

60. Author's interview, July 2013.

61. GARF, fond P-5446, opis 136, delo 458.

62. On dam displacement in a colonial context, see Isaacson and Isaacson, *Dams, Displacement and the Delusion of Development,* 95–121.

63. Letter from the committee on use and preservation of water resources to Khrushchev, (undated, but between September 1961 and May 1962), RGANI, fond 5, opis 45, delo 302, 37. See also Marshall I. Goldman, *The Spoils of Progress: Environmental Pollution in the Soviet Union* (Cambridge, MA: MIT Press, 1972), 77–120.

64. Ibid., 35, 43–44.

65. RGANI, fond 5, opis 45, delo 403, 12–15.

66. TsGART, fond 27, opis 15, delo 3, 3.

67. TsGART, fond 27, opis 15, delo 8, 332–358.

68. TsGART, fond 27, opis 15, delo 1, 38.

69. TsGART, fond 27, opis 15, delo 3, 4.

70. Ibid., p. 7–8.

71. TsGART, fond 27, opis 15, delo 8.

72. Goldman, *Spoils of Progress,* 114–115.

73. TsGART, fond 27, opis 15, delo 8, 20–23.

74. Ibid., 111–112. On farm managers expanding land on their own initiative, see also Abashin, *Sovetskii kishlak.*

75. TsGART, fond 27, opis 15, delo 1, 85.

76. Ibid., 86, 89.

77. TsGART, fond 27, opis 15, delo 1, 106.

78. TsGART, fond 27, opis 15, delo 1, 112.

79. Unpublished memoir by Mamlakat, a former brigade leader on a farm near Ordzhonikidzeabad, provided to the author. (This is not the individual's real name.) Mamlakat writes this in the context of her frustration in the late 1970s and early 1980s with officials who were great at sloganeering and confident in their assessments but did not understand the actual situation on the farm.

80. RGAE, fond 399, opis 1, delo 168, 24, 35–36.

81. TsGART, fond 27, opis 15, delo 1, 86. See also Olbertreis, *Imperial Desert Dreams.*

CHAPTER 5. NUREK, "A CITY YOU CAN WRITE ABOUT"

1. TsGART, fond 1501, opis 1, delo 179, 15.

2. Paul R. Josephson, *The Conquest of the Russian Arctic* (Cambridge, MA: Harvard University Press, 2014), 240.

3. As Mark B. Smith notes, "Local city planning was the result not of Olympian professional logic, but of intra-bureaucratic struggles and technical doubts. It was modulated by popular pressures, stubborn city identities and the persistence of urban chaos. The state relied on citizens to exercise their individual initiative to get things done." Mark B. Smith, "Faded Red Paradise," 598.

4. R. Antony French, *Plans, Pragmatism and People: The Legacy of Soviet Planning for Today's Cities* (London: UCL Press, 1995), 36–37.

5. Peter Hall, *Cities of the Future: An Intellectual History of Urban Planning and Design in the Twentieth Century* (Oxford: Blackwell, 2002).

6. French, *Plans, Pragmatism, and People,* 37–38.

7. Stephen Kotkin, *Magnetic Mountain: Stalinism as Civilization* (Berkeley: University of California Press, 1995).

8. N. A. Miliutin, *Sotsgorod: The Problem of Building Socialist Cities,* trans. Arthur Sprage (Cambridge: MIT Press, 1974), 20.

9. Some of them would come to Nurek to start their lives anew, but that topic is beyond the scope of this chapter.

10. Mark B. Smith, *Property of Communists: The Urban Housing Program from Stalin to Khrushchev* (DeKalb: Northern Illinois University Press, 2010), 8. On the housing

program, see also Stephen Harris, *Communism on Tomorrow Street* (Washington, DC: Woodrow Wilson Center Press, 2013).

11. French, *Plans, Pragmatism, and People,* 69.

12. RGASPI, fond M-1, opis 8, delo 1069.

13. Alan Barenberg, *Gulag Town, Company Town: Forced Labor and Its Legacy in Vorkuta* (New Haven: Yale University Press, 2013); Kate Brown, *Plutopia: Nuclear Families, Atomic Cities, and the Great Soviet and American Plutonium Disasters* (Oxford: Oxford University Press, 2013).

14. Kate Brown, "Gridded Lives: Why Kazakhstan and Montana Are Nearly the Same Place," *American Historical Review* (February 2001): 46–47; Lewis Siegelbaum, "Modernity Unbound: The New Soviet City of the Sixties," in *The Socialist Sixties: Crossing Borders in the Second World,* ed. Anne E. Gorsuch and Diane Koenker (Bloomington: Indiana University Press, 2013), 66–83; Esther Maier, "On the Streets of a Truck-Building City: Naberezhnye Chelny in the Brezhnev Era," in *The Socialist Car: Automobility in the Eastern Block,* ed. Lewis Siegelbaum (Ithaca: Cornell University Press, 2011), 105–122.

15. Stephen Collier, *Neoliberalism, Social Modernity, Biopolitics* (Princeton: Princeton University Press, 2011); Smith, "Faded Red Paradise."

16. See Katherine Lebow, *Unfinished Utopia: Nowa Huta, Stalinismm, and Polish Society, 1949–56* (Ithaca: Cornell University Press, 2014). On Stalinist city planning, see also Heather D. Dehaan, *Stalinist City Planning: Professionals, Performance, and Power* (Toronto: University of Toronto Press, 2014).

17. An MKA pamphlet promised "Every effort will be made to furnish our employees American standard camp accommodations, including water-proof quarters, comfortable furnishings and American food prepared under the direction of American cooks," as well as recreational facilities, a commissary, and access to health care provided by an American doctor. Jones, *Afghanistan Venture,* 9.

18. Robert Vitalis, *America's Kingdom: Mythmaking on the Saudi Oil Frontier* (Stanford: Stanford University Press, 2006).

19. See Elidor Mehilli, "The Socialist Design: Urban Dilemmas in Post-War Europe and the Soviet Union," *Kritika* 13, no. 3 (2012): 635–665; Lukasz Stanek, "Architects from Socialist Countries in Ghana (1957–1967): Modern Architecture and Mondialisation," *Society of Architectural Historians Journal* 74, no. 4 (2015): 416–442; Lukaz L. Stanek, "Mobilities of Architecture in the Late Cold War: From Socialist Poland to Kuwait, and Back," *International Journal of Islamic Architecture* 4, no. 2 (2015): 365–398; Stephan F. Miescher, "Building the City of the Future: Visions and Experiences of Modernity in Ghana's Akosombo Township," *Journal of African History* 53, no. 3 (2012): 367–390.

20. On Tashkent, see Paul Stronski, *Tashkent: Forging a Soviet City, 1930–1966* (Pittsburgh: Pittsburgh University Press, 2010). Stronski sees Soviet planners as the main protagonists in the transformation of Tashkent. In fact, Nuritdin Mukhitdinov, then first secretary of the Uzbek Communist Party, writes in his memoirs that it was Uzbek party cadres in the 1950s who complained about the "old" Uzbek city falling behind the "new" Russian one in terms of modern buildings and amenities. Nuritdin Mukhitdinov, *Gody provedennye v Kremle,* 245. On rebuilding Tashkent after the 1966 earthquake, see Nigel Raab, "The Tashkent Earthquake of 1966: The Advantages and Disadvantages of a National Tragedy," *Jahrbücher für Geschichte Osteuropas* 62, no. 2 (2014): 273–294.

21. GARF, fond R5446, opis 100, delo 285.

22. ACPT, fond 3, opis 239, delo 18.

23. R. O. Tal'man, *Goroda Tadzhikistana* (Dushanbe: Irfon, 1967), 13.

24. Tajikistan's senior architect, V. Veselovskiy, was already complaining about this in 1962; but moving factories once they were erected was a difficult undertaking and

industry representatives resisted any suggestions they do so. See the discussion on the planning of Dushanbe, October 23–24, 1962, RGALI, fond 674, opis 3, delo 1803, 215–216.

25. See Victoria Koroteyeva and Ekaterina Makarova, "Money and Social Connections in the Soviet and Post-Soviet Uzbek City," *Central Asian Survey* 17, no. 4 (1998): 579–596.

26. Interview with Jura L., Dushanbe, April 2013.

27. "Kakoi byt' arkhitekture Tadzhikistana?," *Kommunist Tadzhikistana,* January 24, 1979.

28. "Arkhitektura i natsional'noe svoeobrazie," *Kommunist Tadzhikistana,* February 18, 1979.

29. See, for example, the full-page debate published in *Kommunist Tadzhikistana* on June 14, 1979; M. Mamadnazarov, "Traditsia i sovremennost' v arkhitekture goroda Dushanbe," *Arkhitektura Sovetskogo Uzbekistana,* May 1981, 8–10. Author's interviews with R. Mukimov and N. Ëkubov, Dushanbe, May 2015.

30. Philipp Meuser, Seismic Modernism: Architecture and Housing in Soviet Tashkent (Berlin: DOM, 2016), 228.

31. See R. Mukimov, M. Karimov, and S. Mamadzhanova, *Preemstvenost' i razvitie traditsii v arkhitekture Tadzhikistana* (Dushanbe: ICOMOS, 2015), 134–164; Salia Mamadzhanova and Sangahmad Tilloev, *Arhitektura obschestvennykh zdanii Dushanbe XX veka* (Dushanbe: ICOMOS, 2007), 81–108.

32. For a detailed breakdown of housing types constructed in this period, see N. H. Iakubov, *Rekonstruktsiia zdanii* (Dushanbe: Tajikistan Technical University, 2013), 60–74.

33. Interview with Olimjon H., Khojand, May 2013. The subject was an engineer and a republic-level Gosplan official in the 1980s.

34. As Mark B. Smith notes, Khrushchev's enthusiasm for company towns harked back to an older Soviet model, "according to which towns should grow and export their qualities to their rural surroundings." Smith, "Faded Red Paradise," 613–614.

35. William Taubman, *Governing Soviet Cities: Bureaucratic Politics and Urban Development in the USSR* (New York: Praeger, 1973), 67–68.

36. Khakel, *Unesennoe vetrom*, ch. 19.

37. See, for example, "Ob uchastii komsomol'skoi molodezhi . . . ," RGASPI, fond M-1, opis 8, delo 1169.

38. Pavel Gorbachev, *Plotina* (Moscow: Politizdat, 1980), 137.

39. Kalizhniuk to Novikov, May 22, 1962, RGAE, fond 9572, opis 1, delo 1928, 154.

40. RGAE, fond 339, opis 6, delo 3368, 221.

41. By early 1961, planners had agreed in principle on a town that would peak at 20,000 residents during construction and decline to roughly 10,000 afterward, with a standard of nine square meters per resident in the initial period ultimately rising to twelve square meters. Most of the houses would be 4 floor apartment blocks, but there would also be some two-floor apartment buildings with personal garden plots. RGAE, fond 339, opis 6, delo 3370.

42. RGASPI, fond M-1, opis 8, delo 1126, 7–19.

43. Khakel, *Unesennoe vetrom*, ch. 19

44. Recollections of Semen Laschenov in N. G. Savchenkov, *Nurekskaia GES: Tadzhikistan. Energogiant na Vakhshshe,* 2nd ed. (Moscow: Tipografia Moment, 2013), 471.

45. Khakel, *Unesennoe vetrom*, ch. 19.

46. Yuri Sevenard's reminiscences in N. G. Savchenkov, *Nurekskai GES. Tadzhikistan. Energogigant na Vakhshe* (Moscow: Tipografia Moment, 2013), 460.

47. ACPT, fond 56, opis 5, delo 42, 83–84.

48. TsGART, fond 1609, opis 1, delo 79, 12.

49. RGASPI, fond M-1, opis 8, delo 1169, 12–23.

50. April 16, 1964, RGASPI, fond M-1, opis 9, delo 1169, 1–11.

288 NOTES TO PAGES 129–135

51. Some 2,000 cubic meters of wood were apparently stolen from the construction site in one year. "V storone ot glavnogo," *Norak,* August 24, 1962.

52. RGASPI, fond M-1, opis 8, delo 1169, 12–23.

53. ACPT, fond 56, opis 5, delo 6, 9.

54. RGASPI, fond M-1, opis 8, delo 1169, 12–23; ACPT, fond 56, opis 5, delo 6, 11.

55. "V storone ot glavnogo."

56. "At the moment we are short 300 laborers for tunneling work, and 400 in various construction organizations and auto depots. . . . Some 1,400 laborers and engineering-technical workers . . . have quit," the head of NurekGesStroy complained in 1967, "[and] as a rule it is the qualified labor that quits." ACPT, fond 3, opis 264, delo 201, 81–82.

57. ACPT, fond 56, ops 7, delo 28, 32.

58. ACPT, fond 3, opis 203, delo 164, 6–8.

59. *Pravda*, July 7, 1963.

60. Seventy-one apartments were supposed to be ready by the end of 1961; in fact, none of them had yet passed inspection and been accepted for residents. Construction on a planned apartment building for the executive committee of the city Soviet had not even broken ground. TsGART, fond 1605, opis 1, delo 79, 1–15.

61. "Narodnaia kopeika schet liubit," *Norak,* January 22, 1963; "Ravnodushiiu, net!," *Norak,* June 18, 1963

62. TsGART, fond 1605, opis 1, delo 79, 1–15.

63. Khakel, *Unesennoe vetrom,* ch. 19.

64. E. Sedykh, "Zhemchuzhina Vakhsha," *Pravda*, March 12, 1967. The numbers that emerge from a census conducted that year suggest that Sedykh exaggerated the size of the population. See also TsGART, fond 1609, opis 1, delo 79, 12.

65. Gorbachev, *Plotina,* 137.

66. RGAE, fond 339, opis 6, delo 3373, 50–53.

67. "Snova v Nureke," *Norak,* June 13, 1969.

68. "Nurek," *Intourist Pamphlet,* no date.

69. Gorbachev, *Plotina*; "Iunomu gorodu dostoinyi oblik," *Norak,* May 17, 1968. "Plany i fakty," *Norak,* September 19, 1968; Vladislav Ianelis, "Goriachii polius Nureka," *Smena,* May 1981, 2.

70. "Iunomu gorodu energetikov—krasotu," *Norak,* October 7, 1969. According to the article, only half of the trees planted that spring survived until the autumn.

71. "Rol' mestnykh sovetov v razvitii Nureka," *Norak,* June 13, 1969.

72. See, for example, "Nurekskaia biblioteka popolniaetsia," *Druzhba Narodov,* no. 6 (1974): 285.

73. Mukhiddin Khodzhaev, *Voda k dobru snitsia* (Moscow: Sovetskiy pisatel', 1982). I did not come across archival evidence regarding local residents leaving for villages in higher altitudes. As I show in chapter 7, however, this was indeed a relatively widespread practice well into the 1970s and probably until the end of the Soviet period.

74. See Kalinovsky, "Tractors, Power Lines."

75. Morits Florin, "Faites tomber les murs! La politique civilisatrice de l'ère Brežnev dans les villages kirghiz," *Cahiers du monde russe* 54, nos. 1–2 (2013): 187–211.

76. See, for example, the various projects for "the layout, construction, and landscaping" of rural settlements submitted to the State Committee for Construction, TsGART, fond 1622, opis 1, delo 390.

77. By 1967, 23 percent of the city's residents were "service personnel," which was the result of the fact that "the city of Nurek, surrounded by more than ten kishlaks, is currently serving as a district center, and its organizations are serving not only the population of Nurek but also the surrounding kishlaks." RGAE, fond 399, opis 6, delo 3373, 57.

78. Gorbachev, *Plotina,* 67–68

79. Ibid., 68.

80. TsGART, fond 1605, opis 1, delo 407, 19

81. Almost none of the people I spoke to recalled any desire to move to the city when it was being constructed, preferring the relative spaciousness of the village. Nor have I seen anything in the archival sources that suggests demand for housing from locals as opposed to the laborers coming from elsewhere.

82. ACPT, fond 56, opis 7, delo 16, 89.

83. ACPT, fond 56, opis 7, delo 30.

84. ACPT, fond 56, opis 7, delo 28, 4.

85. ACPT, fond 56, opis 7, delo 28, 32.

86. A. David′iants, V. Tarasevich, *Svet Nureka,* (Moscow: Planeta, 1980*).*

87. This claim is based on my conversations with residents of New Tutkaul as well as neighboring villages like Kibil. The following statement by an official in 1979 again points to the importance placed in the 1970s on raising the level of services in the city and the villages, as well as the problem of doing so: "Nurek is a city of [power engineers (*energetiki*)], one of the largest power stations is being built here, and so the lighting of its streets, blocks, kishlaks and settlements (*poselki*) that surround it need to live up to the name. This year, thanks to the help of Tajikglavenergo, there has been great work done electrification of Karatosh and the satellite of New Tutkaul. We cannot say the same for the city itself … not one of the 100,000 rubles designated for that purpose has been used." ACPT, fond 3, opis 303, delo 104, 50

88. "Rol' mestnykh sovetov v razvitii Nureka," *Norak,* June 13, 1989. The workings of the kishlak soviets were further explained to me by several officials who worked in them. Allowing for the fact that these individuals may have offered self-serving accounts, what they say is consistent with the documentary record as well as the accounts of other residents I met in the villages.

89. The sheer volume of construction material available provided opportunities. Material that was used for a certain phase of production and then discarded, or proved unnecessary for one reason or another was sold off cheaply to workers, who could then use it to expand or rebuild their own houses.

90. "Vypolniat' nakazy izberatelei," *Norak,* April 19, 1971

91. ACPT, fond 3, opis 303, delo 104, 50

92. Ibid. This included planting 3,100 trees, clearing away 860,000 square meters of rocks and garbage, laying two kilometers worth of water pipes, and the greening of Hafez street in New Tutkaul. The chairman of the city council singled out officials who had mobilized people to do this work: "We should particularly note the initiative of those deputies of the city, kishlak and village soviets who directed the public, and residents for the beautification of the city, villages, and kishlaks."

93. Author's interview with Mirkolon Shodjonov, Dushanbe, July 2013. Shodjonov was the head of the Nurek hospital in the 1970s and 1980s.

94. Interview with Mamalakat Z, who worked on labor recruitment and education issues as a Komsomol activist in the early 1980s, June 2013.

95. On the complex relationship to biomedical practices, see Abashin, *Sovetskii kishlak.*

96. "Vyshe znamia internatsionalisma" (Notes from the city party committee plenum), *Norak,* May 24, 1974.

97. ACPT, fond 3, opis 301, delo 103, 67–68.

98. See Ali Igmen's excellent *Speaking Soviet with an Accent: Culture and Power in Kyrgyzstan* (Pittsburgh: Pittsburgh University Press, 2002), which traces the evolution of these clubs and houses of culture in Kyrgyzstan and their roles in fashioning a new Kyrgyz cultural and intellectual elite in the 1920s and 1930s.

99. Interview with Aziz Amonov, former member of the village soviet, Nurek, July 2013.

100. ACPT, fond 56, opis 11, delo 8, 43–48.

101. ACPT, fond 3, opis 360, delo 321, 43.

102. Mark B. Smith describes the Soviet city of the 1970s as the "Faded Red Paradise." Smith, "Faded Red Paradise."

103. Ferguson, *Anti-Politics Machine,* 256.

CHAPTER 6. SHEPHERDS INTO BUILDERS

1. Shulashov features prominently in a number of books on Nurek, including B. Murtazoev and V. Frolov, *Nuru Nori Vakhshrūd,* (Dushanbe: Irfon, 2006).

2. Mikhail Rozhansky, "Sotsial'naia energiia: ustnaia istoriia udarnykh stroek," *Cahiers du monde russe* 52, no. 4 (2011): 619–657.

3. Z. Shokirov, "Ba sohtmon beshtar kadrhoi mahalli zarurand," *Norak,* March 14, 1969.

4. This has been an ongoing debate in the history of labor and industrial anthropology since E. P. Thompson's classic essay "Time, Work-Discipline, and Industrial Capitalism," *Past and Present* 38 (1967): 56–97. Thompson emphasized the difference between the irregularity of the pre-industrial age with the "time-discipline" of capitalist industry. The anthropologist Jonathan Parry has been among those who challenged Thompson's view of pre-industrial society as well as the applicability of his understanding of "time-discipline" by examining work rhythms in a steel mill. Jonathan Parry, "Satanic Fields, Pleasant Mills: Work in an Indian Steel Plant," *Contributions to Indian Sociology* 33, nos. 1–2 (1999): 107–140. There is no doubt that the rhythm of construction was different than that of the kolkhoz. Yet, for reasons I will not delve into here, this varied largely by profession as well as phase of construction. Complaints of idle time, either because of unforeseen obstacles or the failure of equipment to arrive on time are frequently found in the *Norak* newspaper and in the archives of the NurekGesStroy and the party organization. Moreover, as we see below, workers found ways to incorporate prayer and the preparation of evening meals into their workday.

5. Kotkin, *Magnetic Mountain,* 237.

6. Jochen Hellbeck and Igal Halfin, "Rethinking the Stalinist Subject: Stephen Kotkin's 'Magnetic Mountain' and the State of Soviet Historical Studies," *Jahrbucher fur Geschichte Osteuropas* 55, no. 3 (January 1, 1996): 463.

7. M. P. Cowen and R. W. Shenton, *Doctrines of Development* (London: Routledge, 1996), 373–377.

8. Marshall Berman, *All That Is Solid Melts into Air: The Experience of Modernity* (New York: Verso, 1982), 40.

9. For a comparison of Soviet and American approaches to the creation of subjects in development projects, see Giustozzi and Kalinovsky, "The Professional Middle Class in Afghanistan."

10. On Stakhanovism, see Lewis Siegelbaum, *Stakhanovism and the Politics of Productivity in the USSR, 1935–1941* (Cambridge: Cambridge University Press, 1998).

11. Simon Huxtable, "A Compass in the Sea of Life: Soviet Journalism, the Public, and the Limits of Reform After Stalin, 1953–1968" (PhD diss., Birkbeck, University of London, 2013), 152–164.

12. Nurek worker-biographies followed patterns familiar from earlier Soviet memoirs, which were in turn modeled on narratives of religious conversion. See, for example, Reginald Zelnik, *A Radical Worker in Tsarist Russia: The Autobiography of Semën Ivanovich Kanatchikov* (Stanford: Stanford University Press, 1986).

13. I. Mirfozilov, "Javone az Tutkaul," *Norak,* September 13, 1967.

14. Vl. Deriuzhkin, "Vsegda v stroiu" *Norak,* November 2, 1962.

15. *Peredovye stroiteli Nurekskoi GES* (Moscow: Energia, 1964), 12.

16. Tagay Sobirov, *God v nureke* (Dushanbe: Tadzhikgosizdat, 1962), 7.

17. Sobirov, *God v nureke*, 8.

18. Khodzhaev, *Voda k dobru snitsia,* 17.

19. Savchenkov interview, Moscow, May 2013.

20. Collier, *Post-Soviet Social,* 115.

21. ACPT, fond 3, opis 303, delo 104, 52.

22. Although the strategy seemed to work, young women still left after they became pregnant for the first time, which officials took to mean they needed to improve child-care facilities to prevent turnover.

23. Interview with Mamlakat S.; see also N. Morozova, *Nurekskii kharakter* (Moscow: Detskaia Literatura, 1976), reprinted in Savchenkov, *Nurekskai GES,* 132–133.

24. By the late 1970s, one hundred workers at the factory were members of party or Komsomol groups and 580 took part in various activities organized at the factory. See the remarks of Jumagul Nazarova, head of personnel, ACPT, fond 3, opis 308, delo 99, 19. See also remarks about recruitment for the party and Komsomol activity at the factory, ACPT, fond 3, opis 360, delo 324, 17

25. Nurek was hardly the only place where a stable family was considered important for economic life. Projects like Nurek, which mobilized people from across the country, faced particular difficulties with recruitment, retention, and labor discipline, thus making the family particularly important. For example, a study on the Baikur-Amal Mainline (BAM), another construction project that required mobilization of cadres, also noted the importance of stable family for productivity. See V. G. Alekseeva, "Semia kak factor stabilizatsii kadrov," *Sotsiologicheskie issledovaniia* 2 (1983): 89–96.

26. Rozhansky, "Sotsial'naia energiia," 656.

27. On integrating oral history sources into the study of Soviet subjectivity, see also Helbeck, *Revolution on My Mind,* 223–226.

28. It is not surprising then that some of the most intense debate regarding whether Soviet rule in Asia was imperial concerned the Hujum and policy toward Central Asian women more generally. See Kamp, *New Soviet Woman,* and Norhtrop, *Veiled Empire.*

29. K. Abdusalom, "Orzue baamalomada," *Norak,* September 16, 1971.

30. The first secretary of the Nurek party organization, Pavel Gorbachev, later published his own version of this story as well as some of the letters Jumagul wrote to him about her life after Gorbachev had already left Nurek. See Pavel Gorbachev, "Tri sud'by," *Druzhba Narodov,* no. 4 (1979): 217–218.

31. According to a version of this story told by Morozova in 1976, however, it was only the mother who came to visit Jumagul, and even then relations remained difficult because Jumagul refused to submit to her parents authority and "law." It is not clear whether Morozova was trying to emphasize Jumagul's commitment to a new way of life, or if Jumagul was instead painting a slightly rosier picture of things looking back from 2013. Morozova, "Nurekskii Kharakter," in Savchenkov, *Nurekskaia GES,* 131–132.

32. Khakel, *Unesennoe vetrom,* ch. 21.

33. This is not the individual's real name.

34. Author's interview, May 2013.

35. As Shiringul explained, it was after the visit of some "foreign guests" that she was taken to meet, one of the managers inquired as to how she was getting on, and she explained that her and her husband urgently needed a bigger apartment. He then intervened to make it happen quickly. But others described the importance of prominent workers in getting schools built, helping to acquire building materials, and even extending infrastructure into a village.

36. Although in the press she was often portrayed as a "student" of Jumagul Nazarova, Shiringul insisted that she barely knew her at the time. Like Jumagul, she was apprenticed to Russian women, "my Russian women [*sic*] were like a mother to me."

37. We have an interesting manifestation here of the "double burden," where women were expected to work and play the primary role in childcare and housekeeping. The mobilization of family members to make Shiringul's work and activist life possible is also reminiscent of aspects of Stakhanovism in the way that heroic individual effort that could be celebrated for propaganda purposes actually required quite a great deal of supporting labor.

38. Among the most active in this regard was Natalia Morozova, the editor of *Norak*. A number of the women we interviewed cited her influence or intervention as being particularly important in their lives. She also spoke on these issues frequently at party meetings and addressed them in the newspaper. See, for example "Feudals in Worker's Clothing" (Feodaly v rabochikh spetsovkakh), *Norak,* October 3, 1968, about Nurek workers who did not let their daughters study.

39. Literature on Islam in the Soviet Union tended to see these as oppositions; at best, Islamic practice was a kind of resistance even by people who were outwardly Soviet. For a perspective that shows how they could exist in a kind of hybridity, see Sergey Abashin, "Praying for Rain: Practicing Being Soviet and Muslim," *Journal of Islamic Studies* 25, no. 2 (2014): 178–200.

40. Akobirov, *Nurek,* 250.

41. Ibid.

42. Interview with Nikolai Savchenkov and a former human resources manager who worked in Nurek and Rogun, Moscow, May 2013.

43. "Brigadir Muhabbat Sharipov," *Norak,* December 31, 1971

44. The complex brigades were believed to be more efficient that the specialized brigades that were the main unit of labor organization in the first years of construction.

45. We interviewed him twice—on July 2, 2013 and again on July 15.

46. Interview with Zebonissor Sharipova, July 2, 2013. Her mother was present for most of the interview, periodically leaving and coming back with yet more food. But unlike Zebonissor she did not prove talkative, usually giving only brief answers to our questions. At the same time, she never contradicted what Zebonissor said.

47. Although, as Yurchak reminds us, boredom at a Komsomol meeting did not mean a rejection of the organization's values. Alexei Yurchak, *Everything Was Forever until It Was No More: The Last Soviet Generation* (Princeton: Princeton University Press, 2005).

48. When I spoke to Makhram, he claimed that he was born on June 22, 1941, the day the Nazis and their allies invaded the USSR. Party records indicate he was born in 1944. His attempts to tie his own biography to such a totemic date in Soviet history is telling, however.

49. Author's interview with Makhram, Dushanbe, May 2013.

50. ACPT, fond 3, opis 301, delo 323, 76.

51. Ibid., 82.

52. ACPT, fond 3, opis 301, delo 323, 81.

53. Ibid., 79.

54. Ibid., 92.

55. ACPT, fond 3, opis 301, delo 323, 74, 77.

56. Berman, *All That Is Solid Melts into Air,* 300–301.

57. Abashin, "Praying for Rain," 23.

CHAPTER 7. THE COUNTRYSIDE ELECTRIFIED

1. Mamlakat is not the individual's real name.

2. As Lynne Viola points out, planner's utopian visions even guided the thinking beyond the punitive "special settlements" for kulaks set up during the collectivization drive of the late 1920s and 1930s. See Lynne Viola, "The Aesthetics of Stalinist Planning and the Lost World of Stalin's Special Villages," *Kritika* 4, no. 1 (Winter 2003): 101–128.

3. Lewis Siegelbaum and Leslie Paige Moch, *Broad Is My Native Land: Repertoires and Regimes of Migration in Russia's Twentieth Century* (Ithaca: Cornell University Press, 2014), 124–140.

4. Gregory Gleason, "Marketization and Migration: The Politics of Cotton in Central Asia." *Journal of Soviet Nationalities* 1 (Summer 1990): 66–98.

5. A collection that addresses some of these questions, albeit indirectly, is Stephane A. Dudoignon and Christian Noack, eds., *Allah's Kolkhozes: Migration, De-Stalinisation, Privatisation and the New Muslim Congregations in the Soviet Realm (1950s–2000s),* (Berlin: Klaus Schwarz, 2011)

6. The term is Clifford Geertz's, used to describe the way that Indonesian rice farmers made room for an ever growing labor force, thus upsetting the calculations of development economists who expected a surplus agricultural population to fuel industrialization. Clifford Geertz, *Agricultural Involution: The Process of Ecological Change in Indonesia* (Berkeley: University of California Press, 1970). Jenny Leigh Smith uses the term to describe the labor pattern in Uzbekistan's cotton growing valleys. Smith, however, believes that Soviet officials had given up on mechanization for a substantial period and instead tried to create an industrialized system dependent on manual labor. As I emphasize, however, low labor mobility in Central Asia was seen as a critical problem, not a desirable situation. Jenny Leigh Smith, "Agricultural Involution in the Postwar Soviet Union," *International Labor and Working-Class History,* no. 85 (Spring 2014): 59–74.

7. See, for example, the correspondence in RGANI, fond 5, opis 45, delo 412. Uzbek and Tajik officials pushed for lower targets, citing the damage being done by the cotton monoculture to the soil and to the broader collective farm economy.

8. Hodnett, "Technology and Social Change in Soviet Central Asia," 72–73.

9. TsGART, fond 288, opis 14, delo 5279, 56.

10. RGANI, fond 5, opis 30, delo 331, 14–16.

11. Nikita Khrushchev, *Memoirs,* 349.

12. RGASPI, fond 17, opis 89, delo 649, 13–14.

13. RGANI, fond 5, opis 35, delo 29, 117.

14. Analogous journals were published in other republics. Each was unique both in the technical issues it addressed and the particular visions of ideal collective farm life it promoted.

15. Khrushchev, *Memoirs,* 348.

16. Ibid., 350.

17. For example, a survey conducted in Uzbekistan in 1961 found that only 23 kolkhoz schools had been completed in the previous year, and that out of 237 schools under construction, work had stopped on 65 due to lack of funds or materials. RGANI, fond 5, opis 35, delo 205, 100–101.

18. Thomas P. Hughes, *Networks of Power: Electrification in Western Society, 1880–1930* (Baltimore: Johns Hopkins University Press, 1983), 2.

19. Susan Buck-Morss, *Dreamworld and Catastrophe: The Passing of Mass Utopia in East and West* (Cambridge, MA: MIT Press, 2000), 139-140. See also Jonathan Cooper-smith, *The Electrification of Russia* (Ithaca, NY: Cornell University Press, 1992).

20. M. Matniazov, *Elektrifikatsiia i ee sotsial'nye posledstviia* (Tashkent: Uzbekistan, 1984), 154.

21. State Archives of Tajikistan, fond 1605, opis 1, delo 10.

22. TsGART, fond 1605, opis 1, delo 14.

23. B. V. Iunusov, *Elektroenergetika Tadzhikistana* (Dushanbe, Irfon, 1975), 119.

24. See, for example, the petitions and response from agencies in TsGART, fond 18, opis 13, delo 52, 1–24, and suggestions voiced at a party plenum in 1966, 25–27.

25. TsGART, fond 18, opis 13, delo 52, 33; Z. A. Pirogova, *Elektroenergetika Tadzhikistana* (Dushanbe: Irfon, 1966), 27.

26. Iunusov, *Eletroenergetika Tadzhikistana.*

27. Coopersmith, *The Electrification of Russia,* 163–167, 236–244.

28. Hikmatullo Nasriddinov, *Tarkish* (Dushanbe: Afsona 1995), 21–22. Nasriddinov, a water engineer from Kulob who later became minister of irrigation for the republic, blamed regional politics—a northern dominated republican government that refused to invest in the south. However, the more likely explanation is that the shift to larger power stations made officials reluctant to invest in smaller ones, and they expected that Nurek would be finished in the coming years.

29. TsGART, fond 18, opis 13, delo 52, 3.

30. Ibid., 33.

31. According to a report from 1966, of the 272 collective farms using electricity, 92 percent were using it for production purposes. However, the only sphere of production where machinery was being used to ease the production process was sheep shearing: 214 farms used electric shears. Only 52 farms used electricity to clean seeds, 36 for irrigation, 26 for milking cows. TsGART, fond 18, opis 13, delo 52, 34. The figures were roughly comparable for state and collective farms. In other words, the problem was not lack of electricity but rather how it was used or not used once it reached the farm.

32. RGANI, fond 17, opis 138, delo 11, 87.

33. RGANI, fond 5, opis 31, delo 113, 17–18.

34. Richard Pomfret, "State-Directed Diffusion of Technology: The Mechanization of Cotton Harvesting in Soviet Central Asia," *Journal of Economic History* 62, no. 1 (2002): 170–188.

35. TsGART, fond 18, opis 13, delo 52, 53, September 22, 1966.

36. Ibid., annex, 54–70.

37. TsGART, fond 18, opis 13, delo 61, 28.

38. Ibid., 31.

39. TsGART, fond 18, opis 13, delo 6, 84–86.

40. Without the machine tractor stations, which were eliminated in 1958, the burden of maintenance fell entirely on the farms themselves, and, as with the irrigation system, they either lacked the cadres or were unable to maintain them. RGANI, fond 5, opis 45, delo 255, 1–3.

41. This pattern is by no means unique to the Soviet case. See, for example, Timothy Mitchell's discussion of how Egyptian farmers, after switching to tractors for plowing and carrying sugarcane with USAID subsidies, ultimately switched back to cow and calf drawn plowing, and switching back to camels for carrying sugarcane. Mitchell, *Rule of Experts,* 253–254.

42. ACPT, fond 3, opis 23, delo 183, 39. See also the correspondence in RGANI, fond 5, opis 45, delo 425, 1–16. Note that some officials believed that the problem was not the technology, but how it was being used.

43. TsGART, fond 27, opis 15, delo 1, 125.

44. TsGART, fond 288, opis 14, delo 5279, 67

45. ACPT, fond 3, opis 23, delo 183, 40–41.

46. Pomfret, "State-Directed Diffusion of Technology," 186.

47. Ibid., 184. See also Craumer, "Agricultural Change," 161.

48. See, for example, Donald Filtzer, *Soviet Workers and the Collapse of Perestroika: The Soviet Labour Process and Gorbachev's Reforms, 1985–1991* (Cambridge: Cambridge University Press, 1994).

49. Olivier Ferrando, "Soviet Population Transfers and Interethnic Relations in Tajikistan: Assessing the Concept of Ethnicity," *Central Asian Survey* 30, no. 1 (2011): 40–41. On the early Soviet period, see also Botakoz Kassymbekova, "Humans as Territory: Forced Resettlement and the Making of Soviet Tajikistan, 1920–38," *Central Asian Survey* 30, nos.

3–4 (2011): 349–370. Kassymbekova emphasizes the extent to which settlement was used by officials to secure the southern part of the republic that bordered Tajikistan. The most detailed work on internal migrations produced within Tajikistan is Raqib Abdulhaev, *Ta'rihi Muhojirat dar Tojikiston (solhoi 1917–2000)* (Dushanbe: Pazhuhishgohi ta'rih, bostonshinosi va mardumshinosi Akademiqi Fanxoi Jumhurii Tojikiston, 2012). Abdulhaev is often critical of how resettlements were executed, but believes they led to economic progress and allowed Tajiks to populate land previously dominated by Uzbeks.

50. This is reflected in the reports of various local officials; see, for example, TsGART, fond 1566, opis 1, delo 229, 20–21.

51. TsGART, fond 1566, opis 3, delo 81, 48.

52. TsGART, fond 1566, opis 3, delo 83, 55.

53. TsGART, fond 1566, opis 3, delo 81, 72–73.

54. Ibid. See also similar reports TsGART, fond 1566, opis 3, delo 81, 34–35.

55. Ferrando, "Soviet Population Transfers," 42–43.

56. See the reports in TsGART, fond 1566, opis 1, delo 229.

57. TsGART, fond 1566, opis 1, delo 260, 21

58. Officials from the Council of Ministers chided local officials for allowing such things to take place. TsGART, fond 1566, opis 3, delo 81, 39.

59. TsGART, fond 1566, opis 3, delo 96, 36–38.

60. TsGART, fond 1566, opis 3, delo 83, 26.

61. On Matcha, see also Ferrando, "Soviet Population Transfers," and Ariane Zevco, "From Old to New Macha: Mass Resettlement and the Redefinition of Islamic Practice between Tajikistan's Upper Valleys and Cotton Lowlands," both in Dudoignon and Noack, *Allah's Kolkhozes*, 148–201; Abdulhaev, *Tar'ihi mukhojirot*, 349–351.

62. TsGART, fond 1566, opis 3, delo 83, 77–79.

63. Ibid., 78. The figure for average plot size comes from Peter Craumer, "Agricultural Change, Labor Supply, and Rural Outmigration in Soviet Central Asia," in Lewis, *Geographic Perspectives on Soviet Central Asia*, 169.

64. Ibid., 78–79.

65. TsGART, fond 1566, opis 3, delo 81, 57–59.

66. Abdulhaev, *Ta'rihi mukhojirot*, 375–377.

67. TsGART, fond 1566, opis 3, delo 81, 57–58.

68. TsGART, fond 1566, opis 3, delo 83, 79.

69. See A. Sattarov, "Rasselenie sel'skogo naseleniia v Iuzno-Tadzhikskom Territorial'no Proizvodstvennom Komplekse," *BAST*, no. 3 (1979): 47–53.

70. TsGART, fond 1566, opis 3, delo 96, 45.

71. Ibid.

72. TsGART, fond 1566, opis 3, delo 96, 91–92.

73. TsGART, fond 1566, opis 3, delo 96, 64–65. See also Abdulhaev, *Ta'rihi mukhojirot*, 362–364, 369–373.

74. On the migration of the Yagnobis, see also John Schoeberlein, "Shifting Ground: How the Soviet Regime Used Resettlement to Transform Central Asian Society and the Consequences of This Policy Today," JCAS Symposium Series, no. 9, 2000.

75. Nishanov, *Derev'ia zeleneiut*, 72–73.

76. Poliakov, *Everyday Islam*, 28–29. See Kirill Nourzhanov and Christian Bleuer, *Tajikistan: A Political and Social History* (Canberra: Australian National University Press, 2013), 148–149. See also Beate Giehler, "Maksim Gorki and the Islamic Revolution in the Southern Tajik Cotton Plain: The Failure of Soviet Integration in the Countryside," in Dudoignon and Noack, *Allah's Kolkhozes*. Abashin, studying these relationships from the perspective of farmers and farm management, similarly underlines that household plots "cannot be considered something completely separate or autonomous from the economy

of the collective farm, or even the state economy—they were bound by relationships that were numerous and varied." Abashin, *Sovetskii kishlak,* 388. See also Ajay Patnaik, "Agriculture and Rural Out-Migration in Central Asia, 1960–91," *Europe-Asia Studies* 47, no. 1 (1995): 147–169.

77. RGANI fond 5, opis 30, delo 331, 14.

78. Ibid, 16.

79. Ibid.

80. Shoshanna Keller, "The Puzzle of Manual Harvest in Uzbekistan: Economics, Status and Labor in the Khrushchev Era," *Central Asian Survey* 34, no. 3 (September 2015): 296–309.

81. R. A. Ubaidullaeva, *Zhenskii trud v kolkhozakh Uzbekistana* (Tashkent: Institute of Economics, 1964).

82. Interview with author, February 2013.

83. GARF, fond 7523, opis 106, delo 1146, 60.

84. Ibid., 63.

85. Ibid., 61.

86. Ibid., 63.

87. I. Gordijew, "Soviet Agriculture and the March 1965 Plenum of the C.P.S.U.," *The Australian Quarterly* 39, no. 1, (March 1967): 56–68.

88. TsGART, fond 1739, opis 1, delo 1, 5.

89. Ibid., 6.

90. TsGART, fond 1739, opis 1, delo 65, 2.

91. TsGART, fond 288, opis 13, delo 5857, 15.

92. TsGART, fond 1739, opis 1, delo 5, 9.

93. TsGART, fond 288, opis 14, delo 5857.

94. It seems to have been common, at least in some areas, for the older, usually retired, members of a community to take up practices from which younger members of the community were excused during their economically active years, especially if they held some position of importance. In this way the community's spiritual/moral condition was secured. A similar practice developed in some Old Believer communities. See Douglas Rogers, *The Old Faith and the Russian Land: A Historical Ethnography of Ethics in the Urals* (Ithaca: Cornell University Press, 2009).

95. Other scholars have noted a similar process, but emphasize instead that Soviet institutions and personnel, such as the collective farm leadership or local security officials, as well as social institutions like the family shielded Islamic authorities and limited the possibility of effecting change in the countryside. While this was probably the case, there was a more complicated negotiation and exchange between party/state authorities and rural social institutions which allowed the party/state to partly achieve its "modernizing" goals (expansion of schooling, attendance of girls at school) while at the same time limiting the effects by recognizing and even reifying the power of social institutions and figures whose support they needed to carry out meaningful change. See, for example, Beate Giehler, "Maxim Gorki and the Islamic Revolution in the Southern Tajik Cotton Plain," in Dudoignon and Noack, *Allah's Kolkhozes,* 123–147.

96. Author's interview with Ismoil Tolbakov, Dushanbe, July 2012.

CHAPTER 8. "A TORCH LIGHTING THE WAY TO PROGRESS AND CIVILIZATION"

1. TsGART, fond 1516, opis 1, delo 80, 34–35.

2. Tajikistan's engagement with the Third World was not limited to these countries, but because of geographical proximity and historical and cultural links these relationships were particularly emphasized.

3. Scholars have considered the way Central Asia was presented as a place where Islam and Soviet modernity could exist side by side, and some also looked at the way Central Asian elites were drawn into this process. See, for example, Karen Dawisha and Helene Carrere d'Encause, "Islam in the Soviet Union: A Double Edged Sword?," in *Islam in Foreign Policy,* ed. A. Dawisha (Cambridge: Cambridge University Press, 1983), 165–168; Eren Tasar, "The Central Asian Muftiate in Occupied Afghanistan, 1979–1987," *Central Asian Survey* 30, no. 2 (July 2011): 213–226; Kirasirova, "'Sons of Muslims' in Moscow."

4. Alec Nove and J. A. Newith, *The Soviet Middle East: A Communist Model for Development* (New York: Frederick A. Praeger, 1966).

5. Charles K. Wilber, *The Soviet Model and Underdeveloped Countries* (Durham: University of North Caroline Press, 1969), 198–215.

6. See Norton Dodge and Charles K. Wilber, "The Relevance of Soviet Industrial Experience for Less Developed Economies," *Soviet Studies* 21, no. 3 (January 1970): 330–349. See also Teresa Rakowska-Harmstone, "Soviet Central Asia: A Model of Non-Capitalist Development for the Third World," in *The USSR and the Muslim World,* ed. Yaacov Ro'I (London: George Allen & Unwin, 1984), 181–205.

7. RGANI, fond 5, opis 30, delo 305, 116–288. Cited in Iandolo, "Rise and Fall," 692.

8. Gregory J. Massell, "Modernization and National Policy in Soviet Central Asia" in *The Dynamics of Soviet Politics,* ed. Paul Cocks et al. (Cambridge: Cambridge University Press, 1976), 267.

9. G. Ia. Kurzer. "K voprosu ob ispol'zovanii razvivaiushchimisia stranami opyta sotsialisticheskoi industrializatsii respublik Srednei Azii," *Izvestiia Akademii Nauk Tadzhikskoi SSR,* no. 2 (1965): 45–59.

10. ARAN, fond 1731, opis 1, delo 56, 21.

11. David Engerman, "Learning from the East: Soviet Experts and India in the Era of Competitive Coexistence," *Comparative Studies in South Asia, Africa, and the Middle East* 33, no. 2 (2013): 227–238.

12. Quoted in ibid.

13. Sh. Tursumatov, "Some Features of the Economy of Developing Countries," *BAST,* no. 4 (1978): 71–72.

14. Gafurov to Brezhnev, March 12, 1966, RGANI, fond 5, opis 30, delo 489, 147–153.

15. See also Westad on the international department and different conceptions of détente in the 1970s. Westad, *Global Cold War,* 194–206.

16. ACPT, fond 3, opis 239, delo 114.

17. ARAN, fond 1731, opis 1, delo 157, 74.

18. See Artemy M. Kalinovsky and Michael Kemper, "Introduction," in *Reassessing Orientalism,* 1–15.

19. M. Ibrohimov, *Gorizonty nauki Tadzhikistana* (Dushanbe: Irfon, 2007), 112–113.

20. In 1968, for example, these included: "teachers and candidates of physics and mathematical sciences O. Shokirov, V. Tashbaev, F. Hakimov; docents and candidates of philological sciences comrades Juraev and R. Dodyhudoev, who will be in the country until 1970." GARF, fond 9606, opis 1, delo 3456.

21. Ibrohimov, *Gorizonty nauki Tadzhikistana,* 158–163.

22. Tursunov, "Pomoshch' sovetskikh sredneaziatskikh respublik Afganistanu," *Narody Azii i Afriki,* no. 4 (1971): 127; Robinson, *Aiding Afghanistan,* 80

23. M. Tutiev, "Pomoshch' Sovetskogo Soiuza v razvitii elektroenergetiki Afganistana" *Bulliten' Akademii Nauk Tadzhikskoi SSR, Otdelenie Obshchestvennykh Nauk,* no. 3 (1975): 61–64.

24. D. R. Davliatov, "Iz istorii razvitia kult'urnogo sotrudnichestva SSSR s demokraticheskoi respublikoi Afganistan," *BAST,* no. 4 (1979): 11–14.

25. RGANI, fond 5, opis 30, delo 273, 41.

26. Robert Hornsby, "The Post-Stalin Komsomol and the Soviet Fight for Third World Youth," *Cold War History* 16, no. 1 (2016): 92.

27. TsGART, fond 1505, opis 1, delo 86, 20.

28. Holmorod Sharifov, *Tolei baland* (Dushanbe: Pazhuhishgohi farsi-tojiki, 2010), 32–34.

29. RGANI, fond 5, opis 35, delo 225, 7.

30. RGAE, fond 365, opis 9, delo 185

31. Friedman, *Shadow Cold War,* 97–98.

32. Lyndon Baines Johnson Library, National Security Files, box 37. My thanks to Thomas Field for alerting me to Rashidov's speech and providing the text of the document.

33. Nishanov, *Derev'ia zeleneiut,* 88–92.

34. Ibid., 163.

35. "Volnuiushchiia vstrecha v Tashkente," *Pravda,* May 4, 1956, p.2.

36. Mirzoshoev, *Arzi Dil,* 16–17. See also http://news.tj/ru/news/diplomat-politik-i-drug-genseka-kpss.

37. Mirzo Rakhmatov, *Na diplomaticheskom postu* (Dushanbe: Irfon, 1991), 18–19.

38. Ibid., 87.

39. Ibid.

40. David-Fox, *Showcasing the Great Experiment,* 7–8, 20–21.

41. Ibid., 141.

42. We can see it as a component of the larger effort at Soviet nation-building undertaken through the writing and promotion of "national" histories written within the republic, which, particularly in the Tajik case always included an emphasis on Tajikistan's central role in Persian and Indo-Persian history and culture.

43. Interviews (see chapter 2). See also Holmurod Sharifov, *Tolei Baland*, which discusses the author's travels to Afghanistan, South Asia, and Africa.

44. Mirzo Rakhmatov, *Afrika idet k svobode* (Moscow: Gospolitizdat, 1961).

45. A. Kakhorov and G. Prohorov, *Xamkorii iqtisodi va tekhnikii SSSR bo mamlakat-khoi susttaraqqiardai sharq* (Stalinobod: Nashriete davlatii Tojikiston, 1959), 44.

46. A. Kakhorov, *Dar avstralia va Ceylon (qaydhoi safar)* (Dushanbe: Nashrieti davlatii Tojikiston, 1962).

47. Quoted in Constantin Katsakioris, "The Soviet-South Encounter: Tensions in the Friendship with Afro-Asian Partners, 1945–1965," in *Cold War Crossings: International Travel and Exchange across the Soviet Bloc, 1940s–1960s,* ed. Patryk Babiracki and Kenyon Zimmer (College Station: Texas A&M University Press, 2014), 148.

48. See Diana T. Kudaibergenova, *Rewriting the Nation in Modern Kazakh Literature: Elites and Narratives* (London: Lexington Books, 2017), 123–148.

49. Hudoĭnazar Asozoda, *Afghonistoni shohi* (Dushanbe: Devashtich, 2002), 15.

50. Ibid., 291.

51. Ibrohimov, *Gorizonty nauki Tadzhikistana,* 252–53. It's not clear whether this book was ever published; However, R.G. Gidadhubli did edit a book called *Socio-economic Transformation of Soviet Central Asia* (New Delhi: Patriot Publishers, 1987).

52. Interviews with Umarov, February 2015.

53. Ibid. See the discussion in the following chapter

54. On the Soviet war in Afghanistan, see Rodric Braithwaite, *Afgantsy: The Russians in Afghanistan, 1979–1989* (London: Profile Books, 2011); Artemy M. Kalinovsky, *A Long Goodbye: The Soviet Withdrawal from Afghanistan* (Cambridge, MA: Harvard University Press, 2011); Timothy Nunan, *Humanitarian Invasion: Global Development in Cold War Afghanistan* (Cambridge: Cambridge University Press, 2016); Antonio Giustozzi, *War, Politics and Society in Afghanistan, 1978–1992* (Washington, DC: Georgetown University

Press, 2000); Mark Galeotti, *Afghanistan: The Soviet Union's Last War* (London: Frank Cass, 1995).

55. See Artemy M. Kalinovsky, "Encouraging Resistance: Paul Henze, the Bennigsen School, and the Crisis of Détente," in Kemper and Kalinovsky, *Reassessing Orientalism*, 211–232.

56. Olga Oliker, who has written a comprehensive survey of Soviet military advising, calculates that 'Each unit also had one or two interpreters, with two or three assigned to each division or corps staff. Oliker, "Building Afghanistan's Security Forces," 43.

57. Interviews with translators, Dushanbe, Tajikistan, June–July 2011.

58. Interview with Wali Sairbekov, Dushanbe, Tajikistan, July 2012.

59. See Antonio Giustozzi and Artemy M. Kalinovsky, *Missionaries of Modernity* (New York: Hurst, 2015).

60. Conversations and interviews with Abdurashid Samadov, Dushanbe, Tajikistan, 2011–2015.

61. Interview with M. Khait, Dushanbe, Tajikistan, July 2012.

62. See, for example, Marlene Laruelle and Botagoz Rakisheva, "Interv'iu s voinami-internationalistami Afganskoi voiny 1979–1989 godov," 2015, https://app.box.com/s/umser0gccid0n6cvrl51kuyrsc8ikm8b. For more on veterans, see Markus Balasz Goransson, "At the Service of the State: Soviet-Afghan War Veterans in Tajikistan, 1979–1992" (PhD diss., University of Aberyswyth, Wales, 2015).

63. Jeremy Friedman, "Reviving Revolution: The Sino-Soviet Split, The Third World, and the Fate of the Left" (PhD diss., Princeton University, 2011), 279–283, 297–308. See also Vijay Prashad, *The Poorer Nations: A Possible History of the Global South* (Brooklyn, NY: Verso, 2012).

64. Artemy M. Kalinovsky, "The Soviet Union and the Iran-Iraq War," in *The Iran-Iraq War: New international Perspectives,* ed. Nigel Ashton and Bryan Gibson (London: Routledge, 2013), 230–242.

65. Friedman, *Reviving Revolution,* 311–314; Odd Arne Westad, *The Global Cold War: Third World Interventions and the Making of Our Times* (Cambridge: Cambridge University Press, 2005), 283–287.

66. See, for example, G. F. Kim and Nodari Simonia, eds., *Strukturnye sdvigi v ekonomike i evolutsiia politicheskikh system v stranakh Azii i Afriki v 70e gody* (Moscow: Nauka, 1982). See also K. Brutents, *Nesbyvshiesia: neravnodushnye zametki o perestroike*, (Moscow: Mezhdunarodnye Otnosheniia, 2005), 167–170 and Petr Cherkassov, *IMEMO: Portret na fone epokhi* (Moscow: Ves' Mir, 2004).

67. Ekbladh, *The Great American Mission,* 226–256.

CHAPTER 9. THE POOREST REPUBLIC

1. Ekbladh, *Great American Mission,* 255–264; Latham, *The Right Kind of Revolution,* 175–182.

2. McGlinchey, *Chaos, Violence, Dynasty: Politics and Islam in Central Asia,* 70–72. For a detailed discussion of the "cotton affair" and its effects on Uzbekistani politics, see Riccardo Mario Cucciola, "The Crisis of Soviet Power in Central Asia: The 'Uzbek Cotton Affair,' 1975–1991" (PhD diss., IMT School for Advanced Studies, Lucca, Italy, 2017).

3. On Bromlei, see Ernest Gellner, "Ethnicity and Anthropology in the Soviet Union," *European Journal of Sociology* 18, no. 2 (December 1977): 201–220.

4. On Bromlei and Gumilev, see Mark Bassin, *The Gumilev Mystique: Biopolitics Eurasianism, and the Construction of Community in Russia* (Ithaca: Cornell University Press, 2016), 171–176.

5. Yu. Bromley and O. Shkaratan, "Natsional'nye trudovye traditsii: Vazhnyi faktor intensifikatsii proizvodstva," *Sovetskoe Gosudarstvo i Pravo* 1 (1982): 43–54.

6. Ibid., 45–46.

7. Yu. Bromley and O. Shkaratan, "Natsional'nye traditsii v sotsialisticheskoi ekonomike," *Voprosy Ekonomiki,* no. 4 (April 1983); Yu. Bromlei, "Etnicheskie protsesy v SSSR," *Kommunist,* no. 5 (1983).

8. Ibid., 89.

9. Gorbachev Foundation Archive, Document 14912. I thank Jacob Feygin for sharing this document with me.

10. RGAE, fond 399, opis 1, delo 2054, 7–21.

11. See Chris Miller, *The Struggle to Save the Soviet Economy: Mikhail Gorbachev and the Collapse of the USSR* (Chapel Hill: University of North Carolina Press, 2016), 71–100.

12. "Sredneia azia i Kazakhstan: prioritety i alternativy razvitia," *Kommunist* 1989, no.14: 25.

13. Ibid.

14. Ibid.

15. "Sredneia azia i Kazakhstan," 41.

16. This is evident when comparing local party Politburo and plenum records for the 1970s and early 1980s with what comes particularly after 1987, which I examined for Nurek, Ordzhonikidzeabad, and Dushanbe.

17. *Rasshirennii XVIII Plenum TsK Kompartii Tadzhikistana: Stenografischeskii otchet* (Dushanbe: Irfon, 1990), 35–36.

18. Mahkamov interview.

19. It was a major subject of discussion at a seminar on urban planning in 1962, only several years into the plants operation, and there was serious consideration about moving the plant out of the city altogether. Records of a seminar on city planning in Tajikistan, October 23–24, 1962, RGALI, fond 674, opis 3, delo 1803.

20. 1988 conference of the Dushanbe city party organization, Archive of the Communist Party of Tajikistan, fond 3, opis 300, delo 278, 121.

21. Alfred J. DiMaio, Jr., "Evolution of Soviet Population Thought: From Marxism-Leninism to the Literaturnaya Gazeta Debate," in *Soviet Population Policy: Conflicts and Constraints*, ed. Helen Desfosses (New York: Pergamon Press, 1981), 166–167.

22. Jason L. Finkle and Barbara B. Crane. "The Politics of Bucharest: Population, Development, and the New International Economic Order,' *Population and Development Review* 1, no. 1 (1975): 87–114. See also Corina Dobos, "'For a More Just World': Population and Politics at the World Population Conference, Bucharest 1974," *Romanian Journal of Population Studies* 9, no. 1 (2015), 152–164.

23. Urlanis, who sounded the alarm about the falling population in Russia and other Slavic republics, argued for family planning as early as the 1960s; he argued that lack of access to family planning simply led to more abortions and the inevitable health consequences, thus hindering rather than promoting higher birth rates among the "European" population. See discussions from 1966 and 1968. AAOS, fond 1877, opis 8, delo 737 and 519. He was also among those who argued that for some developing countries a policy aimed at reducing family size was probably necessary to raise living standards. DiMaio, "Evolution of Soviet Population Thought," 173.

24. R. Galetskaia, "Demograficheskaia politika: ee napravleniia," *Voprosy Ekonomiki,* no.8 (1975): 149–152.

25. See V. I. Mukomel', "Vremia otvestvennykh reshenii," *Sotsiologicheskie Issledovaniia,* no. 1 (1989): 9–14.

26. See Hakimova, "Hushbahti va badbahshtihoi serfarzandi," *Tojikiston Soveti,* July 15, 1987; Umarov, "Baplangirii oila zaruriiati ob'ektivist," *Tojikiston Soveti,* October 24, 1987.

27. Umarov recalled Tohir Abdujabbor as one of his most strident opponents on this issue. Interview, 2015.

28. Mirzoev and Gurshumov, "Planirovanie sem'i: za i protiv," *Kommunist Tadzhikistana,* February 28, 1988.

29. "Za zdorovuiu sem'iu" (transcript of a roundtable in the Academy of Sciences of the Tajik SSR), *BAST,* no. 3(1988): 21–31.

30. Kathleen Watters, "The Current Family Planning Debate in Central Asia," *Central Asian Survey* 9, no. 1 (1990): 75–86.

31. "Sredneia azia i Kazakhstan."

32. Derluguian, *Bourdieu's Secret Admirer,* 2-4. See also Giovanni Arrighi, Terence K. Hopkins, and Immanuel Wallerstein, "1989, the Continuation of 1968," *Review* 15, no. 2 (Spring, 1992): 221–242

33. Loiq Sherali, "Modaram . . . ," *Muntahabi ahbor* (Dushanbe: Bunyodi adabii Sadriddin Ayni, 2013), 37. Sherali also dedicated a poem to Professor Sa'diniso Hakimova, which addressed the themes of women's health and how it had been harmed. Loiq Sherali, "Ehdo ba professor Sa'diniso Hakimova," in *Muntahabi ahbor,* 164–165.

34. See, for example, Abdulqodir Mukhiddinov, "Mardumi shahr va atrofi Buhoro Tojikon e Uzbek," *Tojikiston Soveti,* November 26, 1988, reprinted in A. Makhmadnazaar, ed., *Darsi kheshtanshinosi* (Dushanbe: Irfon, 1989), 65–67.

35. Among those historians was Rahim Masov, who would become a Rastohez activist. He later became a neo-Stalinist. Masov, *Istoriia topornogo razdeleniia* (Dushanbe: Irfon, 1991).

36. Ibrohim K., interview.

37. Oushakine, Serguei Alex. "The Terrifying Mimicry of Samizdat," *Public Culture* 13, no. 2 (2001): 191–214.

38. On "village prose," see Kathleen Parthe, *Russian Village Prose: The Radiant Past* (Princeton: Princeton University Press, 1992); Yitzchak Brudny, *Reinventing Russia: Russian Nationalism and the Soviet State, 1953–1991* (Cambridge, MA: Harvard University Press, 1998), 158–169. Zubok, *Zhivago's Children,* 330.

39. See Rossen Djagalov, "Pamiat' vs. Memorial: Rasputin, Aitmatov and the Search for Soviet Memory," *Studies in Slavic Cultures,* no. 8 (2009), 27–42.

40. Author interview, New York, January 2016.

41. Shukuri, *Hikoiathoe akandah az hayat . . . ,* 28–29.

42. Ibid., 34–36. See also "Kto bespomoshchen v sobstvennom iazyke," *Literaturnaia Gazeta,* December 14, 1988.

43. Dushanbe city party conference, December 1988, ACPT, fond 3, opis 300, delo 278, 120.

44. Nourzhanov and Bleuer, *Tajikistan: A Political and Social History.*

45. Ibid., 100.

46. Ibid., 174.

47. Robert J. C. Young, *Postcolonialism: A Historical Introduction* (Oxford: Blackwell, 2001), 2.

48. Hojamamat Umarov, "Regional'nye osobennosti proiavleniia protivorechii sotsialisticheskoi ekonomiki," *Izvestiia Akademii Nauk Tadzhikskoi SSR. Seriia: Filosofia, Ekonomika, Pravovedenie* 3 (1989): 29.

49. Ibid.

50. Ibid.

51. Toirdzhon Dzahabbarov, "Severo-Zapadnaia pogranichnaia provintsia Pakistana: Sotsial'no-ekonomicheskii ocherk" (PhD diss., Institute of Oriental Studies at the Moscow Academy of Sciences, 1974).

52. Akhmadshokhi Kamilzoda, *Me'mori istiqloli Tojikiston* (Dushanbe, 2010), 10.

53. Tohir Abdujabbor, "Muhiti zist va zabon," *Sadoi Sharq,* no. 8 (1989). Reprinted in Kamilzoda, *Me'mori istiqloli Tojikiston,* 165–167.

54. Ibid., 179.

55. Ibid., 189. It was not just ethnic Tajik scholars who held these views. V. I. Vetrov, presumably Russian, writing in the Academy of Sciences' monthly journal, described the previous decades as a period when more advanced republics, like the Baltics, became even more advanced relative to the Central Asian republics, at the same time demanding an ever greater share of raw materials. V. I. Vetrov, "Sotsial'no-ekonomicheskie problemy razvitie respubliki," *BAST,* no. 1 (1990): 3.

56. "Barnomae sozmoni Rastohez—junbishi mardumi Jumhurii Tojikiston," in Komilzoda, *Me'mori istiqloli Tokikiston,* 223–226.

57. John Schoeberlein, "Shifting Ground: How the Soviet Regime Used Resettlement to Transform Central Asian Society and the Consequences of This Policy Today," *JCAS Symposium Series* no. 9 (2000): 41–64.

58. Olbertreis, *Imperial Desert Dreams.*

59. "Prorvalas' plotina," *Pravda,* March 18, 1987, 6.

60. "Plotina," *Pravda,* November 21, 1988, 5.

61. Weiner, *A Little Corner of Freedom,* 427.

62. Quoted in Nurjanov and Bluer, *Tajikistan: A Social and Political History,* 158.

63. Interviews with Zafar A., Dushanbe, May 2013.

64. Interviews collected in Nurek. Party documents suggest that in the perestroika era, at least, officials were becoming aware of this trend. ACPT, fond 3, opis 300, delo 325, 71–75.

65. Emil Nasritdinnov and Phillip Shroder, "From Frunze to Bishkek: Soviet Territorial Youth Formations and Their Decline in the 1990s and 2000s," *Central Asian Affairs* 3, no. 1 (2016): 1–28.

66. Albert O. Hirschman and Michael Bernstein, "The Changing Tolerance for Income Inequality in the Course of Economic Development," *Quarterly Journal of Economics* 87, no. 4 (1973): 544–566.

67. Ibid., 550–552.

68. Samuel Huntington, *Political Order in Changing Societies* (New Haven: Yale University Press, 1968). See also Jeremy Adelman, *Worldly Philosopher: The Odyssey of Albert O. Hirschman* (Princeton: Princeton University Press, 2013), 462–466.

69. Beissinger, *Nationalist Mobilization,* 73–74; McGlinchey, *Chaos, Violence, Dynasty,* 67–70.

70. Charles King, *Ghosts of Freedom: A History of the Caucasus* (Oxford: Oxford University Press, 2008), 211–220.

71. James Critchlow, *Nationalism in Uzbekistan: A Soviet Republic's Road to Sovereignty* (Boulder, CO: Westview Press, 1991); McGlinchey, *Chaos, Violence, Dynasty,* 71–74.

72. Stephane A. Dudoignon, "Political Parties and Forces in Tajikistan, 1989–1993," in *Tajikistan: The Trials of Independence,* ed. Mohammad-Reza Djalili, Frederic Grare and Shirin Akiner (Richmond, UK: Curzon Press, 1998).

73. Nourzhanov and Bluer, *Tajikistan: A Political and Social History,* 203.

74. I. P. Gurshunov and N. H. Honaliev, "Eksperiment po podgotovke ne nuzhnykh spetsialistov," *Sotsiologicheskie Issledovaniia,* no. 1 (1989), 15–20.

75. Nourzhanov and Bluer, *Tajikistan: A Political and Social History*, 180. Isaac Scarborough, "(Over)determining Social Disorder: Tajikistan and the Economic Collapse of Perestroika," *Central Asian Survey* 35, no. 3 (2016): 439–463.

76. See Nourzhanov and Bluer, *Tajikistan: A Political and Social History,* 183–188, for an analysis of the different explanations.

77. *Rasshirennii XVIII Plenum.*

78. An assessment of the violence in Osh noted that the waiting list for housing included 57,000 families, and that 50,000 young persons were unemployed, a number

that had increased three times during the ongoing five-year period. GARF, fond 9654, opis 6, delo 220, 42.

79. *Rasshirennii XVIII Plenum*, 65.

80. Ibid., 68–69.

81. This was not an uncontested point, and depended on one's reading of statistical data and sociological surveys. Some scholars pointed out that the proportion of men who were unemployed and wanted to work was actually quite high, while others insisted that the number of women who wanted work outside the home was also far higher than the number of jobs available.

82. Academy of Sciences roundtable on transition to a regulated market economy, *Izvestiia akademii nauk Tadzhikskoi SSR,* no. 4 (1990).

83. See Scarborough, "(Over)determining Social Disorder:"

84. GARF, fond 9654, opis 6, delo 176, 22–23.

85. Safieva to Gorbachev, March 1, 1990, GARF, fond 9654, opis 6, delo 176, 30.

86. GARF, fond 5446, opis 163, delo 180.

87. GARF, fond 5446, opis 163, delo 180.

88. GARF, fond 5446, opis 163, delo 1818.

89. Ibid.

90. Nourzhanov and Bleuer, *Tajikistan: A Political and Social History,* 151–153.

CONCLUSION

1. Langston Hughes, *A Negro Looks at Soviet Central Asia* (Moscow: Cooperative Publishing Society of Foreign Workers in the USSR, 1934).

2. Hughes, *I Wonder as I Wander;* David Chioni-Moore, "Local Color, Global 'Color': Langston Hughes, the Black Atlantic, and Soviet Central Asia, 1932," *Research in African Literatures* 27, no. 4 (Winter 1996): 49–70.

3. Scott, *Seeing Like a State,* 101.

4. Ibid., 102.

5. Sergey Radchenko, *Unwanted Visionaries: The Soviet Failure in Asia at the End of the Cold War* (Oxford: Oxford University Press, 2014); Miller, *Struggle to Save the Soviet Economy.*

6. Thomas Barfield, *Afghanistan: A Cultural and Political History* (Princeton: Princeton University Press, 2010), 212–213.

7. RGAE, fond 365, opis 2, delo 183.

8. See Giustozzi and Kalinovsky, *Missionaries of Modernity.*

9. See Abrahamian, *Iran Between Two Revolutions,* 419–449.

10. Ekbladh, *Great American Mission,* 227.

11. Li, *The Will to Improve,* 1.

12. Ferguson, *The Anti-Politics Machine,* 273.

13. See Greta R. Krippner, *Capitalizing on Crisis: The Political Origins of the Rise of Finance* (Cambridge, MA: Harvard University Press, 2012).

14. Ira Katznelson, *When Affirmative Action Was White: An Untold History of Racial Inequality in Twentieth Century America* (New York: W. W. Norton, 2005); Robert C. Lieberman, *Shifting the Color Line: Race and the American Welfare State* (Cambridge, MA: Harvard University Press, 1998).

15. Thomas Faist, "Ethnicizatlon and Racialization of Welfare-State Politics in Germany and the USA," *Ethnic and Racial Studies* 18, no. 2 (1995): 219–250.

16. See, for example, John Heathershaw, *The Politics of Peacebuilding and the Emergence of Legitimate Order* (London: Routledge, 2009), 66–67.

17. Cooper, "Writing the History of Development," 6.

18. See Kelly M. McMann, "The Civic Realm in Kyrgyzstan: Soviet Economic Legacies and Activists' Expectations," in *The Transformation of Central Asia: States and Societies*

from Soviet Rule to Independence, ed. Pauline Jones Luong (Ithaca: Cornell University Press, 2004), 213–245.

19. Santiago Levy, *Progress against Poverty: Sustaining Mexico's Progresa-Oportunidades Program* (Washington, DC: Brookings Institution Press, 2007).

20. One of those who has cautiously championed cash transfers is James Ferguson. James Ferguson, *Give a Man a Fish: Reflections on the New Politics of Distribution* (Durham: Duke University Press, 2015).

21. Michael Hobbes, "Stop Trying to Save the World: Big Ideas Are Destroying International Development," *New Republic,* November 18, 2014, https://newrepublic.com/article/120178/problem-international-development-and-plan-fix-it.

22. "An Integrated Approach to Rural Development," United Nations Economic and Social Council Report, 2003, http://www.un.org/en/ecosoc/docs/pdfs/an_integrated_approach_to_rural_development.pdf.

23. Sebastien Peyrouse, "The Russian Minority in Central Asia: Migration, Politics, and Language," Woodrow Wilson International Center for Scholars Working Paper no. 297, 2008.

24. See Ruth Mandel, "Transition to Where? Developing Post-Soviet Space," *Slavic Review* 71, no. 2 (2012): 223–233.

25. Menga, "Building a Nation through a Dam."

26. See John Heathershaw, "Tajikistan amidst Globalization: State Failure or State Transformation?," *Central Asian Survey* 30, no. 1 (2011): 147–168.

27. Jeanne Féaux de la Croix and Mohira Suyarkulova, "The Rogun Complex: Public Roles and Historic Experiences of Dam-Building in Tajikistan and Kyrgyzstan," *Cahiers d'Asie centrale* 25 (2015): 103–132.

28. Branko Milanovic, "The West is Mired in Soft Development, China is Trying the Hard Stuff," *The Guardian*, May 17, 2017, https://www.theguardian.com/global-development-professionals-network/2017/may/17/belt-road-project-the-west-is-mired-in-soft-development-china-is-trying-the-hard-stuff.

29. Marlene Laruelle, *Globalizing Central Asia: Geopolitics and the Challenges of Economic Development* (Armonk, NY: M. E. Sharpe, 2013), 27–42.

30. Dilip Ratha et al., *Migration and Remittance Flows: Recent Trends and Outlook, 2013–2016* (Washington, DC: World Bank, 2013), http://siteresources.worldbank.org/INTPROSPECTS/Resources/334934-1288990760745/MigrationandDevelopment Brief21.pdf.

31. Cooper, "Writing the History of Development," 6. Daniel Immerwahr's *Thinking Small: The United States and the Lure of Community Development* (Cambridge, MA: Harvard University Press, 2015) has similarly shown how attempts to promote community development, which go back to the heyday of modernization, often end up reifying local hierarchies.

A NOTE ON SOURCES

1. For a useful discussion of the problems and opportunities of oral history in post-Soviet central Asia, see Timur Dadabaev, "The Role and Place of Oral History in Central Asian Studies," *Uzbekistan Initiative Papers* (Washington, DC: Elliot School of International Affairs; Barcelona: Center for International Affairs, 2014).

Bibliography of Primary Sources

ARCHIVES

Dushanbe, Tajikistan

Archive of the Communist Party of Tajikistan (ACPT)
    Fond 3, Central Committee of the Communist Party of Tajikistan
    Fond 56, Nurek City Committee (Gorkom)

Central State Archive of the Republic of Tajikistan (TsGART)
    Fond 27, Ministry of Irrigation
    Fond 1483, Ministry of Culture
    Fond 1505, Union of Writers
    Fond 1516, Council on Religious Affairs
    Fond 1561, Ministry of Light Industry
    Fond P-1566, State Committee of the Council of Ministers on the Use of Labor
        Resources
    Fond P-1612, State Electricity Construction Company (Tadzhikgoselektrostroy)
    Fond P-1621, State Committee on Architecture

Moscow, Russia

Archive of the Russian Academy of Sciences (ARAN)
    Fond 174, Council on the Study of Productive Forces (SOPS)
    Fond 378, NurekGesStroy
    Fond 457, History Section
    Fond 591, Council on the Coordination of Research by Academies of Sciences in
        the Union Republics
    Fond 1731, Social Sciences Section
    Fond 1825, Nikolai Nekrasov Papers
    Fond 1849, Economic Department
    Fond 1877, USSR Institute of Economics

Russian State Archive of Contemporary History (RGANI)
    Fond 5, Departments of the Central Committee of the Communist Party of the
        Soviet Union

Russian State Archive of the Economy (RGAE)
    Fond 99, Economics Research Institute of the Committee on State Planning
    Fond 339, State Committee on Construction (Gosstroy)
    Fond 365, State Committee on Economic Ties (GKES)
    Fond 399, Council on the Study of Productive Forces (SOPS)
    Fond 4372, State Planning Committee (GOSPLAN)
    Fond 7854, Main Directorate for the Construction and Assembly of Hydropower
        Stations
    Fond 7964, Ministry of Energy and Electrification
    Fond 9572, Ministry of Hydropower Construction

Russian State Archive of Literature and Arts (RGALI)
Fond 674, USSR Union of Architects

Russian State Archive of Social and Political History (RGASPI)
Fond 17, Central Committee of the Communist Party of the Soviet Union
Fond M-1, Central Committee of the All-Union Lenin Union of Communist Youth
(Komsomol)

State Archive of the Russian Federation (GARF)
Fond P 5446, Council of Ministers
Fond P 9540, Soviet Committee for Solidarity with the Countries of Asia and Africa
Fond P-9606, Ministry of Education
Fond P-9654, USSR Supreme Soviet

PERIODICALS

Adabiët va san'at
Bulleten' Akademii Nauk Tadzhikskoi SSR
Kommunist
Kommunist Tadzhikistana
Maorif va Madaniiat
Norak
Pravda
Sadoi mardum
Sel'skoe khoziastvo Tadzhikistana
Sotsiologicheskie Issledovaniia
Sovetskoe gosudarstvo i parvo
Tojikiston Soveti
Vechernii Dushanbe
Voprosy ekonomiki

MEMOIRS AND PRIMARY SOURCE VOLUMES

Artizov, Andrei, ed. *Nikita Khrushchev, 1964: stenogrammy plenuma TsK KPSS i drugie dokumenty* (Moscow: Demokratiia, 2007).
Asozoda, Hudoĭnazar. *Afghoniston inqilobi* (Duhsanbe: Devashtich, 2003).
Asozoda, Hudoĭnazar. *Afghonistoni shohi* (Dushanbe: Devashtich, 2002).
Asozoda, Hudoĭnazar. *Dostoni zindagi* [3 vols.] (Dushanbe: Devashtich, 2006, 2008).
Cherkassov, Petr. *IMEMO: Portret na fone epokhi* (Moscow: Ves' Mir, 2004).
Chernysh, David Iakovlevich. *Nurek* (Moscow: Planeta, 1980).
Dashekvich, V. I. *Ogni Nureka* (Dushanbe: Irfon, 1974).
Davronov, ed. *Ëdi ëri mehrubon: ëdnomae az ustodi shakhir Abduqodir Matniëzov* (Dushanbe: Pazhueshgohi farkhangi forsi-tojiki, 2008).
Dodkhudoev, Nazorsho. *Vlast' vremeni* (Almaty, 2001).
Gafforova, M. K. *Maktabi man* (Dushanbe: Irfon, 2014).
Gorbachev, Pavel. *Plotina* (Moscow: Politizdat, 1980).
Hakimova, Sa'dinisso. *Zalozhniki Imperii* (Dushanbe, 1998).
Haydarov, Ashur. *Zhizn' v isskustve* (Dushanbe: 2001).
Iakubov, Naim. *Dorogu osilit iduschii* (Dushanbe, 2004).
Iakubov, N. H. *Rekonstruktsiia zdanii* (Dushanbe: Tajikistan Technical University, 2013).
Ibrohimov, M. *Gorizonty nauki Tadzhikistana* (Dushanbe: Irfon, 2007).
Ikromī, Jalol. *On chī az sar guzasht* (Dushanbe, 2009).

Ikromī, Jonon. *Jalol Ikromi: Neizvestnye stranitsy* (Dushanbe: Sharqi ozod, 2010).

Iskandarov,B. I. *Trudnyi put' k znaniiu* (Moscow: Izsdatel'stvo Moskovskogo Universiteta, 1999).

Kamilzoda, Ahmadshohi, *Me'mori istikloli Tojikiston* (Dushanbe, 2010).

Kakhorov, A. *Dar avstralia va Ceylon (qaydkhoi safar)* (Dushanbe: Nashrieti davlatii Tojikiston, 1962).

Khakel, Marat Ianovich. *Unesennoe vekom: Zapiski "sovkovogo" marginala*. www.samlib.ru/hakel_m_j/vek.html.

Khlevniuk, Oleg, et al., eds. *Regional'naia politika Khrushcheva* (Moscow: Demokratiia, 2009).

Khodizoda, Rasul. *Khudoe, khudro bishinosam* (Dushanbe: Devashtich, 2006).

Mirzoshoev, Sulton. *Arzi dil* (Dushanbe: Adib, 1996).

Morozova, N. *Nurekskiy Kharakter* (Moscow: Detskaia Literatura, 1976).

Mukhitdinov, N. A. *Gody provedennye v Kremle* (Tashkent, 1994).

———. *Reka vremeni: Ot Stalina do Gorbacheva* (Moscow: Rusti-Rosti, 1994).

Nasriddinov, Xikmatullo. *Tarkish* (Dushanbe: Afsona, 1995).

Nishanov, Rafiq. *Derev'ia zeleneiut do metelei* (Moscow: Molodaia Gvardia, 2012).

Osimī, Mohammed. *Ëdnomai ustod Osimī* (Khojand: Nuri maorifat, 2005).

Otahonova, Hursheda. *Dil mehohad, ki guiamu giram* (Dushanbe: Irfon, 2011).

Rakhimov, R. K. *O proshlom s gordost'iu, o budushchem s optimizmom* (Dushanbe: NPITsenter, 1997).

Rakhmatov, Mirzo. *Na diplomaticheskoi sluzhbe* (Dushanbe: Irfon, 1991).

Saidmuradov, Kh. M. *Vidnyi uchenniy-ekonomist Srednei Azii (k 70-letiu so dnia rozhdeniia I. K. Narzikulov* (Dushanbe: Irfon, 1981).

Savchenkov, N. G. *Nurekskaia GES: Ocherki, raskazy, stikhi sovremennikov o stroiteliakh Nurekskoi GES* (Moscow: Tipografiia Moment, 2013).

———. *Nurekskaia GES: Tadzhikiztan. Energogigant na Vakshe* (Mosow: Tipografiia Moment, 2013).

Shakuri, Muxamadjo. *Hikoiatxoi okanda az haët* (Dushanbe: Royzanii farhangi Saforati Jumhurii Islomi Eron dar Tojikiston, 2014).

Sharifov, Holmurod. *Tolei Baland* (Dushanbe: Pazhuhishgohi fari-tojiki, 2010).

Sufiën, Kamoli. *Taqdir: khotira va ëddoshtho* (Dushanbe: Adib, 2011).

Sultonov, Shukur. *Ëddoshtho, fehristi osor, va andeshaxo* (Khujand: Khuroson, 2012).

Tomilina, N. G., et al., eds. *Nikita Sergeevich Khrushchev: Dva tsveta vremeni* (Moscow: Demokratiia, 2009).

Yakovlev, Aleksandr, et al., eds. *Molotov, Malenkov, Kaganovich 1957: Dokumenty* (Moscow: Demokratiia, 1997).

Index

communal *(subbotniki)*, 138
cooperatives *(artels)*, 82
cottage labor, 14, 81–84, 223
debates on, 72–74, 77–79, 80–90, 138, 139
on farms, issues with, 184–194, 192–194
forced, 30, 96, 102
hoarding of, 186–187, 188, 192
productivity, 177, 178–179, 184–185
reallocation to industry, issues with, 5,
    13–14, 68, 77–79, 87–90, 106–107,
    176–176, 233, 255; housing and, 121,
    123–124, 126, 245; successes in address-
    ing, 107–109, 152–153
"surplus," 72, 81, 192, 239, 293n6
unemployment and underemployment,
    235–236, 237, 238, 239, 302n78, 303n81
See also resettlement
Lahuti, Abdulqasim, 46
language
    Arabic *vs.* Cyrillic script, 205, 230
    higher education, as challenge for, 55–56
    Russian: expectation of locals learning,
        110, 246; fluency levels, 231; in military
        service, 59; teaching in, 108, 230; teaching
        of, 41; travel and, 61
    Tajik: education and, 55–56, 79; elevation
        of, 228; Middle East languages and, 52;
        teaching of, 110; in Uzbekistan, 228
Latifi, Otahon, 234
Lenin, V. I., 23, 182, 208
Leningrad, studying in, 59–62
Leninobod, 62–63
Leontieff, Wasily, 67
Lewis, Arthur, 69, 72–73, 80
Likhachov, Dmitry, 230
Lilienthal, David, 96
"linear city," 119, 122, 123
literary evenings, 57–58
living standards. *See* standard of living
local elites
    de-Stalinization and, 12, 19–24
    developing countries, as links to, 203–214;
        role of in Afghanistan invasion, 214–217
    disillusionment of, 12, 219, 220, 224–235,
        237, 239
    emigration of, 252
    expansion of education and, 51–56
    Khrushchev and, 19–20, 36–42
    local development, involvement in, 8, 12,
        19–20, 69–79, 81–90, 100, 121, 126,
        246–247; by influential workers, 147–148,
        160, 161, 166–167, 170–172
    resistance by, 237
    social mobility and, 53–55, 62–66
    under Stalin, 45–47, 49–50

travel and, 53–54, 59–62
workers' transformation into, 146, 147–148,
    160–168, 170
See also economists; intelligentsia
localism/regionalism, 62–66
local party. *See* Communist Party (local)

Magnitogorsk, 146–147
mahalla, 16
Mahkamov, Qahhor, 60, 86–87, 221, 225, 230,
    238, 241, 242–243
Malenkov, Georgy, 37–38
"mankurt," 229
marriage, 151–152, 153, 156–157, 159
Marx, Karl, 134
Massell, Gregory, 9
Massoud, Ahmad Shah, 216–217, 252
McNamara, Robert, 74
mechanization, 33, 40, 177–179, 184–185, 294n31
Melnikov, R.E., 27
migration
    to cities, 177
    for education, 53–54, 59–62, 237, 275n49
    emigration by Tajiks, 73, 252, 254–255
    of Europeans into Tajikistan, 87, 105, 106,
        127–128, 129, 131, 134, 135, 136–137,
        141, 235; prioritization of housing for,
        121, 123–124, 127–129, 289n81
    of Europeans out of Tajikistan, 246
    See also resettlement
Milanovic, Branko, 254
Miller, Chris, 247
Milyutin, Nikolay, 119, 121, 134
Mirshakar, Mirsaid, 155–158
Mirsky, Georgy, 224, 236
Mirzoshoev, Sulton, 238
Mitchell, Timothy, 265n22, 270n65
model villages, 134–135, 208–210
model workers, 148–151, 155–168
modernity, 5, 6–7
Molotov, Vyacheslav, 37–38
Morocco, 199
Morozova, Natalia, 292n38
Morrison-Knudsen (MK), 97–98
Morss, Susan Buck, 182
Moscow, studying in, 59–62
mosques, 138, 140, 196–197
Mukhitdinov, Nuritdin, 22–23, 24, 37–38, 39,
    40, 207, 286n20
Mukimov, Rustam, 125, 126
Murray Li, Tanya, 12, 249
Muslims
    accusations of oppression of, 208
    as Soviets, 138, 140, 161–164, 196–197, 292n39
    in USSR, official attitudes to, 26–27